Georg Meggle (Ed.)
Ethics of Terrorism & Counter-Terrorism

Philosophische Forschung
Philosophical Research

Herausgegeben von / Edited by

Johannes Brandl • Andreas Kemmerling
Wolfgang Künne • Mark Textor

Band 3 / Volume 3

Georg Meggle (Ed.)

Ethics of Terrorism
&
Counter-Terrorism

ontos
verlag

Frankfurt I Paris I Ebikon I Lancaster I New Brunswick

Bibliographic information published by Die Deutsche Bibliothek
Die Deutsche Bibliothek lists this publication in the Deutsche
Nationalbibliographie;
detailed bibliographic data is available in the Internet at http://dnb.ddb.de

North and South America by
Transaction Books
Rutgers University
Piscataway, NJ 08854-8042
trans@transactionpub.com

United Kingdom, Ire Iceland,
Turkey, Malta, Portugal by
Gazelle Books Services Limited
White Cross Mills
Hightown
LANCASTER, LA1 4XS
sales@gazellebooks.co.uk

©2005 ontos verlag
P. O. Box 15 41, D-63133 Heusenstamm nr. Frankfurt
Tel. ++(49) 6104 66 57 33 Fax ++(49) 6104 66 57 34
www.ontosverlag.com

ISBN 3-937202-68-4

2005

Printed on acid-free paper
ISO-Norm 970-6

Printed in Germany.

TABLE OF CONTENTS

PREFACE

We are supposed to wage war against Terrorism – but exactly what we are fighting against in this war, there is nearly no consensus about. And, much worse, nearly nobody cares about this conceptual disaster – the main thing being, whether or not you are taking sides with the good guys.

This volume is an attempt to end this disaster. What is Terrorism? Are terrorist acts to be defined exclusively on the basis of the characteristics of the respective actions? Or should we restrict such actions to acts performed by non-state organisations? And, most important, is terrorism already by its very nature to be morally condemned?

But, having a clear idea of what Terrorism is, would be only the beginning. Rational moral assessment still needs two further components: The relevant facts; and the relevant values and norms.

Now, in a field where systematic disinformation has been even proclaimed to be the official policy, facts are obviously very hard to get at. This volume is mainly interested in Ethics: What's wrong with Terrorism? And what is morally right or morally wrong, respectively, with all the different means of Counter-Terrorism? What are the moral boundaries for waging war against terrorism? What are the right ways of dealing with terrorists? And what about the alleged anti-terrorism wars on Afghanistan and Iraq?

Even just asking these questions is frowned upon by quite a few people.

Therefore, I guess, asking and discussing these questions is a necessary and worthwhile occupation – the job (and duty) primarily of philosophers, especially analytic philosophers, in cooperation with colleagues from at least some of the other related fields, e.g. from international law, media and public relation departments, social psychology etc.

We, the contributors of this volume, have deliberately and consciously tried to do this job.

Again, we received the best assistance possible by three institutions: By the University of Bielefeld's ZiF (ZENTRUM FÜR INTERDISZIPLINÄRE FORSCHUNG / CENTER FOR INTERDISCIPLINARY RESEARCH) which hosted our conference on *Ethics of Terrorism & Counter-Terrorism*, October 2002; by the CAPPE (CENTRE FOR APPLIED PHILOSOPHY AND PUBLIC ETHICS), Australia, cooperating with the ZiF; and by the DFG (DEUTSCHE FORSCHUNGSGEMEINSCHAFT / GERMAN RESEARCH FOUNDATION) which partially funded our conference.

Our sincere thanks goes to these institutions for their ongoing support. Thanks in particular to *Anja-Marleen Krause*, who managed the ZiF's organisation of this conference and who made our working and living there a pleasure; to *Daniel*

Meßelken, who was responsible for checking incoming papers and did a good deal of the correspondence with the contributors; and to the very person I am most happy to be assisted by in all matters relating to my academic life: *Andrea Busch*. And, of course, also to *Rafael Hüntelmann*, Ontos's publishing manager, as well as to the distinguished members of this series' editorial board. Contrary to some other publishers & editors, they had the courage to accept and publish this volume without any restrictions on the material presented to you.

Leipzig, Januar 2005`   Georg Meggle

ABSTRACTS

I Terrorism & Counter-Terrorism / Semantics

TOMIS KAPITAN
'Terrorism' as a Method of Terrorism

Since September 11 and the onset of the U.S.-led "war on terrorism", increased attention has been given to the very concept of terrorism. What exactly is terrorism? Who practices it and why? What are the appropriate responses to this form of violence? I contend that the issues raised, particularly by this last question, are obscured by the prevalent rhetoric of "terror", a discourse that is routinely employed to dehumanize selected groups and to deflect attention away from a critical examination of the moral and political issues underlying their grievances. The rhetoric has thereby contributed to the increasing spiral of hatred and atrocity in the world and, in many cases, has only prepared the ground for further terrorism. I illustrate this thesis by focusing on the Israeli-Palestinian conflict, and argue that the rhetoric of "terror" ought to be avoided if conflicts like this are to be examined and resolved in an intelligent and just manner.

OLAF L. MUELLER
Benign Blackmail: Cassandra's Plan or What is Terrorism?

What do we mean when we label an activity "terrorist"? And what is the appropriate ethical evaluation of such activity? These are the two questions which I intend to address in the present paper. One of my aims is to convince you that even if a certain course of action is deemed "terrorist", it is still an open question whether or not that very course of action is morally wrong.

My second aim is to show that strict condemnation of terrorism implies pacifism. To show this, I shall propose an extreme thought experiment: Cassandra's plan. Cassandra foresees that sooner or later one of the nuclear powers might take the liberty to use atomic bombs. From fright she founds an NGO for blackmailing the statesmen who are in charge of nuclear weapons; she announces in public that all ministers and leaders of any government shall be hunted down, and executed, whose soldiers drop but one atomic bomb. (Cassandra's NGO keeps killer teams in constant training so as to increase the effect of the threat; this is being financiated from private donations).

I claim: Cassandra's plan is morally wrong – no more and no less than any military action.

G. Meggle (ed.), Ethics of Terrorism & Counter-Terrorism, 9-18.
© 2005 Ontos, Heusenstamm.

DANIEL MESSELKEN
Terrorism and Guerrilla Warfare – A Comparative Essay

Over the last few years, virtually all forms of non-state violence have been labeled as "terrorism". As a result, differences between various forms of war and violence are lost in the analysis. This article proposes a conceptual distinction between terrorism and guerrilla warfare by analyzing their differences and similarities. Definitions of terrorism and guerrilla warfare are presented. Starting with these definitions, the question of the legitimacy of terrorism and guerrilla violence is answered with reference to just war theory. Particular attention is paid to the issue of the so called "innocent victims" of terrorism.

IGOR PRIMORATZ
State Terrorism and Counterterrorism

While everyday discourse and the media assume, as a rule, that terrorism is something perpetrated by non-state groups and organizations, the author defines "terrorism" in terms of the nature and aims of the act, rather than with reference to the agent. The definition makes it possible to speak of state terrorism too. The paper sketches a typology of state involvement with terrorism, and goes on to focus on the moral standing of terrorism. It is argued that state terrorism is, by and large, morally worse than terrorism employed by non-state agencies. The paper offers four arguments in support of this claim. It ends with a discussion of the moral aspects of counterterrorism, and in particular of the "war against terrorism" currently being waged by the United States and its allies. In view of the amount of "collateral damage" caused by the operations in Afghanistan and Iraq, it is argued that the "war against terrorism" is seriously morally compromised – although it still falls short of state terrorism.

CHARLES P. WEBEL
Terror: The Neglected but Inescapable Core of Terrorism

On Sept. 11, 2001, during the first year of this new millennium, the cities of New York and Washington D.C. were attacked by what most political and military leaders and Western citizens have described as "terrorists". The loss of life – approximately 3,000 civilians – was exceeded in American history only by battles during the Civil War, although cities in other countries experienced far greater civilian casualties during World War II. And exactly 911 days later, on March 11, 2004, almost two hundred civilians were killed by a terrorist attack on commuter trains in Madrid, Spain.

How might we try to account for this lamentable state of affairs, unique in human history yet nonetheless illustrative of the usage of "terrorism" as a political tactic and of terror as a predictable human response to the violence, and threats of violence employed by terrorists against innocent people? Is there a common core experience of terror that links the victims of contemporary terrorist attacks to populations who were terrorized during the twentieth century? For example, are the survivors of bombing raids conducted during the Second World War psychologically, ethically, and/or phenomenologically similar to the concentration camp survivors of the Nazi and Stalinist periods, and/or to the surviving victims of terrorism at the dawn of this new millennium? What, if any, obligations do the victors of counter-terrorist "wars" have to the often-traumatized victims of such terrorizing military operations as precision bombing? And what measures – psychotherapeutic, socioeconomic, legal, political, and diplomatic – should taken to aid the victims of terrorism and to minimize the risks of future terrorist attacks?

In this article, I explore the contested lexical and ethical terrain of "Terrorism", and I present an original, phenomenologically-oriented analysis of "Terror", based largely on my interviews with 52 survivors of political terror in 14 countries. I conclude with some reflections on the relationships between terrorism, and terror – the neglected but inescapable core of terrorism.

SEUMAS MILLER
Terrorism and Collective Responsibility

The definition of terrorism is problematic. Roughly speaking, it is the intentional killing, or otherwise seriously harming, of innocent people to achieve political or military purposes. On this account al-Qaeda is a terrorist organisation. But so are some others friendly to the West.

This definition of terrorism raises issues concerning the 'innocence' of various categories of person who are not combatants or the military or political leaders of combatants, but who nevertheless might be responsible for the real or imagined injustices suffered by those in whose name the terrorist organisations are acting. A neglected category of such 'guilty' persons are those who collectively committed sins of omission, rather than sins of commission. This paper explores this issue.

MARCELO DASCAL
The Unethical Rhetoric of Terror

Terrorism and counter-terrorism involve actions that, in addition to their unbearable price in bloodshed and suffering, purport to be communicative acts. Their performers and those who stand behind them intend to convey to the victims of their attacks and counter-attacks, or to those responsible for their security and well-being, certain "messages", which their respective "addressees" are supposed to interpret and understand. Such an "understanding", in turn, is supposed to be facilitated by a host of other communicative acts, in the more strict sense of the word: declarations, warnings, interviews, and sometimes also secret negotiations, both direct and mediated. A "conversation" involving a full range of violent and less violent communicative acts thus takes place between the opponents. The purpose of this paper is to analyze this peculiar kind of communicative interaction, highlighting its paradoxical nature. In so doing, it tackles an important dimension of the terrorism/counter-terrorism problem that has been generally overlooked. The paradoxes revealed by the communicative analysis, in turn, shed light on what should be expected from the analysis of the other dimensions – notably the ethical –

of the problem, suggesting guidelines for the kind of intervention required for its solution.

II   Terrorism & Counter-Terrorism / Ethics

PER BAUHN
Political Terrorism and the Rules of Just War

Political terrorists often conceive of themselves as warriors, as can be seen from the names their groups adopt: Rote Armee Fraktion, Brigate Rosse, Jihad, and so on. Likewise, the most recent effort to eliminate international terrorism, following the events of September 11, has been designated a war against terrorism. Hence, for terrorists and anti-terrorists alike, it has seemed appropriate to adopt the terminology of war.

In this context, it could be worthwhile to examine to what extent the ideas and principles inherent in the just war theory may apply to the acts of political terrorists and warriors against terrorism, especially in the cases in which innocent bystanders are killed or have their lives put in danger.

In this essay, the focus will be on the principle of non-combatant immunity (which holds that innocent bystanders should not be victimized) and the doctrine of double effect (which may justify certain unintended cases of victimization).

C. A. J. (TONY) COADY
Terrorism, Just War and Right Response

In getting a moral grip on the problems posed by terrorism we need to achieve some clarity about what is meant by terrorism and some moral perspective to judge of it. But the initial problem is that the debates about terrorism, both scholarly and public, are replete with contested definitions of the topic. This paper offers a definition of terrorism that catches one central element in this complex conceptual web and helps link the moral evaluation of terrorism with the moral framework of the just war tradition. It will be argued that it is a mistake to treat all revolutionary or insurgent violence as terrorist (even where it is unjustified) and that what is wrong in the activities of non-state terrorists is also wrong in the parallel activities of states. Defences of state terrorism that rely upon necessity or "dirty hands" seem discredited by the fact that they appear equally available to non-state terrorists. The paper concludes by applying just war considerations to the issue of morally appropriate responses to terrorism and argues that there must be serious moral doubts about the style of response to terrorist attacks that currently goes under the title "war against terrorism".

JANNA THOMPSON
Terrorism, Morality and Right Authority

Terrorist acts are often condemned for violating just war restrictions against harming non-combatants. However, another criticism of terrorism focuses on the question of whether terrorists have a 'right to war' – whether they violate the just war requirement of 'right authority' to engage in war. To answer this question it is necessary to consider the purpose just war theory has traditionally served and whether, and to what extent, its function has changed. In particular, I will discuss the relation between terrorism and what some people call 'the crime of war' and how judgements about whether terrorists have a right to war should affect how they are regarded and treated.

GEORG MEGGLE
Terror & Counter-Terror: Initial Ethical Reflections

The basic T-terms like 'terror', 'terrorism' and 'terroristic activity' are explained in this contribution. In doing so, one has to distinguish the descriptive (and value-neutral) components of these terms from those which make for the judgemental component of words often used for moral combat. Once I have secured this distinction, I turn to the just-war-theory to explain how the T-acts (of different kinds) are to be judged morally. What does this mean for the US American strategy of war against terrorism?

HAIG KHATCHADOURIAN
Counter-Terrorism: Torture and Assassination

The paper has two main themes: (1) the ethics of the assassination of suspected terrorists as a form of counterterrorism, by the military forces of a country targeted by presumed terrorists; and (2) the ethics of the torture of suspected terrorists in custody as a further form of counterterrorism.

(1) The paper focuses on Israel's ongoing "targeted killings" of Palestinian militants as a putative form of national self-defense, in the ongoing al-Aqsa Palestinian intifada. It argues that assassination in all circumstances is morally wrong. Moreover, state assassination of suspected terrorists is nothing other than extra-judicial murder: the state acts as judge, jury and executioner, in violation, among other things, of the fundamental moral-legal principle that a suspect is presumed innocent until proven guilty in a fair and just trial. Act-utilitarianism, justifies political assassination under certain circumstances, but is unsatisfactory as an ethical theory. By contrast, the more adequate rule-utilitarianism would reject the admissibility of a general state policy or practice of assassination.

(2) As in the case of "targeted killings", the paper argues that, under any and all circumstances, both physical and psychological torture are barbaric, morally wrong. They also violate Article I of the U.N. General Assembly RES 39/46 Annex and the 1984 Convention Against Torture, as well as the human right against torture.

Moreover, it is an empirical fact that torture is an unreliable method of extracting information designed to preempt or prevent acts of violence.

PETER SIMPSON
The War on Terrorism: Its Justification and Limits

The evil of terrorism, such as the attacks on the US of September 11, 2001, is manifest. There can be no good reason to deny this. Still it is a fact that admits of examination and analysis. A definition of terrorism is needed. For the sake of clarification I exclude, in this context, the idea of state-terrorism. I define terrorism as acts of violence committed by private individuals with no political authority, and directed indiscriminately against civilians so as to spread fear and terror among them to achieve some limited goal short of the immediate overthrow of the government. That terrorism is unjust is an implication, but not a part, of this definition. Justice means giving each their due, but deliberately attacking the innocent, like civilians, is not due to the innocent. So terrorism is unjust. As such terrorism is a threat to decent and civilized living. It needs to be suppressed, peaceably if possible, but by force if need be. Force, like tolerance, is neither good nor bad in itself but only relative to what it is used for. To those who would use force against the innocent, force is itself due, provided there is no other way to defend civilized life against them. The current war on terrorism has so far fallen under this idea of justice. But other things have not, as notably attacks by Western governments on civil rights and liberties

RÜDIGER BITTNER
Morals in Terrorist Times

The ethics of terrorism and counter-terrorism is a moot subject, for terrorism is evidently wrong, and counter-terrorism practically does not exist, the so-called "war on terrorism" being in fact a series of plain wars. The article therefore turns the question around and investigates the political function of the massive employment of moral notions in the orchestration of current warfare. It also considers the likely political consequences of this reliance of political agents on moral distinctions.

UWE STEINHOFF
The Ethics of Terrorism

I argue that in order to avoid double standards terrorism has to be defined as a method, irrespective of its user or its "good" or "bad" aims. I then show that there are at least three arguments available for the justification of terrorism, understood, roughly, as the deliberate attack on innocents in order to intimidate some other people. The first two are Virginia Held's argument that on grounds of justice it is better to equalize rights violations in a transition to bring an end to them, and Michael Walzer's argument from 'extreme emergency'. Against Georg Meggle's claim that it is always wrong to intimidate others via violent acts which directly attack innocents or accept their foreseeable deaths or injuries – Meggle's definition of 'strong terrorism' – I point out that this is also done by judicial systems. Based on this point I develop a third argument for the justification of terrorism and defend it against possible objections, most notably against one that relies on the doctrine of double effect. I conclude that terrorist acts can be justified in certain circumstances, but that such a justification is more difficult for strong parties than for weak ones.

III   Terrorism & Counter-Terrorism / Law and Politics

CAROLIN EMCKE
War on Terrorism and the Crises of the Political

The paper deals with the form the war against terror calls into question: not only the ethical norms for the treatment of prisoners of war, the limits of just wars, but also our understanding of the justifiability of politics. Once "under attack", the western world responded with a wide-spread, multifaceted, multi-front war, transgressing a set of international norms and laws with reference to a "state of emergency" and "self-defense". I will argue that in the wake of 9/11 the application of "self-defense" and "state of emergency"-logics has triggered legitimacy crises of the political:

a) In the national context, the political was reduced to Carl Schmitt's understanding of politics in state of emergency that allows to trump ethical or moral concerns limitlessly.

b) In the international context a historic abandonment of the classical "no-first-strike-doctrin" is about to be established. "Self-defense" is used as a justification for military action. The legitimation-discourse on all sides in the middle east can serve as an example for the dangerous use of the topos of "self-defense" for actions that range from self-defense to preventive attack, to aggressive attack, to terrorist action. The American nuclear plans can serve as another.

The paper reflects on the crises of the political in times of "self-defense" and will try to offer a normative criterion to judge and criticize political or military action.

ALEKSANDAR PAVKOVIĆ
Terrorism as an Instrument of Liberation: A Liberation Ideology Perspective

An ideology of liberation is a set of beliefs, value judgements and exhortations which provides a framework of justification of political action aiming at the liberation of an oppressed group from its oppressors. In order to control the oppressed, their oppressors use both random and targeted violence against them. In response to this violence, the oppressed are also justified in using violence in order to remove oppression. Within the liberation ideologies framework, terrorism against the oppressor group is thus primarily justified as an effective and 'low cost' instrument of the liberation of the oppressed. The paper explores the liberation ideologies' normative justification of the use of terrorism and contrasts this type of justification with that of universal humanism which asserts that each human life is of equal and supreme value.

LAURENCE LUSTGARTEN
National Security, Terrorism, and Constitutional Balance

This essay looks at the dangers to political freedoms and human rights arising from laws and practices designed to control terrorism. These have become more widespread and severe since the attacks on New York and Washington DC in 2001; and nowhere more so than in Britain. Key provisions of the current UK legislation are described, and set in their political and legal contexts. Particular attention is paid to the great constitutional shift of power, originating during the First World War, from the legislature [Parliament] to the executive branch of government, and especially the Prime Minister. This is possible in Britian's unwritten constitution without need for formal amendments or legislation; it is the result of evolving political practice. Ironically that practice has led to more unaccountable and secretive government in the so-called democratic age than was the practice in the 19th century.

The essay also looks at the role of the judiciary which – notwithstanding the enactment into UK domestic [municipal] law of the European Convention on Human Rights – has remained far too differential to executive determinations. It is shown that this attitude also has a long pedigree, derived from cases where the government successfully asserted the need to protect 'national security' as the justification for a range of measures that sharply restricted personal and political freedoms. An outline of principles for redressing the balance, involving a greater role for both legislature and judiciary in the broad area of national security and terrorism, is presented.

THOMAS MERTENS
Criminal Justice after 9-11: ICC or Military Tribunals

The events of September 11th, whether one likes it or not, changed the political climate. Following a short period in which the "end of history" was proclaimed, the Schmittian "political" has reasserted its existential character, both in the acts and the rhetoric of fundamentalists such as Bin Laden, but also those of U.S. president George W. Bush, who declared to the world in the State of the Union address of September 20 that "either you are with us, or you are with the terrorists". On this occasion, President Bush announced that the U.S. would direct every resource to combat terrorism, and this would entail "every instrument of law enforcement". In the ensuing months, the implications of these words have become clear and the establishment of military tribunals has been at the forefront of this legal 'War on Terror'. This contribution uses the technique of a thought-experiment to illustrate the legal process a terrorist could expect to encounter following changes to legal systems in both Europe and the United States. The main elements of military tribunals are sketched, an historical account of their development provided and, finally, such forms of justice are evaluated by the standard of the principles of criminal procedure contained in modern legal systems and embedded in important documents such as the Universal Declaration of Human Rights, the International

Covenant on Civil and Political Rights and the European Convention of Human Rights.

RALF GROETKER
Looking for Mohammed: Data Screening in Search of Terrorists

Data screening in search of terrorists is a violation of information privacy. Why is this so? And should we promote it anyway? After September 11th, police departments all over Germany (and elsewhere) started to search for terrorists using data screening methods: the "Rasterfahndung". I will briefly explain how this approach works and how it differs from other methods also based on data processing (e.g., the screening of flight passengers in the US). My main concern is the ethical legitimacy of this method: how does it harm those whose data have been fed into the search process? Starting with an philosophical outline of the value of "information privacy", I will explore what exactly is at stake in such a search and consider the arguments raised pro and contra the "Rasterfahndung". I will close by asking if there is any rational method or standard by which to decide whether or not the expected increase of security outweighs the damage to information privacy.

FILIMON PEONIDIS
Does the Suppression of Pro-Terrorist Speech Enhance Collective Security?

Although most forms of subversive and deviant political speech are no longer suppressed in liberal democracies, the views expressed by terrorist groups or their sympathizers appear to be the exception. In recent years we have witnessed several legal bans imposed on the broadcasting of pro-terrorist speech in an attempt to fight terrorism more effectively. These policies raise pressing free-speech issues. Is pro-terrorist speech not susceptible to the usual free-speech justifications? Does it constitute an integral part of terrorist acts, which do not deserve special protection? Are all forms of terrorist communication equally objectionable? Is our current "war against terrorism" so different as to outweigh the traditional liberal commitment to free speech? I argue that there is a certain presumption against the suppression of pro-terrorist speech and that considerations of collective security are not in principle strong enough to outweigh this presumption.

VÉRONIQUE ZANETTI
After 9-11 – A Paradigm Change in International Law?

One of the ways that the loss of a state's sovereignty is discernable is through its loss of control over the sources of organized violence. Organized criminality such as the mafia and terrorist organizations brings new actors on the international scene, wearing away the state's inner structures. The classical parameters of organized violence – i.e., its sources of financing, those who wield it, the aims they seek, and the means they use – have changed, and therefore call traditional just-war criteria into question. Such situations dissolve the distinction between a state of peace and a state of war, civilians and combatants, public and private fund raising to finance violence. As a result, traditional answers originating in international law, such as the right of self-defense (Art. 51 of the Charter) or the principle of non-intervention, must be reexamined. The terrorist attacks of September 11 offer a tragic illustration of such changes. The paper focuses on the international reactions immediately following these events, and examines the legal categories that they have called into question.

I

TERRORISM & COUNTER-TERRORISM

SEMANTICS

TOMIS KAPITAN

'TERRORISM' AS A METHOD OF TERRORISM

1. DEFINING "TERRORISM"

Since the onset of the "war on terrorism", increased attention has been given to the very concept of *terrorism*, to what it means to wage war on terrorism, and to whether "war" is the appropriate response to terrorist violence. Virtually all discussions of these matters take for granted that terrorist violence is a problem, and that if things were going as they should be then such violence would not exist. The debates concern how to best resolve this problem

We cannot make much headway on the latter question – the ethical question – without delineating our subject matter. And here we find that there is considerable disagreement on the meaning of 'terrorism'. Often an explicit definition is not even attempted, and when the matter is broached, it is freely admitted that there is no single universally accepted definition of the term – even the various agencies of the U.S. Government are not united. For example, the U.S. State Department takes its definition from Title 22 of the United States Code, Section 2656f(d):

> "The term "terrorism" means premediated, politically motivated violence perpetrated against noncombatant targets by sub-national groups or clandestine agents, usually intended to influence an audience." (The term "noncombatant" is interpreted to include, in addition to civilians, military personnel who at the time of the incident are unarmed or not on duty.) [*Patterns of Global Terrorism* at www.state.gov]

The FBI endorses a definition found in the U.S. *Code of Federal Regulations*:

> "Terrorism is the unlawful use of force and violence against person or property to intimidate or coerce a government, the civilian population, or any segment thereof, in further of political or social objectives." [www.fbi.gov/publish/terror/terrusa.html]

And the U.S. Defense Department says something similar:

> "Terrorism is the unlawful use of threatened use of force or violence against individuals or property to coerce or intimidate governments or societies, often to achieve political, religious, or ideological objectives." [www.periscope.usni.com/demo/termst0000282.html]

G. Meggle (ed.), Ethics of Terrorism & Counter-Terrorism, 21-37.

These latter two definitions automatically make terrorism unlawful, viz., contrary to the laws of whatever country in which the act is committed, though they leave open whether terrorism can ever be morally justified.

Lack of unanimity on definitional matters need not be a problem for rhetorical purposes, but policy-making and scholarship require some sort of definition in order to identify the phenomenon and to justify ascriptions. Otherwise, how can we determine which actions and agents are "terrorist" and which are not? How else can we fashion policies and institute legislation to deal with what some regard as a fundamental challenge to world peace?

To a certain extent, it is arbitrary how one defines any word, including "terrorism". If we view each of the foregoing definitions as a stipulation about how the word "terrorism" is to be used in a certain discourse by persons in a certain group or agency, then there is no need to quarrel. Such definitions might prove useful insofar as they isolate a concept that has actual instances. But to make points about more widespread rhetorical uses of the term, and the effects of this usage, it is important to discern a meaning of the term "terrorism" that helps us to understand contemporary discourse on the topic. As I argue below, the cited definitions from the U.S. agencies are too idiosyncratic for this purpose, and the following is a better attempt at a *reportive* definition of the term as actually used.

> Terrorism is deliberately subjecting civilians to violence, or to the threat of violence, in order to achieve political objectives.[1]

Let me refer to this as the "standard definition" of 'terrorism'. Four things should be noted about it.

First, the occurrence of 'deliberate' suggests that the perpetrator is intentionally using or threatening violence to achieve political objectives *and* are identifying the targets *as* civilians. Some would insist that the targets are also to be described as "innocent", but it seems wrong to require that the perpretrator also identifies the targets as "innocents" (as Primoratz 1990 does). But given that the intentions and beliefs of the perpetrator are essential in determining whether the action is or is not "terrorist", then either requirement might rule out a good number of acts from being terrorist. For one thing, those who act from outrage over perceived injustices may view some civilians as "enemies" deserving of their fate, and not as "innocent people". For another, harm to civilians might be incidental to the main aim, say, to destroy property, to gain attention, to create an atmosphere of fear, or to provoke a military response, in which case a requirement of "targeting" rules out even the attacks on the World Trade Center towers from being "terrorist" – if we can believe those who say that the strikes were directed at these symbols of American dominance.

Second, it is unclear that this definition *implies* that terrorism is never justifiable. It might seem to have that implication given the use of 'civilians', but I think a separate argument is needed to establish that a given act of violence directed upon such targets is unjustifiable. Definitions that *explicitly* make terrorism illegitimate by describing it as 'unlawful' or 'illegitimate' violence make it much more difficult to classify a given action as a "terrorist" act. A definition that avoids this is preferable because a moral assessment can then be defended on an examination of the case rather than being settled by arbitrary stipulation.

Third, the standard definition excludes no kind of person or organization – including a government or state – from being an agent of terrorism. There are serious drawbacks with the U.S. Code's stipulation that terrorism is "practiced" only by non-state agents or clandestine state agencies, never *states*. For one thing, it is questionable as a reportive definition since, etymologically, the term's root "terror" implies nothing about the identity of the agent. For another, historically, the term "terrorism" has been applied to states.[2] Moreover, the restriction to non-state actors is disingenuous. The term "terrorism" has acquired a pejorative connotation, and for better or worse, it has become the term of art in labeling illegitimate methods of political violence. That states can commit criminal acts of warfare has long been recognized, as shown by the emergence of international agreements like the Hague Conventions of the late 19th and early 20th centuries and the Geneva Conventions of 1949. Insofar as terrorism is a moral problem of *jus in* bello – and not of *jus ad bellum* – then is a problem that stems from the nature of its victims and the methods, not the identity of its agents.

Fourth, it might be thought that because of its etymological roots terrorism involves the creation of terror, fear, and alarm. While several writers speak of such psychological effects as essential to terrorism, the use of "deliberately" in the definiens of the standard definition once again requires care. Fear and alarm are typically the byproducts of actions that deliberately expose civilians to violence; certainly the paradigm instances of terrorism have had such effects. But if the perpetrator's aim is simply to cause outrage and to provoke a response in order to achieve political objectives, then fear and alarm may very well be unintended and inessential byproducts of a terrorist action.

Finally, terrorism, so defined, is nothing new; it is probably as old as organized warfare. What is relatively new is the *rhetoric* of "terror" and the political uses made of it. As I shall now argue, any attempt to craft a proper response to terrorism must first come to terms with the fact that this rhetoric is itself part of the contemporary problem of terrorism.

2. THE CONTEMPORARY USES OF 'TERRORISM'

While the standard definition is tentatively adopted herein, the proposals offered below are compatible with a variety of definitions, for they are based on two facts about the contemporary uses of the word in mainstream American (and Western) discourse within the statements by government agencies, mainstream media, corporate "think tanks", and, to an extent, in the educational systems.

The *first* fact is that *the word "terrorist" has acquired an intensely negative connotation in contemporary discourse.* Terrorism is perceived as breaking the rules of legitimate political violence, first, by refusing to respect the distinction between belligerents and civilians, and second, by using methods that should not be employed, for example, hijacking commercial airliners or killing hostages. As such, it can be said to violate some of the standard rules of *jus in bello* (rules about the just conduct of warfare), specifically, the principles of *discrimination* (noncombatants are immune from attack) and *legitimate means* (criminal means of warfare are prohibited, e.g., torture, use of POWs as shields, no quarter). Terrorism is viewed as reprehensible because it employs illegitimate means against those who should be immune from political violence.[3]

The *second* fact is that viewed from the standpoint of most definitions there is a clear inconsistency in ascriptions of "terrorism". Just ask yourself; who gets labeled as a "terrorist"? All and only those who commit terrorist actions? Guess again. In fact, the answer depends on where you are and to whom you are listening. If you are tuned into the mainstream U.S. media, or into the various agencies of the U.S. government, it quickly becomes apparent that the term "terrorism" is ascribed selectively. Let's look at some examples to illustrate this point.

It is generally accepted in the U.S. that those who flew hijacked planes into the World Trade Center towers, or young Palestinians who have turned themselves into suicide bombers amid civilians, were engaged in terrorist activity. But many actions that would qualify as terrorist under most definitions – certainly under the standard definition and under the State Department's definition – are not typically described as "terrorist", nor are their perpetrators referred to as "terrorists". Some of these were committed by sub-national groups, for example,

- the attacks upon civilians in Nicaragua by the U.S. financed "contra" rebels of the 1980s that claimed over 3000 civilian lives;
- the massacre of over 2000 Palestinian civilians by the Israeli-supported members of Lebanese militias in the Sabra and Shatilla refugee camps in Beirut in 1982;
- the massacre of civilians by death squads in Guatemala and El Salvador during the 1980s.

If we broaden our scope and examine some of the overt actions committed by states, then there are numerous examples that are not usually labeled as "terrorist" though they qualify as such under those definitions that allow for *state* terrorism. These include,

- the destruction of Grozny by Russian forces during the Chechnya war in 1999;
- the US invasion of Panama in 1990;
- the US bombing of Tripoli, Libya in April 1986;
- the US naval bombardment of Lebanese villages in the Chouf mountains in October 1983;
- the Israeli aerial and land bombardment of Beirut in the summer of 1982;
- the Syrian army's attack on the city of Hama in the spring of 1982;
- the Iraqi and Iranian missile attacks on each other cities in the mid 1980s;
- the Indonesian invasion and occupation of East Timor, 1975-1998.

The list goes on and on,[4] and this is to say nothing about more large-scale campaigns such as,

- the U.S. bombing of North Vietnam and Cambodia during the Vietnam war;
- the Allied bombing of German and Japanese cities near the end of WWII;
- the Soviet purges of the 1930s;
- the Nazi mass murders of civilian populations during WWII;
- the cultural revolution of Mao Zedong in the 1960s.

If we consider the provisions of jus in bello as part of international law, then the U.S. Government has repeatedly used – in the words of the FBI definition – "force or violence" unlawfully "to intimidate or coerce a government, [a] civilian population, or [a] segment thereof", in order to achieve "political or social objectives".

State-terrorism can take other forms. For example, there is the institutionalized violence exercised against Palestinian civilians throughout Israel's 37-year occupation of the West Bank and Gaza Strip. The occupation has featured widespread abuses of human rights, including torture, deportation, collective punishment, economic strangulation, destruction of property, confiscation of land, and killing unarmed civilians, actions that are routinely designed to intimidate a civilian population in order to secure political objectives (in this case, control over territory). Yet, this brand of structural violence against civilians is almost never referred to as "terrorism". The same can be said about the US-led campaign against Iraq throughout the 1990s, including both the bombing of Iraqi technological infrastructure in 1991 and the subsequent policy of sanctions that have led to the deaths of over a million Iraqis.[5]

At the opposite extreme, some actions are routinely labeled "terrorist" that do not qualify as terrorist under the standard definition nor under the definitions championed by U.S. governmental agencies. For example, the U.S. media is replete with references to "terrorist" actions by the Lebanese group, Hezbollah, against the Israeli military in southern Lebanon, or by Palestinians against Israeli soldiers in the occupied territories, targets that hardly qualify as civilians or noncombatants. Apart from the State Department's unusually strict definition of "noncombatant", the same can be said for actions directed against the U.S. military, say, the bombing of the USS Cole in Yemen in October 2000, or the bombing of the U.S. Marine barracks in Beirut in October 1983 (see note 1).[6]

One way to explain, and even justify, the inconsistent ascriptions of terrorism, is to argue that the term "terrorist" has an *indexical* or *egocentric* character, essentially dependent upon a speaker's point of view, much like the word "enemy" or the phrase "the enemy". No one is an *enemy* as such, but only an enemy *to* someone or other, so that when I use "enemy" and "the enemy" I am talking about *my* enemy or *our* enemy. Similarly, when we hear people speaking of "terrorism", in actual practice they are talking about violence directed against "themselves", or, in first-person terms, against "us".[7]

Some newspaper editors are up front about this. For example, in an article on the T-word, subtitled "When is it OK to label an event a terrorist act?" (March 21,

2002), the Public Editor of the *Chicago Tribune*, Don Wycliff, pointed out that while his paper routinely refers to the attacks of September 11 as acts of terrorism, it withholds that designation from actions in other places where some argue it is warranted. He explained the *Tribune*'s policy as follows:

> "We routinely refer to the attacks of Sept. 11 as acts of terrorism, but withhold that designation from other actions in other places (mainly the Middle East) where some people argue it is warranted. How to justify the difference? Well – and this is just one journalist's view – the *Tribune* is an American newspaper written principally for an American audience and owing its existence and independence to the American Constitution. Our perspective is inescapably American (which is not to say it is necessarily the same as that of the U.S. government). Inevitably, as the news of Sept. 11 is reported and interpreted, *that perspective is reflected in the product*. Indeed, it almost has to be if we are to speak intelligibly on those events to our audience."

Here we can see, in one article, an explicit admission by an editor of a major American newspaper that the term "terrorism" has both an egocentric character as well as a negative connotation. The best that can be said is that the *Tribune*, at least, is candid about its selective usage.

Neither the *Tribune*, the American media in general, nor the U. S. Government, is unique in its speaker-oriented bias; who receives the "terrorist" label depends on where you are and to whom you are listening. The U.S. is not alone in this regard; other countries, including Israel, Great Britain, Russia, India, and Egypt routinely do the same, and so might any state in describing militant insurgents opposed to its policies, for example, the Nazis in describing resistance fighters in the Warsaw ghetto (Herman and O'Sullivan, *ibid.*, p. 261).

Yet, unlike the term "enemy", it is doubtful that anything in the *semantics* of "terrorism" warrants the egocentric usage. Even if we do allow it, a problem arises the moment one wishes to ascribe terrorism to certain individuals and groups *and*, at the same time, make moral claims about terrorism, e.g., that it is an unjust or immoral use of violence. Just as there is no automatic moral taint to being an *enemy* – many good people have been enemies to someone or other – then if a terrorist act is wrongful, it is not *because* it is politically motivated violence directed *at us*. If an action is illegitimate, it is because it possesses some universalizable morally relevant characteristic, e.g., that it violence directed at civilians, or against innocent people, or that it uses improper means, or that it is politically motivated violence, or – from a pacifist perspective – that it is violence. For the purposes of making a moral claim, the egocentric character of the term "terrorism" is irrelevant.

These subtleties of indexical usage and moral relevance are lost upon the general public. As a consequence, the two features of the contemporary rhetoric of "terror", its pejorative overtones and its egocentric orientation, serve to seriously distort the average person's conception of who is and who is not carrying out wrongful actions in the world. What's worse, the distortion is deliberate, not an innocent or accidental byproduct of linguistic usage, as I shall now explain.

3. 'TERRORISM' AS A TERRORIST WEAPON

If we are to judge by the actual amount of damage, state terrorism is by far the more prevalent and deadly form of terrorism. The weaponry and organization that modern states have brought to bear in pursuing their ends through violence consistently dwarfs any amount of harm to civilians done by non-state actors engaged in terrorist activity. What is not often understood, is that the rhetoric of "terror" is one of the means whereby states carry out their terrorism.

It is important to understand how this is accomplished. The discriminatory ascriptions of "terrorism" and "terrorist" by the U.S. Government, echoed by the mainstream American media and the corporate "think tanks", illustrate that there is no real concern with consistency, completeness, and accuracy in their application. *Instead these labels are used selectively by governments, their associated media, and their agencies of propaganda, to describe those who forcefully oppose governmental policies.* Because of its negative connotation, the "terrorist" label automatically discredits any individuals or groups to which it is affixed, dehumanizes them, places them outside the norms of acceptable social and political behavior, and portrays them as "evil" people that cannot be reasoned with. As a consequence, the rhetoric discredits any individuals or groups that are described as "terrorist", and thereby,

–   erases any incentive an audience might have to understand their point of view so that questions about the nature and origns of their grievances and the possible legitimacy of their demands will not even be raised;
–   deflects attention away from one's own policies that might have contributed to their grievances;
–   repudiates any calls to negotiate with them;
–   paves the way for the use of force and violence in dealing with them, and in particular, gives a government "freedom of action" by exploiting the fears of its own citizens and stifling any objections to the manner in which it deals with them;
–   obliterates the distinction between national liberation movements and fringe fanatics.

The general strategy is nothing new; it is part and parcel of the war of ideas and language that accompanies overt hostilities. The term 'terrorism' is simply the current vogue for discrediting one's opponents, to pave the way for action against them, *before* the risky business of inquiry into their complaints can even begin. If individuals and groups are portrayed as evil, irrational, barbaric, and beyond the pale of negotiation and compromise, then asking why they resort to terrorism is viewed as pointless, needlessly accommodating, or, at best, mere pathological curiosity.[8]

Rhetoric of this magnitude is bound to produce results in a context of political turmoil, especially among agitated people looking for solutions. The language of "terror" fosters shortsighted belligerence among those oblivious to its propagandistic employment, while increasing the resentment of those who are so labeled. Far from contributing to a *peaceful* resolution of conflict, it prepares both types of person for more violence. Moreover, by so effectively erasing any incentive to understand the motives behind terrorist violence or to critically examine governmental policies, the rhetoric serves to silence meaningful political debate. Those normally inclined to ask "why?" are fearful being labeled "soft" on terrorism, while the more militant use the "terrorist" label to deface the distinction between critical examination and appeasement.

Obviously, to point out the causes and objectives of particular terrorist actions is to imply nothing about their legitimacy – that is an independent matter – nor is it a capitulation to terrorist demands. To *ignore* these causes and objectives is to seriously undermine attempts to deal intelligently with terrorism, since it leaves untouched the factors motivating recourse to this type of violence. More dramatically, the rhetoric of "terror" actually *increases* terrorism in four distinct ways. *First*, it magnifies the effect of terrorist actions by heightening the fear among the target population. If we demonize the terrorists, if we portray them as arbitrary irrational beings devoid of a moral sense and beyond all norms, we are amplifying the fear and alarm among civilians that is generated by terrorist incidents, regardless if this forms part of the political objectives of the perpetrators.

Second, those who succumb to the rhetoric contribute to the cycle of revenge and retaliation by endorsing violent actions of their own government, not only against those who commit terrorist actions, but also against those *populations* from whose ranks the terrorists emerge, for the simple reason that terrorists are frequently themselves civilians, living amid other civilians not so engaged. The consequence has been an increase in politically motivated violence against civilian targets – "terrorism" under any other name – under the rubric of "retaliation" or "counter-terrorism".[9]

Third, short of genocide, a violent response is likely to stiffen the resolve of those from whose ranks terrorists have emerged, leading them to regard their foes as people who cannot be reasoned with, as people who, because they avail themselves so readily of the rhetoric of "terror", know only the language of force. As long as they perceive themselves to be victims of intolerable injustices and view their oppressors as unwilling to arrive at an acceptable compromise, they are likely to answer violence with more violence. The latter would appropriately be labeled "terrorist" if it were directed against civilians for some political objective. But if the perpetrators have given up hope, it would be more appropriately labeled the violence of despair or revenge.

Fourth, and most insidiously, those who employ the rhetoric of "terror" for their own political ends, are encouraging actions that they understand will generate or sustain further violence directed against civilians. Inasmuch as their verbal behavior is *intended* to secure political objectives through these means, then it is an *instance* of terrorism just as much as any direct order to carry out a bombing of civilian targets. In both cases, there is purposeful verbal action aimed at bringing about a particular result through violence against civilians. Here, "terrorism" becomes a terrorist weapon and, therefore, part of the problem of terrorism.

In his futuristic novel, *1984*, George Orwell described *doublethink* as "the power of holding two contradictory beliefs in one's mind simultaneously, and accepting both of them", and he portrayed it as a device for destroying the capacity for independent critical thinking. Something like doublethink is occurring as the result of the rhetoric of terror. In condemning terrorism, well-meaning people think of it as something bad and to be eliminated at all costs. But in knowingly sanctioning the use of force against civilian populations in order to achieve this end, they are advocating the very thing they condemn – and this is closer to doublethink that we should ever wish to be.

4. AN EXAMPLE: THE ISRAELI-PALESTINIAN CONFLICT

The paradigm instance of the political use of the term "terrorism" is the manner in which this term has been employed in the Israeli-Palestinian conflict. Politically motivated violence against civilians has accompanied the Israeli-Palestinian conflict since its inception in the late 19th century. In the first half-century of this conflict, there were numerous incidents resulting in casualties to hundreds of Arab and Jewish civilians battling over the future of British-governed Palestine. Violence against unarmed civilians was practiced by both sides, sometimes with monumental results. Perhaps the most notorious incident occurred in April of 1948 when Jewish irregulars massacred more than 250 Arab villagers from Deir Yassin, causing widespread panic among Arab villages throughout Palestine and precipitating the flight of over 300,000 Arabs from their homes.[10]

After the establishment of Israel in 1948, and the dismantling of large segments of the Palestinian community and the creation of the Palestinian refugee problem, organized struggle against Israel took time to develop among the Palestinian refugees. It was not until after the 1967 War and the occupation of the remaining portions of Palestine that Palestinian resistance fighters began to make international news. In the late 1960s, Palestinian militants, working within groups like *Al-Fatah,* were described in the international press as "guerrillas", "commandos", and "fedayeen" (sacrificers). It was not until after the September 1970 civil war in Jordan, that the Israeli designations of Palestinian fighters as 'murderers', 'saboteurs' and 'terrorists' became more widespread, at least in the western media. This was partly due to notorious actions by some of the militants themselves, viz., airplane hijackings by PFLP members in 1968-1970, and the attempted kidnapping of Israeli athletes at the Munich Olympics in 1972 that led to the deaths of eleven Israelis and five Palestinians.

It is estimated that over 500 million people witnessed these events on television (Wierinka 1993, p. 43). As another Palestinian spokesman put it: the Munich operation was like "painting the name of Palestine on the top of a mountain that can be seen from the four corners of the earth" (Hirst 1984, p. 311). The Palestinian's recourse to terrorism succeeded in placing Palestinian grievances and aspirations on the World's agenda. But, too often, their complaints were lost in the sensationalism of the deed. In the minds of many, disgust with the means outpaced sympathy with plight of Palestinian refugees and trumped the patience needed to understand core grievances. As the 1970s wore on, and various leftwing groups in Europe and elsewhere made headlines with similar sorts of violence, the "terrorists" came to be viewed as a new type of barbarians whose willingness to hijack airplanes, to take hostages, and especially, to carry their struggle into foreign lands, placed them outside the bounds of civilized behavior. When the Reagan Administration came into power in January 1981, combating this brand of "international terrorism" emerged as a foremost goal of U.S. foreign policy.

Government officials realized that the rhetoric of "terror" had now become a preeminent propaganda device, one that could be used not only to discredit their opponents, but also to obfuscate and to deflect attention away from their own controversial policies. A prime example, relevant to the Israeli-Palestinian conflict, is a well-known book edited by Benjamin Netanyahu entitled, *Terrorism: How the West Can Win* published in 1986, featured in *Time* Magazine shortly thereafter, and used in political science courses in American universities during the late 1980s and 1990s.

While Netanyahu's book offers a standard definition of "terrorism", the editor and the contributors apply the term selectively, and argue that the only way to combat terrorism is to "to weaken and destroy the terrorist's ability to consistently launch attacks", even at the "risk of civilian casualties" (pp. 202-205). Very little is said about the possible causes of terrorist violence beyond vague allusions to Islam's confrontation with modernity (p. 82), or passages of this calibre from Netanyahu's own pen:

> "The root cause of terrorism lies not in grievances but in a disposition toward unbridled violence. This can be traced to a worldview that asserts that certain ideological and religious goals justify, indeed demand, the shedding of all moral inhibitions. In this context, the observation that the root cause of terrorism is terrorists is more than a tautology." (p. 204)

The scholar can pass off comments like these as pure propaganda – if not a brand of psychological lunacy – but it is significant that Netanyahu's book has reached a large audience, especially since its contributors include not only academics and journalists but important policy makers as well. Netanyahu himself went on to become the Israeli Prime Minister, and among the American contributors were the Secretary of State George Schultz, U.N. Ambassador Jeanne Kirkpatrick, and Senators Daniel Moynihan and Alan Cranston, each of whom voiced sentiments similar to those of Netanyahu. The upshot was that a terrorist is portrayed as a carrier of "oppression and enslavement", having "no moral sense", "a perfect nihilist" (pp. 29-30), and whose elimination is the only rational means for the West to "win".

Netanyahu's book conceals an unspoken agenda. By classifying Palestinian resistance to Israeli policies as "terrorism", and by portraying "terrorists" as some sort of monsters unworthy of moral dialogue, the effect of his book, if not its intent, is to shift political focus away from the designs, policies, and actions of the Israeli Government in the occupied territories, e.g., its land confiscations, settlement building, human rights abuses, blatant violations of Security Council resolutions – in a word, its slow but steady policy of territorial expansion – towards the more sensational reactions by the Palestinians. Its strategy manifests this logic: *to get away with a big crime, demonize your victims.*[11]

Netanyahu's exhortation to violence is advanced under the principle that the only way to deal with terrorism is with counter-terrorist violence. This has characterized the policy of successive Israeli governments since the early 1950s, but the result has only *increased* the amount of terrorism in the Near East, especially over the past quarter-century. For example, during the ten-year period from 1978-1987, eighty-two Israelis were killed in terrorist attacks perpetrated by Palestinians, a rate of a little more than eight Israelis per year, including both civilians and security personnel. Yet, in 1982 alone, approximately 18.000 Arab civilians lost their lives in the Israeli invasion of Lebanon. Within the next ten-year period, 1988-1997, the number of Israeli civilians killed jumped to 421, that is, to an average of 42 Israeli deaths per year. During this time same ten-year period, at least 1.385 Palestinians in the Occupied Territories were killed by Israeli security forces (all but 18 of these were civilians). In the first three and a half years since the second Intifada began in late September 2000 approximately 900 Israelis have lost their lives – a rate of more than 250 Israeli deaths per year – whereas about 3000 Palestinians have been slain. Again, the vast bulk of the fatalities on both sides have been civilians.[12]

Figures like these indicate that Israeli "reprisal" killings of Palestinians have not deterred Palestinian violence directed at Israelis. That most Israelis have died in suicide attacks refutes Netanyahu's claim that terrorists will rarely engage in terror tactics if the risks to their own survival are too great. They go directly against his argument that "counter-terrorist" deterrence will put a stop to terrorism and protect innocent civilians from terrorist violence. Despite Israel's policy of retaliatory deterrence, Israelis are less secure today than they were ten years ago, and certainly less than twenty years ago. If any causal claim is to be made, it is that Israeli attacks against Palestinian leaders, institutions, towns, villages, and camps, have only intensified Palestinian anger and stiffened Palestinian resolve. And because honor, and its offspring, revenge, can override fear of death, the average Israeli is in more danger of being harmed by politically-motivated violence than ever before.[13]

Yet, as the figures show, in terms of sheer numbers the Palestinians have been even more victimized by the rhetoric of 'terror'. Not only have they lost more people, their entire infrastructures – their political, economic, educational, and medical institutions, their technological and agricultural resources – have been devastated by the Israeli military campaign. Unemployment and malnourishment are rampant, curfews and checkpoints strangle their movement, and increasingly, the last refuge of civilians, their houses, have been destroyed as they watch, or, in some cases, over their heads.

The most devastating uses of 'terrorism' in the Israeli-Palestinian conflict have been to justify horrific actions by the IDF against Palestinians in refugee camps. In September 1982, for example, after the evacuation of PLO fighters from Beirut, Israeli officials contended that some "2000 terrorists" remained in the refugee camps Sabra and Shatilla in southern Beirut, a claim repeated in the Israeli press. On September 15, the Israeli Defense Minister, Ariel Sharon, authorized entry of what were presumed to be members of the Lebanese militia into the camps that were then sealed off by Israeli tanks. The only resistance they encountered came from a few lightly armed boys. For the next 38 hours, aided by Israeli flares at night, the militiamen raped, tortured, mutilated and massacred over 2000 civilians under the eye of IDF personnel.

As Prime Minister of Israel since March 2001, Sharon, once again, has been able to act on his ambitions, refusing to negotiate with the Palestinian leadership, intensifying settlement building in the West Bank, and adopting an iron fist approach to Palestinian resistance. After the on-going battles of the Al-Aqsa Intifada led to a rash of suicide bombings in Israel in March 2002, Sharon sent IDF troops, tanks, and helicopter gunships into the Palestinian-controlled areas of the West Bank, vowing to destroy the Palestinian "terrorist infrastructure". The assault of the Jenin refugee camp in April 2002, was the most devastating attack on a Palestinian population center in the West Bank during 35 years of Israeli occupation. As with Sabra and Shatilla, the Israelis claim to be fighting terrorism, but the principal result has been the destruction of Palestinian civilian property, homes, institutions, and lives.

That the Israeli government could so easily succeed in convincing people that Israel was eliminating the "terrorist infrastructure" of the Palestinians – rather than a good deal of the institutional structure of Palestinian society – illustrates how the rhetoric of 'terror' is a causal factor in generating even more terrorism. On one side, the bulk of the Israeli public and the American Congress were led to endorse Sharon's actions, giving a green light for a continuation of his offensive against "terrorism", an offensive that continues as I write. On the other side, the flames of outrage and revenge have been fanned, once again, among Palestinians and their sympathizers. The upshot has increased – and will continue to increase – the shedding of innocent blood on both sides, hence, to *more* terrorism, not less.

5. MOVING BEYOND THE RHETORIC: THE PROPER RESPONSE TO TERRORISM

In the absence of a negotiated settlement, the continuation of tit-for-tat violence between Israelis and Palestinians is guaranteed. This has long been forseen. Already in 1956, the U.N. Secretary-General, Dag Hammarskjold, informed Israel's Prime Minister, David Ben-Gurion, that Israel's retaliatory actions against Palestinians would postpone indefinitely peaceful coexistence between Israelis and Arabs. Hammarskjold's advice went unheeded as successive Israeli governments added retaliation to retaliation, with deterrence offered as the standard justification (Dayan 1968, Netanyahu 1993). As Hammarskjold predicted, the effect has been the very opposite. The journalist, Raymond Close, summarized the situation accurately as follows:

> "The state of Israel has been committed for 50 years to a policy of massive and ruthless retaliation – deliberately disproportional. "Ten eyes for an eye", the Israeli like to say. And still their policy fails, because they have not recognized what the thoughtful ones among them know to be true – that terrorism will thrive as long as the Palestinian population is obsessed with the injustice of their lot and consumed with despair." (Close 1998)

The United States has edged ever closer to mimicking Israeli strategy in its confrontation with terrorism (cf., the example of the State Department guidelines on dealing with terrorism noted above). Yet, as Close went on to write, for America to adopt the Israeli model would "weaken its leadership position in the world" and undermine the most effective defenses we have against terrorism, namely, "a commitment to the rule of law, dedication to the fairness and evenhandedness in settling international disputes, and a reputation as the most humanitarian nation in the world". Former Assistant Secretary of State George Ball argued in the same manner in *The New York Times* on December 16, 1984:

> "... let us take care that we are not led, through panic and anger, to embrace counter-terrorism and international lynch law and thus reduce our nation's conduct to the squalid level of the terrorists. Our prime objective should clearly be to correct, or at least mitigate, the fundamental grievances that nourish terrorism rather than engage in pre-emptive and retaliatory killing of those affected by such grievances."

Yet, ever since 1981, when Secretary of State Alexander Haig announced that "terrorism" would replace "human rights" as the main foreign policy concern of the Reagan Administration, the U.S. Government has focused its energies on a military response to terrorism while systematically ignoring the grievances that have spawned the recourse to political violence. Edging ever closer to the Israeli strategy, the State Department developed just "four basic policy tenets" for dealing with terrorism:

> *First*, make no concession to terrorists and strike no deals.
> *Second*, bring terrorists to justice for their crimes.
> *Third*, isolate and apply pressure on states that sponsor terrorism to force them to change their behavior.
> *Fourth*, bolster the counterterrorist capabilities of those countries that work with the United States and require assistance.

Nowhere does the State Department call for investigating the *causes* of persistent terrorist violence, or for any sort of policy review. This is surprising given that the State Department is a policy-making sector of the U.S. Government – unlike the law-enforcement agencies for whom these guidelines are more understandable. Its refusal to deal squarely with the *political* origins of terrorism has led it to adopt a position of dealing with the symptoms while ignoring the causes. The rhetoric of "terror" might not have caused the development of this curious stance, but it has paved the way for its acceptance by the general public.[14]

There are legitimate ways of responding *to* terrorist actions without responding *with* terrorism. Assuming that an act of terrorism is wrongful and intolerable, then attempts must obviously be made to identify, apprehend, and prosecute the individuals and organizations responsible. Yet, any resort to force must abide by the standard provision of *jus in bello*, being careful to target only those for whom one has firm evidence of terrorist activity and, above all, avoiding the kind of "counter-terrorism" that only intensifies hatred and the passion for revenge.

More importantly, steps must be taken to examine and address the *causes* of persistent terrorism steming from a given population. Such violence is symptomatic of a serious political problem and feeds on outrage over perceived injustices to an entire people. As long as the members of that population feel they have a legitimate cause worth dying for, and decide that terrorism is the *only* viable response, then retaliation, coupled with a persistent failure to address grievances, will only intensify resentment and hatred. Rather than solve the problem, the parties will be wrapped in an ever-increasing spiral of violence.

To deal with terrorism in a rational manner, we must first remove the obstacles to clear thinking about the problem, always keeping in view the fact that language moulds thought and thought precipitates action. We must recognize the rhetoric of "terror" is itself a political weapon. Its victims are typically civilians whose grievances are ignored and who suffer from reprisals against their communities because some of their members have found violence to be the only way to react in a desperate hope that somehow, someone with enough sense and power will realize that these grievances must be addressed. When this rhetoric succeeds in cutting off rational inquiry into the grievances of entire communities, when it becomes an obstacle to a clear moral assessment of political conflicts, then it only contributes to further terrorism. This is the principal lesson to be drawn from the persistent use of "terrorism" and "terrorist" in depicting the conflict between Israelis and Palestinians. If we wish avoid plunging the entire world into a similar cycle of strike and reprisal, then we must learn that the first target in a real "war on terrorism" should be the rhetoric of "terror".

NOTES

[1] Noam Chomsky uses 'terrorism' to refer to "the threat or use of violence to intimidate or coerce (generally for political ends)" (quoted in Shafritz 1991, p. 264), and Paul Wilkinson describes terrorism as "the systematic use of coercive intimidation, usually to service political ends", that commonly targets "innocent civilians" (Wilkinson 2000, pp. 12-13). See also, Netanyahu 2001, p. 8 which defines terrorism as "the deliberate and systematic assault on civilians to inspire fear for political ends", and Chasdi 2002, p. 9, who characterizes terrorism in terms of the "threat, practice, or promotion of force for political objectives". While "civilians" is used more commonly than "noncombatants" in defining "terrorism", one might suppose that the two terms are coextensional. However, since some military personnel are noncombatants, I will take "civilians" to specify a narrower category that excludes members of a military organization. Here, *political objectives* have to do with control over certain regions or organizations.

[2] The Jacobins first employed the term during the French Revolution, applying it to the actions of the revolutionary government in eradicating its enemies. By the mid-nineteenth century, it was used to signify anti-government activities, for example, the campaigns of Irish dissidents in the 1860s and of Russian revolutionaries of the 1880s (Laqueur 1987, chp. 1; White 2002, chap. 5). That there are no semantic grounds for restricting terrorism to non-state agents is also evident in the most recent editions of the *Oxford English Dictionary*, *Webster's Dictionary of the English Language*, the *Encyclopedia Britannica*, and the *Encyclopedia Americana*.

[3] The terms "terrorist" and "terrorism" have not always been associated with a negative connotation. While the Jacobins used "terrorist" with a positive connotation, a negative sense was associated with the term in the writings of Edmund Burke (Laqueur 1987, p. 11). Geoffrey Nunberg has noted that "… the word "terrorism" led a double life – a justified political strategy to some, an abomination to others". The Russian revolutionaries who assassinated Tsar Alexander II in 1881 used the word proudly. As late as 1947, the Jewish Stern Gang in Palestine referred to themselves as 'terrorists' and Ben Hecht wrote approvingly of the Jewish "terrorists of Palestine" in their attacks upon British targets in Palestine (Hirst 1984, p. 119).

[4] The failure to recognize such instances of state terrorism is pointed out in many places, for instance, in Chomsky 1988a and 1988b, Herman 1982, and Falk 1991. See also the examples listed in Herman and O'Sullivan 1991, George 1991, and Budiardjo 1991.

[5] Documentation concerning both cases can be found on the websites of several human rights organizations, including, Human Rights Watch, Amnesty International, Voices in the Wilderness, The

World Health Organization, and the Israeli human rights organization, B'tselem. See also Clark, et. al. 1992. U.S. Secretary of State Madeleine Albright admitted that the sanctions were intended to serve a political purpose despite acknowledged harm to civilians. When asked what she felt about the deaths of 500.000 Iraqi children caused by the sanctions, Albright replied that it was "a very hard choice", but, all things considered, "we think the price is worth it" (*60 Minutes* interview, aired May 12th 1996).

[6] See for example, the State Department's *Patterns of Global Terrorism-2000* (reprinted in Yonah Alexander and Donald J. Musch, *Terrorism: Documents of International and Local Control*. Volume 26 (Dobbs Ferry, NY: Oceana Publications INC, 2001), pp. 1-126. In it one finds the Hezbollah attacks on the Israeli targets described as "terrorist" despite the fact that these attacks were directed upon the Israeli military in southern Lebanon (p. 39). Again, the actions of Palestinian groups Hamas and Islamic Jihad are described as "terrorist" even when directed against Israeli occupying forces, whereas Israel's undercover assassinations of Palestinian figures were not so described (pp. 41-45).

[7] Among scholars this has been known for some time. In 1977, C. C. O'Brien wrote: "The words "terrorism" and "terrorist" are not terms of scientific classification. They are imprecise and emotive. We do not apply them to all acts of politically motivated violence or to all people who commit such crimes. We reserve their use for politically-motivated violence of which we disapprove." (O'Brien 1977, p. 91) Noam Chomsky has repeatedly pointed out that there is a "propangandistic usage" in which "the term 'terrorism' is used to refer to terrorist acts committed by enemies against us or our allies" (Interview Number 5 with Chomsky on Znet at www.znet.com.) Similar points are made by Oliverio 1998, chp. 1. Robert Picard writes that it "has become an axiom that terrorism describes acts of violence committed by others, and the similar violence committed by one's own nation or by those with whom one sympathizes, is legitimate" (Picard 1993, p. 3). See also John Collins 2002, pp. 163-166 who argues that it is essential that the US not define 'terrorism' at all, since otherwise the US and its allies would be deemed guilty of terrorism as well. There have been studies that confirm this egocentric usage of "terrorism" in major American media, for example, a study by Brian K. Simmons, "U.S. News magazines' Labeling of Terrorists", in: A. O. Alali, and K. K. Eke (eds.), *Media Coverage of Terrorism*. London: 1991, pp. 23-39. (I thank Erich Schulte for bringing to my attention the indexical character of "terrorism".)

[8] Israel and the Western Democracies adopted the use of "terrorism" in the 1970s to describe those who opposed their policies (see Herman and O'Sullivan 1991, pp. 43-46). During this period, terrorists were portrayed as anti-democratic forces supported by Soviet style communism. In the 1990s, after the fall of the Soviet Union, the pro-communist gloss was submerged and terrorists were seen as an expression of radical Islam. In 1999, the Russians themselves began to use the label, calling the Chechnya rebels "terrorists" during the second invasion of Chechnya. Previously, Moscow had identified the rebels as "bandits" *Chicago Tribune*, Nov. 3, 2002, Section 2, p. 5.

[9] See Alon 1980, pp. 68-81, which mentions that the Israeli policy of combating "international terrorism" included the proviso that civilian populations that "shelter anti-Israeli terrorists" will not be immune from punitive action. See also Gal-Or 1994, for a discussion of Israeli policy, and also the earlier study of Blechman 1971. Ever since the early 1950s, Israeli "reprisals" for violence against Israelis committed by Palestinians has routinely resulted in the deaths of more Arab civilians (see Hirst, *op. cit.*, chapters 6, 8, 9, 10, and also, the statistics of B'tselem at www.btselem.org). The same thinking was evident in the U.S. According to a *New York Times* poll published on September 16, 2001, 59.9% of Americans supported the use of military force against terrorism even if it were to cause the deaths of thousands of innocent civilians.

[10] See Khalidi 1971, Part IV; Flapan 1987, pp. 83-109; and Morris 1987, chp. 3. One objective of the Jewish underground during the 1947-49 war between Jews and Arabs was to induce as many Palestinian Arabs to flee from their homes in Palestine as was possible. Through a few well-timed massacres, notably of some 250 civilians in the Palestinian village of Deir Yassin in April 1948, over 300.000 Palestinians fled from their homes, villages, and lands in the areas that eventually became part of Israel, paving the way for the establishment of a decisive Jewish majority in these areas (Chaim Weizmann, Israel's first president, described this flight of Palestinians, and the forced removal of some 400.000 others, as "a miraculous clearing of the land: the miraculous simplification of Israeli's task" (Hirst, *op. cit.*, p.143). Menachem Begin, head of the Jewish terrorist group, Irgun, wrote: "Of the about 800.000 Arabs who lived on the present territory of the State of Israel, only some 165.000 are still there. The political and economic significance of this development can hardly be overestimated." (Menachem Begin, *The Revolt*, London: W. H. Allen, 1951, p. 164.)

[11] Noam Chomsky wrote of this a decade before: "The Palestinians are a particularly natural target for Western racism. They are weak and dispersed, hounded on every side, but they refuse to accept their fate and melt away, an affront to civilization – not unlike the Jews. They must be despised, or how are we to justify their fate?"(Chomsky 1976)

[12] The estimate of Israeli fatalities is that of the Israeli Embassy in the United Kingdom, at www.israel-embassy.org.uk/web/pages/fatal.htm and the Israeli human rights group, B'tselem at www.btselem.org. The figures on the Palestinians are from B'tselem and from the Palestine Monitor at www.palestinemonitor.org/factsheet/Palestinian_killed_fact_sheet.htm.

[13] Palestinian suicide bombings began after the murder of 29 Palestinians by a Jewish settler, Baruch Goldstein, at a mosque in Hebron in 1994. The perpetrators of the Palestinian suicide bombings during the Al Aqsa Intifada have repeatedly cited revenge as a motive. See for example, articles posted at the following URLs: www.scoop.co.nz/mason/stories/HL0112/S00003.htm, and www.theage.com.au/articles/2002/07/23/1027332376744.html.

[14] See "Patterns of Global Terrorism", available at the State Department website at www.state.gov. The U.S. Government's refusal to consider causes and possible grievances, much less engage in policy review, has been matched by media trends. In the three weeks after the 9/11 attacks, for example, of the 46 oped pieces dealing with the attacks that appeared in *The New York Times* and *Washington Post*, 44 argued for a military response, and only two raised other possibilities (FAIR, "Op-Ed Chamber: Little Space for Dissent to the Military Line", Nov. 2, 2001 at www.fair.org/activism/nyt-wp-opeds.html). This same tendency has been carried over to the discussions preceding the build-up of war against Iraq. The State Department's exclusion of any evaluation of policy or examination of causes is echoed in a recent publication from the Center for Strategic and International Studies, *To Prevail: An American Strategy for the Campaign Against Terrorism* (www.csis.org/press/pr01_69.htm).

REFERENCES

Abou Iyad, with Eric Rouleau (1981), *My Home, My Land: a Narrative of the Palestinian Struggle*. New York: Times Books.

Alexander, Yonah and Donald J. Musch (2001), *Terrorism: Documents of International and Local Control*. Volume 26. Dobbs Ferry, NY: Oceana Publications Inc.

Ashmore, Robert (1997), "State Terrorism and its Sponsors", in: Tomis Kapitan (ed.), *Philosophical Perspectives on the Israeli-Palestinian Conflict*. Armonk NY, M. E. Sharpe: 105-132.

Budiardjo, Carmel (1991), "Indonesia: Mass Exterminations and the Consolidations of Authoritarian Power", in: George 1991: 180-211.

Collins, John (2002), "Terrorism", in: *Collateral Language*, edited by John Collins and Ross Glover, NYU Press, 155-173.

Chasdi, Richard J., *Serenade of Suffering: A Portrait of Middle East Terrorism, 1968-1993*. Lanham, MD: Lexington Books.

Chasdi, Richard J. (2002), *Tapestry of Terror: A Portrait of Middle East Terrorism 1994-1999*. Lanham, MD: Lexington Books.

Chomsky, Noam (1991), "International Terrorism: Image and Reality", in: George 1991: 12-38.

Chomsky, Noam. (1988a), *The Culture of Terrorism*. Boston: South End Press.

Chomsky, Noam (1988b), "Middle East Terrorism and the American Ideological System", in: Said and Hitchens 1988: 97-148.

Chomsky, Noam (1976), "Civilized Terrorism", *Sevendays*, July 26, 1976.

Clark, Ramsey, et. al. (1992), *War Crimes: A Report on United States War Crimes Against Iraq*. Washington, DC: Maisonneuve Press.

Cyran, Phillip (2001), "Defining Terrorism", *Counterpunch* November 29, 2001, www.counterpunch.org/cryan1.html.

Dayan, Moshe (1968), "Why Israel Strikes Back", in: Donald Robinson (ed.), *Under Fire: Israel's Twenty Year Struggle for Survival*. New York: Norton.

Falk, Richard (1991), "The Terrorist Foundations of Recent U.S. Policy", in: George 1991: 102-120.

Flapan, Simha (1987), *The Birth of Israel*. New York: Pantheon Books.

George, Alexander (ed., 1991), *Western State Terrorism*. New York, Routledge.

Herman, Edward (1982), *The Real Terror Network: Terrorism in Fact and Propaganda*. Boston: South End Press.

Herman, Edward and Gerry O'Sullivan (1989), *The Terrorism Industry*. New York: Pantheon Books.

Herman, Edward S. and Gerry O'Sullivan (1991), ""Terrorism" as Ideology and Cultural Identity", in: George 1991: 39-75.

Hirst, David (1984), *The Gun and the Olive Branch*. London: Faber and Faber.

Jenkins, Brian (1985), *International Terrorism: The Other World War*. Santa Monica, CA, The Rand Corporation.

Jensen, Robert and Rahul Mahajan (2001), "Draining the Swamp of Terrorists", *Counterpunch*, Sept. 24, 2001. http://www.counterpunch.org/jensen4.html.

Khalidi, Walid (1971), *From Haven to Conquest*. Beirut: Institute of Palestine Studies.

Laqueur, Walter (1987), *The Age of Terrorism*. Boston: Little, Brown and Company.

Levy, Gideon (2003), "Terrorism by any other name", *Ha'aretz* Sunday, March 09, 2003.

Morris, Benny (1987), *The birth of the Palestinian refugee problem, 1947-1949*. Cambridge: Cambridge University Press.

Netanyahu, Benjamin (1986), *Terrorism: How the West Can Win*. New York: Farrar, Straus, Giroux.

Netanyahu, Binyamin (2001), *Fighting Terrorism: How Democracies Can Defeat The International Terrorist Network*. New York: Farrar, Straus & Giroux.

O'Ballance, Edgar (1979), *The Language of Violence*. San Rafael, CA: Presidio Press.

O'Brien C. C. (1977), "Liberty and Terrorism", *International Security*, 2.

Oliverio, Annemarie (1998), *The State of Terror*. Albany, NY: SUNY Press.

Perlman, Diane (2002), "Intersubjective Dimensions of Terrorism and its Transcendence", in: Chris E. Stout (ed.), *The Psychology of Terrorism*. 4 vols. New York: Praeger.

Picard, Robert G. (1993), *Media Portrayals of Terrorism*. Ames, IA: Iowa State University Press.

Primoratz, I. (1990), "What is Terrorism?", *Journal of Applied Philosophy* 7: 129-138.

Said, Edward (1988), "The Essential Terrorist", in: Said and Hitchens 1988: 149-158.

Said, Edward and Christopher Hitchens (1988), *Blaming the Victims, Spurious Scholarship and the Palestinian Question*. London: Verso.

Simmons, Brian K. (1991), "U. S. News Magazines' Labeling of Terrorists", in: A. O. Alali, and K. K. Eke (eds.), *Media Coverage of Terrorism*. London: 23-39.

Valls, Andrew (2000), *Ethics in International Affairs*. Lanham, MD: Rowman & Littlefield.

White, Jonathan R. (2002), *Terrorism*. Belmont, CA: Wadsworth.

Wierinka, Michael (1993), *The Making of Terrorism*. Chicago: University of Chicago.

OLAF L. MUELLER

BENIGN BLACKMAIL: CASSANDRA'S PLAN *OR* WHAT IS TERRORISM?[1]

What do we mean when we label an activity "terrorist"? And what is the appropriate ethical evaluation of such activity? These are the two questions which I intend to address in the present paper. One of my aims is to convince you that even if a certain course of action is deemed "terrorist", it is still an open question whether or not that very course of action is morally wrong. My second aim is to show that strict condemnation of terrorism implies pacifism.

I. THE LEGAL DIMENSION

On first sight there appear to be normative as well as descriptive aspects in the notion of terrorism. Since the normative aspects tend to provoke greater controversy, we shall begin our discussion with them and save the descriptive aspects for a briefer and later discussion (section III).

The first question which comes to mind when thinking about terrorism and its normative aspects is of course: What kind of norms are involved – legal norms, moral norms, or both? In the present section, I will begin to answer this question by concentrating on the legal norms involved and by tracing the analytic connections between these norms and the notion of terrorism. In the following section, I will then proceed to show that moral norms need not necessarily be invoked when defining terrorism.

"Terrorist activity emerges from the underground." I think this is a truism which expresses well what most people feel to be the most important – and most frightening – aspect of terrorism. However, talk about "the underground" is merely a metaphor. How should we understand it? Invisibility comes perhaps first to mind here, but I propose not to follow this line because terrorist activity can be quite visible. It seems to me that underground activity is first of all *illegal*; it involves breaking the law. (And of course, the best way to succeed in breaking the law is to do it invisibly; invisibility is a good strategy for people outside the law.) Less metaphorically, then, our truism can be put as follows:

> Terrorism is, by definition, unlawful.

You may ask: "Unlawful" under the laws of whom? This is indeed a crucial question because our truism leaves room for interpretation, and hence for political exploitation. In other words, the truism runs the danger of playing into the hands of those who invoke the notion of terrorism in order to defend a given legal or political order against violent attempts at change – and it runs the danger of playing into the hands of those who wish to impose their own legal order on everybody else.

G. Meggle (ed.), Ethics of Terrorism & Counter-Terrorism, 39-50.
© 2005 Ontos, Heusenstamm.

The danger is real. It lurks, for example, in an official US-American document which defines terrorist activity as an "Activity [...] which, if committed in the United States, would be unlawful under the laws of the United States."[2]

In order to avoid the severe political (if you want, imperialistic) implications of such a passage, one might be tempted to divorce the notion of terrorism from the legal codex of individual countries. One might choose instead to change the notion of terrorism such that it signifies an activity which (in one's opinion) is simply "immoral" (and which, in addition, falls under certain non-normative descriptions to be discussed later). With such a notion of terrorism the tables are suddenly turned, and it is now only one small step to detecting "terrorism" in the US-Office of the Coordinator for Counterterrorism, in the entire US foreign policy, that of its allies, its armies, secret services etc.

I have three arguments against this way of speaking. First, the inflated usage of the term "terrorism" diminishes its significance and informational value. When used in such a loose manner, the term is devalued to the point of becoming a mere propaganda slogan – unapt for serious, rational discussion.

But secondly, even if you apply the term "terrorism" with more self-discipline than in (my caricature of) leftwing propaganda, you will still cause confusion and fruitless quarrelling about words as long as you use the term "terrorist" as a way to morally criticize – let us say – governments. Moreover it is not necessary to call a government a terrorist government if you wish to criticize it; rather it suffices to state the moral criticism directly, without invoking the term "terrorism".

This leads us to my third reason for not divorcing the term from its legal connotations: Such a divorce is not the only way to counter the US-Coordinator for Counterterrorism and his deplorable definition of terrorism. He and his combatants are only capable of exploiting this term as long as it is taken for granted that terrorism is eo ipso morally wrong and must be fought against. What makes the term dangerous is not its legal connotations alone, but rather the lumping together of its legal and ethical connotations. Once we manage to free the notion of terrorism from ethical connotations altogether, the notion becomes much more difficult to exploit.

In the next section I will demonstrate (on linguistic grounds) that the supposed marriage between terrorism and ethical considerations has been invalid from the start. I will prepare the grounds in the remainder of this section by returning to our initial truism

Terrorism is, by definition, unlawful,

and to the question which we posed but have not yet fully addressed:

"Unlawful" under the laws of whom?

There is only one way to approach this question without bias – and that is to relativize. I would like to propose that an act can only be considered "terrorist" *relative* to the laws of a given country. Of course, in a derivative sense, it is possible to call a terrorist act *absolutely terrorist* if it is considered unlawful under the laws of every country. Or we can speak of terrorism relative to the laws of Western democracy. But whether or not we employ derivative notions of terrorism or stick to the original, relative notion, we can only gain clarity in our discussions about terrorism when we explicitly state whose laws we have in mind when we use the term.

And the clarity so gained will have a side-effect which we should welcome: It will prevent us from hasty moral judgments since we are all (I hope) aware that reference to some country's legal system alone is morally irrelevant.

To be sure, I do not intend to imply that all legal systems are morally on a par. What I have said implies only that legal considerations (within, say, our own political order) cannot replace moral considerations – even when we speak about terrorism.

II. THE MORAL DIMENSION: AN ADDITIONAL COMPONENT IN THE NOTION OF TERRORISM?

In the preceding section I first appealed to the truism "Terrorist activity emerges from the underground" in order to convince you that the norms to be invoked when defining terrorism must be of a *legal* sort. I also indicated that it would be politically dangerous to invoke moral norms when defining terrorism. Someone could of course object to this latter point and argue that when explicating a given term, undesirable political consequences should not play any role whatsoever: An explication must be sensitive to the actual usage of the term in question, even if certain political dangers do in fact result.

Fair enough; let us look at actual linguistic practice and try to determine whether or not our notion of terrorism might have ethical aspects after all. The following proposal is at issue:

> "By definition, an activity is terrorist if it falls under such and such description [to be specified], and if, *in addition*, it is immoral."

To refute this proposal I want to direct our attention to three characteristics of the way we use the term "terrorism".

(a) In everyday language, it is easier to agree that a given act is terrorist than to agree that the very same act is immoral.

For example, during the Seventies and Eighties there was a far-reaching consensus in West Germany that the members of the Red Army Fraction (RAF) were terrorists. (If I am not mistaken, the RAF is still a paradigm case of terrorism in the eyes of most Germans). Nevertheless there have been quite a few debates in which it was not taken for granted that the terrorist RAF actions deserved unequivocal moral condemnation. Although the majority of Germans have thought that they deserve to be morally condemned, there has been a small number of people who have not agreed that the RAF actions, which they themselves have labeled "terrorist", were immoral. This would not be the case if moral condemnation was part of the meaning of the term "terrorism".

It is important to see that by simply providing one example of this sort I have already proven my point. I do not imply that whenever people agree to call a certain activity "terrorist" there is always ethical disagreement about the act in question (the attack on the Twin Towers could be well cited as a perfect counterexample for such a broad claim). I am only urging that it is possible to label an activity "terrorist" without implying that that particular activity is also immoral. For my purposes it suffices to insist that not all attributions of terrorism are in this respect similar to the example of September 11th.

Someone could counter that the example of linguistic usage cited above to prove my point is not convincing because it exemplifies a deviant usage of language, or worse, a misuse of language. And indeed, isn't it a little suspicious to cite linguistic behavior of an extremely small group of political radicals in order to analyze *our* notion of terrorism? Had we not better take a closer look at our own linguistic habits?

This is a sensible suggestion. It brings us to my next piece of linguistic evidence (which parallels G.E. Moore's famous argument of the "open question", see Moore [PE]:66-68 (§13)):

(b)   We are not puzzled when we hear someone saying: "This is an act of terrorism, but is it morally wrong?"

Let us focus on *our own* reaction to someone else's questions of that sort. I claim that we do not react as if we are witnessing linguistic incompetence. Rather we feel dragged into moral controversy, which could not be the case, if we did not understand what our interlocutor meant to say in the first place.

It could, for example, be the case that the speaker approves of the good motives behind the terrorist act in question and that she subscribes to a moral point of view in which nothing else matters but the agent's motives. We can *understand* this point of view even if we do not share it.

My third piece of linguistic evidence which speaks against including issues of morality in the definition of "terrorism" is connected to the two linguistic observations we have been looking at:

(c)   A terrorist can describe her own acts as "terrorist" – and nevertheless insist that the very same acts are morally good.

Self-ascriptions of terrorism occur quite frequently. If the meaning of the term "terrorism" contained an element of moral condemnation it would follow that any self-*ascription* of terrorism would entail moral self-accusation. To be sure, it may well be that a terrorist considers her own deeds morally wrong. But this is not the rule. (And if it occurs, then usually from an ex-post perspective, which is in a way external). Are terrorists, who call themselves so, insensitive to moral considerations, then? Quite the reverse. I believe that often they are sensitive to moral considerations – but unfortunately they are sensitive to moral considerations which most of us find preposterous. They picture themselves as being driven by morals. And if this is compatible with self-ascriptions of terrorism then obviously moral condemnation cannot be a part of what is meant by that word. To the contrary, the word's meaning seems to include the morality of the agent's motives – in the eyes of the agent herself. Unlike ordinary criminals she does not break the law for personal gain but because her motives are directed to something "higher". Although this may be considered a moral component in the notion of terrorism, it is, strictly speaking, an element of description: it describes which moral quality the terrorist attributes to her own motives.

If we were to summarize the results from sections I and II, we would have to say that terrorist activity emerges when moral motivations lead an agent to break the positive law. Both legal and moral norms are involved when we speak of terrorism – but the latter are involved only on a purely descriptive level: What happens to be the law of such and such a country is violated due to motives, which agent so and so happens to find morally superior.

This is not yet a complete definition of terrorism because there are – for example, non-violent – ways of breaking the law for moral reasons which cannot be subsumed under the label "terrorism". To complete our account we have to include an element that highlights the role of violence and horror in terrorist activity. Here, then, is my complete proposal:

III. A PROPOSED DEFINITION OF TERRORISM

By definition, any illegal use (or threat) of violence is terrorist activity if

(a) it is performed in the light of motives which the agent considers morally good (rather than for mere personal gain);
(b) its aim is directed against a given legal or political order (or decision);
(c) it tries to reach that aim *via* horrifying those who benefit from, are involved in, or support the order (or decision) in question.[3]

This proposal needs some comment. First of all: According to the definition, legal use of violence cannot be labeled "terrorist". It can however be morally equivalent to terrorism. As we shall see in the next section, it is even possible for legal political action to be morally worse than terrorism. My definition is morally neutral.

Secondly: According to part (b) of our definition, the aim of terrorist activity need not be constructive. I think this captures well how we speak and think about terrorism. Terrorism is destructive rather than constructive. When we call an activity terrorist we do not need to know much about its positive or constructive goals. And yet it would seem strange if we couldn't at least tell *against* whom or what the terrorist act was directed.

True, it could very well be the case that we know more than that. But even when we know something about the terrorist's positive goals, we are likely to know much more about her negative goals. This is because the terrorist thinks she can reach her positive goals only on the *via negativa* – by way of removing hindrances. Destruction comes first on the terrorist agenda. If we want to put the same point less tendentiously we might choose to say that the terrorist is essentially interested in initiating changes; the actual, positive result of the change comes later and need not play a prominent role in the terrorist's deliberations and activities.

Once we look at things from this perspective it becomes obvious that the destructive aspect of terrorism might not necessarily lie in the terrorist's goals. This leads us to my last comment, which concerns part (c) of our definition. In my understanding, terrifying people through horrific acts need not be the ultimate goal of terrorists; rather and as a rule, it is supposed to be an effective means to some other goal. This is not to say that horrifying people *cannot* be the ultimate goal of a terrorist act. The attack on the Twin Towers is perhaps the best example of terrorism where no other goal was present than the goal of terrifying a complete city. Still I want to insist that this extreme case is the exception and that there can be and indeed are numerous cases of terrorism where horror is not the final goal of the act but merely an instrument.

IV. IS TERRORISM *ALWAYS* MORALLY WRONG? A COMPARISON TO WAR

In the previous sections I have proposed an understanding of terrorism that gives us semantic room for attributing the term "terrorism" without built-in moral disapproval. The sentence "Terrorism is always morally wrong" is not an *analytic* truth. Still the sentence might be true; it might be the case that all instances of terrorism just happen to be morally wrong. So our next question must be: Is terrorism always morally wrong?

I want to consider four possible reasons for believing that the answer should be to the positive. These reasons will later turn out to be inconclusive; yet this is not my main concern at present. Rather I hope to show that those reasons – if convincing – not only provide moral ammunition against terrorism, but against war as well. The lesson from this will be that strict counter-terrorism implies pacifism. This is most easily seen with respect to the first moral reason against terrorism:

(a) "Terrorism is always morally wrong just because it involves *violence.*"

Those who find this convincing have to claim that violence is always morally wrong no matter what the case. Since this carries over to any military action, such arguments imply a strictly pacifistic position. I have nothing to say against strict pacifism in the present paper. I only want to remind you that reason (a) has quite extreme implications and cannot be appealed to by those who support a war against terrorism.

Be that as it may, you might find counter-terrorist reason (a) too extreme, because you believe that violence should be permissible at times – at least in cases where it is directed against criminal mass murderers and where there is no other way to prevent the worst. This may lead you to contemplate our next counter-terrorist reason, which is less extreme than the previous one.

(b) "Terrorism is always morally wrong because *de facto* it always involves violence against *innocent* people (that is, against people who have nothing to do with the political order or decision against which the terrorist act in question is directed)."

This moral reason against terrorism is compatible with permitting limited usage of violence in police action. But again, it is incompatible with any actual instance of military action. Violence against innocent people seems more characteristic of military than of terrorist action. (Some of the German RAF's first terrorist activities, for example, were committed without *great* danger to innocent people, see Aust [BMK].) Let me be more specific about this: There have been many military enterprises in recent history whose death poll among civilians was much higher than in the case of, say, the Western intervention in Kosovo during 1998. But there have not been many terrorist courses of action whose lethal effects among "innocent people" have reached a comparable dimension.[4] Surely, there have been *some* terrorist acts of that dimension; the attack on the Twin Towers is a case in point, yet its dimension is the exception, not the rule.

To prevent misunderstandings, I do not mean to imply that since we have become accustomed to collateral damage in the course of military action we should stop complaining about the victims of an average terrorist atrocity. The point is intended to mean just the opposite: If we cannot and do not want to accept terrorist activity because of its lethal consequences for innocent victims, then, *a fortiori*, we should also be against war because there the situation is far worse.

For those who wish to prevent inferring strict pacifism from moral counter-terrorism it might be helpful to try and detect crucial ethical differences between military and terrorist actions. One such difference is of course that terrorism emerges from the underground while war can be quite official. Does this difference matter when considering the morality of the deed in question? According to our next counter-terrorist reason, it does:

(c) "Terrorism is always morally wrong because it involves *illegal* violence."

This view is implausible, because it implies what one might call strict legalism: "Whatever is illegal within a given legal order is *eo ipso* morally wrong." We should never subscribe to views of this sort, since we know all too well that there can be and have in fact been legal systems so wicked that obedience to their positive laws must be considered evil.

The counter-terrorist of our time, who is sensitive to this observation, does not have to give up yet. She does not need to be opposed to all varieties of terrorism; she can content herself with being opposed to the branch of terrorism which matters the most to us (the citizens of Western democracy). She can restrict her counter-terrorist reasoning so as to be only directed against terrorism *relative to the Western democracies*. As a result, she will only have to refer to our legal systems – thus circumventing the unfortunate reference to *all* systems of law, even to the evil ones, which troubled us in (c). The result is this:

(d) "Terrorism *relative to our Western democracy* is always morally wrong because it involves action which is unlawful under a law with moral backing."

I believe that this is a counter-terrorist point of view which many Western citizens find plausible. To be sure, it is not a view which disapproves of terrorism *tout court*. Therefore, it is less vulnerable to criticism than the counter-terrorist reasons considered earlier. Let us, however, see what happens when we bring the issue of military action and warfare into play again. As we shall see, doing so appears to shake the robust trust in the moral superiority of our own legal systems.

True, Western legal systems pay high regard to the value of human life – at least to that of their own citizens (and to that of those who happen to be within their borders). But it must be admitted that these high standards are not granted world-wide. It may happen that legal procedures *within* our own countries lead to decisions and activities of disastrous consequence *outside* these very same countries. Military action "out of area" is the most prominent example of that sort. And once we reflect on the fact that atomic warfare is still legal under the laws of (at least some of) the Western countries, we may hesitate before subscribing to Western legalism (as exhibited in counter-terrorist reason (d)).

Let us try to test these intuitions by means of an extreme example, which I shall call Cassandra's Plan. My friend Cassandra has founded a terrorist organization whose exclusive goal it is to prevent atomic warfare. A noble goal indeed, if it were not for the henous methods involved …

When Cassandra first told me about her plan I immediately thought to myself: Her organization could be considered one of the best counter-examples – I have ever come across – for the claim "Terrorism (relative to the Western democracies) is always morally wrong".

V. TERRORISM AGAINST ATOMIC WAR: CASSANDRA'S PLAN

Let me begin by quoting some crucial passages from an underground paper which Cassandra wrote for fund-raising purposes. As we shall see, Cassandra seems to be quite pessimistic about recent history:

> "As a matter of good coincidence, the world's political leaders have abstained from the military usage of nuclear weapons for the last 56 years. There is no guarantee that this will continue to be so for the next 50 years."

In the text which follows Cassandra cites examples of major leaders who were tempted to play with atomic fire for military reasons. The examples range from 1962 (the time of the Cuban Missile Crisis) to the present. Cassandra includes analyses of the British war in the Falklands, of the conflict between Pakistan and India, and addresses the alarming question as to what has become of the former Soviet Union's nuclear arsenal. It is in fact the end of the Cold War which troubles Cassandra the most. She is afraid that the only remaining super-power might someday find it convenient to solve certain military problems with nuclear arms. Cassandra invites us to reflect briefly on the recent counter-terrorist war in Afghanistan: When entire terrorist armies remain undetected in a labyrinth of mountain caves, then surely a well-placed atomic explosion would put an end to the matter, wouldn't it? According to Cassandra it is precisely considerations of this sort which have already led to a change of strategic doctrine in the United States. So-called "mini-nukes" – atomic arms of limited effect – are being developed so as to increase the options for restricted atomic warfare.[5]

Not too many people seem worried by this. We are so accustomed to the non-usage of nuclear arms that we can hardly imagine being woken up by an abrupt change. But Cassandra's imaginative powers are not asleep, otherwise she wouldn't be Cassandra.[6] The question is, should we diagnose Cassandra with hysterical pessimism – or rather with reasonable realism? Looking at her list of examples, I cannot help thinking that it would be a miracle if in the future (say, within the forthcoming five decades) we were not made to witness the military usage of nuclear arms. Needless to say, Cassandra refuses to believe in miracles. Her next step is what I call Cassandra's moral axiom:

> "Any military usage of nuclear weapons is evil and must be prevented at [almost] any price. (We should not wish to lead our lives in a world where a third atomic catastrophe has been produced for military reasons.)"

Cassandra does not really try to *prove* her moral axiom. Her paper is addressed to people who find it obvious that nuclear warfare is perverse.

There is of course always going to be a small group of people who do not want to subscribe to Cassandra's axiom, and I do not think these people are likely to be convinced by moral reasoning alone. Perhaps it would therefore be more effective to make them *see and feel* what unheard-of evil was brought about by atomic explosions in Hiroshima and Nagasaki in 1945. This is a task for historians, museum directors, biographers, photographers, painters, poets, and film-makers. But as I have said, Cassandra's concern lies somewhere else. I propose joining Cassandra to see what her moral axiom implies for those who subscribe to it.

Cassandra does not succumb to fatalism. She wants to prevent the nuclear danger that she alone sees lurking. But how? Here is what she has learned from Western nuclear strategy (as practiced during the Cold War Era):

> "Deterrence by means of mutually assured destruction may decrease the probability of atomic warfare."

In Cassandra's eyes it is more than a little dubious to gamble in such a way with the survival of the whole human race. (And anyway, such a game is beyond Cassandra's powers.) Still she thinks that *some* deterrence, or blackmail, might be helpful in preventing a third nuclear catastrophe. At this point Cassandra comes up with an innovative idea:

> "It would be sufficient to direct the effects of deterrence precisely towards those who decide about military usage of nuclear weapons."

The crucial question is, who exactly must be the target of Cassandra's threat? Her answer is quite simple. It is first of all *governments* who are in charge of and responsible for nuclear arms. Thus she thinks it most promising to issue an announcement of the following sort to all members of government of the nuclear powers:

> "We have founded an NGO whose aim it is to compel all leaders and governmental members of the nuclear powers to abstain from the actual usage of nuclear weapons. In the event that the soldiers of a nuclear power drop but one atomic bomb, our killer teams shall hunt down and execute this government's ministers and its leader."

We may well doubt whether this would be sufficient. There have been crazy politicians in the past and there may be crazy ones in future. Happily, however, *most* politicians care about their own well-being. They are likely to avoid decisions which will produce the life-long danger of assassination, since such a threat would turn their lives into a living nightmare even if the assassination itself could be prevented. The nightmare Cassandra has in mind here does not spring solely from her imagination but also from very recent history; Salman Rushdie lived through it. It does not seem that an impossible sum of money is needed to produce similar effects on politicians.

If Casssandra's threat could be made credible (which in her mind is only a matter of sufficient financial backing), it would certainly diminish the danger of nuclear warfare. True, it would not erase the danger altogether; just think of crazy politicians again – or of soldiers out of government control. Cassandra does not pretend to have a solution for stopping them. Her ambition is more modest. Her ambition is to make the world a safer place – safer at least for those of us who do not belong to certain governments. She admits that it appears a little unfair to threaten without difference *all* members of government of the nuclear powers. But then, justice is not her concern. She wants to issue a threat which is effective, clear-cut, and easily understood. And she wishes to avoid endless discussions about the targets of action, should it turn out that her threat was ineffective. In this case, Cassandra will announce the following:

> "The following people belong to the government which is responsible for yesterday's atomic explosion: [List of names to be inserted]. Each of them was priorly informed about our plan of action; each of them was free to resign from his post before the fatal decision was made. From now on, they are to be considered outlaws, they are to be hunted down and executed. WARNING to secretaries, bodyguards, drivers, friends, and family members: We cannot guarantee for your safety as long as you stay in the vicinity of the people listed above."

This is Cassandra's final announcement; her next steps will be non-verbal.

VI. CONCLUDING REMARKS

Cassandra's NGO is *unlawful* (under the law of the Western democracies), it involves *violence* (or the threat of violence), its *motives* are honorable (at least when judged from Cassandra's own perspective), and it tries to reach its political aim by means of *terrifying* statesmen, especially those from the Western democracies.[7] Therefore, Cassandra's NGO is a terrorist organization (in the sense of "terrorism" that was defined in section III). The NGO is a terrorist organization relative to the laws of the Western countries.

Question: Is Cassandra's plan morally wrong? I can see three possible views for those who think so and who nevertheless subscribe to Cassandra's moral axiom:

(a) You have *complete* trust in the moral wisdom of Western military policy and find Cassandra's NGO superfluous or even disturbingly dangerous.

This I find a little naive, and I do not think that I have to say much more against it.

(b) You do not have moral objections to the military logic of deterrence, or to the war against terrorism in Afghanistan, or to some of the Western humanitarian interventions (such as in Kosovo); but you find Cassandra's plan morally wrong.

To me it appears difficult to formulate this view in any coherent way. What exactly is the essential difference between Cassandra's methods and ordinary military practice? The main difference seems to be that Cassandra's NGO is not an official army, and thus, cannot be controlled legally. But Cassandra finds the legal control of those who might decide in favor of nuclear warfare to be insufficient. And: Her plan is much less dangerous for civil populations than almost any military action.

(c) You find Cassandra's plan brutal, inhuman, cruel, full of hatred, and thus, morally unacceptable.

In my eyes this view is correct. It is an accurate and convincing moral description of Cassandra's plan. The creator of the plan exhibits a frame of mind which I find deplorably cynical. To see this I propose that you look, for example, at the brute way she exploits Salman Rushdie's fate – a fate that ought to elicit our solidarity and sympathy.

Of course, utilitarians and consequentialists will not be disturbed by observations of this kind. And although I think their position is wrong, it would go beyond the scope of this paper to present a full-fledged argument against their way of calculating moral issues.[8] I can only ask them to imagine what it would be like if they themselves were to found or belong to an NGO like the one projected by Cassandra. Even if you do not find the personal danger involved in belonging to such an NGO frightening, ask yourself the following question:

> Would you like to be the sort of person who is capable of playing Cassandra's part? Would you like to be as fanatic as Cassandra and her friends?

Let me conclude the paper with a comment for those who (like me) disapprove of Cassandra's plan because in their eyes it exhibits an inhuman, cruel, cold, in short: ugly frame of mind. I invite you to look with the very same eyes at whatever military action you wish. If I am not mistaken you will discover Cassandra's ugly traits in all those who wage war – the same traits, but escalated. The politician who initiates military action differs from Cassandra in only two aspects. He has more power, and his power is legal. The first aspect makes him more dangerous while the second does not offer any antidote for his lack of virtue. And indeed, if in the course of war he coolly risks the lives of (foreign) civilians, who have not authorized him to do so, and if in addition he calls this "collateral damage", then his lack of virtue is more than obvious. Conclusion: Terrorism is bad, war is worse.

NOTES

[1] I am grateful to Michael Haarkötter, Sybille Haupt, Thomas Schmidt, Matthias Schote, Cassandra da Troia, and Sylwia Trzaska for controversial discussions of the ideas from which this paper originated. Thanks to Cynthia Myers for linguistic advice. Last but not least, I would like to thank the symposion's participants for both challenging and constructive criticism.

[2] US-Office of the Coordinator for Counterterrorism. See the "2001 Report on Foreign Terrorist Organizations", released by the Office of the Coordinator for Counterterrorism, October 5th, 2001. (The formulation quoted above occurs also in the *Immigration and Nationality Act*.)

[3] There are, of course, more possibilities of defining "terrorism". My definition covers what Georg Meggle calls political terrorism in the broad sense, see Meggle [TGT], sections 1.5-1.6.

[4] Such comparisons may seem to depend on a prior decision as to how many seperate terrorist acts are to be considered a *complete* "terrorist course of action". (A terrorist underground war, for example, may last many years, and the longer it lasts, the more victims it is likely to produce.) I think, however, that even if we look at complete civil wars (in which often one side labels the other one "terrorist"), we must admit that their consequences tend to be less disastrous than the consequences of ordinary, official wars between nations. (For a similar observation see Schleichert ([MSIo], section 2), who refers to Schlick ([NK]:101.)

[5] See Bromley et al [BB].

[6] See Wolf [K].

[7] Her threat is, of course, also directed to the statesmen of Russia, India, Pakistan etc. I neglect this aspect of her threat because we are interested in terrorism relative to the law of Western democracy; in this context it is more significant to consider threats against the democratic leaders.

[8] Elsewhere I have tried to argue against consequentialism and utilitarianism. On the one hand, I have detected an incoherence within radical forms of consequentialist or utilitarian ethics (see [CTSW]). On the other hand, I have tried to show that consequentialist or utilitarian ethics presuppose a sharp division between fact and value: a division which cannot be drawn when matters of peace and war are at issue (see [RP]).

REFERENCES

Aust, Stefan [BMK]: *Der Baader-Meinhof-Komplex* (Hamburg: Hoffmann und Campe, Enlarged edition, 1997).

Bromley, Mark / Grahame, David / Kucia, Kristine [BB]: *Bunker Busters: Washington's Drive for New Nuclear Weapons* (British American Security Information Council, Research Report 2002.2).

Meggle, Georg [TGT]: "Terror & Gegen-Terror. Erste Ethische Reflektionen", *Deutsche Zeitschrift für Philosophie* 50 Heft 1 (2002), pp. 149-162.

Meggle, Georg (ed.) [EoHI]: *Ethics of humanitarian interventions* (Heusenstamm: Ontos, 2004).

Moore, George Edward [PE]: *Principia ethica* (Cambridge: Cambridge University Press, revised edition, 1993).

Mueller, Olaf L. [CTSW]: "Can They Say What They Want? A Transcendental Argument against Utilitarianism", *The Southern Journal of Philosophy* 41 No. 2 (June 2003). pp. 241-259.

Mueller, Olaf L. [RP]: "Reconstructing Pacifism. On Different Ways of Looking at Reality", in: Meggle (ed.) [EoHI]: 57-80.

Schleichert, Hubert [MSIo]: "Moritz Schlick's Idea of Non-Territorial States", Eröffnungsvortrag zum Symposion *The Vienna Circle and Logical Empiricism* (Vienna, July, 12th, 2001), in: Stadler (ed.) [VCLE]: 49-62.

Schlick, Moritz [NK]: *Natur und Kultur* (aus dem Nachlass des Autors herausgegeben von Josef Rauscher. Wien: Humboldt-Verlag 1952). (= *Sammlung die Universität*, Vol. 30)

Stadler, Friedrich (ed) [VCLE]: *The Vienna Circle and Logical Empiricism* (Dordrecht: Kluwer, 2002). (= *Vienna Circle Institute Yearbook* 10 (2002))

Wolf, Christa [K]: *Kassandra* (Frankfurt / Main: Luchterhand, 1990).

DANIEL MESSELKEN

TERRORISM AND GUERRILLA WARFARE –
A COMPARATIVE ESSAY

1. INTRODUCTION

"Even more recently, the term "terrorism" (like "guerrilla") has been
used in so many different senses as to become almost meaningless,
covering almost any, and not necessarily political, act of violence."[1]

This observation made by Laqueur about 25 years ago is still of topical interest.
Perhaps it is even more modern then ever, as, since the events of 9/11/2001, nearly
every use of force by non-state actors is referred to as terrorism. And nobody seems to
care that the most divergent forms of violence are summed up under this term,
especially when the implications for political action and military response are
immense. The so-called "war against terrorism"[2] is fully understood to be a war
against evil; what constitutes evil thus may not be questioned and makes, finally, any
further distinctions impossible. Against terrorists (guerrilla fighters are not
distinguished anymore) war is allowed and, they say, must be fought.

In this paper, I will try to analyze the key elements of terrorism and guerrilla
warfare. I will not give a historical overview, but my aim will be to reach a theoretical
description that includes the crucial features of the two treated forms of violence. On
the one hand, a possible connection between them has to be investigated, and, on the
other hand, the question whether one can usefully speak of war in any of the
concerned cases has to be answered. First, I will delimit the terms terrorism and
guerrilla warfare from each other. Their distinct uses and – if they are elaborated –
their theoretical concepts shall be analyzed and discussed. Further on, I shall compare
the two strategies of war or violence and make some remarks about common and
different characteristics they possess. Finally, a prospect of these forms of violence
shall be dared.

2. GUERRILLA WARFARE – "SMALL WAR"

"Surprise is the essential feature of guerrilla war; thus the ambush is the
classic guerrilla tactic."[3]

Leading surprise attacks on one's enemy is a strategy that has been used in nearly all
wars that mankind has known. The resort to ruse and camouflage is also part of
"normal" military strategy and, thus, is not sufficient to fully describe guerrilla

51

G. Meggle (ed.), Ethics of Terrorism & Counter-Terrorism, 51-68.
© 2005 Ontos, Heusenstamm.

warfare. Therefore, the matter here is to show the differences of guerrilla strategy vis-à-vis classic warfare. Organized guerrilla warfare and its theoretic foundations are relatively young: the first time "this way of combat has been applied in a relevant and militarily decisive degree has been in the 1808 rebellion of the Spanish people against Napoleon".[4] This is the first time, too, that the expression "guerrilla" was used, which originated from the Spanish and literally translated means *small war*. I will analyze guerrilla strategy following the contributions of its most important theoretical founders and writers. From the beginning of the twentieth century on, during the Chinese wars against Japan and subsequently on the side of the red army, Mao Tse Tung developed a detailed theory of guerrilla warfare. Later on, Ernesto "Che" Guevara, descending from an aristocratic family, adapted these ideas to his experiences of the different kind of conditions he had to face in Latin America.

Both in the example from Spain and the historically more important and better-known cases of guerrilla wars in Latin America or Vietnam (in our days e.g. in Chechnya), the confrontation with the militarily superior opponent is searched by the guerrilla fighters in the country.[5] By shifting the theatre of war and through an activity marked by "constant surprise", the militarily inferior party manages to create for itself advantages that, at best, iet it win the war. There are two main reasons for the geographical shift of the war theatre utilized by the guerrilla: on the one hand, control is harder to establish in rural areas than in conurbations for the regular armed forces. On the other hand, the guerrilla, according to Walzer, "fight where they live".[6] Two decisive strategic advantages follow from this last point: first, the guerrilla fighters have the better local knowledge and, second, they are part of the population. Thus, camouflage among the civil population and surprise attacks becomes possible, i.e. those kind of action which go to make up guerrilla warfare in the broader sense. Mao has given the image that guerrilla fighters have to swim in the popular crowd like fishes in the water.[7] They live in an environment they are dependent upon and which, at the same time, is inhospitable for others. As fish need water, so do the guerrillas need the population; their symbiosis is even somehow more intimate than that of fish to water and, in addition, is bound to some conditions. That is what Guevara recognizes when he says that

> "the absolute cooperation of the people and a perfect knowledge of the ground are necessary. [...] Therefore, [...] intensive popular work must be undertaken to explain the motives of the revolution."[8]

It is enormously important to enlighten the population among whom support is sought and to convince them of the guerrilla's motives to revolt. The aim is not so much to mobilize all people for the armed struggle, but to garner enough support so as to protect the identity of the clandestine fighters who need to disguise among the civilians. Thus, the relation between guerrilla fighters and civilian population is mixed between seeking protection on the one hand and hostage-taking on the other hand:

> "[The guerrilla fighter] does respect the status of non-combatant insofar as he does not attack civilians himself, and at the same time he does not respect it insofar as he forces everybody who wants to attack him to also attack civilians."[9]

The guerrilla, who respects international laws in this respect, does not directly threaten the population. The danger comes from the other side that is led to attack despite the impossibility of discriminating between civilian and "commando". In doing so, they will not be able to avoid killing civilians as a kind of collateral damage. In the words of Walzer:

> "They [the guerrillas] seek to place the onus of indiscriminate warfare on the opposing army."[10]

That way, the guerrilla seeks both to steer the population's hatred on the enemy's forces and to gain support for its own endeavors. After all, it is the others who are (directly) responsible for the inflicted grief. However, this calculation is quite dangerous as realized by Fanon within the context of African struggle of liberation:

> "But the leader realizes, day in day out, that hatred alone cannot draw up a program. You will only risk the defeat of your own ends if you depend on the enemy (who of course will always manage to commit as many crimes as possible) to widen the gap, and to throw the whole people on the side of the rebellion. At all events as we have noticed, the enemy tries to win the support of certain sectors of the population, of certain districts, and of certain chiefs. [...] The native is in fact made to feel that things are changing."[11]

The described tactics thus have to be built upon strong enough ideological foundations, especially in view of possible concessions or new strategies from the opposing side. That is why Guevara emphasized the absolute necessity of the "intensive popular work" as cited above. Haffner, in an introductory essay to Mao, describes guerrilla warfare even as a "democratic war", opposing it to the "aristocratic and absolutist wars of the Europeans", because guerrilla warfare in his opinion is a sort of "daily plebiscite".[12] One has to understand him in the sense that the civilian population can decide, on every new day, whether they want to continue the (passive or active) cooperation with the guerrilla or whether they prefer to divulge the identity of the fighters. According to Waldmann, "an embedding in large sections of the population"[13] is a requirement for the use of the term guerrilla (in contrast to rebels).

Keeping good relations with the population is all the more difficult, considering that the guerrilla fight is only part of a general strategy orientated on the long term and on the attrition of the enemy. A quick decision – and thus the end of the war – exist only in very few cases. This is very clear in the writings of Mao. He describes guerrilla warfare (opposing it to classic warfare marked by the striving for a fast decision) as no permanent military campaign and no strategy of blitzkrieg but a strategy of permanent war with military blitz-campaigns.[14] Unlike the regular forces, the guerrilla does not seek a temporary or geographical delimitation of the battlefield, their struggle is "ubiquitous and permanent".[15] Due to the duration of combat and their own scant resources, many guerrilla movements have to rely on an external force,[16] which directly helps them with goods or may support them on the diplomatic level.

A typical method of guerrilla warfare is sabotage. Its aim is mostly to cut off enemy communication[17] and supplies. It is part of the strategy of attrition, which is meant to weaken the opposing forces and induce them to surrender.

> "All factories, all centers of production that are capable of giving the enemy something needed to maintain his offensive against the popular forces, ought also to be liquidated."[18]

But explicitly, a differentiation between acts of sabotage and terrorism is made. While sabotage is seen as an important and effective means, terrorist acts are refused except in some rare cases[19] because of their indiscriminate nature and because often innocents (!) are harmed.

But not only in view of attrition guerrilla warfare is out for a long duration. Starting as a numerically small group, the aspect of numeric growth also plays an important role. In time, the guerrilla develops to a larger group and models itself on the regular forces they are fighting. The original guerrilla tactic is only the initial stage in a development and will be replaced later on, as the final victory cannot be achieved with it:

> "[Guerrilla warfare] is one of the initial phases of warfare and will develop continuously until the guerrilla army in its steady growth acquires the characteristics of a regular army. [...] Triumph will always be the product of a regular army, even though its origins are in guerrilla army."[20]

In the writings of Mao as well as of Guevara, guerrilla groups are seen as an important but transitional stage on the way of establishing a regular army. Concerning the organizational structure, this means that, at the beginning, all comrades in arms are nearly on the same hierarchic level. Only during the (successful) course of the struggle, new structures, which resemble a state armies' chain of command, develop. Münkler describes this tendency as an "evolutionarily aimed hierarchic monocephaly".[21]

The importance of guerrilla strategy therefore lies in creating, among the population, the conditions for mass mobilization against the suppressor. The implicit teleological conception of history is, at least partly, a result of the Marxist background which influenced the theories of Mao and Guevara.

An important factor in achieving mass mobilization is the guerilleros' motivation. One does not enter the highly risky commitment of a guerrilla war for material but only for ideological reasons, that is because of political convictions. According to Allemann, fighting in a guerrilla movement is the form of "an individual or collective coming out against a social context resented as intolerable and burdening; as a manifestation of a violent protest against the law of the ruler, which neither the *bandolero* nor the *guerillero* wants to resign to".[22] In that context, the guerrilla fighters consider the resort to force as reasonable and also necessary.[23]

Different kinds of motivations can lead to distinguish between at least two current subtypes of guerrilla warfare; it can on the one hand be revolutionary with the aim of changing the social order, or, on the other hand, be the reaction to the occupation of one's own country by foreign forces. This distinction is very clear in the writings of Guevara, who himself represents the social-revolutionary guerrilla theory:

> "It should be noted that in current interpretation there are two different types of guerrilla warfare, one of which – a struggle complementing great regular armies […] – does not enter in this analysis. We are interested in the other type, the case of an armed group engaged in struggle against the constituted power, whether colonial or not, which establishes itself as the only base and which builds itself up in rural areas."[24]

Concerning the concrete way of fighting, this differentiation is less important. And, evidently, it cannot be drawn with an absolute clear dividing line. Mao even represents both alternative forms, as his thoughts originate as much from the war against the occupier Japan, as from the communist revolution and the civil war in China. Another example of a mixed form, given by Fanon, is the struggle for national liberation of the North African colonies, in which – in addition to national feelings – social aspects also played a crucial role.

To sum up, one may say that "the guerrilla is a military strategy in the classic sense, but which does not ignore certain social and psychological circumstances".[25] So, one can call it a form of warfare, which nonetheless differs from "classic" warfare in some important points: (1) its organizational structure, (2) in the way of combat and the employed means, (3) in the motivation of the combatants and (4) in the widely-ranged embedding in the civil life. While the motivation for the struggle is marked by ideology, the strategic drawing up is deliberate and subordinated to the only aim of final victory. The military usefulness of possible alternatives and the anticipated respective reactions are weighed out. The widespread use of the term "guerrilla" might come from its identification with any occurrence of underground movements. It should have become clear, that such kind of simplification does not do justice to the very idea of guerrilla, which, at least in its theory, proves a high sense of responsibility and will to gain legitimacy.

3. TERRORISM – A FORM OF WAR?

Unlike in the case of guerrilla warfare, theories of terrorism have not been written. Even though many writings of terrorists exist, they are merely ideological pamphlets against a system, etc., and do not give us a theory of the terrorists' action. Thus, the description I will try to give has to be based on the analysis of terrorist action.

Before speaking on a definition of terrorism, I will give a short overview of the historical and semantic development this term has passed. The word "terrorism" has been introduced and used for the first time during the French Revolution, at that time actually as a self-description the Jacobin gave to their *Régime de Terreur*. Then,

> "Primitively, a terrorist is someone who legitimizes and practices the Terror [*la Terreur*]. It is an objective designation that is only infamous for political adversaries."[26]

The revolutionary circumstances make it necessary to employ drastic means. The question is not whether the way (*how*) is good, but if the aim (*what*) can be achieved that way. In 1848, the German radical democrat Heinzen even proclaimed, that, if it was about defending democracy against barbarians, every mean (i.e. including suicide attacks) would be justified, even if half of a continent needed to be blown up.[27] He proposed to offer a price for the invention of new and suitable weaponry.[28] So terrorism was seen both as a legitimate means and as a form of violence which could possibly be employed by the state. But this has changed with the course of history, and the sense of the term "terrorism" has made a significant shift.

> "It is remarkable that, little by little, the term 'terrorism', which clearly qualified a particular form of the state's exercise of power, succeeded in meaning exactly the contrary. Since a long time, actually, 'terrorist' is the word by which the states name every violent and / or armed adversary, precisely because of his non-state character."[29]

This semantic shift has been fixed, for example in the definition given by the US-law, which settles in article 22 that terrorism is "politically motivated violence perpetrated [...] by subnational groups or clandestine agents".[30] In this and many similar definitions, a state cannot act in a terrorist way, just because it is a state. Obviously, such kinds of restriction always reflect some influence of political interests. And no state leader nowadays would claim to be a terrorist. The formerly objective character of the term has been completely lost in its semantic development over the time:

> "[A]t the end of its semantic evolution, 'terrorist' today is an intrinsically propagandist word. It has no neutral reading at all. It dispenses political situations from any rational examination, from their causes and their consequences. [...] 'Terrorist' does not describe a political orientation or the possibility of such or such situation anymore, but exclusively the form of action."[31]

After this short overview of the semantic history of the term "terrorism", I will now work out a definition. In the above quotation, Badiou criticizes the fact that "terrorism" and "terrorist" are used exclusively to describe a *modus operandi*, i.e. a form of action. In my opinion, the advantage accrues from such a use where no fixed link to a concrete group of actors or type of action is already implied in the definition.

Looking for a generally valid definition of "terrorism", the US-American social scientists Schmid and Jongman gathered 101 different descriptions and filtered the common points. They found 22 different factors characterizing terrorism, but none of them was included in all definitions. Even the use of violence or force figured in "only" 83,5 % of the investigated samples. The definition then proposed by Schmid and Jongman themselves that includes 16 of the factors reaches the scope of an entire page.[32] This clearly illustrates the breadth of the difficulty of description. Laqueur, who was one of the first to treat the issue of terrorism from a theoretical point of view, has doubts about the possibility of defining it in a useful way. However, this may be because he represents a very broad conception of terrorism, including nearly every form of politically motivated violence.

Indeed, there are, in my opinion, certain aspects which are well-suited to describe terrorist action and to distinguish it from other violent forms of action, and which therefore can help to define terrorism. I will now go into the most important of those aspects, which in my opinion are defining features of terrorist action.

Near-unanimity prevails on the fact that terrorist action implies the use of violence, or, at least, the credible threat of its use (see above). Nevertheless, the use of violence made by terrorists differs from other occurrences of its uses in a decisive point: terrorist violence is not originally directed against its victims, the physical damage of the targeted persons is not the final objective. To make it clear: a murderer kills a certain person out of hatred, vindictiveness etc., his crime could not be directed towards a different victim. Terrorists, on the contrary, *personally* do not have anything against their victims, often (or most of the time) they do not even know them. Thus, *personal* hatred is irrelevant.

> "Unlike the soldier, the guerrilla fighter, or the revolutionist, the terrorist therefore is always in the paradoxical position of undertaking actions the immediate physical consequences of which are not particularly desired by him. [...] [A] terrorist will shoot somebody even though it is a matter of complete indifference to him, whether that person lives or dies."[33]

The victim is selected only because he is part of a certain group or community. At the end, who exactly is hit (or who will be hit next) cannot be predicted. Walzer remarks that "[r]andomness is the crucial feature of terrorist activity".[34] In a similar context, Waldmann quotes a "Spanish" who states quite aptly the relation between the terrorist and his victim:

> "It would be less bad, if they killed somebody because they hate him personally; the inhuman comes from them killing him without having anything against him."[35]

In the words of Nagel:

> "When this background [i.e. the attack on a real or assumed quality or conduct of the victim] is absent, hostile or aggressive behavior can no longer be intended for the reception of the victim as subject."[36]

The random choice and the absence of any personal relationship are important grounds why terrorism is so repugnant to us. There is no good reason, why just these people have become victims of the terrorist, and that is where the somewhat clueless accusation that terrorism targets the so-called innocent comes from. I will get back to this point later in this essay. Nevertheless, for the moment I want to settle, what objective the terrorists' violence pursues when it is not the direct physical damage of its victims.

The possible gain that terrorists see in using violence is more complicated to grasp, because it does not correspond to the classic instrumental employment of force we are habituated to. "Terrorism, primarily, is a communication strategy."[37] That is to say: violence "is not the first aim, but only a step on the way to occupy the thinking".[38] Not instrumental, but communicative violence, not physical damage, but psychical influencing are the goals pursued by terrorist attacks.

> "Not the *violentia* itself, but the resulting *terror*, the horror is what terrorist strategy in its core is about."[39]

So, the first aim of terrorist violence is the production of fear, horror etc. among a broad group of persons, which stands in an appropriate relation to the direct physical victims of the violence. In our modern world, mass media support this intention by reporting fast and in detail on the occurred atrocities. The fact, that the media do not intend to support the terrorist but only want to serve the desire for sensations, does not matter in view of the result. The live-coverage from New York and Washington on 9/11/2001 has not only caused consternation in the face of the destruction's new scale, but has also led to a feeling of insecurity and consequently to wide-spread fear.[40] If one has understood that the first level of the terrorist calculation consists precisely in this causing of horror and fear, the reason for the unpredictable and random violence becomes evident. If it can never be foreseen when and where the next plot will appear or who will be victimized, both the existential insecurity and the resulting fear are maximized. To sum up: the production of horror and the feeling of insecurity constitute the first level of what is called the terrorist calculation.

As the second and more decisive level in this calculation, the following is assumed: through the intimidation of a group of persons, achieved through violence, this group (or a closely related one) can be induced to actions they otherwise would not have taken. The violence is the starting point in a series of reactions "at the end of which panic-stricken fear and ways of action dictated by this feeling are meant to be".[41] These actions, which are demanded in most of the cases by the terrorists as their claims, are the real objective of the terrorist violence. The people who are to execute these actions are the real target group in the terrorist calculation. According to Fromkin, the terrorist strategy for that reason has something unique, because "it achieves its goal not through its act but through the response to its acts".[42] In that sense, one may speak of it as a form of indirect coercion.

Terrorist acts are composed of three chronological elements (act of violence, emotional reaction, acts as a consequence of these) in which three groups of persons are involved (the perpetrators, the victims of the violence, the actual target group).[43] A relatively short and concise definition by Primoratz including these elements says:

> "Terrorism is best defined as the deliberate use of violence, or threat of its use, against innocent people, with the aim of intimidating some other people into a course of action they otherwise would not take."[44]

It is important, that Primoratz explicitly does not mention or exclude any possible perpetrator; he defines terrorism as a form of action or a strategy. On the basis of the motivation, the scene and the actors, different kinds of terrorism can be distinguished:[45] vigilante terrorism,[46] insurgent terrorism, transnational or international terrorism and state terrorism. In addition, insurgent terrorism can be subdivided into single-issue, separatist, and social-revolutionary. These distinctions are important and worthy of note as they show the very different kind of possible actors and their motivations. All cases have in common the recourse to the above described communicative use of violence, which instrumentalizes its victims according to the terrorist calculation.

However, it is also within that indirect strategy of the terrorist calculation that the decisive weakness of terrorist action lies.

> "The important point is that the choice is yours. That is the ultimate weakness of terrorism as a strategy. It means that, though terrorism cannot always be prevented, it can always be defeated. You can always refuse to do what they want you to do."[47]

A terrorist never has a *direct* influence on the person(s) whose behavior he wants to change or provoke in a concrete way. He tries to achieve his goals through the roundabout way of coercion. Thus, he depends on the (forced) cooperation of his adversaries. This cooperation can be refused and, with that, the achievement of the terrorists' goal is thwarted; however, only with the proviso that the terrorist strategy is seen through.[48] Both the application of the terrorist strategy and the response to a terrorist threat therefore require a high level of rationality among its actors.[49]

Finally, I would like to make some remarks on the quite common presumption of a connection between terrorism and poverty. According to this thesis, poverty, if not being the root cause of terrorism, would at least be a useful condition for it. In a recent study, Krueger and Maleckova refute this assumption in the case of the Israeli-Palestinian conflict. On the basis of a comparative statistical analysis they show that the Palestinian suicide attackers of Hezbollah on average have at least a secondary school education and come from economically advantaged families. The authors see terrorism as genuinely politically motivated and thus estimate that education and a sufficient social position are even a condition for it, while poverty was more likely an obstacle:

> "More educated people from privileged backgrounds are more likely to participate in politics, probably in part because political involvement requires some minimum level of interest, expertise, commitment to issues and effort, all of which are more likely if people are educated and wealthy enough to concern themselves with more than mere economic subsistence."[50]

In fact, members of terrorist groups often come from the society's middle class. That was for instance the case for the German *Rote Armee Fraktion* or also for the perpetrators of the attacks of 9/11/2001. Concerning the latter case, a certain degree of higher education adds to the social condition, as the planning and the execution of the deed took place in a foreign country and, furthermore, technical abilities needed to be acquired. Even if terrorist action often aims at favoring oppressed or deprived people, it is not the poor man's weapon it often is said to be.

It is probably wrong to speak of terrorism as a form of warfare, because in fact there are incontestably many more differences than common ground between them. Many of the terrorist groups conceive(d) themselves as warriors (cf. Rote *Armee* Fraktion, *Brigate* Rosse, …). However the choice of their strategy and means does not correspond with those made in a (classic) war. Terrorism as a strategy did and does occur in many wars on all sides; but, as part of a whole and not as a whole itself.

4. GUERRILLA AND TERRORISM – A COMPARISON

"A logical extension of guerrilla war is the terrorist war."[51]

"We sincerely believe that terrorism is of negative value, that it by no means produces the desired effects, that it can turn people against a revolutionary movement."[52]

In this section, I will examine the commonalities and also the differences between guerrilla warfare and terrorism. This chapter will be restricted to insurgent terrorism, which seams to be most appropriate to be compared with guerrilla warfare. I will investigate the question why these two terms are quite often mentioned in the same breath. My analysis will be led by the four features composing the below diagram, of P. Waldmann:[53]

	[Political] Terrorism	*Guerrilla warfare*
Function of the violence	Mostly symbolic, communicative use	Military use
Social support	Restricted to radical splinter groups from the middle class	Inclusion of broad social classes, in particular of the rural population
Territorial factor	No territorial basis	Territorial basis
Dynamic	No chance of military or political seizure of power, more likely to be counterproductive	Possible chance of military or political seizure of power

Function of the violence
While both use violence, terrorism and guerrilla pursue different tactics. The guerrilla wants to occupy a certain territory, terrorists want to occupy the thinking.[54] When terrorist violence is called symbolic, this is not meant to trivialize its proportions, since clearly it consists "of many acts which are not symbolic at all".[55] What is meant is that terrorists do not achieve their objectives directly by means of violence, but indirectly via intimidation. This distinguishes them considerably from all guerrilla strategies which aim "to achieve their political and military objectives straight through the use of violence"[56] and therefore put their hopes on the physical effects of violence. This is also true concerning sabotage. When the guerrilla destroys, for instance, a railway line, they do it for the sake of the damage directly resulting from the act, in this case to cut off the supplies' ways. In the final consistency, the guerrilla's struggle finds his end in a "decisive battle",[57] which is a comparative showdown between the contending forces of direct violence. As the tactics used by the guerrilla before do not always conform to international war conventions, guerrilla warfare is not respected as a regular form of combat.

This difference becomes clear also in the fact that a guerrilla movement can win its struggle without the support of the media, whereas terrorists rely heavily on media transmissions to bring their matter to public attention.

Social support

In most of the cases, the leadership of guerrilla, as well as of terrorist movements, comes from educated and radicalized middle classes.[58] However, guerrilla groups, before starting the armed resistance, secure their support of the population, because they cannot win their struggle without the popular support. The first step of a guerrilla struggle is the (in most of the time non-violent) construction of a sufficiently broad material and ideological basis. Terrorists, on the contrary, often conceive themselves as an avant-garde, enlightening others by violent messages when other means have no longer met with success. They, too, want to gain the support of the population, but often they do not get there with just those groups, whose interests the terrorists claim to defend. For instance, the *Rote Armee Fraktion* never had a significant support among the German working class. With regard to the ethnically motivated violence of the Spanish ETA or the Irish IRA, this point looks slightly different. They differ from the RAF in the fact that "the militant middle class avant-garde of the two minorities anyhow did not only project their own problems and visions of the future into a society concerned with different questions, but [...] gave expression to an extremely explosive conflict."[59] These two groups, who without any doubt used terrorist strategies and means, were nevertheless able to gain a considerable degree of popular support.

Territorial factor

A terrorist group can survive quite a long time without possessing any territory, as they aim to occupy the thinking. The guerrilla, though, needs on the one hand, for military and strategic reasons, to occupy a real space in view of its aim to control a whole country. On the other hand, the control of a territory is necessary to be able to guarantee the security of the supporting population, who cannot leave their land, against the enemy troops.

Here, too, IRA and ETA go off the path of terrorism and get closer to guerrilla warfare because "at least basically a thinking in spatial categories" exists. It manifests itself in the choice of the attacks' locations that mainly "are concentrated in particular regions, in which the rebels feel strong enough to face the state's security forces".[60] The violence of these groups finally has the real objective to drive out the "occupiers". The credibility of such a demand depends on the continuity of its backing by the population. After a concession on the part of the state to the minority, which then stops to see the necessity of violent resistance only in order to achieve the maximal aims, the guerrilla-like resistance group changes in its aims and size back to a terrorist group.

Dynamic

At last, guerrilla warfare offers a long-term prospective to the seizure of power, which the terrorist strategy does not have. Empirically, political and insurgent terrorism, so far, have remained unsuccessful, while the history of guerrilla struggles can look back on several victorious cases. But this is not only a historical difference. Concerning the moral evaluation, this dynamic gives the political movement guerrilla the perspective of full legitimacy even before the end of their struggle. Once again Walzer:

> "At some point along that continuum, guerrilla fighters acquire war rights, and at some further point, the right of the government to continue the struggle must be called into question."[61]

If the guerrilla movement gains a sufficient degree of support, they may not only be militarily in the position to take over political power, but they are then also morally legitimated in doing so. The war against them becomes an unjust war.

As result of the comparison made between guerrilla strategy and terrorism, the following can be stated together with Laqueur:

> "There are basic differences between the strategy of rural guerrilla warfare and urban terrorism."[62]

Mutual overlapping is possible when one strategy makes use of the other one, as shown for the cases of ETA and IRA. Whether terrorism or guerrilla is the chosen strategy and whether it might be successful depends decisively on geographical, demographical, social and political circumstances and cannot be stated once for all cases. But here resides at least partly an explanation why, in Europe, terrorism and, in Latin America, guerrilla was respectively more frequent.

Nevertheless, it must be given in, that this comparison is made up rather on ideals than on empiric occurrences. At least in recent years, the purely political guerrilla fighting for a just world and utopia has not existed anymore. The passage from politically motivated guerrillas to criminal forces with the objective of enrichment has, in time, become fluid. This development is furthered by the growing number of mercenaries who do not risk their lives and kill others in order to defend convictions, but instead for the aim of accruing their own wealth. It becomes quite clear on the level of the "rebels'" leadership, which is no longer composed of charismatic idealists but where profit-seeking so-called warlords have the say.[63]

5. ON THE NOTION OF "INNOCENT VICTIMS"

In the definitions of terrorist acts, virtually always the so-called *innocent victims* are evoked.[64] And most of the authors, who do not reject violence unconditionally and *a priori*, see just in the attack on the *innocent* the blameworthy feature of terrorism. In this section, I will go into the term of innocence in some more detail, which in my opinion is misleading for its vagueness and thus used in an inadequate way.

"Innocent" describes the conduct of a certain person relative to one *selected* system of values, mostly a system of laws. Obviously, when we speak of innocent victims of a terrorist act, not such a kind of relation is meant. A terrorist act on a prison full of convicted felons would still be a terrorist act. Violence against the so-called innocent is wrong for a different reason, the adjective "innocent", in this context, has another sense. The victims of a terrorist attack are innocent in the sense that:

> "They are not guilty of any action (or omission) the terrorist could plausibly bring up as a justification of what he does to them. [...] They are not responsible on any plausible understanding of responsibility, for the (real or alleged) injustice, suffering, or deprivation that is being afflicted on him [i.e. the terrorist] or on those whose case he has adopted, and which is so grave that a violent response to it can be properly considered."[65]

"Innocent", here, first changes to "not guilty" and then to "not responsible" for the terrorists' causa. Even if at first glance this distinction may seem irrelevant, I do take it for a decisive turn, because the highly emotional and never universal term "innocent" is replaced by a more neutral adjective that in particular is not relative to a system of *values*. The victims' specific relation to the terrorists' acts and demands, too, becomes much more plain. He cannot be called upon to account for the reason of the terrorist action personally[66] and, even if asked to, would be incapable of complying with the terrorists' requests. Therefore there is no apparent reason why one should continue to speak of the victims' innocence, which is a completely different idea. The problem is that we do not have, in our normal languages, any appropriate term to fully describe this relationship.

A different possibility to replace the term "innocent" is to take into account the classic discrimination between combatants and noncombatants, codified in the Geneva conventions. Their being guilty or not does not count; what matters is their belonging to the military apparatus or their responsibility for the military's acts. Terrorism, then, would be characterized by deliberately ignoring this discrimination and attacking, *in extremo*, only noncombatants – namely, against unprotected people. Even though this distinction without doubt contains some borderline cases,[67] it is sufficiently clear enough what it wants to say. Murphy proposes the following description:

> "Combatants [...] are all those of whom it is reasonable to believe that they are engaged in an attempt at your destruction. Noncombatants are all those of whom it is not reasonable to believe this."[68]

Attacking or using violence against noncombatants is generally not allowed, according to the Geneva convention, as well as according to moral standards, because those benefit from immunity against attacks, even in wartime. Bauhn proposes to shift the focus when describing the status of noncombatant:

> "Instead of trying to distinguish between innocence and non-innocence, or between various degrees of non-innocence, we could formulate the concept of *a recipient non-deserving of violent interference*. This concept would denote a person whom it would be morally wrong to subject to violent interferences."[69]

Bauhn's concept is based on the idea of noncombatant-immunity, but the emphasis is not on the person as an agent, but as a recipient (of violence). This stresses the central element of the noncombatant-immunity: the *prima facie* right to freedom from bodily harm of those who do not use violent means shall be strengthened. This kind of argumentation can also claim validity in the context of other violent conflicts,[70] as it mainly makes topical the classic just war theory.

6. CONCLUSION AND OUTLOOK

In this paper, I have shown that guerrilla warfare and terrorism are two fundamentally different matters. Differences notwithstanding, they do not exclude each other on the short term, that means each of these strategies *can* make use of the other one or parts out of it from time to time. Yet, such a mutual overlapping does not affect the theoretical separation between the two different strategies.

Guerrilla struggle can be seen as a variation of "classic" warfare and therefore can be morally judged according to the classic just war theory for the most part. If it is led with broad popular support, it can become, following the theory, a just war.

Terrorism should not be referred to as a form of war, since two many features separate these two types of violence. Not long ago, nobody would have used the term war in the context of terrorism[71] and the indubitably shocking change in the dimension of terrorist violence should not lead us to do so. Terrorist violence should continue to be called criminal[72] "privatized violence".[73] The proceeding against terrorist movements, too, must take into account that it is not directed against a warlike attack. The response to terrorist attacks or threats has to differentiate itself from their criminal nature, otherwise the vicious circle of violence will be infinite:

> "Who wanted to achieve something like the 'complete extermination of the terrorism worldwide', would […] hit so many innocent, hurt and humiliate so many people, that constantly new terror would become unavoidable."[74]

He who wants to proceed against terrorism must distinguish himself from his target exactly by *not* using violent means against noncombatants. If not, at least he cannot claim for himself to defend this moral principle or to act in the name of it. One could even go further and say that "a state which has itself been involved in or with terrorism to any significant degree, lacks the moral standing for *bona fide* moral criticism of terrorism".[75]

In the future, the well-mannered guerrillas, fighting on the side of the population and for their country, will become rare. Rather, the importance of political motivations will continue to decrease as a reason for conflicts or the outbreak of violence. Obviously, ideological justifications will not cease to be evoked. Nevertheless, economical and/or personal reasons will continuously play a more and more central role. The phenomenon of the warlords gives quite a good example for the potential development. Neither are these conflicts fought on the side of the population, on the contrary they may even be lead against it, in any case not in its interests anymore. The theatre of war is intentionally moved to residential regions and near the civilian population, which does not enjoy protection or immunity anymore. It is no longer possible to speak of guerrilla, as the methods of combat and the securing of power have become increasingly dictatorial or terrorist.

With regard to the more and more transnational terrorism two completely different dangers arise. On the one hand, the often discussed threat exists, that terrorists could use more dangerous weapons for even more perilous attacks. Besides this vital danger, another fundamental change threatens, largely unnoticed, our modern democratic societies in an insidious and subtle way. Not only by real destruction can harm be inflicted on a society:

> "The new form of war will consist to use, instead of troops and aircraft, exclusively the means of emotions – and with these new arms not to try the conquest of such bulky and unwieldy things as territories and cities, but, through the smallest possible costs cause the greatest possible devastation in the enemy state: the distraction of the feelings of its citizens in order to damage the basis of the society."[76]

When daily tasks and activities, like opening a letter or taking the public transports, cannot be done without the tormenting feeling of fear, the conditions of social life and relationships are jeopardized or even destroyed. And moreover, crucial changes of social structures (such as mutual confidence) are initiated by the state, that restricts the hard-won liberty of its citizenry by the reinforcement of surveillance in all fields, without being able to guarantee definite security. But precisely when the lifestyle and the habits of a whole civilization may be manipulated, the terror shows to advantage.

NOTES

[1] Laqueur (1977b: 6).
[2] According to P. Sloterdijk (*Luftbeben*. Frankfurt a. M., 2002: 25) a wording without meaning. Cf also Eppler (2002: 20).
[3] Walzer (1977: 176).
[4] Allemann (1974: 15). Many other authors agree on this point. [Quotation translated by the author. Original text: "[Das erste Mal] in bedeutendem und militärisch zum mindesten mitentscheidenden Umfang ist diese Kampfweise [...] von 1808 an im Volksaufstand der Spanier gegen [...] Napoleon erprobt worden."
[5] It's true that Carlos Marighella developed a concept of urban guerrilla (*Mini Manual de Guerrilheiro Urbano*) that influenced for example the German *Rote Armee Fraktion*. This form of action however is far more comparable to terrorism than to guerrilla warfare and therefore does not enter into account here.
[6] Walzer (1977: 184).
[7] Tse Tung (1966: 68).
[8] Guevara (1997: 56).
[9] Münkler (1992: 112). [Quotation translated by the author. Original text: "[Der Partisan] respektiert den Nonkombattantenstatus, indem er selbst Zivilisten nicht angreift, und er respektiert ihn zugleich nicht, indem er jeden, der ihn angreifen will, zwingt, Zivilisten mitanzugreifen."]
[10] Walzer (1977: 180).
[11] Fanon (1968: 139 f).
[12] Haffner, Sebastian (1966): *Der neue Krieg*. In: Tse Tung (1966: 22).
[13] Waldmann (1993: 76). [Quotation translated by the author. Original text: "Verankerung in breiteren Bevölkerungsschichten".]
[14] Cf. Tse Tung (1966: 19).
[15] Münkler (1992: 116). [Quotation translated by the author. Original text: "ubiquitär und permanent".]
[16] Cf. Hahlweg (1968: 19). *Anlehnungsmacht*.
[17] In the historical context, in which the guerrilla developed, this has to be taken literally (cut off telegraph lines).
[18] Guevara (1997: 118).

[19] Cf. Guevara (1997: 60). An exception to the refusal may according to Guevara be the murder of a particularly cruel enemy leader. I will show later in this paper that such kind of action has not to be counted as terrorism in its narrow sense.

[20] Guevara (1997: 54 f).

[21] Münkler (1992: 113). [Quotation translated by the author. Original text: "evolutiv angestrebte hierarchische Monokephalie".]

[22] Allemann (1974: 21). Allemann intentionally draws a parallel line between guerrilla and bandits in South-America, because in his opinion both are based on similar elements (such as individualism, machismo) and originate from these. [Quotation translated by the author. Original text: Die Form "eines individuellen oder kollektiven Heraustretens aus einem als unerträglich und lastend empfundenen sozialen Zusammenhang; als Ausdruck eines gewaltsamen Protestes gegen das Gesetz des Herrschenden, dem sich weder der Bandolero noch der Guerillero fügen will".]

[23] Cf. Hahlweg (1968: 20).

[24] Guevara (1997: 53).

[25] Waldmann (1993: 72). [Quotation translated by the author. Original text: "die Guerilla eine militärische Strategie im klassischen Sinn [ist], die allerdings gewisse soziale und psychologische Gegebenheiten nicht außer acht lässt".]

[26] Badiou (2002: 12). [Quotation translated by the author. Original text: "Primitivement, un terroriste est celui qui légitime et pratique la Terreur. C'est une désignation objective, qui n'est infamante que pour des adversaires politiques."]

[27] Cf. Heinzen, Karl (1848): *Der Mord*. Cited as in Ramonet, Ignacio (2002: 53): *Les guerres du XXIe siècle*. Paris.

[28] Cf. Laqueur (1977b: 27). Laqueur remarks in a cynical way that Heinzen himself never became a terrorist but settled down in one of the most civilized cities of America.

[29] Badiou (2002: 12 f). [Quotation translated by the author. Original text: "Il est remarquable que, peu à peu, le mot 'terrorisme', qui qualifiait clairement une figure particulière de l'exercice du pouvoir d'Etat, réussisse à signifier exactement le contraire. Depuis longtemps, en effet, 'terroriste' est le mot par lequel les Etats désignent tout adversaire violent, et / ou armé, précisément au vu de son caractère non-étatique."]

[30] 22 U.S.C. 2656 f (d). The CIA's definition also explicitly speaks of "individuals and groups", the definition given by the FBI is less clear on that issue.

[31] Badiou (2002: 13). [Quotation translated by the author. Original text: "[A]u terme de son évolution sémantique, 'terroriste' est aujourd'hui un vocable intrinsèquement propagandiste. Il n'a aucune lisibilité neutre. Il dispense de tout examen raisonné des situations politiques, de leurs causes et de leurs conséquences. [...] 'Terroriste' ne désigne plus une orientation politique, ou une possibilité de telle ou telle situation, mais, exclusivement, la forme de l'action."]

[32] Therefore I do not quote it here. Nevertheless it is one of the best and most complete definitions.

[33] Fromkin (1975: 693).

[34] Walzer (1977: 197).

[35] Waldmann (1998: 12).

[36] Nagel (1972: 136).

[37] Waldmann (1998: 13). [Quotation translated by the author. Original text: "Es wäre weniger schlimm, wenn sie jemanden umbrächten, weil sie ihn persönlich hassen; das Unmenschliche besteht darin, dass sie ihn töten, ohne eigentlich etwas gegen ihn zu haben."]

[38] Wördemann (1977: 152).

[39] Münkler (1992: 154). [Quotation translated by the author. Original text: "Nicht die violentia selbst, sondern der von ihr ausgehende Terror, der Schrecken, ist es, worum es der terroristischen Strategie im Kern geht."]

[40] In addition, geographical distances nowadays do not represent insurmountable obstacles. This new reality, caused widely by new technologies, which is true above all for information, adds to the possibility of addressing a large group of people, too.

[41] Waldmann (1993: 71). [Quotation translated by the author. Original text: "an deren Ende panikartige Angst und von diesem Gefühl diktierte Handlungsweisen stehen sollen".]

[42] Fromkin (1975: 692).

[43] Cf. Waldmann (1998: 29).

[44] Primoratz (1990: 135).

[45] Cf. Barkan / Snowden (2001: 66).

[46] This term comes from the "vigilante committees". As a current form of vigilante terrorism, Barkan / Snowden give the example of the Ku Klux Klan.

[47] Fromkin (1975: 697).

[48] As an example, Fromkin describes the reaction to the FLN's attacks of the French colonialist regime. In suspecting all non-Europeans they unwillingly emphasized the national difference which forced the national Algerian solidarity. This was exactly what the FLN terrorists originally intended to achieve (cf. Fromkin 1977). This is also an example for the use of terrorist strategy at the beginning of a guerrilla movement.

[49] Concerning the terrorists, the rationality is required for the planning, nevertheless, the motivation may be irrational (e.g. religious). One has to make a difference between the cause and the carrying out of an action.

[50] Krueger / Maleckova (2002: 32).

[51] Margiotta, Franklin D. (ed.) (1994: 106): *Brassey's Ecyclopedia of Military History and Biography.* Washington, London.

[52] Guevara (1997: 116).

[53] Waldmann (1993: 71).

[54] Cf. Wördemann (1977: 145).

[55] Laqueur (1977a: 51). [Quotation translated by the author. Original text: "aus vielen Handlungen, die überhaupt nicht symbolisch sind".]

[56] Münkler (1992: 153). [Quotation translated by the author. Original text: "ihre politisch-militärischen Ziele durch die Anwendung von Gewalt unmittelbar zu erreichen suchten".]

[57] Tse Tung (1966: 74). This logic is also present in the writings of Guevara.

[58] Cf. Waldmann (1993: 73).

[59] Waldmann (1993: 96). [Quotation translated by the author. Original text: "dass die militante Mittelschichtenavantgarde der beiden Minderheiten jedenfalls nicht nur ihre eigenen Probleme und Zukunftsutopien in eine Gesellschaft hinein projizierte, die mit anderen Fragen beschäftigt war, sondern einem [...] äußerst brisanten Konflikt Ausdruck verlieh."]

[60] Waldmann (1993: 97). [Quotation translated by the author. Original text: "in bestimmten Zonen konzentrieren, in denen sich die Rebellen offenbar stark genug fühlen, um den staatlichen Sicherheitskräften die Stirn zu bieten".]

[61] Walzer (1977: 195).

[62] Laqueur (1977b: 217).

[63] Cf. Eppler (2002: 31 ff).

[64] Cf. the definitions given above.

[65] Primoratz (2003).

[66] According to Wilkins, terrorism may be justified as defensive ultima ratio, if the victims belong to a group that is collectively responsible for the causa. Cf. Wilkins, Burleigh Taylor (1992): *Terrorism and collective responsibility.* London.

[67] Just think about the "naked soldiers" Walzer (1977: 138 ff) refers to, or the Guantanamo P.O.W., called illegal combatants.

[68] Murphy (1973: 536).

[69] Bauhn (2003).

[70] The discrimination between combatants and noncombatants keeps on losing its relevance in "normal" wars, too. By 1900, 1 killed civilian was opposed to 10 killed soldiers, today, this relation is nearly inverted: 8 times more civilians are killed in warlike conflicts than soldiers. In addition, in so-called (post-) modern wars, the victims are mourned on the weaker side almost exclusively (cf. the wars in Kosovo 1999, Afghanistan 2002/03, etc.).

[71] In 1993, the failed attack on the WTC rightly was called a terrorist act and not an act of war.

[72] Even if one can imagine some very rare cases, where terrorism might eventually be justified. Cf. for instance Wilkins (op. cit.), Bauhn (2005), Pavković (see his article in this volume).

[73] Cf. Eppler (2002: 11): Violence that wants to injure and thus is illegal, but which poses to be legitimated.

[74] Eppler (2002: 20). [Quotation translated by the author. Original text: "Wer so etwas wie die 'restlose Ausrottung des Terrorismus auf der Welt' erreichen wollte, müsste [...] so viele Unschuldige treffen, so viele Menschen verletzen und demütigen, dass immer neuer Terror unausweichlich würde."]

[75] Primoratz (2005).

[76] Ankowitsch, Christian: "Angst ist ein Gefühl mit Zukunft", in: *Frankfurter Allgemeine Sonntagszeitung*, 1.12.2002, p. 71. [Quotation translated by the author. Original text: "Die neue Form des Krieges wird darin bestehen, sich statt Truppen und Flugzeugen ausschließlich der Mittel der Gefühle zu bedienen – und mit dieser neuen Waffen nicht die Eroberung so sperriger und unhandlicher Dinge wie Territorien und Städte zu versuchen, sondern unter geringstem Aufwand die größtmögliche Verheerung im feindlichen Staat anzurichten: die Verstörung der Gefühle seiner Bürger, um in der Folge die Basis der Gesellschaften zu beschädigen."]

REFERENCES

Allemann, Fritz R. (1974): *Macht und Ohnmacht der Guerilla*. München.

Badiou, Alain: "Considérations philosophiques sur quelques faits récents", in: *lignes 08*, may 2002, Paris: Editions Léo Scheer, pp. 9-34.

Barkan, Steven E. / Snowden, Lynne L. (2001): *Collective Violence*. Boston.

Bauhn, Per (2005): "Political Terrorism and the Rules of Just War", in this volume.

Eppler, Erhard (2002): *Vom Gewaltmonopol zum Gewaltmarkt?* Frankfurt a. M.

Fanon, Frantz (1968): *The wretched of the earth*. New York: Grove Press.

Fromkin, David (1975): "The strategy of terrorism", in: *Foreign Affairs*, July, New York, pp. 683-689.

Funke, Manfred (ed.) (1977): *Terrorismus. Untersuchungen zur Struktur und Strategie revolutionärer Gewaltpolitik*. Düsseldorf.

Gilbert, Paul (1994): *Terrorism, security and nationality*. London / New York.

Guevara, Ernesto (1997): *Guerilla Warfare*. Wilmington: SR Books.

Hahlweg, Werner (1968): *Guerilla. Krieg ohne Fronten*. Stuttgart.

Hoffman, Bruce (1999): *Terrorismus – der unerklärte Krieg. Neue Gefahren politischer Gewalt*. Frankfurt a. M.

Krueger, Alan B. / Maleckova, Jitka (2002): "Education, Poverty, Political Violence and Terrorism. Is there a Causal Connection?", *NBER Working Paper Series*. Working Paper 9074. http://www.nber.org/papers/9074/.

Laqueur, Walter (1977a): "Interpretationen des Terrorismus", in: Funke (1977), pp. 37-82.

Laqueur, Walter (1977b): *Terrorism*. Boston.

Münkler, Herfried (1992): *Gewalt und Ordnung. Das Bild des Krieges im politischen Denken*. Frankfurt a. M.

Murphy, Jeffrie G. (1973): "The Killing of the Innocent", in: *The Monist*, 57, LaSalle, Illinois, pp. 527-550.

Nagel, Thomas (1972): "War and Massacre", in: *Philosophy and Public Affairs*, Vol. 1, No. 2, pp. 123-144.

Primoratz, Igor (1990): "What is Terrorism?", in: *Journal of Applied Philosophy*, Vol. 7, No. 2.

Primoratz, Igor (2005): "State Terrorism and Counterterrorism", in this volume.

Schmid, A. P. / Jongman, A. J. ([2]1988): *Political terrorism*. Amsterdam/ New Brunswick.

Tophoven, Walter / Becker, Horst (1979): *Terrorismus und Guerilla*. Düsseldorf.

Tse Tung, Mao (1966): *Theorie des Guerilla-Krieges*. Reinbek.

Waldmann, Peter (1977): *Strategien politischer Gewalt*. Stuttgart.

Waldmann, Peter (1993): "Terrorismus und Guerilla – Ein Vergleich organisierter antistaatlicher Gewalt in Europa und Lateinamerika", in: Backes/Jesse (ed.): *Jahrbuch Extremismus und Demokratie*. Bonn.

Waldmann, Peter (1998): *Terrorismus. Provokation der Macht*. München.

Wördemann, Franz (1977): "Mobilität, Technik und Kommunikation als Strukturelemente des Terrorismus", in: Funke (1977), pp. 140-157.

Walzer, Michael (1977): *Just and Unjust Wars*. New York.

IGOR PRIMORATZ

STATE TERRORISM AND COUNTERTERRORISM

1. INTRODUCTORY

When it first entered political discourse, the word "terrorism" was used with reference to the reign of terror imposed by the Jacobin regime – that is, to describe a case of state terrorism. Historians of the French Revolution have analyzed and discussed that case in great detail. There are also quite a few historical studies of some other instances of state terrorism, most notably of the period of "the Great Terror" in the Soviet Union.

In a contemporary setting, however, state terrorism is apparently much more difficult to discern. Discussions of terrorism in social sciences and philosophy tend to focus on non-state and, more often than not, anti-state terrorism. In common parlance and in the media, terrorism is as a rule assumed to be an activity of non-state agencies in virtue of the very meaning of the word. If one suggests that the army or security services are doing the same things that, when done by insurgents, are invariably described and condemned as terrorist, the usual reply is: "But these are actions done on behalf of the state, in pursuit of legitimate state aims: the army, waging war, or the security services, fending off threats to our security." In other words,

> Throwing a bomb is bad,
> Dropping a bomb is good;
> Terror, no need to add,
> Depends on who's wearing the hood.[1]

As far as everyday discourse and the media are concerned, this can perhaps be explained by two related tendencies. One is the widely shared assumption that, at least normally, what the state does has a certain kind of legitimacy, while those challenging it tend to be perceived as the forces of disorder and destruction, engaged in clearly unjustifiable pursuits. The other is the double standard of the form "Us vs. Them". In states facing insurgency, the general public and the media find themselves on the side of the state. This tends to affect the usage. An offshoot of this tendency is that when insurgents abroad are sponsored by our state, we do not call them terrorists, but rather guerrillas, freedom fighters, and the like.

The focusing on non-state terrorism in social sciences is given a different explanation: that whatever the similarities between state and non-state terrorism, the dissimilarities are more prominent and instructive. Walter Laqueur, a leading

A shorter version of the paper was first published in Igor Primoratz (ed.), *Terrorism: The Philosophical Issues*, Basingstoke and New York: Palgrave MacMillan, 2004, pp. 113-127. Reproduced with permission of Palgrave MacMillan.

69

G. Meggle (ed.), Ethics of Terrorism & Counter-Terrorism, 69-81.

authority on the history and sociology of terrorism, tells us that the two "fulfil different functions and manifest themselves in different ways", and that "nothing is gained by ignoring the specifics of violence".[2] I am not convinced that this approach is to be preferred in social science;[3] but be that as it may, it certainly will not do in philosophy. If some acts of state agents are basically similar to and exhibit the same morally relevant traits as acts of non-state agents commonly termed terrorist, that will clearly determine our moral understanding and evaluation of both. Thus philosophers have been less reluctant than sociologists and political scientists to recognize and discuss state terrorism.[4]

But the philosophical work on the subject done so far leaves room, and indeed suggests the need, for a typology of state involvement in terrorism, and a fuller statement of the argument for the claim philosophers sometimes make in passing that state terrorism is worse, morally speaking, than terrorism by non-state agents. My aim in this paper is to offer some comments on these two topics. In the light of these comments I shall then make a few remarks on counterterrorism. But I must start with a few words on the definition of terrorism.

2. WHAT IS TERRORISM?

I have argued elsewhere that, for the purposes of philosophical discussion, terrorism is best defined as the deliberate use of violence, or threat of its use, against innocent people, with the aim of intimidating some other people into a course of action they otherwise would not take.[5]

Defined in this way, terrorism has two targets. One person or group is attacked directly, in order to get at another person or group and intimidate them into doing something they otherwise would not do. In terms of importance, the indirect target is primary, and the direct target secondary. The secondary, but directly attacked target, are innocent people. In the context of war, according to the mainstream version of just war theory, this includes all except members of armed forces and security services, those who supply them with arms and ammunition, and political officials directly involved in the conflict. In the context of political conflict that falls short of war, the class of the innocent has similarly wide scope: it includes all except government officials, police, and members of security services.

What is the sense in which the direct victims of terrorism are "innocent"? They are not guilty of any *action* (or *omission*) the terrorist could plausibly bring up as a justification of what he does to them. They are not attacking him; therefore he cannot justify his action in terms of self-defense. They are not waging war on him, nor on those on whose behalf he presumes to act; therefore he cannot say that he is merely waging war. They are not responsible, on any plausible understanding of responsibility, for the (real or alleged) injustice, suffering, or deprivation that is being inflicted on him or on those whose cause he has adopted, and which is so grave that a violent response to it can be properly considered. Or, if they are, the terrorist is in no position to know that.

Notice the qualification: "real *or imagined* injustice, suffering, or deprivation." This qualification is necessary because I am not referring to the innocence of the terrorist's victims from a point of view entirely different from, and independent of,

70

that of the terrorist. Such an external approach makes for arbitrariness and talking at cross-purposes. The killing of a certain politician can then be seen, and judged, as an act of terrorism by most of us, while its perpetrators can, in good faith, reject both the classification and judgment, and say that what they did was political assassination. For most of us, although perhaps not subscribing to the politician's policies, might deny that they were so extremely unjust or otherwise morally intolerable as to make him deserving to die on account of them, while those who killed him will claim that they were. Most of us might think of the politician as innocent in the pertinent sense of the word, while those who killed him will claim that he had been guilty. That is, this approach generates too high a degree of relativism in discussions of terrorism: to paraphrase the hackneyed *cliché*, one person's terrorist is another person's political assassin. In order to avoid this, I take the innocence of the victims of terrorism to mean innocence of real injustice *or* innocence of injustice the terrorist believes is being perpetrated, although others see things differently. On my definition of terrorism, the terrorist's victim is innocent even if we grant the terrorist his assessment of the policies at issue.

If the terrorist subscribes to some plausible understanding of responsibility, that means that he kills or maims people he himself, in his heart, believes to be innocent. This, I think, captures the distinctive obscenity of much terrorism. To be sure, there are terrorists who adhere to extremely crude notions of collective responsibility that take mere membership in an ethnic or religious group or citizenship of a state as a sufficient ground for ascription of such responsibility. The perpetrators of the attacks in New York on September 11, 2001, seem to have held such views. Still others are amoralists, and will not be bothered by questions of responsibility. Terrorists belonging to these two classes do not believe their victims to be innocent. The distinctive obscenity of their type of terrorism must be located elsewhere: in their preposterous positions on responsibility and the gory consequences these positions have in their practice.

Along these lines we can distinguish between terrorism, on the one hand, and war and political violence, on the other. This is not to say that political violence cannot intimidate and coerce (it often does), nor that an army cannot employ terrorism (many armies have done so, and that, indeed, is one of the main types of state terrorism).

The definition acknowledges the historical connection of "terrorism" with "terror" and "terrorizing". It does not confine terrorism to the political sphere, but makes it possible to speak of non-political (e.g. criminal) terrorism.

The definition is politically neutral: it covers both state and anti-state, revolutionary and counterrevolutionary, left-wing and right-wing terrorism. It is also morally neutral at the fundamental level of debate. I believe it captures the elements of terrorism that lead most of us to judge it as gravely wrong: the use or threat of use of *violence* against the *innocent* for the sake of *intimidation* and *coercion*. But it does not prejudge the moral question of its justification in particular cases. For it entails only that terrorism is *prima facie* wrong, and thus does not rule out its justification under certain circumstances.

Another virtue of the definition is that it relates the issue of the moral standing of terrorism to just war theory. For the central tenet of that theory, under the heading of *ius in bello*, is that we must not deliberately attack the innocent.

Clearly, the definition is both narrower in some respects and wider in others than common usage would warrant. Attacks of insurgents on soldiers or police officers, which the authorities and the media depict, and the public perceives, as terrorist, would not count as such, but rather as political violence or guerrilla warfare. The bombing of German and Japanese cities in World War II, or numerous Israeli Army attacks on Lebanon, on the other hand, are commonly presented as acts of war, but would count as terrorism on my definition.

If it is said that this tells against the definition, my reply is that it need not. My point is that, if what we hope for is more discerning and critical moral understanding of these matters, we should not be unduly bound by conventional usage. What matters is that in the former case, the targets are soldiers or police officers, and not innocent people. In the latter case, innocent people are deliberately targeted with the aim of intimidation and coercion. The former case does not involve the four morally problematic components the definition singles out; the latter does. On the other hand, whether the bomb is planted by hand or dropped from an aircraft, and who does or does not wear the hood, can hardly matter, morally speaking.

3. VARIETIES OF STATE INVOLVEMENT WITH TERRORISM

Philosophers tend to be perceived as given to introducing all manner of distinctions where none were acknowledged before. With respect to state terrorism this has been the case to a lesser degree than on most other issues. Thus Alan Ryan discusses the claim that "a terrorist state" is logically impossible by virtue of the definition of "state", and brings up Nazi Germany and Stalin's Soviet Union as obvious counterexamples. Further on he writes: "If Syria paid for, protected, equipped, and assisted hijackers and would-be bombers of El Al aircraft, that makes the Syrian regime a terrorist regime."[6] This looks rather like a leaf from the US State Department's book; for the purpose of moral assessment, it is clearly much too rough. However repugnant Syria's sponsorship of Palestinian terrorism may have been, it is certainly not in the same moral league with the regimes of Hitler and Stalin. Surely we ought to differentiate more carefully.

When speaking of state involvement in terrorism, there are distinctions to be made both in terms of degree of such involvement and with regard to its victims.

Concerning the degree of state involvement in terrorism, we should withstand the temptation to classify every state that has made use of terrorism, either directly or by proxy, as a *terrorist state*. I suggest that we reserve this label for states that do not merely resort to terrorism on certain occasions and for certain purposes, but employ it in a lasting and systematic way, and indeed are defined, in part, by the sustained use of terrorism against their own population. These are *totalitarian states*, such as Nazi Germany, Soviet Union in Stalin's times, or Cambodia under the rule of the Khmer Rouge.

A totalitarian regime aims at total domination of society and total unanimity of its subjects. Such an aim can only be pursued by an appropriately radical means: incessant terrorism, inflicted by an omnipresent and omnipotent secret police on an atomized and utterly defenseless population. Its efficiency is due, for the most part, to its arbitrary character: to the unpredictability of its choice of victims. Students of totalitarianism have pointed out that both in the Soviet Union and in Nazi Germany, the regime at first brutally suppressed all its opponents; when it no longer had any opposition to speak of, it deployed its secret police against "potential opponents". In the Soviet Union, it was eventually unleashed on masses of victims chosen at random. In the words of Carl J. Friedrich and Zbigniew K. Brzezinski, totalitarian terrorism

> "aims to fill everyone with fear and vents in full its passion for unanimity. Terror then embraces the entire society ... Indeed, to many it seems as if they are hunted, even though the secret police may not touch them for years, if at all. Total fear reigns. [...] The total scope and the pervasive and sustained character of totalitarian terror are operationally important. By operating with the latest technological devices, by allowing no refuge from its reach, and by penetrating even the innermost sanctums of the regime ... it achieves a scope unprecedented in history. The atmosphere of fear it creates easily exaggerates the strength of the regime and helps it achieve and maintain its façade of unanimity. Scattered opponents of the regime, if still undetected, become isolated and feel themselves cast out of society. This sense of loneliness, which is the fate of all but more especially of an opponent of the totalitarian regime, tends to paralyze resistance ... It generates the universal longing to 'escape' into the anonymity of the collective whole."[7]

While only totalitarian states use terrorism in this way and with such an aim, many states that are clearly not totalitarian, including many basically democratic and liberal states, have used terrorism on a much more limited scale and for more specific purposes. They have done so directly, or by sponsoring non-state agencies whose *modus operandi* is, or includes, terrorism. But as their resort to terrorism is occasional rather than sustained, let alone essential, they should not be termed terrorist states. When they are, an important moral, political, and legal divide is blurred.

Another distinction is that between the use of terrorism by a state *against its own citizens*, and the use of terrorism *abroad*, as a means of foreign policy, war, or occupation. Other things being equal, state terrorism of the former type seems worse, morally speaking, than that of the latter type. For in the former case the state is attacking the very population for which it should be providing order, security, and justice.

Quite a few non-totalitarian states have made use of terrorism against their own population. Some have done so directly, by having state agencies such as the armed forces or security services employ terrorism. Many military dictatorships in South America and elsewhere are examples of this; the most extreme cases are, of course, Chile under Pinochet and Argentina under the generals. Other states have done the same indirectly, by sponsoring death squads and the like.

Many states, both totalitarian and non-totalitarian, have used terrorism abroad, as a means of achieving foreign policy objectives, in the course of waging war, or as a method of maintaining their occupation of another people's land.

These types of state involvement in terrorism are not mutually exclusive; indeed, they are often complementary. A terrorist state will see no moral reason for hesitating to use terrorism beyond its borders too, whether in the course of waging war or in peacetime, as a means of pursuing its foreign policy objectives. Both Nazi Germany and the Soviet Union provide examples of that. But the same is true of states that do not qualify as terrorist, but do resort to terrorism against their own population on certain occasions and for some specific purposes. Such states, too, are not likely to be prevented by moral scruples from using terrorism abroad as well, whether directly or by proxy, when that is found expedient.

On the other hand, the fact that a state has resorted to terrorism in the international arena need not make it more prone to do the same at home, as there is a fairly clear line between the two. But it might. Since its establishment, Israel has often made use of terrorism in its conflict with the Palestinians and the neighboring Arab states. The suppression of the second Palestinian uprising (*intifada*) has been carried out, in part, by state terrorism. (Israel's neighbors, on their part, have supported Palestinian terrorism against Israel.) The way Israeli police put down the demonstrations of Palestinians living in Israel proper, as its citizens, in October 2000 – by shooting at them with rubber-coated and live ammunition and killing thirteen – may well qualify as state terrorism. If it does, that shows how the willingness to resort to terrorism abroad can eventually encourage its use at home.

To be sure, in practice the dichotomy of state and non-state terrorism does not always apply. Attempts at drawing hard and fast lines cannot succeed because of the widespread phenomenon of terrorist organizations receiving various types and degrees of support by states. Since in such cases a simple division of terrorism into state and non-state is no longer feasible, the moral assessment too becomes much more complex.

4. STATE TERRORISM IS MORALLY WORSE THAN NON-STATE TERRORISM

All terrorism is *prima facie* extremely morally wrong. But not everything that is extremely morally wrong is wrong in the same degree. State terrorism can be said to be morally worse than terrorism by non-state agents for at least four reasons.

First. Although unwilling to extend the scope of his discussion of terrorism to include state terrorism, Walter Laqueur remarks that "acts of terror carried out by police states and tyrannical governments, in general, have been responsible for a thousand times more victims and more misery than all actions of individual terrorism taken together".[8] He could also have mentioned terrorism employed by democracies (mostly, but not exclusively, in wartime), although that would not have affected the striking asymmetry very much. Now this asymmetry is not just another statistical fact; it follows from the nature of the state and the amount and variety of resources that even a small state has at its disposal. No matter how much non-state terrorists manage to enrich their equipment and improve their organization, planning, and methods of action, they stand no chance of ever significantly changing the score. No insurgent, no matter how well funded, organized, determined, and experienced in the methods of terrorism, can hope to come close to the killing, maiming, and overall destruction on the scale the RAF and US Air Force visited on German and Japanese cities in World

War II, or to the psychological devastation and subsequent physical liquidation of millions in Soviet and Nazi camps.

The terrorist attacks in the United States carried out on September 11, 2001, were in some respects rather unlike what we had come to expect from non-state terrorism. The number of victims, in particular, was unprecedented. Mostly because of that, I suspect, the media have highlighted these attacks as "the worst case of terrorism ever". So have quite a few public intellectuals. Thus Salman Rushdie, in his monthly column in the Melbourne daily *The Age*, wrote of "the most devastating terrorist attack in history".[9] The number of people killed, believed to be approaching seven thousand at the time, was indeed staggering. Yet "the worst case of terrorism ever" mantra is but another instance of the tendency of the media to equate terrorism with non-state terrorism. When we discard the assumption that only insurgents engage in terrorism – as I submit we should – the overall picture changes significantly. Let me give just one example from the Allies' terror bombing campaign against Germany. In the night of July 27, 1943, the RAF carried out the second of its four raids on Hamburg, known as the "Firestorm Raid". In the morning, when both the attack itself and the gigantic firestorm it had created were over, some forty thousand civilians were dead.[10]

Second. In one way or another, state terrorism is bound to be compounded by secrecy, deception, and hypocrisy. When involved in terrorism – whether perpetrated by its own agents or by proxy – a state will be acting clandestinely, disclaiming any involvement, and declaring its adherence to values and principles that rule it out. Or, if it is impractical and perhaps even counterproductive to deny involvement, it will do its best to present its actions to at least some audiences in a different light: as legitimate acts of war, or acts done in defense of state security. It will normally be able to do that without much difficulty, given the tendencies of common usage mentioned in Section 1 above.

Those engaging in non-state terrorism, on the other hand, need not be secretive, need not deceive the public about their involvement in terrorism (except, of course, at the operational level), and need not hypocritically proclaim their allegiance to moral principles that prohibit it. Some of them are amoralists, possibly of the sort exemplified by the notorious declaration of the nineteenth-century anarchist writer Laurent Tailhade: "What do the victims matter if the gesture is beautiful!" Others exhibit what Aurel Kolnai has called "overlain conscience":[11] conscience completely subjected to a non-moral absolute (the Leader, the Party, the Nation), which will permit and indeed enjoin all manner of actions incompatible with mainstream moral views, including terrorism. Still others adhere to some version of consequentialist moral theory, which will readily justify terrorism under appropriate circumstances.[12] In none of these cases will there be a need for deception and hypocrisy concerning the performance of specific terrorist acts or the adoption of policies of terrorism.

Third. Virtually all actions that constitute terrorism are prohibited by one or another of the various international human rights declarations or conventions and agreements that make up the laws and customs of war. The latter provide for immunity of civilians in armed conflict and thus prohibit terrorism by belligerent sides. Most, if not all, remaining types of terrorism – terrorism in wartime perpetrated by groups not recognized as belligerent parties, and terrorism in time of peace perpetrated by anyone at all – are covered by declarations of human rights. Now those engaging in non-state terrorism are not signatories to these declarations and conventions, while virtually all states today are signatories to most if not all of them. Therefore, when a state is involved in terrorism, it acts in breach of its own solemn international commitments. This particular charge cannot be brought against those resorting to non-state terrorism.

Fourth. Non-state terrorism is often said to be justified, or at least that its wrongness is mitigated, by the argument of no alternative. In a case where, for instance, a people is subjected to foreign rule with the usual attendant evils of oppression, humiliation, and exploitation, which is utterly unyielding and deploys overwhelming power, a liberation movement may claim that the only effective method of struggle at its disposal is terrorism. To refrain from using terrorism in such circumstances would be tantamount to giving up the prospect of liberation altogether.

This argument is often met with criticism. For one thing, since terrorism is extremely morally wrong, the evils of foreign rule, grave as they may be, may not be enough to justify, or even mitigate, resort to it. After all, its victims would by definition be innocent people, rather than those responsible for these evils. Furthermore, one can hardly ever be confident that terrorism will indeed achieve the aims adduced as its justification or mitigation. What people has ever succeeded in liberating itself by terrorism?

These objections are weighty, and may be enough to dispose of most attempts at justifying particular cases and policies of terrorism; but they do not show that the "no alternative" argument will *never* work. Persecution and oppression of an ethnic, racial, or religious group can reach such an extreme point that even terrorism may properly be considered. And the question of its efficiency, being an empirical one, cannot be settled once and for all. So it is possible that a liberation movement should be facing such circumstances where resort to terrorism is indeed the only feasible alternative to the continuation of persecution and oppression so extreme as to amount to an intolerable moral disaster. In such a situation, the "no alternative" argument would provide moral justification for terrorism, or at least somewhat mitigate our moral condemnation of its use. On the other hand, it seems virtually impossible that a state should find itself in such circumstances where it has no alternative to resorting to terrorism.

The only counterexample that comes to mind is the terror bombing campaign of the RAF against the civilian population of Germany in World War II, inasmuch as it can be seen as a case of "supreme emergency" allowing one to set aside even an extremely grave moral prohibition in order to prevent an imminent moral catastrophe.[13] Yet even this example is of a very limited value. The supreme emergency argument may have been valid only during the first year of the campaign: in 1942, the victory of Nazi Germany in Europe – a major moral disaster by any standard – might have been thought imminent. However, after German defeats at El Alamein (November 6, 1942) and at Stalingrad (February 2, 1943), that was clearly no longer the case. But the campaign went on almost to the very end of the war. As Michael Walzer says, "the truth is that the supreme emergency passed long before the British bombing reached its crescendo. The greater number by far of the German civilians killed by terror bombing were killed without moral (and probably also without military) reason."[14]

My argument might be challenged by pointing out that what I have called terrorist regimes can maintain themselves only by employing sustained, large-scale terrorism against their own population. Furthermore, a state that would not qualify as terrorist in this sense may be waging a war whose aims can be achieved only by means of terrorism. The successive Serbian onslaughts on Croatia, Bosnia-Herzegovina, and Kosova in the 1990s are a clear example. Their aim was conquest, "ethnic cleansing", and annexation of territories whose inhabitants included a non-Serb majority or large minority. Under the circumstances, and given the constraints of time, the "cleansing" had to be accomplished by large-scale terrorism. The Serbs had no alternative.[15]

All this is true, but not to the point. In such cases terrorism is indeed the only efficient option and, if the aim is to be achieved, there is no alternative to its use. But in such cases, unlike at least some conceivable cases of non-state terrorism justified or mitigated by the "no alternative" argument, the aim itself – the continuation of a Nazi or Stalinist regime, or the setting up of a greatly expanded *and* "ethnically homogeneous" Serbia – can justify or mitigate nothing. Its achievement, rather than failure to achieve it, would amount to an intolerable moral disaster.

Another objection would refer to the "balance of terror" produced by the mutual threat of nuclear attack that marked the Cold War period. The type of such threat relevant here was the threat of attacking the other side's civilian population centers. (In Cold War jargon, this was known as "countervalue deterrence".) If that threat was morally justified, it was a case of state terrorism justified by the "no alternative" argument.

I am not convinced that it was justified. Clearly, carrying out the threat and actually destroying major population centers of the enemy and killing hundreds of thousands, if not millions, of enemy civilians, could never be morally justified. But does that mean that a threat to do so – made with the aim of preventing the chain of events that would make such destruction a serious option – is also morally impermissible? A positive reply to this question assumes that, if it is wrong to do X, it is also wrong to intend to do X, and therefore also to threaten to do X. This assumption has been questioned.[16] I have not made up my mind on this matter. Perhaps the problem can be circumvented by arguing that the threat need not involve the intention of ever carrying it out; a bluff will do. Yet one might well wonder if a threat of this sort can be both credible and a bluff. Of course, if the threat is not credible, it will not be morally justified either.

But this is too large a subject to go into on this occasion. Therefore I will only say, in conclusion, that even if the "balance of terror" generated by the threat of use of nuclear weapons against civilian targets turned out to be a convincing counterexample to my fourth argument for the claim that state terrorism is morally worse than terrorism employed by non-state agents, the first three arguments would still stand and, I trust, suffice.

5. COUNTERTERRORISM

This discussion of state terrorism has some fairly straightforward implications with regard to moral assessment of and constraints on counterterrorist measures in general, and the "war against terrorism" the United States and its allies are currently waging in particular.

One concerns the moral high ground the state usually claims in the face of insurgent terrorism. What is at issue is a certain policy contested by the insurgents or a certain political setup the state wants to maintain and the insurgents want to do away with. But at the same time the conflict is seen as much more basic: since the insurgents have resorted to terrorism, the conflict is also about the very fundamentals of the political and social order, and indeed about certain moral values and principles, which terrorists are challenging and the state is defending. Now it is true that terrorism challenges some of our fundamental moral beliefs and rides roughshod over some highly important moral distinctions. Therefore opposition to terrorism can and indeed should be motivated, above all, by moral concern.

But that is not the only condition for claiming the moral high ground in the face of terrorism. The other, equally necessary condition is that of moral standing. A thief does not have the moral standing required for condemning theft and preaching about the paramount importance of property. A murderer does not have the moral standing necessary for condemning murder and pontificating about the sanctity of life. By the same token, a state which has made use of terrorism, or sponsored it, or condoned it, or supported governments that have done any of the above – in a word, a state which has itself been involved in or with terrorism to any significant degree – lacks the moral standing required for *bona fide* moral criticism of terrorism.

This simple point bears emphasizing since, more often than not, it is completely ignored. As a result, we are treated, time and time again, to moral condemnations of terrorism by representatives of states that have much to answer for on the same count. Much of the quaint moralistic rhetoric that accompanies the "war against terrorism" currently waged by the United States and its allies is as good an example as any.

Another point has to do with the nature of counterterrorism. Insurgency that makes use of terrorism poses a difficult challenge to the state. Not only does it contest the state's monopoly of violence – any violent opposition activity does that – but also demonstrates that the state is no longer capable of performing efficiently enough its most important task, that of providing basic security to its citizens. For the indiscriminate nature of terrorism poses a threat of deadly violence to virtually everyone; there is next to nothing a citizen can do to ensure her lasting physical security.

Faced with such a challenge to its very *raison d'être* and the difficulties of fighting terrorism while remaining within the bounds of morality and the law, the state may well be tempted to resort to terrorism itself, as Israel has done in response to Palestinian terrorism. Since the 1950s, a central part of Israel's response to terrorism have been reprisals in which civilian targets in the neighboring countries were attacked in order to force their governments to restrain Palestinian terrorists operating from their soil. Israel occasionally acknowledged the terrorist nature of its strategy, most memorably when its Prime Minister (and Defense Minister) Yitzhak

Rabin explained that the aim of shelling and bombing south Lebanon was "to make it uninhabitable" and thereby force the Beirut government to suppress the activities of the Palestinian liberation movement on its territory. Israel has also made extensive use of state terrorism in its rule over the Palestinian territories occupied in 1967 and its fight against Palestinian resistance terrorism; it is doing so at the time of writing. But the temptation to fight terrorism with terrorism ought to be resisted. This type of counterterrorism may well prove a dismal failure in political terms, as it has done in the Israeli case. More to the point, it is utterly indefensible from the moral point of view. Israel has certainly had other options, and so does virtually every state.

What of the current "war against terrorism" prosecuted by the United States and its allies? It raises a number of serious moral, political, and legal concerns about citizens' rights at home and the treatment of enemies taken prisoner.[17] But surely, it will be said, it does not present an example of state terrorism. There have been civilian casualties in the course of attacks on the Taliban and al-Qaida targets in Afghanistan. But the innocent have not been attacked intentionally; civilian casualties have been foreseen, but not intended side-effects of attacks on legitimate military targets. Such casualties – known as "collateral damage" in American military jargon – are inevitable in modern war. Actions that bring them about do not qualify as terrorism, on my own or any other definition of "terrorism" I find helpful, and do not constitute a violation of the relevant principle of just war theory, that of discrimination. If the principle ruled out unintentional harming of civilians too, given the conditions of modern warfare, the theory would enjoin renunciation of all war. It would no longer deserve the name of just *war* theory, since it would turn out to be, for all practical purposes, indistinguishable from pacifism.

It is true that the United States and its allies are not guilty of state terrorism, since terrorism is by definition *intentional* attack on the innocent. But that is not the end of the matter. Concerns about the scale of "collateral damage" the "war on terrorism" has been inflicting surfaced early on, as the war was initially conducted exclusively from the air, and from very high altitudes at that. By January 2002, these concerns appeared to be based on good grounds. Under the heading "News of Afghan Dead is Buried", the US correspondent of *The Age* reported:

> "University of New Hampshire economics professor Marc Herold was so disturbed by the lack of coverage of civilian deaths in the war in Afghanistan that he began keeping a tally. [...] Professor Herold says, on average, 62 Afghan civilians have died each day since bombing began. The total was now close to 5000, far more than the 3000 killed in the terrorist attacks in America on September 11. [...] According to Professor Herold, America's strategy of using air strikes to support local ground forces is designed to minimize American casualties. Only one American soldier has died from enemy fire."[18]

Now just war theory does not prohibit harming the innocent *simpliciter*. In this matter it applies the doctrine of double effect, and accordingly prohibits harming them intentionally, while leaving room for deliberate attacks on military targets that also have the foreseen but unintended effect of harming the innocent. But it does not leave room for unintentionally harming *any number* of civilians. Acts of war that unintentionally harm civilians must also satisfy another requirement of the doctrine: the harm must be proportionate to the importance and urgency of the military objective that cannot be attained in any other way. It will not do, say, to shell a village in order to take out a handful of enemy soldiers who have taken up position in it if that also involves the unintended, but foreseen killing of scores of innocent villagers.

This much is clear in any mainstream version of just war theory. The version elaborated by Michael Walzer in his influential book *Just and Unjust Wars* adds an important qualification. When performing an act of war that will also have the unintended but foreseen consequence of harming the innocent, we must seek to reduce that harm to a minimum, and must accept risk to life and limb of our own soldiers in order to do so:

> "Simply not to intend the death of civilians is too easy ... What we look for in such cases is some sign of a positive commitment to save civilian lives. Not merely to apply the proportionality rule and kill no more civilians than is militarily necessary – that rule applies to soldiers as well; no one may be killed for trivial purposes. Civilians have a right to something more. And if saving civilian lives means risking soldiers' lives, the risk must be accepted."[19]

Mark the words "right" and "must": taking risks to ensure that harm to the innocent is reduced to a minimum is not a matter of supererogation, but rather a *duty* of soldiers and a correlative *right* of civilians. The right of the innocent not to be killed or maimed is the point of departure of just war theory and, indeed, of any plausible ethics of war. Since it is the soldiers who put the civilians' life and limb in danger, it is only fair that they should accept some risk in order to minimize that danger.[20]

Now our repugnance of terrorism is generated, primarily, by the value we place on human life and bodily integrity, and in particular by our commitment to the right of the innocent not to be killed or maimed. This right is violated in the most radical way when the terrorist intentionally kills or maims them in order to achieve his or her aims. But it is also violated in a morally unacceptable way when their death or grave physical injury is not brought about as a means, but as an anticipated side-effect, if the harm they sustain is out of all proportion to the aim achieved, and those who do the killing and maiming refuse to take any chance of being harmed themselves in the process. The latter is not terrorism, and is less repellent, morally speaking, than the former. But not *much* less.

If this is granted, it means that terrorism may not be fought by terrorism. Nor may it be fought by means of a strategy that does not amount to terrorism, but must be condemned on the ground of the same moral values and principles that provide the strongest reasons for our rejection of terrorism. In this respect, so far the record of the "war on terrorism" has been very poor indeed.[21]

NOTES

[1] R. Woddis, "Ethics for Everyman", quoted in C. A. J. Coady, "The Morality of Terrorism", *Philosophy*, vol. 60 (1985), p. 52.

[2] W. Laqueur, *The Age of Terrorism*, Boston: Little, Brown & Co., 1987, p. 146. In a more recent book, *The New Terrorism: Fanaticism and the Arms of Mass Destruction* (New York: Oxford University Press, 1999), Laqueur remains faithful to this approach. The book includes a chapter on "State Terrorism", but its scope is clearly circumscribed in its first sentence: "State-*sponsored* terrorism, warfare by proxy, is as old as the history of military conflict" (p. 156, emphasis added). State terrorism in the strict sense is still beyond Laqueur's ken: "Terrorism seldom appeared in brutal dictatorships such as in Nazi Germany or Stalinist Russia, for the simple reason that repression in these regimes made it impossible for the terrorists to organize." (p. 6)

[3] For a sample of social science research illustrating a different approach, see M. Stohl and G. A. Lopez (eds.), *The State as Terrorist: The Dynamics of Governmental Violence and Repression*, Westport, CN: Greenwood Press, 1984.

[4] See J. Glover, "State Terrorism" and A. Ryan, "State and Private; Red and White", in R. G. Frey and C. W. Morris (eds.), *Violence, Terrorism and Justice*, Cambridge: Cambridge University Press, 1991; P. Gilbert, *Terrorism, Security and Nationality*, London: Routledge, 1994, chapter 9; R. B. Ashmore, "State Terrorism and Its Sponsors", in T. Kapitan (ed.), *Philosophical Perspectives on the Israeli-Palestinian Conflict*, Armonk, NY: M. E. Sharpe, 1997.

[5] See my "What Is Terrorism?", *Journal of Applied Philosophy*, vol. 7 (1990), and "The Morality of Terrorism", ibid., vol. 14 (1997), pp. 221-222.

[6] A. Ryan, op.cit., p. 249.

[7] C. J. Friedrich and Z. K. Brzezinski, *Totalitarian Dictatorship and Democracy*, 2nd edn., Cambridge, MA: Harvard University Press, 1965, pp. 169-170.

[8] Laqueur, *The Age of Terrorism*, p. 146.

[9] S. Rushdie, "How to Defeat Terrorism", *The Age*, October 4, 2001, p. 15.

[10] See M. Middlebrook, *The Battle* [sic] *of Hamburg*, Harmondsworth: Penguin Books, 1984, chapter 15.

[11] A. Kolnai, "Erroneous Conscience", *Ethics, Value and Reality*, London: Athlone Press, 1977, pp. 14-22.

[12] See my "The Morality of Terrorism".

[13] See M. Walzer, *Just and Unjust Wars: A Moral Argument with Historical Illustrations*, 3rd edn., New York: Basic Books, 2000, chapter 16.

[14] Ibid., p. 261. For an account of the terror bombing of Germany, see J. Friedrich, *Der Brand. Deutschland im Bombenkrieg 1940-1945*, München: Propyläen Verlag, 2002, and the accompanying volume of photographs, J. Friedrich, *Brandstätten. Der Anblick des Bombenkriegs*, München: Propyläen Verlag, 2003. For a discussion of the moral issues involved, see S.A. Garrett, *Ethics and Airpower in World War II: The British Bombing of German Cities*, New York: St. Martin's Press, 1993.

[15] See N. Cigar, *Genocide in Bosnia: The Politics of "Ethnic Cleansing"*, College Station, TX: Texas A&M University Press, 1995, chapter 5.

[16] See e.g. G. Kavka, "Some Paradoxes of Deterrence", *Journal of Philosophy*, vol. 75 (1978).

[17] See e.g. R. Dworkin, "The Threat to Patriotism", *The New York Review of Books*, February 28, 2002; "The Trouble with the Tribunals", ibid., April 25, 2002; "Terror and the Attack on Civil Liberties", ibid., November 6, 2003.

[18] G. Alcorn, "News of Afghan Dead Is Buried", *The Age*, January 12, 2002, p. 17.

[19] M. Walzer, op.cit., pp. 155-156.

[20] Ibid., p. 152.

[21] The paper has benefited from the discussion at the conference on "Ethics of Terrorism and Counterterrorism", held at the Center for Interdisciplinary Research (ZiF), University of Bielefeld, Germany, on October 28-30, 2002, and from correspondence with Stephen Nathanson.

CHARLES P. WEBEL

TERROR: THE NEGLECTED BUT INESCAPABLE CORE OF TERRORISM

"We are determined to answer the call of history and we will defeat terror."
    U.S. President George W. Bush

"Only by the elimination of terrorism's root causes can the world hope to succeed in greatly reducing it if not putting an end to it."
    Haig Khatchadourian, *The Morality of Terrorism*

"What can be done against force, without force?"
    Cicero, *Letter to his Friends*

THE SETTING

On Sept. 11, 2001, during the first year of this new millennium, the cities of New York and Washington D.C. were attacked by terrorists. The loss of life – approximately 3.000 civilians – was exceeded in American history only by battles during the Civil War, although cities in other countries experienced far greater civilian casualties during World War II.

A number of factors make the events of 9/11/01 and their aftermath unprecedented in American history: First, the attacks were perpetrated by foreign terrorists on American soil. Second, U.S. civilian airplanes were transformed into weapons of mass destruction. Third, the U.S. was not in a declared state of war at the time. Fourth, the identities of the perpetrators were unknown and were probably "non-state actors". Fifth, no one has claimed responsibility for the events of 9/11, in contrast to most other terrorist attacks and acts of violence committed against civilian populations during wartime and since 1945. Finally, millions of Americans, as well as many civilians in other countries, have felt unprecedented levels of stress, anxiety, trauma, and related feelings of having been "terrorized" by these attacks.

According to a study conducted by the RAND corporation and published in the November 15, 2001 issue of *The New England Journal of Medicine*, 90 percent of the people surveyed reported they had experienced at least some degree of stress three to five days after the initial attacks on 9/11, while 44 percent were trying to cope with "substantial symptoms". These symptoms include the respondents' feeling "very upset" when they were reminded of what happened on 9/11; repeated, disturbing memories, thoughts, and/or dreams; difficulty concentrating; trouble falling and/or staying asleep; and feelings of anger and/or angry outbursts. Furthermore, the RAND

G. Meggle (ed.), Ethics of Terrorism & Counter-Terrorism, 83-93.
© 2005 Ontos, Heusenstamm.

study found that 47 percent of interviewed parents reported that their children were worried about their own safety and/or the safety of loved ones, and that 35 percent of the respondents' children had one or more clear symptoms of stress. The survey concluded with a list of measures taken by these randomly selected American adults to cope with their feelings of anxiety and stress.

How generalizable are these findings? Would these findings be comparable to studies of other populations terrorized and traumatized by political attacks? How long will people feel this way, even in the unlikely event that no significant additional acts of terrorist violence are perpetrated on American soil? And how will everyday citizens and policy-makers behave if there are more events like September 11, 2001?

How might we try to account for the usage of "terrorism" as a political tactic and of terror as a predictable human response to the violence, and threats of violence, employed by terrorists against innocent people? And what might we all learn about terror from the experiences of people around the world who underwent and survived terrifying acts of political violence during the twentieth century?

Is there a common core experience of terror that links the victims of contemporary terrorist attacks to populations who were terrorized during the twentieth century? For example, are the survivors of terrifying acts of political violence committed during the Second World War psychologically and ethically similar to the concentration camp survivors of the Nazi and Stalinist periods? To what degree do their experiences resemble those of the surviving victims of acts of state-sponsored terrorism, such as "ethnic cleansing" and genocide, committed in Eastern and Central Europe during the twentieth century? And what measures – psychotherapeutic, socioeconomic, legal, political, and diplomatic – should taken to aid the victims of terrorism, to prosecute the perpetrators of mass political violence, and to minimize the risks of future terrorist attacks?

These are the questions that orient my phenomenological and cross-cultural inquiry into *terror and terrorism*. In this essay and in the recently published book (*Terror, Terrorism, and the Human Condition*, St. Martin's/Palgrave/Macmillan Press 2004), I will also report and analyze the feelings and thoughts of survivors of terrorist and related attacks, both in the Western Hemisphere and in Europe.

UNRAVELING THE HISTORY AND SCOPE OF TERROR AND TERRORISM

The events of 9/11 and their aftermath constitute a unique variation on an all-too-common historical theme, one played out in terrifying variations in Europe during the twentieth century. These historical events offer us the opportunity to explore and to try to come to terms with our most basic needs, feelings, thoughts, and desires – including vulnerability, rage, meaninglessness, dread, revenge, hostility, conviction, hope, fortitude, courage, faith, and solidarity.

I take a novel approach to understanding the multiple dimensions of terror and terrorism, and I situate and assess the diverse and often divergent meanings and interpretations of these terms, experiences, and events within a comparative and historical framework.

My methods for approaching terror and terrorism are multidisciplinary. They are drawn from phenomenological and trauma psychology, psychoanalytic and political theory, comparative politics, ethnography, and oral history. They are informed and undergirded by a conviction that the kinds of nonviolent theory and practices articulated and exemplified by Gandhi and Martin Luther King, as well as by the peace movements of the early 1980's and by the "Velvet Revolutions" in Germany and Eastern Europe in the late 1980's and early 1990's, offer us today a practicable model for confronting both the terrorist "wars" outside our persons, and the terrors inside us as well.

The similarities and differences among American, European, Latin American, and Asian interpretations and experiences of terror and terrorism are intriguing and important, especially if we hope to devise culturally appropriate ways of treating the victims of political terror and to facilitate prosecution of the perpetrators of political terrorism.

WHAT IS "TERRORISM"?

"The term 'terrorism' means premeditated, politically motivated violence perpetrated against noncombatant targets by subnational groups or clandestine agents, usually intended to influence an audience."

DCI Counterterrorist Center, Central Intelligence Agency, p. 3.

"... it (terrorism) is distinguished from all other kinds of violence by its 'bifocal' character; namely, by the fact that the immediate acts of terrorist violence, such as shootings, bombings, kidnappings, and hostage-taking, are intended as means to certain goals.., which vary with the particular terrorist acts or series of such acts [...] the concept of terrorism is a 'family resemblance' concept [...] Consequently, the concept as a whole is an 'open' or 'open-textured' concept, nonsharply demarcated from other types/forms of individual or collective violence. The major types of terrorism are: predatory, retaliatory, political, and political-moralistic/religious. The terrorism may be domestic or international, 'from above' – i.e., state or state-sponsored terrorism, or 'from below'."

Haig Khatchadourian, *The Morality of Terrorism*, p. 11.

"... terrorism is fundamentally a form of psychological warfare. Terrorism is designed, as it has always been, to have profound psychological repercussions on a target audience. Fear and intimidation are precisely the terrorists' timeless stock-in-trade [...] It is used to create unbridled fear, dark insecurity, and reverberating panic. Terrorists seek to elicit and irrational, emotional response."

Bruce Hoffman, "Lessons of 9/11", RAND, CT-201, October 2002.

"Etymologically, 'terrorism' derives from 'terror'. Originally the word meant a system, or regime, of terror: at first imposed by the Jacobins, who applied the word to themselves without any negative connotations; subsequently it came to be applied to any policy or regime of the sort and to suggest a strongly negative attitude, as it generally does today [...] Terrorism is meant to cause terror (extreme fear) and, when successful, does so. Terrorism is intimidation with a purpose: the terror is meant to cause others to do things they would otherwise not do. Terrorism is coercive intimidation."

> Igor Primoratz, "What is Terrorism?" *Journal of Applied Philosophy*, Vol. 7, No. 2, 1990, pp. 129-30.

"All wars are terrorism!"
Political Slogan.

In searching for a universal definition of "terrorism", a concept that is as contested ("one man's terrorist is another man's freedom fighter ...") as it is "open", I found that "terrorism" has been used most often to denote politically-motivated attacks by *subnational* agents (this part is virtually uncontested in the relevant scholarly literature) *and/or states*, (this is widely debated, but increasingly accepted) on non-combatants, usually in the context of war, revolution, and struggles for national liberation. In this sense, "terrorism" is as old as human conflict.

However, "terrorism", and "terrorists" have become relativized in recent times, since there is very little consensus on who, precisely, is, or is not, a "terrorist", or what is, or is not, an act of "terrorism". Thus, who is or is not a "terrorist", and what may or may not be "acts of terrorism", depend largely on the perspective of the group or the person using (or abusing) those terms.[1]

"Terrorism" is clearly a sub-category of political violence in particular, and of violence in general. Almost all current definitions of terrorism known to me focus on the violent acts committed (or threatened) by "terrorists", and neglect *the effects of those acts on their victims*. My focus is on the *terrifying effects* of certain violent acts on the victims of those acts, rather than on continuing the never-ending debate as to who is, or is not, a "terrorist". Nonetheless, for functional purposes, I propose the following definition of "terrorism":

> *Terrorism is a premeditated, usually politically motivated, use, or threatened use, of violence, in order to induce a state of terror in its immediate victims, usually for the purpose of influencing another, less reachable audience, such as a government.*

Note that under this definition, states – which commit *"terrorism from above"* (TFA) – and subnational entities, individuals and groups alike – which engage in *"terrorism from below"* (TFB) – may commit acts of terrorism. Note as well, that the somewhat artificial distinction between "combatants" and "non-combatants" does not come into play here, since *both* groups may be terrorized by acts of political violence.

My underlying assumption is that unless necessary and sufficient conditions can be provided by perpetrators of "terrorism from above" (i.e. state actors using "terror bombing" to attempt to break the morale of a civilian population and its government, as has been done numerous times since the Italians bombed Tripoli in 1911), and by "terrorists from below" (ranging from the Russian revolutionaries and defenders of "Red Terror" during the late nineteenth and early twentieth centuries to Al Qu'aeda) to justify their acts, *any* act that deliberately inculcates terror is, more or less, unethical. However, there are of course *degrees* of moral culpability. The decisions by Churchill to target the civilian populations (especially the working class neighborhoods of industrial cities) of Germany for "terror bombings" during World War II, and by Truman to "nuke" Hiroshima and Nagasaki (which had no military significance) are, by this criterion, acts of "terrorism from above". But they are not morally equivalent to such acts of "terrorism from below" as the terrorist attacks of September 11, 2001 on the United States, or of the acts of other terrorist groups (such as the "Red Army Faction") during the late twentieth century who targeted civilians as means to achieving perceived political ends. This is not because they are "less unethical", but, on the contrary, because they *more* unethical, for both consequentialist and deontological reasons.

From a consequentialist perspective, terror bombings of civilians during wartime have resulted in many *more* casualties (millions of dead and wounded) than *all* acts of "terrorism from below" combined. Furthermore, they have rarely resulted in achieving their declared political objectives: The firebombings of German and Japanese cities did *not* by themselves significantly induce the German and Japanese governments to surrender, rather, they tended to harden to resolve of the indigenous populations to fight harder (as did the German *Blitz* of England during 1940). Even the nuclear bombings of Hiroshima and Nagasaki did not significantly influence, or accelerate, the outcome of the War in the Pacific, because the Japanese government seems willing to have surrendered *before* the bombings. On the other hand, the terror bombing of Rotterdam in 1940 (which, apparently, may not have been intended by the *Luftwaffe*) was followed almost immediately by the surrender of the Dutch to the Germans; and Serbia did withdraw from Kosovo soon after Belgrade and other Yugoslavian cities were bombed by NATO in 1999. But in these two cases, the bombing was brief and civilian casualties were probably in the hundreds, and not in the hundreds of thousands, as they were in Germany and Japan during World War II.

Accordingly, the terror bombings committed by Great Britain and the United States, as well as by Nazi Germany and by Japan (principally in China), are classic examples of "terrorism from above", (TFA) or "state terrorism", (ST) and they resulted in millions of civilian casualties, without accomplishing their most important political objectives, viz., the profound demoralization of the civilian populations and prompt surrender of their antagonists. But what these state terrorists *did* accomplish, like their "terrorists from below" counterparts, was the *terrorization* of huge numbers of people, the use of persons as means to alleged political ends, and the dehumanization and denial of dignity to the objects of their terror bombings. And this is unethical by any known moral criterion.

To sum up the commonalities and differences between TFA and TFB in terms of their respective degrees of moral culpability for terrorizing and/or killing many innocent (and possibly a few "guilty") people, while both are unethical, TFA usually *exceeds* TFB in its moral reprehensibility in terms of the:

1. *Magnitude, or Scale, of terror*, TFA, or ST, is immeasurably more pernicious than TFB, since nation-states under Hitler and Stalin killed and/or terrorized tens of millions of their own citizens in the 1930s and 1940s, and slaughtered millions of "enemies" during the Second World War. Japan, Great Britain, and the United States also killed and/or terrorized millions of "enemies" in Chinese and German cities

during that war. Latin American, African, and Asian despots and dictators, many with American support, killed and/or terrorized many thousands of their own citizens during the twentieth century. And the United States has used "precision bombing" and "counter-insurgency" campaigns to kill and/or terrorize millions of Vietnamese and other Southeast Asians, as well as civilians in countries ranging from Afghanistan to Somalia. In comparison, the collective efforts of TFB groups, ranging from the IRA and PFLP to Al Qu'aeda, have probably resulted in fewer than 10,000 casualties – a tragedy for all the victims and their families, but in scale not comparable to TFA "collateral damage".

2. The *Culpability, or Degree of Legal and/or Ethical Responsibility*, of the people who made the decisions to terrorize and/or kill people unfortunate enough to be living in states at war with their own is also disproportionately skewed toward TFA. Such decision-makers as Hitler, Stalin, Truman, Churchill, Pol Pot, and L.B. Johnson, who collectively issued orders resulting in the deaths of tens of millions of non-combatants and the terrorization of millions of their compatriots, rarely if ever engaged in personally overseeing the soldiers, sailors, and bombardiers who "were just following" (their) "orders". On the contrary: they were distant and detached from the mass killings that resulted from their policies, and would probably have refused to acknowledge their culpability for any "war crimes" and/or "crimes against humanity" – had they ever been called before an institution such as the International Court of Justice. In contrast, most leaders of TFB subnational groups are themselves directly involved in the terrorist operations, and may even put their lives at risk "for the sake of the cause". They may rationalize what they do, and justify mass murder by appeals to political motives (as do TFA decision-makers), but they would be, and have been, held individually legally culpable for their "crimes against humanity", unlike their TFB counterparts (the trials of Serbian leaders may set a notable precedent for a TFA decision-maker to be held legally culpable for crimes against humanity, in this case Bosnians).

TFA and TFB *share comparable degrees* of moral culpability because:

1. They *instrumentalize* the victims of their terrorist tactics. Both TFA and TFB turn civilian noncombatants and combatants alike into disposable means to be used (or terrorized) in order to achieve perceived political ends. Along the way,

2. They *Dehumanize, Objectify, and Demonize* their real and perceived "enemies", including the leaders of other nations or groups ("The Great Satan", "The Evil One", etc.). They also frequently polarize the conflicting parties, esteeming themselves and their followers as "good and virtuous", with "God on our side", and denigrating their opponents as "wicked, evil" and frequently "in-" (or sub-)"human". Citizens of other states who are killed and/or terrorized by their subordinates' tactics are denoted as "collateral damage", and "body counts" of those killed are often employed as quantitative measures of an "operation's" "success".

3. They use or threaten to use *Violence on a Mass Scale*, often disregarding and/or prematurely discarding nonviolent means of conflict resolution. From a crude utilitarian perspective, the "costs" of "inadvertent" and or "unintentional" – but *nevertheless predictable and foreseeable* "friendly fire" and/or "collateral damage" are reflexively seen by many decision-makers to be outweighed by the perceived "benefits" of "victory". Dialogue, negotiation, diplomacy, compromise, the use of

nonviolent tactics and/or of non-lethal force, and the recourse to international institutions, are often regarded by both TFA and TFB as, at best futile, and at worst weak and defeatist.

4. *Weapons of Mass Destruction (WMD)*, including but not limited to chemical, biological, and nuclear weapons, are desirable "assets" to both TFA and TFB, even though the use of such weapons on a significant scale may have global – even omnicidal and therefore suicidal – consequences. WMD Terrorism is the logical extension of the "logic of deterrence" and the "ethics of retaliation" (a version of *lex talionis*).

Consequently, this "Age of Global Terrorism", dating from the early twentieth century, when "total war" and "strategic bombing" became acceptable components of military and diplomatic strategy, has culminated in the progressive obliteration of important previously-held distinctions. Most notably, there has been a gradual collapse of the distinction between "illegitimate" (i.e. civilian non-combatants) and "legitimate" (i.e. military) "targets", as well as of the distinction between "terrorists" and "the states" (and peoples…) that, allegedly, "support them".

Finally, this century-long process is leading to the erosion of the boundary between "terrorism" and "war", to such a degree that, since at least the early days of World War II, for the civilian populations of the affected states, war has, ipso facto, become indistinguishable from terrorism. Terror, or *psychological* warfare, has become a predictable tool to be employed by war planners and policy-makers. This turn of events is on the one hand a regression to the kind of "barbarism" that preceded the rise of "civilization" about 5000 years ago in the Ancient Near East, and on the other hand is a seemingly inevitable consequence of technological "progress" *un*accompanied by a comparable "moral evolution" on the parts of the proponents, practitioners, and apologists for TFA and TFA alike.

WHAT IS TERROR? HOW DOES TERROR FEEL? WHAT ARE ITS SOURCES?

> "The idea that you can purchase security from terror by saying nothing about terror is not only morally bankrupt but it is also inaccurate."
> Australian Prime Minister John Howard.

> "Terror for me was an auditory process. I was terrified all the time but had no words for it."
> German Survivor of the Allied Bombing of Wurms in 1944-45.

> "History is terror because we have to move into it not by any straight line that is always easy to trace, but by taking our bearings at every moment in a general situation which is changing."
> Maurice Merleau-Ponty, *Humanism and Terror,* p. 94.

Unfortunately, despite Australian Prime Minister's assertion, virtually no one has talked in a meaningful way about the root of terrorism – terror. This is an omission that stands out amidst the endless talk of fighting a "war against terrorism/terror". It is also a glaring lacuna in current scholarly investigations (at least in such major Western languages as English, German, and French), which focus *either* on trauma (and Post-Traumatic Stress Disorder, PTSD) and anxiety (the clinical literature), or on terrorism, terrorists, and counterterrorism (the social scientific/policy-oriented literature). But there is virtually no serious analysis of terror in the major Western scholarly discourses, with the glaring exception of Spanish (mostly from Latin America) accounts of political terror from above and below. The rest of this essay will try to begin a conversation about this vital, but neglected, core dimension of terrorism. It is very much a work-in-progress, since the research I am undertaking to understand terror and its vicissitudes is still underway.

Is terror primarily a feeling state, an acute and potentially traumatizing kind of anxiety? Does terror lead to an overwhelming sense of helplessness, to a state of unanticipated and uncontrollable panic?

Is the source of terror primarily intrapsychic, some unresolved and possibly unresolvable unconscious conflict between repressed impulses and desires? Or is terror a situationally-appropriate response to an externally induced, environmental cause, one that triggers overpowering feelings of dread and vulnerability?

What is terror's relation to aggression and violence? Does the intensity of the experience of terror unleash, and even rationalize, aggressive and violent responses to those we blame for our unbearable anxiety?

How do we behave when we feel terrified? Do we seek immediately and automatically to rid ourselves of terror? Do we then transmit this emotionally intolerable condition to others, whom we then brand as "terrorists", the alleged cause and source of our unease? Is terror contagious, spreading uncontrollably among panic-stricken people?

Does the unbearable heaviness of being in terror compel us to expel, split off, and dissociate terror, as quickly as possible and by any means necessary?

Are "terrorists" really "criminals", "fanatics", and "zealots", wholly "other" to us? Or are they to a remarkable degree the "shadow side" of "civilized peoples", the unleashed and unrepressed violence lurking in virtually all of us? Do many "terrorists", especially those with deep ideological and/or religious convictions, have a way of facing death from which we might learn, even if we deplore their taking of human life?

Based on my reading of the extant psychological, psychoanalytic, historical, and social-scientific literature, as well as on a content analysis of 52 interviews I have conducted with survivors of terrifying political violence in 13 nations (ranging from Denmark to Chile, but mostly in Germany, the United States, Spain, and the former Soviet Union), I tentatively conclude: *We don't yet know the answers to these important questions!* This is in part because of the lack of good academic discourse on terror (except in relation to horror films and to PTSD, which I believe is a syndrome that may, or may not, follow as sequelae to one or more terrifying incidents, such as a bombing, a rape, or an accident or assault). It is also due to the overdetermined and complex nature of terror, and of its important, but poorly understood, connections to anxiety, horror, panic, paralysis, and trauma.

To initiate a broad-based, multidisciplinary inquiry into terror and its "family resemblances", I offer the following provisional definition:

The term "terror" denotes both a phenomenological experience of paralyzing, overwhelming, and ineffable mental anguish, as well as a behavioral response to a real or perceived life-threatening danger. Ex post facto (sometimes as much as 80 years after the events occurred) descriptions of terrifying experiences by people I have interviewed cluster around the following themes:

First, the experience is described as having been *overwhelming.* The people felt *helpless and completely vulnerable* during the time of the assault (mostly bombings by airplanes during war).

Second, they described the situation as *uncontrollable, a time of loss of autonomy and surrender of self-control* to an often unseen, and always menacing, "other".

Third, the outcome of the event is universally depicted as *unknowable and unpredictable* – possibly leading to bodily injury and/or death – and the terror is of *indefinite if not infinite duration.*

Fourth, the salient subjective feeling is that of *acute anxiety,* sometimes *panic,* and the cognitive orientation is of *profound spatial/temporal disorientation.*

Fifth, the person feels their body as *frozen, immobilized, and often paralyzed,* incapable of self-direction and mobility.

Finally, the *intensity* of the experience of terror is so great that most people find themselves unable to speak, and later are left wordless when they attempt verbally to describe it. *Terror is profoundly sensory* (often auditory), and is pre- or post-verbal. The *ineffability of terror* is a complement to, and often a result of, the unspeakable horror(s) of war(s).

I do not (yet) know if the sample of people I have interviewed is representative of the victims of politically terrifying events (ranging from sniper to aerial attacks) in their own countries, much less globally. Perhaps we will never know. But I do know that to expose anyone to any of the terrors these people have lived through is to commit a significant transgression of human rights and an inexcusable assault on personal dignity. Accordingly, terrorism in all it forms is deeply unethical. In my recently published book, *Terror, Terrorism, and the Human Condition,* I explore this topic in more detail and in greater depth.

CONCLUSION: THE FUTURE OF TERRORISM, AND THE TERRORS OF THE FUTURE

"Everyone has the right to life, liberty, and security of person."
Universal Declaration of Human Rights, Article 3, United Nations.

"Only by the elimination of terrorism's root causes can the world hope to succeed in greatly reducing it if not putting an end to it."
Haig Khatchadourian, *The Morality of Terrorism,* p. xiii.

"The cardinal principles of humanitarian law are aimed at the protection of the civilian and civilian objects. States must never make civilians the objects of attack and must consequently never use weapons that are incapable of distinguishing between civilian and military targets."
The International Court of Justice, Paragraph 78, *Legality of the Threat Or Use of Nuclear Weapons*, Advisory Opinion, 8 July 1996.

Are terror and terrorism a portal into our common human condition? What do the existence of terror and terrorism reveal about the world, one in which our worst fears may indeed come true? Is the future of terrorism to include an ever-escalating series of attacks and counterattacks culminating in global annihilation? Or can such hypothetical, but foreseeable, terrors be minimized by the judicious application of self-restraint on the one hand, and of nonviolent means of conflict avoidance and resolution on the other hand.

Over two millennia ago, Cicero asked: "What can be done against force, without force?" The answer is "maybe a great deal, maybe very little; it depends on the situation". But to assume that the only, or best, "realistic" response to the use of deadly force, and/or terror, is to reply either "in kind" or with even greater force, is virtually to guarantee that our common future will be even more terrifying than has been our collective history. Is this the future we wish our descendants to have?

NOTES

[1] See my book with David Barash, *Peace and Conflict Studies* (Sage Publications, 2002), pp. 80-83, for a fuller discussion of the semantics and history of "terrorism".

REFERENCES

Arendt, Hannah. *The Human Condition*. NY, 1959.
Attali, Jacques. *Millennium*. NY, 1991.
Barash, David & Webel, Charles. *Peace and Conflict Studies*. Thousand Oaks, 2002.
Barber, Benjamin. *Jihad vs. McWorld*. NY, 1996.
Baroja, Julio. *Terror y Terrorismo*. Barcelona, 1989.
Beck, Aaron. *Prisoners of Hate*. NY, 1999.
Becker, Ernest. *The Denial of Death*. NY, 1973.
Boss, Pauline. *Ambiguous Loss*. Cambridge, 1999.
Brown, Seyom. *The Causes and Prevention of War*. NY, 1987.
Choron, Jacques. *Death and Western Thought*. NY, 1963.
Cooley, John. *Unholy Wars. Afghanistan, America & International Terrorism*. London, 1999.
Crenshaw, Martha (ed.). *Terrorism in Context. University Park*, 1995.
Falkenrath, Richard, et al. *America's Achilles Heel*. Cambridge, 1998.
Freud, Sigmund. *The Problem of Anxiety*. NY, 1956.
Friedrich, Joerg. *Der Brand*. Munich, 2002.
Fromm, Erich. *The Anatomy of Human Destructiveness*. NY, 1973.
Geary, Conor. *Terror*. London, 1991.
Gilligan, James. *Violence*. NY, 1996.
Giorgi, Amedeo. *Phenomenology and Psychological Research*. Pittsburgh, 1985.
Gurr, Nadine & Cole, B. *The New Face of Terrorism*. London, 2000.
Hanle, Donald. *Terrorism*. Washington, 1989.
Hardt, Michael & Negri Antonio. *Empire*. Cambridge, 2000.
Harvard Magazine. *Terrorism*. Jan.-Feb. 2002.
Hobbes, Thomas. *Leviathan*. Baltimore, 1968.
Hoffman, Bruce. *Inside Terrorism*. NY, 1998.
Hoffman, Bruce. "Lessons of 9/11", *RAND*, CT-201, October 2002.
Johnson, Chalmers. *Blowback*. NY, 2001.
Johnson, James T. *Morality & Contemporary Warfare*. New Haven, 1999.
Karr-Morse, Robin & Wiley, M. *Ghosts from the Nursery*. NY, 1997.

Kernberg, Otto. *Aggression*. New Haven, 1992.
Khatchadourian, Haig. *The Morality of Terrorism*. NY, 1998.
Kierkegaard, Soren. *Fear & Trembling and The Sickness Unto Death*. Princeton, 1954.
Kovel, Joel. *Against the State of Nuclear Terror*. Boston, 1983.
Kvale, Steiner. *InterViews*. Thousand Oaks, 1996.
Lake, Anthony. *6 Nightmares*. Boston, 2000.
Laqueur, Walter. *The Age of Terrorism*. Boston, 1987.
Lasswell, Harold. *World Politics & Personal Insecurity*.
Leys, Ruth. *Trauma*. Chicago, 2000.
Lindquist, Sven. *A History of Bombing*. NY, 2001.
May, Rollo, et al. (ed.). *Existence*. NY, 1967.
May, Rollo. *The Meaning of Anxiety*. NY, 1979.
Merleau-Ponty, Maurice. *Humanism and Terror*. Boston, 1969.
Mueller, Daniel. *Measuring Social Attitudes*. NY, 1986.
Pearlstein, Richard. *The Mind of the Political Terrorist*. Wilmington, 1991.
Pincus, Jonathan. *Base Instincts*. NY, 2001.
Primoratz, Igor. "What is Terrorism?", *Journal of Applied Philosophy*, Vol. 7, No. 2, 1990.
Rapoport, Anatol. *The Origins of Violence*. NY, 1989.
Rapoport, David & Alexander, Y. *The Morality of Terrorism*. NY, 1989.
Rapoport, David (ed.). *Inside Terrorist Organizations*. London, 2001.
Reich, Walter (ed.). *Origins of Terrorism*. Cambridge, 1990.
Robins, Robert & Post, Jerrold. *Political Paranoia*. New Haven, 1997.
Rose, Jacqueline. *Why War?* Oxford, 1997.
Saigh, Philip, & Bremner, Douglas. *Post-Traumatic Stress Disorder*. Boston, 1999.
Sebald, W. G. *On the Natural History of Destruction*. NY, 2003.
Shephard, Ben. *A War of Nerves*. Cambridge, 2001.
Simon, Jeffrey. *The Terrorist Trap*. Bloomington, 1994.
Smith, Brent. *Terrorism in America*. Albany, 1994.
Speilhagen, Charles, et al. (ed.). *Cross-Cultural Anxiety*. 4 Volumes. Washington, 1990.
Spiegel, Der. "Als Feuer vom Himmel fiel", 2/2003.
Staub, Ervin. *The Roots of Evil*. NY, 1992.
Stern, Jessica. *The Ultimate Terrorists*. Cambridge, 1999.
Taylor, Max & Horgan, John. *The Future of Terrorism*. London, 2000.
Underhill-Cady, Joseph. *Death and the Statesman*. NY, 2001.
Walzer, Michael. *Just and Unjust Wars*. NY, 1977.
Wieviorka, Michel. *The Making of Terrorism*. Chicago, 1993.
Wilkinson, Paul. *Terrorism vs. Democracy*. London, 2000.
Wilson, John, et al. *Treating Psychological Trauma and PTSD*. NY, 2001.
Yule, William (ed.). *Post-Traumatic Stress Disorder*. 1999.

SEUMAS MILLER

TERRORISM AND COLLECTIVE RESPONSIBILITY

1. OSAMA BIN LADEN, TERRORISM AND COLLECTIVE RESPONSIBILITY[1]

Listening to George W. Bush and most of the world media, one gets the impression that terrorism is both easily identifiable and by definition morally unacceptable. In fact the definition of terrorism is problematic, and terrorism takes a number of not necessarily mutually exclusive forms, e.g. the state terrorism of Saddam Hussein or Pinochet, the anti-state terrorism of Hamas or the IRA, and the state sponsored terrorism of extremist Muslim groups by Gaddaffi or extremist right wing groups or regimes by the USA in Latin America.

The terrorism practised by Osama bin Laden's al-Qaeda appears to be a species of non-state terrorism directed principally at non-muslim western states, especially the US, that are alleged to be attacking Islam. While bin Laden and al-Qaeda found a natural home and ally among the fundamentalist Islamist Taliban in Afghanistan, his organisation is global in character. For bin Laden has put together a loose coalition of extremist Islamist groups based in a variety of locations, including Egypt, Algeria, Afghanistan, Sudan and Pakistan. Peter Bergen refers to it as "Holy War Inc".[2] The global nature of this coalition is evidenced by such terrorist campaigns as that being waged in Algeria by the al-Qaeda linked Islamic Salvation Front (ISF) in which there have been over 100,000 victims of terrorism since 1992, as well as by the September 11th attacks on the World Trade Centre in New York and the Pentagon, and by the Bali bombing in which 200 people, including some 100 Australian tourists, were killed by terrorists almost certainly linked to al-Qaeda.

It is important to note, however, that the brand of Islam propounded by bin Laden has little in common with the more moderate forms of Islam to be found throughout the Muslim world in places such as Indonesia, India and, for that matter, the Middle East and North Africa. For example, bin Laden is anti-democratic, opposed to the emancipation of women, and opposed to the modern secular state with its division between religious institutions and the state. So bin Laden is opposed to more secular Muslim governments such as those in Egypt, and even Iraq. And he is implacably opposed to pro-western Muslim governments such as Saudi Arabia, no matter how religiously conservative they are. Given all this, the prospects of bin Laden and his followers setting up a sustainable long term Islamic state, let alone an Islamic empire of the kind his pronouncements hearken back to, are not good. His role will in all probability remain that of a terrorist; a force for destabilisation only.

Moreover, the fact that al-Qaeda is opposed to democracy and the emancipation of women ensures that it does not have moral legitimacy, objectively speaking. And this

95

G. Meggle (ed.), Ethics of Terrorism & Counter-Terrorism, 95-112.

says nothing of various other morally suspect features of extreme religious fundamentalism, whether it be Islamic, Christian or some other kind. Such features include a lack of respect for individual autonomy, and for truth, and an intolerance of ways of thinking and of living that are not one's own.

In short, al-Qaeda cannot reasonably claim to be speaking and acting on behalf of a majority of the Muslim world, and some of its main goals are morally objectionable. What of its methods?

The preparedness of his followers to commit suicide, and thereby supposedly achieve martyrdom, is an enormous advantage for a terrorist organisation. Moreover, this role is greatly facilitated not only by real and perceived injustices, and already existing national, ethnic and religious conflict, but also by global financial interdependence and modern technology, such as the global communication system and the new chemical and biological weapons of mass destruction that he has been seeking to develop. Perhaps al-Qaeda's success is not dependent on widespread political and popular support for its goals, although it is certainly reliant on disaffection, including with US policies. Rather its success might largely be a function of the psychological preparedness and logistical capacity to perpetrate acts of terror, coupled with the technological capacity to communicate those acts world-wide, and thereby wreak havoc in a globally economically interdependent world. Its methods have proved extraordinarily effective in relation to the goal of destabilisation. The terrorist group from the medieval past has identified the Achilles heal of the modern civilised world.

That said, its methods clearly involve the intentional killing of the innocent, and are not constrained by principles of the proportional use of force or minimally necessary force. Indeed, bin Laden's aim is to maximise the loss of human life. So bin Laden's methods are an affront to accepted moral principles governing the use of deadly force in conflict situations. It remains an open question whether this is so for *all* forms of terrorism.

The definition of terrorism is contested. However, I offer the following one. By definition, terrorism is a political or military strategy that:

1. Involves the intentional killing, maiming or otherwise seriously harming, or threatening to seriously harm, of civilians (and not merely combatants and their leaders);
2. Is a means of terrorising the members of some social, religious or political group in order to achieve political or military purposes;
3. Relies on the killings – or other serious harms inflicted – receiving a high degree of publicity, at least to the extent necessary to engender widespread fear in the target political, religious or social group.

Notice that on this definition civilians might or might not be innocent. Clearly *some* civilians are innocent, e.g. young children. Accordingly, indiscriminate uses of deadly force, such as bombing restaurants or napalming villages, are unjustifiable forms of terrorism because they kill innocent civilians.

However, not all non-combatant civilians are innocent. For example, civil servants directly involved in developing and implementing a policy of genocide – as was the case in Hitler's Germany – are not innocent.

Moreover, there are a number of additional salient points. Firstly, the notion of terrorism being used here is relativised to the specific conflict in question. So a person is innocent if they are not opposing the terrorists by, for example, perpetrating any alleged wrongdoing the terrorists are seeking to redress, or trying to kill or apprehend the terrorists. Secondly, the definition does not rule out the possibility that terrorist tactics might be directed at military personnel as well as civilians. However, it does rule out the possibility that terrorism might be directed exclusively at military personnel.

The September 11 attacks were performed in the name of moral righteousness by people prepared to give up their own lives, as well as the lives of those that they murdered. Osama bin Laden himself may well be principally driven by hatred and a desire for revenge, but he and like minded religious extremists have managed to mobilise moral sentiment, indeed moral outrage, to their cause, and they have done so on a significant scale. In this respect they are, of course, not unique among terrorist groups. Terrorist groups typically come into existence because of, and are sustained by, some real or imagined injustice.

Moreover, in order for Osama bin Laden and his group to mobilise moral sentiment they have had to overcome, at least in the minds of their followers, what might be regarded as commonly held principles of moral acceptability, including the principle according to which only those responsible for injustice or harm should be targeted. Yet the majority of those killed, and intended to be killed by the September 11 terrorists, were – according to commonly held principles of moral responsibility – innocent victims. They included not only civilians, but also children, visiting foreign nationals, and so on. This being so, what possible moral justification could be offered by the terrorists and their supporters?

One justification does not necessarily overthrow all moral principles, rather it simply appeals to the principle that the ends justify the means. It is not that those who are killed by terrorists deserve to die; indeed their death may well be a matter of regret to the terrorists. However, killing these innocent people is the only way to further the righteous cause, and the moral importance of that cause overrides the evil that consists in killing some innocents; or so the argument goes. This argument assumes that the end in question is not only a morally worth one, but also a very morally weighty end; something that is, as we have already noted, far from being the case in relation to al-Qaeda's goals. Moreover, any particular recourse to terrorism may in fact not realise the ends of the terrorists. Consider the failed terror tactics of the Red Brigade in the 1970's in Europe. As far as al-Qaeda's likelihood of realising its ultimate goals is concerned, as I have already indicated, the prospects are not good. Finally, even if terrorism does realise its ends, and they are good ends, it can still be maintained that the ends realised in some given situation do not in fact justify the particular means used.

No doubt the idea that the ends justify the means is a line of reasoning that has considerable weight with terrorists in general, and with bin Laden's al-Qaeda organisation, in particular. And doubtless there have been instances, such as in the French-Algerian colonial conflict and the British-Kenya colonial conflict, where terrorism in fact achieved its ends, whether or not achieving these ends did in fact justify the terrorist methods used. Perhaps in the case of Algeria it was a case in part of activists deploying terrorist tactics as a response to terror directed at themselves.

Certainly, bin Laden needs to rely *in part* on the ends-justify-the-means argument. If the ultimate ends of terrorism are not good ends then it is immoral. And if terrorism does not realise its ends then it seems both irrational and immoral. However, bin Laden himself no longer seems to rely *exclusively* on the argument. For bin Laden denies, at least implicitly, that so-called innocent victims of his terrorist attacks are in fact innocent. For example, on 22 February 1998 in announcing the formation of the World Islamic Front for Jihad against the Jews and the Crusaders he said:

> "All those crimes and calamities are an explicit declaration by the Americans of war on Allah, His Prophet, and Muslims... Based upon this and in order to obey the Almighty, we hereby give Muslims the following judgment: The judgment to kill and fight Americans and their allies, whether civilians or military, is an obligation for every Muslim who is able to do so in any country."[3]

Accordingly, perhaps bin Laden believes that his brand of terrorism is both likely to realise its ends, and that it is morally acceptable by virtue of the guilt of its victims; it is essentially self-defence against terrorism. Is there any real or alleged basis for this latter belief?

Evidently, the justification for denying the innocence of US civilians is collectivist in character. The idea seems to be that certain collectives, namely Islam and the US or Islam and Communist Russia in Afghanistan – or perhaps Islam and Christianity or Islam and the Jews or even fundamentalist Islam and moderate Islam – are locked in struggle in the manner that two individual human agents might be.

Osama bin Laden and thousands of other Arab Muslims went to Afghanistan in the 1980's to join the Afghans in their fight against the godless communist invaders from Russia. According to bin Laden, Islam won a great victory against the Russian superpower. Thus he apparently thinks that he can repeat the same feat in relation to the US. For Afghanistan provided a breeding ground for terrorism, fundamentalist Muslims from many countries came to fight the Afghanistan war, and then returned to their home countries, including Algeria, Egypt and the like, to wage terrorist campaigns against the governments in those countries.

Now bin Laden claims that Islam is fighting the US in order to defend itself against the threats to its existence posed by the US, and specifically its ongoing support of Israel, the US military bases in Saudi Arabia (the country in which are located the two most holy Islamic sites, Mecca and Medina) and US led invasion of Iraq.

Moreover, allegedly this attack upon Islam is a longstanding one, and the attackers have simply refused to listen to reasoned argument, but have instead subjected Islam to the considerable weight of western economic and military power. (Hence bin Laden's choice in the September 11 attacks of symbols of that power, namely the World Trade Centre and the Pentagon.) Given this collectivist conception, all US citizens (and citizens of their allies) can be regarded as a collective threat to Islam, and as being collectively guilty for the ongoing attacks on Islam. Accordingly, so the logic seems to run, there can be nothing wrong in killing US citizens, irrespective of whether they are combatants, or otherwise intentionally supporting US military actions.

What are we to make of this justification of terrorism by recourse to collective moral responsibility? Osama bin Laden's pronouncements are objectionable on a number of counts. For one thing, his account and analysis of US actions and policies are simplistic and in large part fallacious. For example, the US bases in Saudi Arabia were presumably established for the purpose of protecting the flow of oil, rather than to undermine Islam, and presumably the US invasion of Iraq was in large part motivated by a desire to remove the authoritarian dictator, Saddam Hussein, and the threat posed by his (alleged) possession, or probable future possession, of weapons of mass destruction.

Nor has the US waged war against Islam as such; although bin Laden has sought to present US support for Israel, the US led occupation of Iraq and war against the Taliban in Afghanistan, as war on Islam itself. On the other hand, given Israeli occupancy of Palestinian territory, including by way of the resettlement program, and Israeli bombing of civilian targets, including in Lebanon, US' support for Israel is at the very least questionable. Moreover, the US led invasion of Iraq seems to have been ill conceived and may well have a bad outcome for the Iraqis and the region more generally. Nevertheless, whatever the rights and wrongs of specific US policies against particular Muslim states and communities, including the war against Iraq, the US cannot seriously be accused of engaging in a terrorist campaign against Islam as such.

Moreover, the US' alleged protagonist, namely Islam, seems far from the unitary agent referred to in bin Laden's pronouncements. Consider the Iran/Iraq war, or the role of Pakistan in destabilising Afghanistan. On the other hand, the US support for Israel in its war with Palestine, and for autocratic regimes, such as the Saudi regime, that repress ordinary Arab and Islamic people, and various other US policies, such as the invasion of Iraq, provide fertile ground for anti-US feeling in the Islamic world. Indeed, if the recent work of the well-known scholar Samuel Huntington is to be given any credence, bin Laden's conception of a Western versus Islamic confrontation are not entirely without foundation. Huntington's view is essentially collectivist in character. It is just that whereas bin Laden seems to think Islam is the object of the threat, Huntington thinks it is the source.

For another thing, bin Laden's pronouncements on the collective guilt of all Americans are facile, and evidently inconsistent with the Koran itself, e.g. on the issue of killing non-combatants.

Nor is bin Laden alone in holding some sort of collectivist conception of the moral conflict he is involved in. Saddam Hussein, for example, spoke in the same way.

The collectivist conception in question manifests a number of tendencies that need to be noted here. First, collective entities, such as states or ethnic or religious groups, are often assumed not only to have interests, but also to be necessarily and exclusively self-interested. Thus Islam must fight in order to preserve its identity and influence in certain regions of the world, and yet bin Laden seems at least implicitly to believe that Islam does not need to accommodate the interests or respect the rights of the non-Islamic world; perhaps he even believes that the interests and rights of the moderate Islamic world do not need to be respected. Perhaps this is because the non-Islamic world – and non fundamentalist Islamic world – are unworthy unbelievers, or some such. Second, these collective entities have, so to speak, hearts and minds of their own. They are in some sense agents, albeit supra-human agents. The US is an agent seeking to attack and undermine Islam. It is not simply a matter of specific US government leaders having specific policies at particular times that might be contrary to Islamic interests. Third, these collective entities are moral agents, in the sense that they do good and evil, they can be held morally responsible and therefore praised and blamed.

Sometimes these tendencies come into conflict. For example, it is sometimes asserted that international relations, and waging war in particular, are outside any moral normative framework; it is simply a matter of power and the pursuit of national self-interest. This view has had a good deal of currency in foreign policy sectors of the US administration. But it is inconsistent with being morally outraged by terrorist attacks on US citizens, and seeking to convince the rest of the world that they also ought to be morally outraged. And the claim that waging war or pursuing a terrorist campaign is somehow a non-moral activity, is not typically assented to by those on the receiving end of the rights violations and other harms visited upon them. They know that the issues are profoundly moral in character.

Further, in so regarding groups of individual human beings in this collectivist light, or lights, it is arguable that certain untoward consequences follow, or at least are facilitated. For one thing, terrorists, and military organisations more generally, can more easily justify the killing of innocents. For innocent victims are typically at least members of the collective, the state or ethnic or religious group or whatever, that is the object of the terrorists' anger. Accordingly, they can be killed qua members of, say, the US citizenry. Indeed, in the case of many extremist fundamentalist Islamic groups, even moderate Muslims are not innocents; so they become legitimate targets. Moreover, the value of the lives of these individual innocent victims can be given a discount, and in the limiting case of genocide, can be regarded as having no value. Consider the Holocaust or the Rwandan genocide.

Nor is this tendency restricted to terrorist organisations. Consider the My Lai massacre. Again, policies of pursuing military tactics that involve killing innocent victims rather than risking lives of one's own combatants seem to partake of this logic. Consider the atomic bombs dropped on Hiroshima and Nagasaki, or the recent bombing by NATO in Kosovo rather than deploying ground troops. Apparently, the life of one of one's own country's combatants is worth many times that of an innocent civilian who happens to be of another country with whom one is at war, or indeed of another ethnic group one is supposedly protecting. This inconsistent view was implicit in the policy of sanctions against Iraq, notwithstanding the fact that it was leading to the starvation and death of hundreds of thousands of Iraqi children – albeit through the refusal of Saddam Hussein to capitulate.

At this point it might be useful to explicitly distinguish my notion of collective *moral responsibility* from the above-mentioned strong collectivist conceptions – conceptions that manifest what might be termed the *morality of collective identity.*

According to the morality of collective identity the members of some oppressor or enemy group are guilty purely by virtue of membership of that national, racial, ethnic or religious group. So a white South African who opposed apartheid was nevertheless guilty in the eyes of extremist anti-apartheid groups simply by virtue of being white. All Americans are guilty of oppressing Muslims simply by virtue of being American citizens, according to some extremist al-Qaeda pronouncements.

The morality of collective identity determines the moral worth or guilt of a person not by what they choose to do or not do, but by virtue of what they cannot choose to be or not be, namely a member of some racial, ethnic, religious or national group.

As such, the morality of collective identity elevates the category of membership of racial, ethnic, and national groups above the category of human moral personhood; a person is first and foremost (say) a white or black or Jew, and only secondly a human being who is morally responsible for their actions.

In seeking to make sense of the notion of collective moral responsibility I am not endorsing the morality of collective ethnic, racial, national or religious identity; indeed I reject this notion.

So much for the collectivist features and tendencies implicit in the pronouncements, policies and actions of terrorists such as bin Laden, and to a much lesser extent in that of their protagonists, such as the US. What we now need to do is directly address the philosophical issue of collective responsibility and terrorism. Under what conditions, if any, can a group of so-called victims of terrorism be regarded as guilty by virtue of their collectively responsibility for the injustices that the terrorists in question are seeking to redress?

As it happens, there are a number of philosophical theories of collective responsibility that might be deployed to justify some acts of terrorism, though presumably not those perpetrated by Osama bin Laden and his followers. These include the theories of David Cooper[4] and Peter French.[5] A more moderate collectivist theoretical account, and one that explicitly addresses the issue of terrorism, is that offered by Burleigh Taylor Wilkins. According to Wilkins, under certain conditions terrorism is morally justifiable, and the key element of that justification is the collective, but not individual, guilt of the victims of terror.

Before turning directly to claims concerning the collective responsibility of 'innocent' victims, let me put forward the basic account of collective moral responsibility that I have developed in more detail elsewhere.[6] For my intention is to make use of this account to clarify some of the central normative issues and claims regarding terrorism. As will become evident, I am opposed to collectivist accounts of collective moral responsibility, and will defend an individualist account. Moreover, I want to see how far such an individualist account can go in offering a moral justification for at least some limited forms of terrorism in certain contexts. It will turn out that the limited forms of 'terrorism' in question are not forms of terrorism by virtue of the fact that they involve the targeting of the innocent, properly understood; but rather by virtue of their targeting of morally culpable non-attackers. I do so against the following assumptions: (i) the terrorist tactics in question are in the service of very morally weighty goals; (ii) the tactics are likely to realise those goals; (iii) the terrorist group using them is in some sense a legitimate representative of the people on whose behalf they are deploying the tactics; (iv) there is no other alternative to these terrorist tactics; (v) the specific tactics are minimally necessary to attain the goals in question. I take it that in the case of al-Qaeda none of these conditions are met. Accordingly, the September 11 attack on the World Trade Centre, the October

12th Bali bombing and the like, are unjustified and inexcusable moral atrocities. However, it would not follow that there were not morally justified acts or campaigns of terrorism; it would not follow that *some* forms of terrorism were not morally justified under some conditions.

2. COLLECTIVE MORAL RESPONSIBILITY AS JOINT MORAL RESPONSIBILITY[7]

My suggestion is that collective moral responsibility can be regarded as a species of joint responsibility, or at least one central kind of collective moral responsibility can be so regarded.

Here we need to distinguish four senses of collective responsibility. In the first instance I will do so in relation to joint actions.

What is a joint action?[8] Roughly speaking, two or more individuals perform a joint action if each of them intentionally performs an individual action, but does so in the true belief that in so doing they will jointly realise an end which each of them has. Having an end in this sense is a mental state in the head of one or more individuals, but it is neither a desire not an intention. However, it is an end that is not realised by one individual acting alone. So I have called such ends collective ends. For example, the terrorists who hijacked American Airlines flight 11 and crashed the plane into the North Tower of the World Trade Centre in New York performed a joint action. At least one terrorist operated the controls of the plane, while another navigated, and the remaining terrorists, by violence and the threat of violence, prevented the cabin crew and passengers from intervening. Each performed a contributory action, or actions, in the service of the collective end of crashing the plane into the building and killing passengers, office workers and themselves.

Agents who perform a joint action are responsible for that action in the first sense of collective responsibility. Accordingly, to say that they are collectively responsible for the action is just to say that they performed the joint action. That is, they each had a collective end, each intentionally performed their contributory action, and each did so because each believed the other would perform his contributory action, and that therefore the collective end would be realised.

Here it is important to note that each agent is individually (naturally) responsible for performing his contributory action, and responsible by virtue of the fact that he intentionally performed this action, and the action was not intentionally performed by anyone else. Of course the other agents (or agent) *believe* that he is performing, or is going to perform, the contributory action in question. But mere possession of such a belief is not sufficient for the ascription of responsibility to *the believer* for performing the individual action in question. So what are the agents *collectively* (naturally) responsible for? The agents are *collectively* (naturally) responsible for the realisation of the (collective) *end* which results from their contributory actions.

Further, on my account to say that they are collectively (naturally) responsible for the realisation of the collective end of a joint action is to say that they are *jointly* responsible for the realisation of that end. They are jointly responsible because: (a) each relied on the other to bring about the state of affairs aimed at by both (the collective end), and; (b) each performed their contributory action on condition, and only on condition, the other(s) performed theirs. Here condition (b) expresses the *interdependence* involved in joint action.

Again, if the occupants of an institutional role (or roles) have an institutionally determined obligation to perform some joint action then those individuals are collectively responsible for its performance, in our second sense of collectively responsibility. Consider the collective institutional responsibility of the members of the Fire Department of New York City to put out fires in high rise buildings in New York. Here there is a *joint* institutional obligation to realise the collective end of the joint action in question. In addition, there is a set of derived *individual* obligations; each of the participating individuals has an individual obligation to perform his/her contributory action. (The derivation of these individual obligations relies on the fact that if each performs his/her contributory action then it is probable that the collective end will be realised.)

The *joint* institutional obligation is a composite obligation consisting of the obligation each of us has to perform a certain specified action in order to realise that end. More precisely, I have the obligation to realise a collective end by means of doing some action, believing you to have performed some other action for that self-same end. The point about joint obligations is that they are not be discharged by one person acting alone.

Notice that typically agents involved in an institutional joint action will discharge their respective individual institutional obligations and their joint institutional obligation by the performance of one and the same set of individual actions. For example, if each of the members of an anti-terrorist task force performs his individual duties having as an end the locating of a terrorist cell then, given favourable conditions, the task force will locate the cell. But one can imagine an investigating agent who recognises his individual institutional obligation, but not his jointly held · obligation to realise the collective end in question. This investigator might have an overriding individual end to get himself promoted; but the head of the task force might be ahead of him in the queue of those to be promoted. So the investigator does not have locating the cell as a collective end. Accordingly, while he ensures that he discharges his individual obligation to (say) interview a particular suspect, the investigator is less assiduous than he might otherwise be because he wants the task force to fail to locate the cell.

There is a third putative sense of collective responsibility. This third sense of individual responsibility concerns those in authority. Here we need to distinguish two kinds of case. If the occupant of an institutional role has an institutionally determined right or obligation to order other agents to perform certain actions, and the actions in question are joint actions, then the occupant of the role is *individually* (institutionally) responsible for those joint actions performed by those other agents. This is our first kind of case; but it should be set aside, since it is not an instance of *collective* responsibility.

In the second kind of case it is of no consequence whether the actions performed by those under the direction of the person in authority were joint actions or not. Rather the issue concerns the actions of the ones in authority. In what sense are they collective? Suppose the members of the Cabinet of the UK government (consisting of the Prime Minister and his Cabinet Ministers) collectively decide to exercise their institutionally determined right to order the Royal Air Force to attack Afghanistan during peacetime. The air force does what it was ordered to do, and the Cabinet is collectively responsible for starting the war in some sense of collective responsibility. Moreover, depending on the precise nature of the institutional arrangement, it might be that the Prime Minister orders the commander of the Air Force to launch the attack, and does so as the representative of, or under instructions from, the Cabinet of which the Prime Minister is the head. If the decision is the Cabinet's to make, then there is full-blown collective responsibility. If the decision is the Prime Minister's to make, albeit acting on the advice of the Cabinet, or even subject to the veto of the Cabinet, then matters are more complex; the Prime Minister has individual responsibility, albeit individual responsibility that is tempered or constrained by a layer of collective responsibility.

There are a couple of things to keep in mind here. First, the notion of responsibility in question here is, at least in the first instance, institutional – as opposed to moral – responsibility.

Second, the 'decisions' of committees, as opposed to the individual decisions of the members of committees, need to be analysed in terms of the notion of a joint institutional mechanism that I have introduced elsewhere.[9] So the 'decision' of the Cabinet – supposing it to be the Cabinet's decision, and not simply the Prime Minister's – can be analysed as follows. At one level each member of the Cabinet voted for or against the military attacking Afghanistan; and let us assume some voted in the affirmative, and others in the negative. But at another level each member of the Cabinet agreed to abide by the outcome of the vote; each voted having as a collective end that the outcome with a majority of the votes in its favour would be pursued. Accordingly, the members of the Cabinet were jointly institutionally responsible for the decision to order the military to attack Afghanistan. So the Cabinet was collectively institutionally responsible for starting the war against the Taliban; and the sense of collective responsibility in question is *joint* (institutional) responsibility.[10]

What of the fourth sense of collective responsibility, collective *moral* responsibility? Collective moral responsibility is a species of joint responsibility. Accordingly, each agent is individually morally responsible, but conditionally on the others being individually morally responsible; there is interdependence in respect of moral responsibility. This account of collective moral responsibility arises naturally out of the account of joint actions. It also parallels the account given of individual moral responsibility.

Thus we can the following claim about moral responsibility. If agents are collectively responsible for the realisation of an outcome, in the first or second or third senses of collective responsibility, and if the outcome is morally significant then – other things being equal – the agents are collectively morally responsible for that outcome, and can reasonably attract moral praise or blame, and (possibly) punishment or reward for bringing about the outcome.

Here we need to be more precise about what agents who perform morally significant joint actions are collectively morally responsible for. Other things being equal, each agent who intentionally performs a morally significant *individual* action has *individual* moral responsibility for the action. So in the case of a morally significant joint action, each agent is *individually* morally responsible for performing *his contributory* action, and the *other* agents are *not* morally responsible for his individual contributory action. But, in addition, the contributing agents are *collectively* morally responsible for the outcome or *collective end* of their various contributory actions. To say that they are collectively morally responsible for bringing about this (collective) end is just to say that they are *jointly* morally responsible for it. So each agent is individually morally responsible for realising this (collective) end, but conditionally on the others being individually morally responsible for realising it as well. So in the World Trade Centre example, terrorist A might be individually morally responsible for navigating the plane, terrorist B individually morally responsible for piloting the plane into the building, and terrorists C, D and E for using and threatening to use violence to prevent the cabin crew and passengers from intervening. However, A, B, C, E and E are jointly morally responsible for the destroying the plane and building, and for killing the passengers and office workers.

Moreover, whatever the reason why each came to have the collective end in question, once each had come to have that collective end then there was interdependence of action. That is, each played his role in the attack only on condition the others played their role. So the full set of actions performed by the individual members of the terrorist group can be regarded as *the means* by which the collective end was realised; and each individual contributory action was a *part of* that means. Moreover, in virtue of interdependence, each individual action is an integral part of the means to the collective end. Accordingly, I conclude that all of the members of the terrorist group are jointly – and therefore collectively – morally responsible for the destruction of the building and the attendant loss of life. For each performed an action the service of that (collective) end, and each of these actions was an integral part of the means to that end.

Note the following residual points. First, it is not definitive of joint action that each perform his/her contributory action on the condition, and only on the condition, that *all* of the rest of the other perform theirs. Rather, it is sufficient that each perform his/her contributory action on the condition, and only on the condition, that *most* of the others perform theirs. So the interdependence involved in joint action is not necessarily *complete* interdependence. Nevertheless, if the action of one agent (or more than one agent) is not interdependent with *any* of the actions of the other agents, then the action of that first agent (or agents) is not part of the joint action. So if one (or more) of the members of the group of terrorists in fact performed his action independently of the rest, and if the rest performed their actions independently of that one agent, then the action of the latter would not be part of the joint action. The action of the latter agent would not be part of the means to the *collective* end; and the agent could not be said to have had the destruction of the building and the loss of life as a *collective* end.

Second, in my view, if an action is a means to some end, and if the action is sufficient for the realisation of that end, then the agent who performed the action has (natural) responsibility for bringing about the end. So the fact that the outcome in question might be overdetermined by virtue of the existence of some second action performed by some second agent, does not remove the responsibility of the first agent for the outcome in question. Consider two assassins who work entirely independently. By coincidence each assassin fires a bullet at the President of the USA, and the two bullets lodge simultaneously in the brain of the President killing him instantly. Assume further that either one of the bullets would have been sufficient to kill the President. I take it that each of the assassins is guilty of murder, and each is guilty by virtue of having intentionally (and individually) shot the President dead.

We can conceive of two joint actions that are analogous to the assassin example. There are two independent actions, albeit two joint actions performed by the members of two separate groups, respectively; and each of these (joint) actions is sufficient for some outcome. I conclude that just as the two assassins are both morally responsible for the murder of the President, so are the members of both of the two groups morally responsible for the two envisaged joint actions. The only difference is that each of the assassins is *individually* responsible for the death of the President, whereas the members of the first group are *jointly* responsible for the outcome in question, as are the members of the second group.

Third, an agent has moral responsibility if his action was intentionally performed in order to realise a morally significant collective end, and the action causally contributed to the end. The action does not have to be a necessary condition, or even a necessary part of a sufficient condition, for the realisation of the end.

Fourth, agents who intentionally make a causal contribution in order to realise a morally significant collective end, are not necessarily fully morally responsible for the end realised.

The second problem in relation to collective moral responsibility for actions arises in the context of the actions of large groups and organisations.

Consider the al-Qaeda terrorist organisation. The actions of the members of al-Qaeda are interdependent in virtue of the collective end viz. destroy, or at least badly damage, the World Trade Centre, and kill numerous passengers and office workers. Naturally, this interdependence is far more complex than simple cases of joint action, given the existence of an hierarchical organisation, and its more loosely structured extensions. Moreover, the contribution of each individual to the outcome is far more various, and in general quite insignificant, given the large numbers of people involved.

At this point the notion of, what I have elsewhere termed, a layered structure of joint actions needs to be introduced.[11] Suppose a number of 'actions' are performed in order to realise some collective end. Call the resulting joint action a *level two* joint action. Suppose, in addition, that each of the component individual 'actions' of this level two joint 'action', is itself – at least in part – a joint action with a second set of component individual actions. And suppose the member actions of this second set have the performance of this level two 'action' as their collective end. Call the joint action composed of the members of this second set of actions a *level one* joint action. An illustration of the notion of a layered structure of joint actions is in fact an army fighting a battle. At level one we have a number of joint actions. The pilots of (say) the US squadron of planes bomb a Taliban position in Afghanistan, and members of (say) the Northern Alliance move forward on the ground, killing Taliban combatants and taking the position. So there are two level one joint actions. Now, each of these two (level one) joint actions is itself describable as an *individual* action performed (respectively) by the different military groups, namely, the action of bombing the position, and the action of overrunning and occupying the position. However, each of these 'individual' actions is part of a larger joint action directed to the collective end of winning the battle against the Taliban. For each of these individual attacks on the position is part of a larger plan coordinated by the US and Northern Alliance commands. So these 'individual' actions constitute a *level two* joint action directed to the collective end of winning the battle.

Accordingly, if all, or most, of the individual actions of the members of the US airforce squadron and of the Northern Alliance army were performed in accordance with collective ends, and the performance of each of the resulting level one joint actions were themselves performed in accordance with the collective end of winning the battle, then, at least in principle, we could ascribe joint moral responsibility for winning the battle to the individual pilots of the US air force and to the individual members of the Northern Alliance.

At any rate, we are now entitled to conclude that agents involved in complex cooperative enterprises can, *at least in principle*, be ascribed collective or *joint natural* responsibility for the outcomes aimed at by those enterprises, and in cases of morally significant enterprises, they can be ascribed collective or *joint moral* responsibility for those outcomes. This conclusion depends on the possibility of analysing these enterprises in terms of layered structures of joint action. Such structures involve: (a) a possibly indirect and minor causal contribution from each of the individuals jointly being ascribed responsibility; (b) each individual having an intention to perform his or her contributory (causally efficacious) action; and (c) each individual having as an ultimate end or goal the outcome causally produced by their jointly performed actions.

The upshot of the discussion in this section is that the undoubted existence of the phenomenon of collective moral responsibility for actions is entirely consistent with individualism in relation to moral responsibility. For an acceptable individualist account of collective moral responsibility is available.

3. COLLECTIVE OMISSIONS AND TERRORISM

I hold that terrorist groups fighting for a just cause might be morally entitled to target persons individually and/or collectively responsible for perpetrating the rights violations the terrorists are seeking to redress. However, according to the conception of collective moral responsibility that I favour the legitimate targets in question would be – in the paradigm case – persons who had intentionally causally contributed to the rights violations in question. Here the assumption is that the intention is under the control of the agent in question.

There are various other theoretical or quasi-theoretical forms of individualism that I would find unacceptable. One such view rests on the claim of causal inter-relatedness. If we take harm as including both direct and indirect harm, then, for example, a US citizen who paid taxes that were used to train a pilot who bombed a Taliban stronghold might be held to be responsible for the deaths of the civilians killed. Clearly, moral responsibility cannot be ascribed merely on the basis of possibly very indirect, and entirely unforeseen, causal contributions. Moral responsibility implies agency, and agency implies intention, ends and the like.

Permissive causal accounts of moral responsibility are as unpalatable as ones ascribing moral responsibility on the basis of membership of the group.

As thing stand, the category of innocent victims would consist of all those who have not intentionally individually performed any rights violations and who have not intentionally contributed to rights violations, either as a member of a group and/or as the occupant of a role in the context of a layered structure of joint actions.

Here it is important to note that there might be a further category or categories of persons with diminished moral responsibility who nevertheless might be legitimate targets for terrorist groups engaged in justified armed struggles. Such persons with diminished responsibility might include ones who had lesser or subordinate roles in the rights violations, e.g. minor clerical staff at Nazi headquarters, or ones who should have known, but did not know, what the consequences of their actions would be, e.g. a person who provided information concerning the whereabouts of an African National Congress (ANC) member to the South African Police during the apartheid years.

However, the addition of such a category, or categories, of persons with diminished moral responsibility while it complicates the basic account in terms of individual intention and causal contribution, it does not constitute a significant theoretical addition to it. However, I now want to turn to a somewhat different category of persons who might be legitimate targets for terrorists, namely, culpable non-attackers. The inclusion of this category represents a considerable extension to the set of legitimate targets, and it does constitute a significant theoretical addition.

By a culpable non-attacker I mean someone who intentionally refrains from undertaking some action that they are morally obliged to perform. In other words, a victim might be (at least in large part) innocent in respect of the actions that they have performed; however, they might not be innocent in respect of their inactions. They might be guilty of omissions; they might be culpable non-attackers.

There are two general reasons that a bystander might be considered to be guilty of an act of omission. Firstly, the wrong being done is of such a magnitude that someone ought to intervene, and as a bystander they are in a position to see what is going on, and to intervene. Secondly, they are not mere bystanders, but bystanders who are in effect benefiting from the wrong that is being done. Perhaps the US economy, and therefore US citizens, are benefiting from US government policy of propping up autocratic regimes in the Middle East, such as Saudi Arabia, in order to ensure the requisite continuing flow of reasonably cheap oil.

The fact that someone is benefiting from some wrongdoing, while not causally contributing to it, is not sufficient to ascribe to them any responsibility for the wrongdoing. Here we need to be careful, since there are cases where the fact that someone benefits from some wrongdoing *indirectly* causally contributes to the wrongdoing. For example, men who pay young women for sex may not be directly contributing to the situation whereby these young women are coerced into working as prostitutes. However, the fact remains that a causally necessary condition for the young women being thus coerced is the willingness of men to pay for their sexual services. Naturally, the men may falsely suppose that the young women voluntarily work as prostitutes.

At any rate, let us focus exclusively on culpable omissions.[12]

Assume that there are large numbers of people whose lives are at risk, and there are bystanders who could successfully intervene without significant risk or cost to themselves. Assume also that these bystanders are the only persons who could effect the rescue. Consider a scenario in which a boat at sea is sinking and hundreds of its passengers (who are refugees from war) are about to drown. Assume that there is a second large merchant vessel that could rescue the passengers, but its captain is refusing to order it to do so; he despises the refugees. Would not a third party – say, the captain and crew of a small naval vessel – which is itself unable to effect the rescue, be morally entitled to use deadly force to enforce the moral right to be rescued, by (say) shooting the culpable captain – a civilian – in the course of attempting to commandeer the large vessel?

Now consider another kind of case. There is a destitute African person who is dying of HIV AIDS.[13] Drugs are available which would enable him to live, however they are far too expensive for him. Moreover, let us assume that the drug could be produced cheaply, but that the company wants to guarantee exorbitantly high profits, and is therefore refusing to allow cheap production of the drug which would only guarantee reasonable profits. And let us further assume that everyone, including the government knows this. At any rate, he unsuccessfully pleads with the drug company's managers to provide him with the drugs. Next he seeks legal means, and even petitions the government. However, he lives in a lawless society governed by a corrupt and authoritarian regime, and all his efforts in this regard inevitably fail. He then considers trying to ask for money to pay for the drugs. However, all the members of his community are destitute, and in any case AIDS is ravaging the community; if anyone had enough money they would use it to buy drugs for themselves or AIDS stricken members of their family. As for members of the alternative community, while most are reasonably affluent and many are wealthy, they despise the poor and especially AIDS sufferers; they regard them as less than human, and AIDS as a fitting punishment for their sexual promiscuity. Moreover, the alternative community lives in a separate area in heavily fortified homes; it is an apartheid-style society. Theft is not an option. Accordingly, in desperation and with all other avenues closed, he goes to the pharmaceutical company demanding the drugs that will enable him to live. Predictably, he is yet again refused, on the grounds that he must pay for the highly priced drugs. However, this time he grabs the gun from the guard and threatens to kill one or more of the three company managers responsible for the high price. The managers refuse to hand over the drugs and the AIDS sufferer knows that this is his last and only chance to procure the life-saving drugs; self-evidently, he will never be admitted into this building again. The AIDS sufferer fires a warning shot but still his request for the drugs in denied. He then shoots the first manager in the leg, but even this act of malicious wounding fails to move the managers. He is running out of bullets and also out of time; soon the police will arrive. Finally, he shoots one of the managers dead, doing so in order to instil such fear in the second and third manager that they will hand over the drugs. He gets the drugs, escapes and is cured of AIDS.

I believe that that the AIDS sufferer's action is morally justified, given this action was the only way to preserve this life, and given that the assistance required could have been provided at minimal cost to the drug company. For he had a positive right to be assisted, and the 'bystanders' – the manager of the drug company – was refraining from carrying out his duty to respect that right even though he could do so at minimal cost to himself. So the case is analogous to those involving negative rights, such as the right not to be killed, or the right not to have one's freedom interfered with. But for those who might still want to resist the claim that the AIDS sufferer's action was morally justified, let me gesture at additional moral considerations. For example we could assume that AIDS sufferer would distribute the stock of drugs he was seeking to procure in order to save the lives of tens, hundreds or thousands of AIDS sufferers in his community. Let us further assume that the pharmaceutical company had actually been given a monopoly in the country in question on the condition it would sell the drugs cheaply; however, it was paying off corrupt government officials to turn a blind eye to the high prices it was charging.

So deadly force can in principle be used to enforce some positive rights, including presumably rights to subsistence, as well as to enforce negative rights. Here I am assuming the usual principles of proportional and minimum force, and the principle of necessity.

Moreover, as is the case with negative rights, third parties – at least in principle – have rights, and indeed duties, to use deadly force to ensure that positive rights are respected.

This point is especially clear in the case of governments who intentionally refrain from respecting the positive rights, including subsistence rights, of their citizens. For governments have a clear institutional responsibility to provide for the well-being of their citizens. Accordingly, the moral responsibility based on need – and the fact that those in government could assist if they chose to – is buttressed by this institutional responsibility that they have voluntarily taken on. Consider Saddam Hussein's refusal to distribute much needed food and medicine to his own citizens, albeit in the context of UN sponsored sanctions. The citizens, or third parties, are entitled to use deadly force against these governments. Perhaps such use of deadly force, including assassination, is to be regarded as terrorism on the grounds that the victims of terrorism are not themselves attackers. If so, then terrorism can be morally justified in some circumstances. However, the victims in this kind of scenario are not innocent; their acts of omission constitute intentionally violations of the positive rights of their citizens.

In the case of members of a group or institutional entity we need to focus on the collective role of bystanders. So the members of the group or institution are said to be collectively morally responsible for a collective omission. But here we need some theoretical account of collective responsibility for omissions. Elsewhere I have elaborated such an account.

According to that account, members of some group are collectively responsible for failing to intervene to halt or prevent some serious wrongdoing or wrongful state of affairs if: (1) the wrongdoing took place, or is taking place; (2) the members of the community intentionally refrained from intervening; (3) each or most of the members intervening having as an end the prevention of the wrongdoing probably would have prevented, or have a reasonable chance of halting, the wrongdoing; (4) each of the members of the community would have intentionally refrained from intervening – and intervening having as an end the prevention or termination of the wrongdoing – even if the others, or most of the others, had intervened with that end in mind; (5) the members of the community had a collective institutional responsibility to intervene. Note that on this account, if an agent would have intervened, but done so only because the others did, i.e. not because he had as an end the prevention or termination of the wrong, then the agent would still be morally responsible, jointly with the others, for failing to intervene (given conditions (1)-(3) and (5)).

Now there are additional theoretical complications that arise when the intervention in question has to be performed by representatives of a group or community, rather than by the members of the group or community themselves or by third parties who are mere bystanders. Thus in democracies, the government has to enact policies to intervene; the citizens cannot themselves intervene as a community. Moreover, some organisation – authorised by the government – has to implement these policies, has to actually do the intervening. This being so, we need to help ourselves to the notion of a layered structure mentioned above.

In the light of this definition, it might well be the case that members of governments, such as the Iraqi government, who fail to meet their responsibilities to their own citizens, and South African officials in the days of apartheid who arguably had a pre-existing responsibility to assist destitute blacks in the 'homelands', are collectively morally responsible for omissions of a kind that might justify the use of deadly force to ensure that the rights to assistance in question are realised.

However, it might be argued that in the case of liberal democracies – as opposed to authoritarian regimes – the citizens themselves can at least in principle be held collectively morally responsible for the rights violations of their governments.[14] The salient contemporary example here is the Israeli citizenry. Arguably, the Israeli government is responsible for violating the rights of Palestinians, including establishing Israeli settlements on Palestinian land, shooting dead stone-throwing youths during the Intifada (armed uprising), and so on. So let us assume that the Palestinians are morally entitled to used deadly force against the Israeli government and its armed forces. However, on the view that holds the citizens of a democracy morally responsible for the actions of its government, the citizens themselves might be regarded as legitimate targets. On this view, at least in principle, Israeli non-combatant citizens might well be legitimate targets for Palestinian gunmen. It is important to note that even on this view there will be innocent persons, e.g. children and members of the citizenry who actively opposed the policies of the government.

This move to include the citizenry of contemporary liberal democracies as legitimate targets is unwarranted, and an unacceptable extension of the category of legitimate targets even in the case of otherwise morally justified armed struggles. (I am not claiming that the PLO, for example, is in fact engaged in a morally justified armed struggle.) In the first place, in general in representative democracies citizens votes are cast for representatives not policies. (An exception here would be a democracy in which there were referenda on specific policies, such as the decision to go to war.) Governments can and do implement policies that citizens as a whole may object to, e.g. evidently a majority of UK citizens now think the UK armed forces ought not to have invaded Iraq. In short, citizens do not have a clear and direct institutional responsibility for the specific policies of governments; rather the members of the government have a clear and direct responsibility for these policies. In the second place, the size of the citizenry of most contemporary democracies is such that each citizen must be held to have very considerably diminished responsibility for the election of the government; to cast one vote among millions is hardly sufficient to establish full moral responsibility for a particular government being in power.

NOTES

[1] An earlier version of the first section of this paper appeared under the title "Osama bin Laden, Terrorism and Collective Responsibility", in: T. Coady and M. O'Keefe (ed.): *Terrorism and Justice*, Melbourne University Press, 2002.

[2] Bergen, op.cit.

[3] Quoted in Bergen, op.cit., p. 105.

[4] David Cooper: "Collective Responsibility", in: *Philosophy* XLIII July 1968.

[5] Peter French: *Collective and Corporate Responsibility,* New York, 1984.

[6] See, for example, Seumas Miller: "Collective Responsibility", in: *Public Affairs Quarterly* vol.15 no.1 2001.

[7] An earlier version of the material in this section appeared in "Terrorism and Collective Responsibility: A Response to Narveson and Rosenbaum", in: *International Journal of Applied Philosophy* 2004.

[8] See Seumas Miller: *Social Action: A Teleological Account,* Cambridge University Press, 2001, Chapter 2.

[9] ibid., Chapter 5.

[10] This mode of analysis is also available to handle examples in which an institutional entity has a representative who makes an individual decision, but it is an individual decision which has the joint backing of the members of the institutional entity e.g. an industrial union's representative in relation to wage negotiations with a company. It can also handle examples such as the firing squad in which only one real bullet is used, and it is not know which member is firing the real bullet and which merely blanks. The soldier with the real bullet is (albeit unknown to him) *individually* responsible for shooting the person dead. However, the members of the firing squad are *jointly* responsible for its being the case that the person has been shot dead.

[11] Seumas Miller: "Collective Responsibility, Armed Intervention and the Rwandan Genocide", in: *International Journal of Applied Philosophy* vol.12 no.2 1998 and Seumas Miller: *Social Action*, op.cit., Chapter 5.

[12] I am not claiming that being a beneficiary of wrongdoing never warrants retaliation on the part of those wronged.

[13] This example is taken from my "Collective Responsibility and Terrorism: A Reply to Narveson and Rosenbaum", op.cit.

[14] See Igor Primoratz' contribution to this volume.

MARCELO DASCAL

THE UNETHICAL RHETORIC OF TERROR[*]

Terrorism is not an abstract subject matter – at least not for me. My family and me, our friends, the restaurants where we eat, the theaters and museums we visit, the discotheques where we dance, the streets we walk and the buses we ride – all of them have been and are likely to continue to be actual targets of terror attacks. The topic of this lecture, therefore, cannot be for me an academic topic just like any of the many others I talk about.

As I set out to write the n-th draft of this lecture (it was never so difficult for me to write down a lecture!), the news of the November 21st suicide attack in a bus in the Kiryath Menachem neighborhood in western Jerusalem break through the self-imposed walls of my peace of mind. The bus exploded at 7:28 a.m. There is no doubt about the target: children, young girls and boys going to school, eager to learn and to play. Twelve lives – including that of the young suicide bomber – cut down before they were given the chance to blossom. Forty-eight lives scarred forever. The lives of dozens of families disrupted forever. Trauma, fear, and hatred once more got their heavy toll. Calls for vengeance, for more death and horror, are sure to lead to more deaths in an absurd action-reaction dialectics of horror. As long as these voices prevail on both sides, the senseless bloodbath will no doubt continue.

SILENCE OR WORDS?

My first reaction was to shut off the computer and to withdraw to silence. What could I, what could anyone, say in the face of this macabre spectacle? Do any words – other than the expression of absolute disgust, of total, unrestricted and unequivocal condemnation of such an act and of similar ones – make sense? And didn't even such condemnations already become a sort of routine reaction that makes they sound hollow and without effect? Is any analysis, any lecture, any form of discourse about such a monstrosity even permissible? Aren't such analyses rather dangerous, for they may provide some sort of "understanding" of the causes and motives of what was done, which in turn may lead, if not to justifying it, at least to moderating one's rejection of it?

No. I definitely do not want to take part in this game. I ought perhaps simply to express my utter moral refusal to admit this kind of acts by shutting up. I should stand here tonight, with you, in total silence, for a full hour, in memory of these most recent victims, as well as of the hundreds of other victims, of this absolutely immoral expression of human imbecility. Sometimes silent protest is incomparably more powerful than thousands of words. The people of Leipzig demonstrated in 1989 how what begins as silent protest is capable to bring down mighty walls. But can we be sure our silent protest, here and now, would be correctly interpreted, as it

G. Meggle (ed.), Ethics of Terrorism & Counter-Terrorism, 113-120.

was in 1989? Can't it be that what we are protesting against is not quite clear for each one of us, and perhaps even quite different if not opposite?

Without the help of words, I confess that I see no way to answer these questions. I happen to believe in the usefulness of words, of discussion, of dialogue, of argument, of understanding. I think the way of dialogue is the only way to stop the bloodshed – in my country, and in any other region where terror has raised its head and is deemed by some people to be a legitimate and efficient means to achieve political ends. I believe that we should make an effort to overcome our instinctive – and justified – repulsion vis-à-vis such actions and to engage in dialogue. We owe this to the victims. We owe this to the would-be future perpetrators, as a last minute effort to divert them from their murderous intentions. We owe it to ourselves in order to know what to do, to decide towards what to address our protest as well as our constructive action.

DEBATING AND MORALITY

The use of words for clarifying our thoughts and for understanding a neighbor or an adversary is not without its dangers. The same words can mean one thing for David and a completely different thing for Ahmed. Words can be truthful, but they can also lie. Argument can serve to widen the gap between the opponents rather than to bring them closer to each other. Debate and criticism can contribute to acknowledging that the opponent has got it right at least on some points, and thereby lead to problem solving; but it can also become a mere eristic exercise of the art of proving that I am absolutely right and my opponent absolutely wrong – an exercise that only leads to the perpetuation of disputes. Although the chances of success are not assured, the risk is nevertheless worthwhile. Not only because talking is the only alternative to violence, but also because the readiness to talk with a person amounts to recognizing that person as a human being, and thus to refusing to de-humanize her. And the de-humanization of the adversary is a well-known strategy of terrorism and of some counter-terrorist measures, as we all know.

Arguing with an opponent is a particularly important form of talking, from this point of view. For, in order to confront successfully the adversary's claims and arguments one must make a serious effort to understand them properly. This means identifying their presuppositions and implications and detecting their eventual theoretical inconsistencies and unacceptable practical consequences. By granting the opponent's arguments their due weight, one *eo ipso* becomes aware of one's own assumptions and discovers their weaknesses. Self-criticism may then lead to the modification of one's position and to stronger counter-argumentation in its support. This whole process forces one to "put oneself in the place of the other", i.e., to see the conflict as the opponent sees it, thus gaining a less self-centered perspective on it. This does not necessarily require *accepting* the opponent's reasons, but it certainly requires *understanding* them *qua* reasons that, in the opponent's eyes at least, lead to the conclusions s/he draws.

The compilers of the Talmud were aware of the importance of the whole process of argumentation and counter-argumentation for the proper understanding of the conclusion reached. Accordingly, they recorded, in addition to the conclusion, the arguments of both the winner and the loser, in each particular debate. When asked why so much effort should be spent in preserving the winning and losing arguments, when what matters for practical purposes is the conclusion reached, their reply was: אלה ואלה דברי אלוהים חיים – "both are the words of the living God".

In the Talmudic framework, where the topics that were debated concerned legally binding decisions about the daily conduct of life, conclusions had to be reached, and they had to be accepted by winners and losers. In other contexts, argumentation not always leads to compelling decisions. But in the case we are discussing here, can we afford hesitation? After weighing all the arguments, the scales will unequivocally point to the immorality of the deliberate sacrifice of innocent human lives in the altar of political objectives. In fact, I would take this as the hallmark of a morally acceptable argument or assumption: if the argument leads to a conclusion that justifies such a sacrifice, then either its premises are morally unacceptable, or the argument is logically invalid, or both. In this sense, the examination of the arguments, enlightening as it surely is, cannot yield a justification for such acts. Therefore, the purpose of such an examination cannot be (as it often is) the weakening or cancellation of the condemnation through "but" statements of the form "We condemn this act, but we should not forget that p" – whatever the content of p. They must be examined, rather, in order to clear up the mistakes and other confusing factors that – whether deliberately or involuntarily – may grant such dubious "but" statements an appearance of plausibility.

I have singled out some of these confusing factors by means of contrived or hyphenated expressions such as 'discommunication' and 'pseudo-morality'. I will pursue my analysis by trying to explain these expressions and related ones. Notice that the prefixes I chose function as hedges, which modify the meaning of the noun to which they are attached in the following way: in the cases under analysis, the thing denoted by the modified noun is not in fact what is usually called by that name, although it has some resemblance with what the noun usually denotes. 'Discommunication', for instance, refers to something similar in some respects to communication, but lacking some central feature thereof. The task of the analysis is to determine how the phenomenon analyzed – in our case, terrorism – on the one hand resembles human communication and makes deceptive use of this resemblance and, on the other, violates some of its most basic norms. Furthermore, we must inquire what are the moral consequences – if any – of such a violation.

DISCOMMUNICATION: FROM MANIPULATION TO BLOCKING COMMUNICATION OPTIONS

The actions performed in terrorist and counter-terrorist operations are, on the face of it, communicative acts. Through the direct material and human damage they cause, they are supposed to convey certain "messages", which their respective "addressees" are supposed to interpret and understand, as well as to act upon. Such an "understanding", in turn, is supposed to be facilitated by a host of other communicative acts, in the strict sense of the word – communiqués, warnings, threats, demands – performed through a variety of channels, such as the media, mediators, overt and covert negotiations, etc. The opponents seem to be, thus, engaged in an ongoing "conversation", involving a full range of verbal and non-verbal, extremely violent and less violent, communicative acts. This conversation seems even to follow the rules of normal conversation, such as the turn-taking principle and the maxims of cooperation: the interlocutors "speak" each in their turn; each intervention by one of them is followed by a "relevant" response by the other; and special concern for the full intelligibility of the message conveyed is manifest, each side making a point of "speaking" in what it takes to be the "language" best understood by the other (usually, the language of violence) and making its intentions crystal clear.

This semblance of communication, however, breaks down as soon as one scrutinizes it closely. What sets acts of terror radically apart from normal human communication is the way in which they seek to achieve their "communicative" aims. Whereas in communication the addressee's recognition of the speaker's communicative intention is what is supposed to lead to his/her change of mind and subsequent behavior, in a terrorist attack this aim is principally achieved by the direct impact the attack has upon the population's emotions. Overwhelmingly frightened, raging, insecure, disoriented – in short, "terrorized" – the target population is emotionally coerced to react as the perpetrators wish. Under these circumstances, the effort to understand the message and its motivation, the consideration of alternative possible responses, and the other cognitive operations that are routinely performed in a communicative exchange, are paralyzed or overruled by automatic emotional responses. Nothing could be farther from the autonomous, self-conscious, and self-critical partner of a true communicative exchange than the debased and manipulated "interlocutor" of a terrorist attack. On the other extreme, nothing could be farther from that human partner than the cool, disciplined and precise – but no less manipulated – perpetrator of such attacks, be it by using homemade explosives or tanks.

Yigal Brunner is one of the few hundreds of Israeli soldiers who courageously refused to serve in the occupied territories, who refused to become a trigger-squeezing robot. In his letter to the general who summoned him to duty, Yigal begins by quoting Bertold Brecht:

> "General, your tank is a powerful vehicle.
> It smashes down a forest, it crushes a hundred persons.
> But it has one defect.
> It needs a driver."

After describing the dispossession and repression of the Palestinians resulting from the Israeli government's support of the settlements, and the role of the army in implementing these policies, he writes:

> "The tank commander observed a number of persons residing in a suspicious manner in their homes, and ordered the gunner to blast off a round. I'm the gunner. I'm the final small cog in the wheel of this sophisticated war machine. I am the last and least link in the chain of command. I am just supposed to obey orders. To reduce myself to

stimulus-and-response. To hear the command "Fire!" and squeeze the trigger. To burn it into the awareness of every Palestinian. To complete the grand demarche. And do it all with the natural simplicity of a robot who senses nothing beyond the shaking of the tank as the shell is ejected from the gun barrel and flies to its target."

But – he continues – as Brecht wrote further:

> "General, man is very useful
> He can fly, and he can kill.
> But he has one defect.
> He can think.

> And so, mon general, I am capable of thought. ... I can see where you're leading me. I can understand that we shall kill and crush, wound and die, and it will never end. ... Therefore I have to turn down your summons to duty. I won't come along to squeeze the trigger on your behalf."

Yigal Brunner exemplifies the small number of individuals who manage to preserve their autonomy and their critical faculties under the enormous social pressures that engender and are engendered by terror and counter-terror. But, regardless of whether it succeeds in curtailing the individual's autonomy or not, such a coercive and manipulative pressure is morally unacceptable because it runs, of course, against the fundamental ethical principles of individual freedom and responsibility.

Let us consider also other ethical consequences of the 'discommunication' effects of terrorism and counter-terrorism. I have coined this term by analogy with the term '*dys*functional', to suggest that acts of terrorism distort and impair communication to such an extent that the basic conditions of its functionality are called into question.

One of the reasons often mentioned by those who resort to terrorism is that there is "no partner", no one worth communicating with on the "other side". This assertion's truth is carefully guaranteed by silencing potential candidates for partners in either camp, and by blocking the communication channels between the two camps. The former is achieved by tagging as 'collaborators' those who communicate in any way with "the enemy" and as "traitors" those who denounce their own camp's atrocities. The latter is achieved by planning the succession of terrorist operations in such a way that communicative channels across the camps are permanently flooded with the noise of explosives and of the emotions they unleash. Each group thus becomes self-enclosed in a circle of solidarity and amen-saying that solidly excludes inner criticism as well as any contact with the other side's point of view. Discommunication of this kind, coupled with indoctrination and preserved by forceful social pressure, amounts to a sort of mental imprisonment that violates the basic human right of free access to information and freedom of thought.

THE ACTION-REACTION DIALECTICS OF TERROR

Another similarity the cycle of terror displays with a familiar phenomenon is its dialogical or dialectical nature: a terrorist attack is followed by reprisals, which in turn yield further terrorist attacks, which in turn lead to further reprisals, and so on – as if through the voice of the explosions the opponents were making statements, raising objections, rebuking these objections, and so on. I should perhaps make clear that this dialectical semblance is no more than a caricature by using inverted commas around the word 'dialectics'. In my preferred usage, 'dialectics' refers to the art of dialogue practiced by Plato's Socrates, to the art of grounding reasonable arguments on largely shared opinions, practiced by Aristotle, and to the art of reconciling apparently incompatible positions, practiced by Leibniz. The action-reaction 'dialectics' of terror, however, has nothing to do with any of these, for the simple reason that it has hardly anything to do with dialogue and argumentation, just as it displays only a semblance of communication. It is a 'dialectics' where the participants are acted upon rather than agents. They are pawns in an action-reaction interplay of forces that seem to be beyond their control, like the laws of nature or the alleged laws of history. Brute causality determines their contribution to this interplay, not free agency. But if this is the case, then there is no room for moral judgment and for the ascription of moral responsibility regarding the acts of the participants in such a dialectics. The terrorist may not *want* to perpetrate his act, but he is persuaded that he is *compelled* to do it, by virtue of the divine order of the world, the absolutely true ideology, or the course of history. As applied to the cogwheels of action and reaction in terror and counter-terror, perhaps it is in the Marxian sense, rather than in the Socratic, Aristotelian and Leibnizian senses, that 'dialectics' is the appropriate word.

PSEUDO-MORAL ARGUMENTS

Last but not least, let me turn now to the pseudo-morality characteristic of many – if not all – arguments justifying acts of terror. One of the arguments most often invoked in order to justify such acts consists in pointing out the situation of material and/or cultural dispossession, oppression, humiliation, physical danger, and other grievances of a group of people as the ultimate cause of such acts. These acts are considered morally legitimate because the situation that causes them is unjust and must be redressed, and the 'balance of power' between oppressed and oppressor is so asymmetric in favor of the latter that the former have no alternative other than terror to fight their legitimate, injustice-redressing war. It is important, however, to discern the different spheres to which the various components of this argument belong, in order to assess its due weight.

At the factual level, the causal analysis that identifies a particular individual, group, or state as the cause of the grievances listed must be objectively ascertained. It is not unheard of that factors within the dispossessed group are themselves at least partly responsible for the dispossession. Also, the question "who threw the first stone?" may yield endless dispute, as the questions "who is the rightful original owner of this land?" or "who is the victim?" do too. Nevertheless, it is essential to identify correctly the causes if one wishes to redress their effects without thereby generating similarly unjust effects vis-à-vis another group. Assuming this identification is satisfactorily done, a further factual question arises: what is the most effective way of removing the causes of the situation one wants to redress? This is a typical means-ends rationality issue, which requires a careful comparison of the different possible means (and their predictable effects) to achieve the desired aim without undesirable results. In addition to questions such as whether to use negotiation or military action, whether an all-out revolution would be more effective than a piecemeal improvement policy, etc., one should include in this category the factual question whether the oppressed or dispossessed themselves rather than some third party are the most appropriate candidates to conduct the redressing action.

This last question is related to the 'balance of power' issue mentioned before, as well as to the – also factual question – of whether acts of terror are indeed (a) the only available alternative to redress the injustice and (b) capable of actually achieving this aim. Regarding (a), if a third party's intervention (e.g., the "international community") is a real possibility, then the "only alternative" argument collapses, and with it the factual justification for acts of terror. Regarding (b), if it turns out that acts of terror are rather counter-productive, say, because they rally the oppressor's camp around harder policies, then, again, the justification of these acts dwindles on the basis of mere efficacy considerations, even prior to discussing their moral acceptability. In any case, the moral justification of acts of terror as means of redressing injustice depends upon the demonstration that they indeed are able to do so. Since the argument as usually presented pays little or no attention to this requirement, it fails to provide the moral justification it purports to provide, and therefore is a pseudo-moral argument, catering on the sympathy one naturally feels towards the underdogs.

Turning now to the moral sphere, the first question is, of course, whether warfare is morally justified in the combat against the injustice under consideration. This question lands us squarely at the center of the highly elaborated and hotly debated 'just war' theory. I have no intention to expound or discuss this theory here. Whatever its merits, however, some of its insights are useful for our discussion. Firstly, the theory specifies conditions for the moral assessment not only of waging war but also of the ways of conducting the war. Determining that a war is 'just' does not mean issuing a blank check for the performance of any military or paramilitary action within the framework of the just war in question. In terms of just war theory, therefore, each operation must be morally scrutinized on its own, and it is perfectly possible to view as morally unacceptable certain kinds of operations even if the objectives of the war are morally justified. Acts of terror clearly fall within this category. So that, even if they were to pass all the factual-efficacy tests mentioned above, and even if they were performed as part of a just war, they should not be admitted as morally justifiable acts. To argue that they are, because they allegedly serve the objectives of a just war, is to argue invalidly.

Secondly, it is important to note that the use of the adjective 'just' next to the noun 'war' clearly reveals the presumption of modern thought that war as such is to be avoided, being only permitted under stringent conditions. Morally acceptable wars are thus exceptional, and should be used only exceptionally, as a last resort. They should not be used if a last minute alternative is found, nor should they be converted into routine or semi-permanent means to deal with conflicts. To argue that because a war is just it ought to be fought is to violate the basic anti-war presumption of just war theory.

Thirdly, the considerations of just war theory, as well as the efficacy-factual analysis employed above, apply also to another argument, adduced particularly in justification of counter-terror operations – the argument invoking the right and duty of self-defense. Here too, it must be borne in mind that (a) the conditions for the exercise of this unquestionable right are quite precise and restricted in scope, (b) the fact that they obtain does not amount to issuing a blank check for indiscriminate operations against all those presumably involved in the conception, planning, preparation, logistic support, execution, and divulgation of the attack, and (c) whenever non-violent alternatives are available, they should be preferred as a means of self-defense. To grant oneself rights and moral legitimacy that one denies the opponent in similar circumstances is no doubt the most worrying example of pseudo-morality one all too often encounters in discussions about terrorism and counter-terrorism. For it is to hide under the mantle of moral judgment a shameless use of double standards to foster one's interests.

CONCLUSION

I have begun this talk in a highly emotional tone, prompted by recent events. I have nevertheless tried to tone down my emotional involvement to a minimum, ending up with a rather dry analytic discussion. Let us not be deluded, however, by the tone of my discussion, for its conclusions are clear-cut and far reaching: the unequivocal condemnation of acts of terror, whatever their provenance, perpetrators, causes, alleged efficacy, and presumed justification. No "buts" toning down this conclusion are allowed.

NOTES

* This is, with minor modifications, the text of my lecture in the Cycle of Conferences "Terror and the War Against It", organized by Georg Meggle at Leipzig University, delivered on November 26, 2002. The present text does not overlap that of of my talk in the colloquium "Ethics of Terrorism and Counter-Terrorism" (Bielefeld, October 2002; org. Georg Meggle).

II

TERRORISM & COUNTER-TERRORISM

ETHICS

PER BAUHN

POLITICAL TERRORISM AND THE RULES OF JUST WAR

Political terrorists often conceive of themselves as warriors, as can be seen from the names their groups adopt: Rote *Armee* Fraktion, *Brigate* Rosse, Islamic *Jihad*, and so on. Likewise, the most recent effort to eliminate international terrorism, following the events of September 11, has been designated as a *war* against terrorism. Hence, for terrorists and anti-terrorists alike, it has seemed appropriate to adopt the terminology of war.

In this context, it could be worthwhile to examine to what extent the ideas and principles inherent in the just war theory may apply to an analysis of the moral problems of the acts of those who perform acts of political terrorism, as well as of those who try to fight political terrorists, especially when fighting political terrorism requires attacking areas where there are also innocent civilians.

In this essay, the focus will be on a modified version of the principle of non-combatant immunity (which holds that innocent bystanders should not be victimized) as well as on the principle of double effect (which may justify certain unintended cases of victimization).

First a brief comment on the issue of how to define the term "political terrorism". Acts of political terrorism are physically violent acts performed by an agent or group of agents (who may represent a state government or a movement fighting against a state government) against a certain group of individuals (the victim group) with the purpose of intimidating a certain other group of individuals (the target group), and thereby bringing about a desired political outcome.[1]

Accordingly, a distinctive feature of political terrorists, in contrast to political assassins generally, is that the victims of their violent acts are only instrumentally important, as a means to intimidate the target group. While the political assassin's mission is completed when he has killed his victim, the political terrorist's task remains unfinished as long as his killings have not realized the double purpose of intimidating the target group and thereby bringing about a certain political outcome.

Now, I have deliberately refrained from including in my definition of acts of political terrorism any moral judgement. Likewise I have refrained from making the innocence of the victims a defining characteristic of acts of political terrorism. For one thing, even if the victims of terrorist acts often, and perhaps most of the time, indeed are morally innocent in a sense relevant to the context of the acts in question, we should not make this a matter of definition. It would seem arbitrary to hold that of two acts which both involve violence directed against a group of victims with the purpose of intimidating a target group for political reasons, one should be categorized as an act of political terrorism and the other not, because we judge the victims of the

G. Meggle (ed.), Ethics of Terrorism & Counter-Terrorism, 123-134.

first act to be innocent and the victims of the second act as lacking that characteristic. That these two acts may differ in their *moral* properties is one thing, but this should not cause us to place them in two different *descriptive* categories. A justified political terrorist act is still a political terrorist act, for the same reason that a just war is still a war.

Moreover, I believe it is more fruitful for the theoretical discussion of political terrorism to separate the question of whether a particular act is an act of political terrorism from the question of whether that act is morally justified or not. By distinguishing these two questions we enable ourselves to sidestep the notorious difficulty that "one man's terrorist is another man's freedom-fighter", which precludes any agreement as to whether a particular act is an act of political terrorism or not as long as there is no agreement about its moral status.

Now, while it is not a matter of conceptual necessity that acts of political terrorism must involve innocent victims, I believe it is true to say that much of the controversy surrounding acts of political terrorism hinges on the moral indifference often evidenced by political terrorists, whether they are agents of a repressive state or agents of a movement fighting against a particular state, when it comes to their choice of victims. Placing bombs on buses or in shopping centres, abducting, torturing, and killing the inhabitants of some village just to "send a message" to the other party, are actions carried out with no consideration for the individual victim's moral status, that is, whether or not she has done anything to deserve this kind of treatment.

The sacrificing of victims that are innocent in the sense that they have done nothing to deserve to be killed or physically harmed or coerced often occurs in the context of wars, especially civil and ethnic wars, where hatred does not seem to need any other background than the intended victim's identity. In fact, acts of ethnic cleansing are in most cases also acts of political terrorism, whereby some terrorist militia kills and persecutes certain members of an ethnic group in order to intimidate the rest of that group into giving up some piece of territory desired by the terrorists. And since terrorist groups in general often invoke the terminology of war to justify their existence as well as their activities, we may well argue that to the extent that their actions actually approximate the atrocities committed in wars, we should judge them according to those moral standards that we apply to war crimes, although we may be reluctant to accord to political terrorists the status of soldiers.

War and political terrorism, for all their other differences, are both species of the more inclusive category of politically motivated armed violence. And, for the purpose of moral evaluation, we may find it more rewarding to focus on what the innocent victims of war crimes and the innocent victims of acts of political terrorism have in common, rather than on what separates war criminals from political terrorists.

Given that we accept a description of the innocent victims of acts of political terrorism as people who should enjoy an immunity against politically motivated armed violence, we may easily extend the application of the principle of non-combatant immunity belonging to the just war theory to cover this category of victims as well. However, it is by no means evident who is "innocent" in the relevant sense here.

Against the idea that "non-combatants" simply means "civilians" it has been objected that persons in uniform may well be non-combatants (serving as, for instance, cooks or drivers), while civilians may organize or contribute to the war effort in various ways (as, for instance, political leaders, administrators, or workers in munitions factories).[2]

It has also been argued that the soldiers who fight for a just cause (for instance, defending their democratic state against a ruthless aggressor) are "innocent" in the sense that they are doing the morally right thing and that it therefore would be morally wrong to kill them, although they are certainly not non-combatants.[3]

Moreover, it could be argued that even if an intended victim of an act of political terrorism is *not* "innocent" in the contextually relevant sense of the word, this does not necessarily imply that it is right to kill or physically harm her. A person might, for instance, be employed in some important administrative capacity by a repressive government, thereby being a "part of the system", although she herself has never committed or ordered others to commit any atrocities. This person is obviously not completely innocent (since she is, after all, employed by oppressors to maintain their rule), but is her non-innocence sufficiently strong to justify killing or harming her? Here the objection focuses not only on the issue of innocence and non-innocence, but also on the kind of response appropriate to different forms of non-innocence. Political terrorists may be accused of lacking proportion in their violent actions even when their victims are not (fully) innocent.[4]

Now since the important point in the idea of non-combatant immunity is that there are people who should be *immune* from the violent acts of other people, I believe it would be fruitful to shift our focus from the question of innocence to the question of immunity. Instead of trying to distinguish between innocence and non-innocence, or between various degrees of non-innocence, we could formulate the concept of *a recipient non-deserving of violent interference*. This concept would denote a person whom it would be morally wrong to subject to violent interferences such as kidnapping, torture, or killing. The concept includes the completely innocent victim as well as the victim who is not sufficiently non-innocent to warrant her being subjected to violent interference. By describing the person as a recipient rather than as an agent, we point to the moral issue that the principle of non-combatant immunity is intended to capture, namely that we should strive to secure certain rights of people who may be the *objects* or the *receivers* of the violent actions of others, and who are not themselves agents of violence.

Before we proceed, we should note that it has been suggested that, among the criteria of a just war, it is not the principle of non-combatant immunity but rather the principle of legitimate authority that deserves our attention with regard to acts of political terrorism.[5] The idea here is that the question of who has the right to wage a war is logically prior to the question of who is entitled to the status of combatant. Moreover, if an agent does not have the right to wage a war and hence has no right to the status of a combatant, she cannot call her killings acts of war, regardless of whether her victims are civilians or persons in uniform. This applies to agents of governments that are oppressing their own peoples with military means as well as to terrorist groups fighting against democratically representative governments. Hence, the idea of legitimate authority sets limits to the exercise of state power as well as to the right to resist that power.

Now, while I agree that the principle of legitimate authority is indeed an important factor in political philosophy in general, I remain convinced that the question of non-combatant immunity is the most relevant moral issue in the discussion of acts of political terrorism. For one thing, the question of the legitimacy of an authority ordering acts of political terrorism (be it a government or an anti-government group) seems to derive its significance from the effects of these acts on the well-being of recipients non-deserving of violent interference: 'What *right* do they have to kill the innocent?' What we find appalling is that innocent people are being killed, not that the agent who kills them lacks legitimate authority. And it is our questioning of the agent's killing of the innocent that makes us question the legitimacy of the agent's authority, not the other way round.

Second, legitimate authority may be *lost* by an agent who kills indiscriminately. That is, a government that initially possesses legitimate authority, for instance by being democratically elected, may deprive itself of its legitimacy by responding with excessive force to public discontent, ordering, for instance, its security forces to kill people in a random manner. The legitimacy of any authority will depend not only on the origins but also on the exercise of its powers. Hence, I believe that, far from being an independent standard against which we may morally assess acts of political terrorism, the idea of legitimate authority is itself affected by that assessment.

The concept of a recipient non-deserving of violent interference relies on the idea of persons having *moral rights* to basic goods, such as life, freedom, and physical integrity. These rights should not be thought of as being merely the expression of contingent intuitions that we may or may not have regarding what we owe to other people. As Alan Gewirth has argued, right-claims can be given a non-arbitrary and logically compelling structure if we analyse them as necessary claims made by rational agents regarding the freedom and well-being that constitute the generally necessary conditions of successful action. The rational agent's perception of herself as necessarily requiring of all other agents that they should not interfere with her having these necessary goods of agency is universalized into a moral prescription that all agents should act in accord with the rights to freedom and well-being of their recipients as well as of themselves.[6]

However, even if we accept that persons have moral rights to basic goods such as life, freedom, and physical integrity, we have not thereby committed ourselves to the view that these rights are *absolute*. A's right to physical integrity may, for instance, be overridden by B's right to defend herself in the case of A assaulting B. And starving C's right to life overrides affluent D's right to his property if C can avoid starving to death only by stealing a loaf of bread from D, since life is generally more important to successful agency than is having all of one's property left intact.

Hence, we may best conceive of moral rights as *prima facie*, not denying that they may be overridden, but leaving the burden of proof with the person who wants to override them. For a deontologist a moral right can only be overridden by a more basic right. For a consequentialist, to the extent that she accepts the terminology of moral rights at all, the goal of maximizing certain valued outcomes may, in case of a conflict, justify overriding particular rights.

Now, given that we conceive of moral rights as prima facie rather than as absolute, would it not be possible to justify acts of political terrorism even when they are directed against a recipient non-deserving of violent interference? The answer is yes, it is theoretically possible, but it is indeed difficult to see what could constitute a justifying reason. Consider this case:

A political terrorist has reason to believe that he can make a ruthless dictator resign, thereby saving the lives of 1.000 people awaiting their execution in a state prison, by abducting, torturing, and abusing the dictator's daughter who is not in any way involved in her father's activities. The dictator, whose only soft spot is his daughter, can be expected to yield when he is presented with a video film of the terrorist's abuse of his daughter, followed by the terrorist's threat to kill the girl if the dictator does not release his prisoners and resigns.

Now would not the political terrorist be justified in torturing and abusing the dictator's daughter? After all, from the deontological perspective it could be argued that the girl's prima facie right to physical integrity is overridden by the equally important rights of the 1.000 prisoners. And from a consequentialist point of view, the saving of 1.000 lives seems clearly to outweigh the harm done to the girl.

However, what is missing in the analysis so far is a proper account of the relation in which the terrorist agent stands to the girl he is about to torture and abuse, compared to the relation in which he stands to the 1.000 prisoners he expects to have released as a consequence of his action. The political terrorist seems to assume that both the dictator's daughter and the prisoners are prospective recipients of his action, and that it is up to him to either sacrifice one life or sacrifice many lives. But this is simply not true.

If he refrains from torturing and abusing the dictator's daughter, and the prisoners subsequently are executed, this does not imply that they are executed *because* of his inaction, nor does it imply that he is morally responsible for their deaths. Between his choice *not* to violently interfere with the girl's right to physical well-being, and the execution of the prisoners, there intervenes the action of the dictator who gives the order to execute the prisoners. It is the dictator, and he alone, who is causally as well as morally responsible for the execution of the 1.000 prisoners (that is, given that nobody would dare to execute the prisoners unless the dictator ordered it, and that nobody would dare to prevent the executions from taking place once they had been ordered by the dictator).

This is an application of *the principle of the intervening action*, one important function of which is to enable us to resist moral blackmail of the form 'Either *you* kill one person, or *I* will kill 1.000 persons'. This kind of blackmail attacks our moral integrity, as the blackmailer, if she is successful, can make us do anything that we find horrible and evil, simply by threatening that she herself will otherwise do something we think is even worse.[7]

Hence, with the introduction of the principle of the intervening action, the political terrorist will be unable to argue that his duty to respect the right to physical integrity of the dictator's daughter is overridden by his duty to respect the right to life of the 1.000 prisoners, since there is no such moral conflict for him to resolve in the first place. His duty is to respect the right of his recipient, i.e., the dictator's daughter, while the 1.000 prisoners are recipients of the *dictator's* action, and it is he, not the political terrorist, that is to be blamed if they are unjustly killed.

Now this line of reasoning may convince a deontologist, as she is supposed to be sensitive not only about the external effects of her actions, but also about her duties to her recipients. But what of a consequentialist who is interested in expected outcomes, whether in the form of the direct effects of her action, or in the form of indirect effects, such as, for instance, what other people will do or refrain from doing as a response to her action?

Well, a careful moral consequentialist would have to take into account what it would mean to subscribe to a *moral principle* with the content that innocent persons may be tortured and abused for the sake of saving the lives of many other persons. What would it be like to live in a world or a society in which such a principle guides moral conduct? The consequentialist is likely to find that the fearful insecurity that is likely to spread in a society in which the immunity against torture and abuse of the innocent is not protected makes this principle an unsuitable candidate for a consequentialist ethic. The traditional deontological maxim regarding the immunity of the innocent has much to say for itself, even on consequentialist terms. But even if this is the case, why not make an exception in a situation in which it actually *would* benefit the greater good to sacrifice the innocent? Perhaps it can be done without anyone finding out about it, and then there would be no negative long-term side effects in the form of distrust and fear. However, the consequentialist must consider the fact that this involves herself in a very complicated calculation indeed, and given what is at stake here – the possibility of widespread fear, distrust, and social instability – she cannot afford to be wrong. Hence, the consequentialist should not be disposed to make exceptions from the rule that protects the immunity of a recipient non-deserving of violent interference. In the words of the utilitarian Richard Hare,

> Perhaps the sheriff should hang the innocent man in order to prevent the riot in which there will be many deaths, if he knows that the man's innocence will never be discovered and that the bad indirect effects will not outweigh the good direct effects; but in practice he never will know this.[8]

Hence, violating the rights of a recipient non-deserving of violent interference will find no support in neither deontology, nor consequentialism. Both types of ethical doctrine point to aspects of the terrorist agent's responsibility that make it virtually impossible for him to morally justify his intended maltreatment of the dictator's daughter. According to deontology his primary responsibility is to respect his recipient's right to physical integrity, regardless of what the dictator may do to *his* recipients. According to consequentialism it is his responsibility to act so as to maximize good effects not only here and now, but universally and in a long-term perspective. Given the destabilizing and unsettling effects of allowing the torture of innocent people, it is his responsibility as a thoughtful consequentialist to refrain from such an action, even when its immediate effect would be the saving of many innocent persons' lives.

Now real life political terrorists may try to escape all arguments about their responsibility by simply pointing an accusing finger in the direction of someone else. So did, for instance, the skyjacker Leila Khaled in 1970:

> If we throw bombs, it is not our responsibility. You may care for the death of a child, but the whole world ignored the death of Palestinian children for 22 years. We are not responsible.[9]

This is simply passing the buck: 'We may be bad, but you should not blame us, but rather those other people who made us bad in the first place.' In the mouth of a political terrorist these are also words of warning: 'You who have ignored our complaints for so long are the ones really responsible. If we kill your friends, you should blame nobody but yourself.'

This will not do as an assessment of terrorist responsibility, however. The political terrorist is an agent who acts for a purpose. She is not supposed to be a robot or a mentally deranged person unable to control her behaviour. Whether she is right or not in believing that she and her people are the victims of oppression, she has made a *choice* when she decides to translate her beliefs into acts of political terrorism (after all, there is no law of nature that by necessity links the experience of being oppressed to the decision of becoming a terrorist) and for that choice she is fully responsible, causally as well as morally.

But perhaps we should understand Leila Khaled's statement as a rejection of moral guilt rather than of moral responsibility. That is, she is not denying that the terrorist indeed is an agent and as such responsible for her actions, but she rejects the idea that the terrorist is to be morally blamed for what she is doing. The idea that Khaled might want to defend is that the political terrorist when she is fighting for the just cause of freeing her nation from occupation is entitled to do what is necessary to realize that goal, including killing recipients non-deserving of violent interference.

However, as Michael Walzer has argued, the fact that you have the right to go to war (the *jus ad bellum*) does not mean that whatever you subsequently do to win the war will automatically be in accordance with the rules of right conduct in war (the *jus in bello*).[10] And it is up to the terrorist to prove not only that her people is indeed being oppressed, but also that the oppression is of a kind that may justify resistance by terrorist means, including attacks on recipients non-deserving of violent interference.

Here the political terrorist may respond by invoking another of Walzer's arguments, namely the one regarding supreme emergency. According to this argument, a political community defending itself against external aggression (and hence fulfilling the requirements of *jus ad bellum*) and facing a danger that is both imminent and serious, may be justified in letting military necessity override the non-combatant immunity requirement of *jus in bello*. That the danger is imminent means that there is no time to look for means of defence that distinguish between combatants and non-combatants; you have to use whatever weapons and tactics that are available, even if they tend to be indiscriminate in their effects. That it is serious means that the entire community faces the risk of being massacred or enslaved; merely suffering a minor loss of territory or having to pay heavy indemnities would not count here.[11] Could not a political terrorist fighting for Palestinian, or Kurd, or Basque national independence refer to supreme emergency as justifying her attacking recipients non-deserving of violent interference, in the same way that Walzer justifies British area bombing of German cities during World War II? (That is, at least for the period 1940-

42 – after that period there was no imminent danger to Britain and hence no supreme emergency, according to Walzer.)[12]

Now, as it stands I believe Walzer's idea of supreme emergency is incomplete. It is, for instance, difficult to see that the area bombing of German civilians had any effect on Britain's supreme emergency during the early years of World War II. It might have contributed to boosting British morale by showing that the Germans were not invulnerable to British attacks. But it does not seem to have made much difference to the military strength of Germany, and it was after all German military strength that caused Britain to face a supreme emergency in the first place. And the fact that the area bombings were directed at targets and people that were not causally related to Britain's supreme emergency seems to deprive the bombings of their moral justification. Hence, we should qualify Walzer's idea of a justified response to a supreme emergency, adding the requirement that the response should be directed against those enemy structures that constitute the sufficient conditions of the supreme emergency in question. Due to the character of the supreme emergency situation we may allow the use of weapons and tactics that may risk the lives of recipients non-deserving of violent interference as a side effect of our attack on military installations, but we should never allow that these recipients are made deliberate targets of our response.

Moreover, as Daniel Statman has pointed out in his criticism of the "no-choice argument", "the fact that I have no other option to achieve my goal but to use means M does not entail that means M is morally justified".[13] For instance, it might be true that my only chance of survival is to kill another person and have his heart implanted in my body. Still, this does not imply that I would be morally justified in killing that person.

Returning to the case of the contemporary nationalist political terrorist, she may perhaps be able to prove that her national group is subjected to discrimination and harassment, but this does not constitute a supreme emergency. And when the conditions of a supreme emergency indeed are satisfied for a national, or ethnic, or religious group that does not have a state of its own (as they were in the cases of the Armenians during World War I and the Jews during World War II), the group in question often lacks the capacity to defend itself with any means, terrorist or non-terrorist. Today, as far as I can see, none of the national movements or governments that carry out or order the carrying out of acts of political terrorism for the sake of having or maintaining an independent national state can justify their actions by referring to a supreme emergency. (That a *terrorist group* or a *terrorist government* may face immediate destruction does not imply that the *nation* they claim to represent is in the same predicament; hence it does not constitute a supreme emergency in the required sense.)

Moreover, *should* a political terrorist be right about her nation facing a supreme emergency she would still not be justified in deliberately directing her violence against recipients non-deserving of violent interference. According to the above argument, she may be justified in attacking a military post, even if that brings with it an obvious risk that innocent people will be killed *as a side effect*. But this is very far from justifying the placing of bombs on buses and in market places, actions which deliberately target recipients non-deserving of violent interference.

It is also important to note that the goals of having or maintaining an independent national state of one's own does not by itself justify *any* act of political terrorism. On the contrary, acts of political terrorism may *deprive* a national project of its moral justification. States can be *instrumentally* justified only to the extent that they protect the human and civic rights of its citizens, while respecting these same rights of the citizens of other states. However, a state that denies its own citizens their rights to life, physical integrity, and political freedom is nothing but a tyranny, and a state that attacks or support attacks against other states and their citizens is nothing but a menace to a civilized world order, and in both cases these states may justifiedly be interfered with by various international rights-protecting agencies and alliances.

Now when agents of a national group that does not yet have a state of its own commit acts of political terrorism against recipients non-deserving of violent interference, not as a response to a supreme emergency, but simply to achieve national independence, they also send a message to the rest of the world that theirs will be a state that is likely to be disrespectful of the rights of individuals. That they care little for the lives of people they think of as foreigners and enemies simply in virtue of their ethnic background or national identity, have already been shown. But the prospect for the human and civic rights of their own people is not very bright either, especially if their future leaders will be persons who have made it a habit to endorse terrorist strategies against recipients non-deserving of violent interference.

As members of the world community, we must ask ourselves why we should contribute to the creation of yet another morally flawed state, built on a politics of despotism and hatred? It should not suffice for leaders of nationalist movements to show that independence is indeed wanted by their people. We must also consider what the effects will be with regard to human rights if we help them realize a state of their own, the politics of which is likely to be inspired by the methods of terrorism. (I believe this has relevance for the question of whether support should be given to the forming of a Palestinian state. A reasonable condition for such a support should be an unconditional ending of all Palestinian terrorist attacks on Jewish civilians in Israel as well as in the rest of the world.)

The moral criticism of political terrorists attacking recipients non-deserving of violent interference has an obvious relevance also for those states and agencies that employ military means to combat terrorism. To the extent that they do not want themselves to be regarded as perpetrators of unjustified acts of political terrorism, they must refrain from indiscriminately killing, maiming, or incarcerating people who are unrelated to the terrorist activities that they are trying to put an end to.

(Douglas Lackey notes, for instance, that if it is true that the American bombing of Libya in 1986 had as one of its targets Colonel Qaddafi's tent, and that it hence was no accident that an adopted daughter of his was killed in the attack, then "the American attack, directed at civilians for political purposes, must be considered an act of terrorism".)[14]

Now the moral restriction placed on anti-terrorist operations applies to means as well as to ends. It does not suffice to declare that one intends to strike only against known terrorist bases. It is also necessary that the manner in which these operations are carried out should be sensitive to whether there is a risk of sacrificing the lives of recipients non-deserving of violent interference. For instance, dropping bombs on a terrorist base situated within a densely populated village makes it more likely than not that there will be innocent victims. And here we cannot invoke the idea of a supreme emergency, since terrorist groups usually are not able to confront us with the immediate massacre or enslavement of a whole nation. However, anti-terrorist agencies aiming for efficiency rather than discrimination may look for support in *the principle of double effect*.

This principle states that an unintended but foreseen morally bad effect of an action can be excused, if the action itself as well as its intended effect are morally permissible. The typical case would be an action of self-defence, having both the permissible effect of warding off a wrongful assault on the agent's life, and the morally bad effect of killing the aggressor. Given that the agent only intended the former effect, the second effect can be excused morally, although the agent may have been aware that the aggressor's death would be a likely outcome of her act of self-defence. (For instance, the agent's only means of defending her life against the aggressor might have been to throw a heavy stone at his head.)

Now, it has been pointed out that the focus on the agent's intentions makes the principle of double effect too malleable in the hands of an unscrupulous agent. Robert Holmes notes, for instance, that this principle "lends itself to the justification of virtually any action its user wants. On the assumption that we can 'direct' or 'aim' intentions as we please, any action whatever can be performed with a good intention or, at any rate, can be described as being performed with a good intention ... This is as true of pillage, rape, and torture as of killing."[15]

Clearly, there is a risk that anti-terrorist agencies will put all innocent victims of their operations down as unintended casualties in a justified war against terrorism. This suggests that the principle of double effect should be modified in a way that extends the agent's responsibility for her recipients. One such modification has been proposed by Michael Walzer, who has argued that soldiers in action should not only *not intend to kill* non-combatants, but also *intend to protect* them from being killed, even if that means risking the lives of the soldiers themselves.[16]

Accepting Walzer's modified version of the principle of double effect implies that anti-terrorist agencies must accept greater risks for their own personnel for the sake of minimizing the risks for those of their recipients that are non-deserving of violent interference. In practice this would mean operations on the ground and face-to-face encounters with the terrorist enemy rather than the use of bomber planes that may be safe from terrorist fire, but which cannot discriminate between terrorists and non-terrorists as they drop their bombs from high altitudes. It also means that operations against terrorist bases must be preceded by a careful collecting and studying of intelligence in order to make it possible to distinguish those targets that are legitimate from those that are not.

Still, even the most carefully planned anti-terrorist operations may have innocent victims. But to the extent that the anti-terrorist agencies have actively tried to *minimize* these innocent casualties, and to the extent that the political terrorists that they are fighting are, on the contrary, committed to a strategy that is *indifferent* to the rights of recipients non-deserving of violent interference, the anti-terrorist agencies cannot be depicted as belonging to the same moral category as the terrorists. In a confrontation of this kind, I would like to suggest that the political terrorists should be held morally responsible also for the killing of those innocent people that occurs as a practically unavoidable side effect of a justified anti-terrorist operation. After all, had it not been for the indiscriminate acts of the terrorists there would have been no moral need for an anti-terrorist operation in the first place, and hence the terrorists are morally responsible for there being a situation in which further innocent people may be killed as an unintended effect of the anti-terrorist operation.

When I say that there is a "moral need" for an anti-terrorist operation against terrorists who sacrifice the rights of recipients non-deserving of violent interference, I mean that the anti-terrorist operation is not only morally justified but also *morally necessary*. This is so for the same reason that it is morally necessary that the police force of any country rounds up and brings to justice murderers and robbers within its jurisdiction. Not to do so would be tantamount to accepting that some people may violate their recipients' most basic rights and get away with it. And this would clearly deprive any state of its moral justification, as this justification depends on the instrumental role of the state in protecting the moral rights, especially the most basic rights, of its citizens. Hence, it is morally unacceptable that political terrorists should be allowed to kill recipients non-deserving of violent interference. Hence, anti-terrorist agencies are not only morally justified but morally obliged to use the force that is necessary to put an end to the activities of these terrorists. However, it cannot be too strongly emphasized that it is also morally necessary that anti-terrorist operations are carried out in a manner consistent with the modified version of the principle of double effect above, and that the burdens of risk that are involved should be shouldered by the anti-terrorist forces rather than by recipients non-deserving of violent interference.

To sum up the discussion of political terrorism and the rules of just war, we have found that while the rule of non-combatant immunity does not rule out all acts of political terrorism, it does rule out terrorist acts directed against recipients non-deserving of violent interference. This conclusion will hold on deontological as well as on consequentialist grounds. It has also been argued that the political terrorist's responsibilities to her victim cannot be overridden or set aside by reasons that refer to what *other* agents do to *their* recipients. As for the argument from supreme emergency, it was concluded that it seems to have little practical relevance, whether we speak of contemporary nationalist terrorists fighting against a state government, or anti-terrorist agencies or alliances fighting against terrorist organizations. Finally, anti-terrorist agencies are morally required to respect the right to physical integrity of recipients non-deserving of violent interference, and the content of that right limits the ways in which it is possible to invoke the principle of double effect to justify killing innocent persons while fighting political terrorists.

NOTES

[1] This is a slightly modified version of the definition proposed in Bauhn (1989), pp. 28-49.
[2] Norman (1995), pp. 159-160.
[3] Norman (1995), pp. 166-167; Holmes (1989), p. 186.

[4] Fotion & Elfstrom (1986), pp. 222-223.
[5] Coates (1997), pp. 123-145.
[6] Gewirth (1978), pp. 78-82, 109-112, 134-140.
[7] Gewirth (1982), pp. 229-231.
[8] Hare (1981), p. 164.
[9] Quoted in Schmid & Jongman (1988), p. 86.
[10] Walzer (2000), p. 21.
[11] Walzer (2000), pp. 251-255.
[12] Walzer (2000), p. 261.
[13] Statman (1997), p. 141.
[14] Lackey (1989), p. 91.
[15] Holmes (1989), p. 199.
[16] Walzer (2000), pp. 155-156.

REFERENCES

Bauhn, Per (1989), *Ethical Aspects of Political Terrorism*, Lund University Press.
Coates, A. J. (1997), *The Ethics of War*, Manchester University Press.
Fotion, Nicholas & Elfstrom, Gerard (1986), *Military Ethics*, Routledge & Kegan Paul.
Gewirth, Alan (1978), *Reason and Morality*, The University of Chicago Press.
Gewirth, Alan (1982), *Human Rights*, The University of Chicago Press.
Hare, Richard (1981), *Moral Thinking*, Oxford University Press.
Holmes, Robert (1989), *On War and Morality*, Princeton University Press.
Lackey, Douglas P. (1989), *The Ethics of War and Peace*, Prentice Hall.
Norman, Richard (1995), *Ethics, Killing and War*, Cambridge University Press.
Schmid, Alex P. & Jongman, Albert A. (1988), *Political Terrorism. A New Guide to Actors, Authors, Concepts, Data Bases, Theories and Literature*, North-Holland.
Statman, Daniel (1997), "*Jus in Bello* and the Intifada", in: Kapitan, Tomis (ed.), *Philosophical Perspectives on the Israeli – Palestinian Conflict*, pp. 133-156, M. E. Sharpe.
Walzer, Michael (2000) *Just and Unjust Wars*, Basic Books.

C. A. J. (TONY) COADY

TERRORISM, JUST WAR AND RIGHT RESPONSE

WHAT IS TERRORISM?

There are three important questions about terrorism that require philosophical attention. These concern the nature of terrorism, the kind of wrong involved in it, and the right way to respond to it. In what follows I shall discuss each of these in turn.[1]

Although some theorists are dismissive of attempts at defining terrorism, it seems to me that a well-grounded definition can help us avoid much of the confusion that surrounds discussion of the topic. After all, stating clearly what you take the subject of discussion to be should avoid the sort of talking at cross-purposes that is all too common in heated public debate about terrorism. The slogan "One man's terrorist is another's freedom fighter" is deeply misleading if it suggests that nothing substantive is at issue in debates about terrorism, or if it gestures at some sort of moral relativism, but it is accurate enough as a description of the confused points of view that disputants often bring to the debate. The confusion is of course partly a product of the polemical context in which the term "terrorism" is employed, and we should not expect to be able to isolate "the" meaning of terrorism in a way that decisively captures what anyone must mean who uses the term. Some degree of conceptual regimentation is bound to be involved, but a useful definition should fulfil two criteria: it should capture central common elements in a wide range of usages of the expression, and it should help advance moral and political discussion of the topic. Of course, the mere statement of a definition is not likely to advance matters unless the definition is clear, thoroughly defended and understood by one's fellow discussants. Often enough, vague definitions are simply declared and nothing is done to relate them to other ways of thinking about the topic. It is estimated that there are more than 100 different definitions in the scholarly literature, but many give the impression of being sloppy or cobbled together to advance a particular political interest.[2] Brian Jenkins, for instance, defines terrorism as "the use or threatened use of force designed to bring about political change".[3] This has the consequence that all forms of war are terrorist which surely collapses far too many important distinctions. Other definitions rely heavily upon the idea that terrorism is an illegitimate or unlawful use of force or violence, but the fact that terrorist acts are against some domestic law is too superficial a fact to be given such prominence, as can be seen by reflecting that armed internal resistance to Hitler by the victims of his brutal regime would certainly have been against German law, but, for all that, would arguably have been morally justified and not necessarily terrorist. The adjective "illegitimate" may fare better, but it suffers from two problems. In the present context, it is too vague because we need to know what it is about terrorism that makes it illegitimate, and, in any case, a definition of

G. Meggle (ed.), Ethics of Terrorism & Counter-Terrorism, 135-149.

terrorism should at least leave some room for further debate about when, if ever, terrorism can be justified. It is a reasonable presumption, if possibly a rebuttable one in some circumstances, that issues of justification should not be settled by definition.

Rather than further reviewing the varieties of definition, I propose to concentrate on one focal element in common responses to and fears about terrorism, namely the idea that it involves 'innocent' victims. This element features in many of the definitions in the scholarly and popular literature though often mixed with other materials. It was recently overtly invoked by Yasser Arafat's condemnation of terrorism when he said:

> "... no degree of oppression and no level of desperation can ever justify the killing of innocent civilians. I condemn terrorism, I condemn the killing of innocent civilians, whether they are Israeli, American or Palestinian."[4]

I cite Arafat with no interest in endorsing or rejecting his sincerity. His view is important as one articulated by someone involved in a violent struggle and who is often accused of supporting terrorism and often accuses others of using it. These facts suggest that his implicit equation of terrorism with the killing of civilians has a strong connection with common instincts about what is at issue in talk of terrorism. These instincts were also very much in evidence after the September 11 attacks on New York when the innocence of the civilians in the planes and in the buildings were prominent in discussions of these terrorist acts. But in addition to yielding a reasonable match to ordinary discourse, the emphasis on the killing of innocent civilians provides a useful point of connection with the moral apparatus of just war theory, specifically the principle of discrimination and its requirement of non-combatant immunity. Of course, terrorism does not always take place in the context of all-out international war, but there are other forms of war than that, for example, civil wars and wars of secession, and terrorism usually has a war-like dimension. There is much that is misleading and much that is metaphorical about the expression 'war against terrorism' but it is not surprising that it is invoked with some literal meaning in talk of responding to the political violence of terrorist attacks. I shall say more of this later, but I will for now take the connection of terrorism with a form of war as initially plausible. I will define terrorism as follows: 'the organised use of violence to attack non-combatants ('innocents' in a special sense) or their property for political purposes.'

This definition has several contentious consequences. One is that states can themselves use terrorism, another is that much political violence by non-state agents will not be terrorist. As to the former, there is a tendency, especially amongst the representatives of states, to restrict the possibility of terrorist acts to non-state agents. But if we think of terrorism, in the light of the definition above, as a tactic rather than an ideology, this tendency should be resisted since states can and do use the tactic of attacking the innocent. This is why allegations of terrorism against Israeli government forces in parts of Palestine during the current anti-terrorist campaign make perfect sense even if the truth of the claims is disputed.

Some theorists who think terrorism cannot be perpetrated by governments are operating with a definition that differs markedly from the tactical definition. They define terrorism as the use of political violence by non-state agents against the state or its agents. Some would restrict it to violence against a democratic state. This is the way many political scientists view terrorism. Call this the political status definition to contrast with the tactical definition.

Those in the grip of the political status definition tend to think that terrorism is wrong because all political violence directed against the state or its agents is wrong. On my definition, this remains an open question, as indeed does the morality of terrorism, but the fact that the tactical definition is narrower than the political one leaves room for the possibility that terrorism is morally wrong (as a violent tactic) whereas other forms of political violence may be morally permissible. And this is surely a more plausible beginning to philosophical and ethical debate about these matters, since, for example, the possibility of a morally justifiable revolution should not be excluded from the beginning. Indeed, my own view, as elaborated below, is that terrorism, as I define it, is morally objectionable although a violent revolution may not be. I should stress that I am no enthusiast for violent revolution since I think that the vast majority of violent revolutions, like the vast majority of interstate wars, have been morally and politically disastrous. Nonetheless, it is arguable that some violent revolutions have been legitimate and that there are imaginable circumstances in which others might be. Moreover, full-scale revolution is not the only possible use of political violence against the state. Where there is no other option, a group may surely defend itself against a tyrannical government agency bent upon its physical destruction even though the group has no interest in wholesale revolution. In all these contexts, the question of whether the group's behaviour is terrorist is a question of what violent tactics they employ, not a question of whether they resort to violence at all. And this distinction is indeed recognised by many revolutionary groups, even if they do not honour it in their practice. The Cypriot revolutionary, General George Grivas, showed his sensitivity to the distinction in his memoirs when he wrote of the EOKA campaign:

> "We did not strike, like the bomber, at random. We shot only British servicemen who would have killed us if they could have fired first, and civilians who were traitors or intelligence agents."[5]

Whether Grivas truly described EOKA practice is less important for our discussion than his acknowledgment of the possibility and desirability of directing revolutionary violence at morally legitimate targets.

A further consequence of the tactical definition is that it implies a degree of purposiveness that terrorism is thought to lack. Some theorists have claimed that terrorism is essentially 'indiscriminate' or 'random', others that it is essentially 'expressive'. In both cases, the suggestion is that a reference to political purposes is inappropriate. In reply, it can be argued that talk of terrorism as random is generated by the genuine perception that it does not restrict its targets to the obvious military ones, but this does not mean that it is wild and purposeless. Similarly with the epithet 'indiscriminate' which is consistent with the tactical definition if it indicates a disregard for the principle of discrimination, but is quite misleading if it suggests that terrorists give no thought to the political impact of their attacks. Indeed, most terrorists think that the best way to get certain political effects is to aim at 'soft' non-

137

combatant targets. Similarly, there can be no doubt that many terrorist attacks are expressive and symbolic, involving the affirmation of the attitude: 'We are still here; take notice of us.' Yet the expressive need not exclude the purposive. You can warn someone by an utterance that also expresses horror as when shouting "Fire!" So terrorist acts can be, and usually are, both expressive and politically purposive. It is a further question whether these purposes are particularly realistic. The idea that terrorist acts are merely expressive is partly sustained by the belief that when viewed as purposive the acts are basically futile. The futility is often real enough, but purposive acts abound that are in fact futile. There is also the problem that has become prominent in recent discussions of extremist Islamic terrorism that the terrorist political agenda may be so vast and fantastic as to make the term "political" seem inappropriate. This is a point that I will pursue in the last section of the chapter. Note again that I am not *defining* terrorism as immoral: it needs discussion and some background moral theory to show that it is immoral.

THE JUST WAR BACKGROUND

The just war tradition provides much of that background. Its development has been strongly influenced by Catholic philosophers and theologians in the West, but also by people of quite different commitments, such as Aristotle, Grotius, Locke, and in modern times Michael Walzer. There are also parallel lines of thought in the ancient Chinese and Hindu philosophical traditions. This is not surprising, because, unless one takes the view that war is entirely beyond moral concern or that it is simply ruled out by morality, then one has to give some account of what can morally justify it. Just war theories constitute a major line of response to this need; another is provided by utilitarian thinking and another by the so-called realist tradition. In the just war tradition, this account has two key divisions – the Jus ad bellum and the Jus in bello. The former (which I'll abbreviate as the JAB) tells us the conditions under which it can be right to resort to war; it includes such conditions as just cause, the need for legitimate authority, and the requirements of last resort and reasonable prospect of success. The latter (which I'll call the JIB) is concerned to guide us in the permissible methods by which we should wage a legitimate war. It includes conditions relevant to determining legitimate targets and tactics during war and it puts limits on the degree of violence to be deployed even in a just war. The JIB is of primary interest here because it is directly relevant to the moral assessment of terrorism as defined by the tactical definition.

Under the JIB, there are basically two governing principles:

1. The Principle of Discrimination. This limits the kind of kind of violence that can be used, principally by placing restrictions on what count as legitimate targets.

2. The Principle of Proportionality. This limits the degree of response by requiring that the violent methods used do not inflict more damage than the original offence could require.

The conditions specified by the JAB and JIB raise many philosophical and practical problems but they also have a direct intuitive and ethical appeal. I shall concentrate on the Principle of Discrimination since it is the principle most relevant to my approach to terrorism. As my colleague Janna Thompson has noted elsewhere in developing Coates's comments on terrorism, the approach embodied in what I have called "the political status definition" could also connect with just war theory through a particular interpretation of the requirement of legitimate authority. Coates wants to define terrorism in terms of the resort to political violence without the possession of "legitimate authority". This makes it difficult for him to treat revolutionary violence as anything but terrorist since the primary paradigm of "legitimate authority" is a certain sort of state authority. In this he echoes a significant strand in medieval thinking on the just war which is hostile to "private" war. But he recoils from adopting a "political status" definition that would make all revolutionary violence terrorist. Even so, defining terrorism in terms of the resort to political violence without "legitimate authority" surely stacks the odds too greatly against the possibility of a justified revolution. Coates wants to allow that just war thinking can apply to revolutions, and that, as applied, there can be a just revolution, but he has great difficulty specifying a sense of "legitimate authority" that can apply to units other than states. He is justifiably sceptical of romantic attitudes to revolutionary violence, but his approach to terrorism takes him too close to the problems of the political status definition. In any case, if terrorism is defined in terms of the lack of 'legitimate authority' alone, then those revolutions that do have legitimate authority cannot, by definition, employ terrorism. This is both counter-intuitive and theoretically unsatisfactory. For we surely want to leave room for discussing the question whether a properly authorised revolution is nonetheless using terrorist tactics.[6]

Against any connection with the JIB and the thought that there should be moral restrictions on the conduct of war, there is a certain tough-minded reaction that expresses itself in the demand that you should do whatever needs to be done to win. But here, as elsewhere, the tough-minded are often unrealistic. The unrealism comes out in the way this stance ignores so many common human responses to war, in particular, the horror at and rejection of atrocities. This rejection registers something significant about the way morality continues to exert force even in the most extreme of circumstances, for the most evil of regimes continues to insist in wartime that it avoids certain activities even when it engages in them. This is part of the tribute that vice pays to virtue, and in its very hypocrisy this tribute acknowledges something deep in human responses. Even that very tough warrior, the US war ace General Chuck Yeager writes in his memoirs that he suffered genuine moral revulsion at orders to commit 'atrocities' that he was given and complied with in World War II. He was especially 'not proud' of his part in the indiscriminate strafing of a 50-mile square area of Germany that included mainly non-combatants.[7]

It is also unrealistic to dismiss without argument the long tradition of just war thinking and related utilitarian forms of thinking that set limits to the conduct of war. A further lack of reality can be seen in the way the tough-minded reaction, even as it purports to be pragmatic, ignores the pragmatic consequences of the ruthless pursuit of victory. For where both sides of a conflict acknowledge no moral constraints on the pursuit of victory, the likely upshot is a sort of mayhem that suits no one's longer term interests. The situation in war generally is like that applicable to the detention and interrogation of prisoners of war. The pragmatic and moral costs of ignoring the relevant moral restraints on obtaining information from helpless prisoners have been dramatically illustrated by events in the Abu Ghraib prison in Iraq.

The principle of discrimination offers one important elucidation of moral constraints on the conduct of war by insisting that the right to go to war conveys no right to employ any means of attack or defence that you regard as effective. Just as, in the case of individual conflict, the right to defend yourself against an attacker does not license you to direct violence against an innocent bystander whose death may distract your attacker, so, in collective self-defence or other legitimate resort to violence, there are restrictions on whom may be targeted and attacked. A major part of the discrimination principle concerns the immunity of non-combatants from direct attack. This is a key point at which utilitarian approaches to the justification of war tend to clash with the classical just war tradition. Either they deny that the principle obtains at all, or, more commonly, they argue that it applies in virtue of its convenience. The former move is associated with the idea that war is such 'hell' and victory so important that everything must be subordinated to that end, but even in utilitarian terms it is unclear that this form of ruthlessness has the best outcomes, especially when it is shared by the opposing sides. Hence, the more common move is to argue that the immunity of non-combatants is a useful rule for restricting the damage wrought by wars. Non-utilitarians (I shall call them 'intrinsicalists' because they believe that there are intrinsic wrongs, other than failing to maximise good outcomes) can agree that there are such extrinsic reasons for the immunity rule, but they will see this fact as a significant additional reason to conform to the principle. Moreover, they will hold that the principle remains valid even where such extrinsic reasons might somehow fail to gain a grip. Intrinsicalists will argue that the principle's validity springs directly from the reasoning that licenses resort to war in the first place. This resort is allowed by the need to resist perpetrators of aggression (or, on a broader view, to deal with wrongdoers) and hence it licenses violence only against those who are agents of the aggression.

This prohibition on attacking the non-perpetrators (non-combatants or the innocent as they are often called) has been a consistent theme in the just war tradition. So John Locke says in Chapter XV of his *Second Treatise of Civil Government* that a conqueror with a just cause "gets no power" over those amongst the enemy populace who are innocent of waging the war. Locke's emphasis on the importance of defending the innocent and preserving innocent life is pronounced. It is perfectly clear that legitimate violence should be directed against perpetrators (whom he characterises as "beasts of prey" like the lion or the wolf) and not those who have no part in the offence. So when he says in Chapter XV, that a conqueror with a just cause "gets no power" over innocent people in the enemy country, he goes on to explain their immunity as follows:

> "they ought not to charged as guilty of the violence and injustice that is committed in an unjust war any farther than they actually abet it."[8]

Locke is actually discussing the post-war entitlements of a conqueror rather than the limits on how he wages the war, but his comments apply naturally to the latter and are clearly in the tradition of just war thinking. This licenses violence only against those perpetrating the injustice that makes the war legitimate in the first place. As Vitoria, in similar spirit to Locke, had earlier put it:

> "... the foundation of the just war is the injury inflicted upon one by the enemy, as shown above; but an innocent person has done you no harm."[9]

NON-COMBATANTS AND IMMUNITY

It is nonetheless understandable that various questions have been raised about the making of the combatant/non-combatant distinction in the context of modern war.[10] The first point of clarification is that when we classify people as non-combatants or innocents we do not mean that they have no evil in their hearts, nor do we mean that combatants are necessarily full of evil thoughts. The classification is concerned with the role the individual plays in the chain of agency directing the aggression or wrongdoing. And it is agency, not mere cause, that is important since the soldier's aged parents may be part of the causal chain that results in his being available to fight without their having any agent responsibility for what he is doing. The combatant may be coerced to fight, but he or she is still prosecuting the war, even if the greater blame lies with those who coerce. On the other hand, the young schoolchild may be enthusiastic about her country's war, but is not prosecuting it. Neither is the farmer whose products feed the troops, for he would feed them (if they'd buy) whatever their role. It should be added that the combatant/non-combatant distinction is not equivalent to the soldier/civilian distinction even though they overlap considerably. Some civilians, such as political leaders and senior public servants, will be legitimate targets if they are actively directing or promoting unjust violence whether or not they wear uniforms or bear arms.

But even when these distinctions are made there seems room not only for doubt about the application of the distinction to various difficult categories of person such as slave labourers coerced to work in munitions factories, but also its applicability at all to the highly integrated citizenry of modern states. Some people say that it is surely anachronistic to think of contemporary war as waged between armies; it is really nation against nation, economy against economy, peoples against peoples. But although modern war has many unusual features, its 'total' nature is more an imposed construction than a necessary reflection of changed reality. Even in World War II not every enemy citizen was a combatant. In any war, there remain millions of people who are not plausibly seen as involved in the enemy's lethal chain of agency. There are, for instance, infants, young children, the elderly and infirm, lots of tradespeople and workers, not to mention dissidents and conscientious objectors. This challenge to the distinction requires there to be no serious moral difference between shooting a soldier who is shooting at you and gunning down a defenceless child who is a member of the same nation as the soldier. The conclusion is perhaps sufficiently absurd or obscene to discredit the argument.

In fact there has been a remarkable change on this issue in the strategic doctrine and military outlook of many major powers since the end of the Cold War. It is now common to pay at least lip service to the principle, as evidenced by certain restraint shown or announced during the Gulf War, and the bombing of Serbia, and by the widespread condemnation of Russian brutality in Chechnya. The rhetoric, at least, of the recent US-led wars in Afghanistan and Iraq is also respectful of the distinction. The real question is not so much whether it is immoral to target non-combatants (it is), but how 'collateral' damage and death to non-combatants can be defended. This was always a problem in just war theory, often solved by resort to some form of the principle of double effect. This allowed for the harming of non-combatants in some circumstances as a foreseen but unintended side-effect of an otherwise legitimate act of war. The 'circumstances' included the proportionality of the side-effect to the intended outcome. Not everyone agrees with the principle but the conduct of war in contemporary circumstances is morally impossible unless the activities of warriors are allowed to put non-combatants at grave risk in certain circumstances. Some modification to the immunity principle to allow indirect harming seems to be in line with common sense morality in other areas of life, and to be necessitated by the circumstances of war. If it is not available then pacifism, as Holmes has argued seems the only moral option.[11]

On the other hand, the double effect principle (or some surrogate) is dangerously open to abuse, to what the philosopher Elizabeth Anscombe once called "double-think about double effect".[12] One form of this abuse is a tendency to ignore the proportionality requirement built into the principle, so that in wiping out a whole village of mostly innocent people one can plead that the target was really the one terrorist in the place and the death of the other 400 was merely "collateral damage". The concept of intention tends to collapse under this sort of weight; it's as if someone saw a fly on the head of bald man, grabbed a sledgehammer, killed the fly but smashed the man's head open, then declared his death to be an unintended side-effect of a legitimate action. After all, you're not in favour of flies are you? Another problem is the tendency of the double-effect principle to desensitise military and political agents to the death and suffering of innocents. The thought can easily be insinuated that because we are entitled sometimes to put innocent people at risk of death and injury then we can simply shrug off the deaths and maimings that we cause. To many, the phrase "collateral damage" has just this flavour of indifference. Yet indifference to the killing of the innocent (even where it is not intended) displays a failure to appreciate the value and dignity of innocent human life. It is inconsistent with that regard for the dignity of individual human life that is so central to Kant's ethics and indeed to much in the mainstream religious traditions of human kind. Any proposal to inflict "collateral damage" needs to bear in mind the accelerating rate of non-combatant casualties in the wars of the last century. According to one source, the ratio of soldiers to civilian casualties shifted in the course of the 20th century from 9 to 1 to 1 to 9.[13] Much of this resulted from the direct targeting of civilians, but "collateral damage" has certainly played its part.

The tactical definition of terrorism faces the problems already discussed concerning the meaning of the term 'non-combatant', but even more acutely. In guerrilla war, for instance, insurgents may not be easily identifiable as combatants and will seek to enlist or involve the villagers and local inhabitants in the campaign thereby blurring their status as non-combatants. On the other hand, many state officials who are not directly prosecuting the campaign against the insurgents may be plausibly viewed as implicated in the grievances the revolutionaries are seeking to redress. There are certainly problems here, but they do not seem insurmountable. In the heat and confusion of battle, it may be difficult and dangerous to treat even children as non-combatants, especially where children are coerced or seduced into combatant roles (as is common in many contemporary conflicts). Nonetheless, a premeditated campaign of bombing regional hospitals to induce civilian lack of co-operation with rebels is in palpable violation of the JIB. So are the murder of infants, and the targeting of state officials, such as water authorities or traffic police, whose roles are usually tangentially related to the causes of the conflict. It is true that some ideologies purport to have enemies so comprehensive as to make even small children and helpless adults into 'combatants'. Western advocates of strategic bombing of cities in the name of 'total war' share with the Islamic fanatics who incorporate American air travellers and sundry citizens of Manhattan into their holy targets a simplistic and Manichaean vision of the world. This vision is at odds with the just war tradition's attempt to bring some moral sanity to bear upon the resort to political violence.

MORAL JUDGEMENT

Asking the question whether terrorism is wrong may seem superfluous in light of the widespread condemnation it usually receives, and I have no wish to offer a moral defence of terrorism. Nonetheless, I have argued that the tactical definition does not make it wrong by definition and we have reviewed a moral background precisely in order to form a reasoned moral assessment of it. Is terrorism wrong? Given just war theory and the tactical definition, the answer is clearly yes. And if one takes the principle of non-combatant immunity to invoke an absolute moral prohibition, as just war thinkers have commonly done, then it is always wrong. Yet many contemporary moral philosophers, sympathetic to just war thinking, are wary of moral absolutes. They would treat the prohibition as expressing a very strong moral presumption against terrorism and the targeting of non-combatants, but allow for exceptions in extreme circumstances. So, Michael Walzer thinks that in conditions of 'supreme emergency' the violation of the normal immunity is permissible in warfare though the violation still constitutes a wrong that imposes a heavy burden of remorse. He thinks the Allied terror bombing of German cities in World War II (in the early stages) was legitimated by the enormity of the Nazi threat. John Rawls has recently endorsed this view while, like Walzer, condemning the bombings of Hiroshima and Nagasaki.[14]

I have examined the supreme emergency exemption in more detail elsewhere. Here I shall merely point out several of its implications. The first is that it is not equivalent to a simple utilitarian attitude to morality. This would always allow exceptions to moral rules since it views all of them as merely "rules of thumb". By contrast, the doctrine of "supreme emergency" is propounded by those who reject utilitarianism but insist on the depth of such prohibitions as that on the intentional killing of the innocent. Even so, they believe that in emergency situations the prohibitions may, with a heavy heart, be ignored. For these thinkers, there is a sense in which the exemption means that the agent has still done wrong, but a necessary wrong. Here, it may be helpful to explore briefly the similarities and differences with the rejection of absolutism about the wrong of lying. Famously, theorists like St. Augustine and Immanuel Kant held that the wrong of lying was so deep that no circumstances at all could justify it. But critics have countered by claiming that there are surely circumstances in which refusing to lie would itself be morally wrong. Suppose the only way of concealing an innocent fugitive from pursuers bent on her torture and death involves lying to her pursuers (as might well have been the case in the Rwanda conflict), then it seems obvious this would be the right thing to do. The critic's voice here is not necessarily that of a utilitarian since a non-utilitarian might stress that a duty to rescue or to protect the innocent is overriding in the circumstances. Absolutists have often responded with ingenious suggestions about ways of frustrating the pursuers without lying to them, but sometimes there are no such plausible paths, and, in any case, the lying route may be easily the more effective.[15] It seems to me clear that the critics have the best of this debate: absolutism about lying is mistaken. But the parallel with the prohibition on killing the innocent is remote. With all due respect to Augustine and Kant, the two prohibitions are not in the same class. This is clear from the fact that the necessity to lie to the violent Hutu or Nazi pursuer should leave no trace of remorse or conviction that one has done wrong, where, at the very least, the necessary murder (as its "supreme emergency" defenders insist) does. Moreover, the case for legitimate lying exists not only at the gravely serious end of the spectrum of circumstances, but at the trivial end also. Certain jokes or benign arrangements may require the momentary deception of the audience in contexts that make the absolutist position appear simply fanatical. There is no parallel here to the prohibition on killing the innocent.

Second, the emphasis of writers like Walzer and Rawls is on the need for the occasional relaxation of the moral constraint in the case of states faced with supreme emergency, but it is hard to see how they can rule out the application of this doctrine to sub-state agents as well. Walzer's view of terrorism conforms broadly to the tactical definition and, consistent with that, he treats the Allied city bombings of World War II as examples of terrorism. Yet some of them were justified by supreme emergency. This clearly implies that there may sometimes be overriding reasons to engage in terrorism even though it somehow remains morally wrong. One needs some powerful argument to show that only states may avail themselves of this reasoning. Walzer tries to supply such an argument, but I find his effort unpersuasive, as I have argued elsewhere.[16] Third, there is a serious worry about the consequences of allowing such exemptions to deep constraints on the conduct of war or other forms of political violence. After all, the principles of the just war are supposed to provide public guidance to all participants in violent conflict, and, although they are not justified merely by convention or utility, they operate in a context where it can be extremely dangerous for parties to a conflict to be able to grant themselves exemptions from the basic ground rules. The dangers concern both a temptation for the party that first breaks the rule and a temptation for the other party (or parties) to the conflict. As to the former, there is likely to be an increased tendency for the scope of resort to supreme emergency to expand under the pressure of the many exigencies of warfare. This can be seen in the continued bombing of civilian populations in World War II long after a supreme emergency story could be plausibly told. As to the latter, the resort of one party to the exemption is all too likely to encourage their enemy to similar behaviour. At the very least, any advocacy of a supreme emergency argument must take account of these effects. For these reasons, I am sceptical of the value of the supreme emergency exemption. I think it better to condemn the recourse to terrorism unconditionally whether it be urged on behalf of states, revolutionaries or religious fanatics.

MORAL RESPONSE

The problem of responding to terrorism is partly a question of effective strategy or tactics, and on this a philosopher has no particular claim to speak. But it is also a matter of morality since, once more, the urgency of the problem cannot permit morally unconstrained reactions. In what follows, I shall be principally concerned with responses by states to sub-state terrorism directed against them, though a good deal of the discussion is also relevant to the problem of responding to state terrorism. The first thing to say about the moral legitimacy of responses to terrorism is that the use of terrorism to combat terrorism should be ruled out. It is both immoral and very often ineffective. One reason for the ineffectiveness is that meeting terror with terror tends to lend an air of legitimacy to the original outrage. It also creates resentment amongst those who survive the terrorist response and this is likely to breed widespread sympathy for the enemy terrorists where it might not otherwise have existed. Even actions that fall short of terrorism, but show a lack of concern for the safety of non-combatants, are likely to create this reaction. As mentioned earlier, a casual or indifferent attitude to "collateral damage" to non-combatants is immoral and can exhibit a spirit close to that of terrorism. The resentment and the reactive sympathy generated by counter-terrorist campaigns that are themselves terrorist (or akin to terrorist) are clearly illustrated in certain aspects of state responses to terrorism in Israel, Chechnya and Iraq. The dramatic revelations about the abuse and torture of detained Iraqi suspects by American forces in Bhagdad illustrate the problem. These suspects were either innocent of any offences or possibly former combatants who were now prisoners or in some category in between, but, in any case, were close enough to non-combatants at the time to warrant immunity from the sort of violent and degrading treatment routinely given to them. The behaviour of their jailers is partly to be explained in terms of the meeting of terror with terror. It is particularly ironic that the growth of an Islamic terrorist movement that obscenely treats everyone in the world of the infidel (and many fellow Muslims with the wrong religious outlook) as legitimate targets can create a mindset in which attempts to counter the movement mimic the very obscenity of their thinking and tactics.

Second, the use of violence to capture or even kill terrorists is legitimate if it accords with the conditions of the JAB and JIB that govern the morality of resort to war. One of the crucial conditions is that of last resort. If you have means of dealing with a terrorist threat, short of the use of military might, then those means are to be preferred to widespread death and destruction. True, the idea of last resort has its mysteries since, first, there are epistemological puzzles about how we can know whether we have exhausted the list of effective alternatives to the use of violence. And, second, there are tactical problems about reducing the effectiveness of resort to military force while you search around for more peaceful alternatives, since you may be giving the wrong-doers valuable time to repel or avoid your violence when it eventually comes. Nonetheless, the condition of last resort expresses an important ethical underpinning of just war theory, and indeed, common-sense morality, namely, the moral superiority of peace over war. The condition emphasises that the resort to war must be reluctant, and reluctance is not compatible with the failure to consider realistic alternatives to widespread violence. This reluctance has hardly been evident in the increased reliance on massive military campaigning in the US reactions to the outrage of September 11 culminating in the invasion of Iraq.

Another condition, especially relevant to the present 'war against terrorism', is whether the exercise is likely to achieve success. Here it is difficult to know what success amounts to. Venting of rage or grief is hardly sufficient. Bringing the agents of terrorist attack to justice or destroying them would seem a legitimate aim, as would diminishing the future prospect of terrorist attacks. The war in Afghanistan certainly did some damage to al Queda but its main effect was to disperse rather than destroy the organisation, and much of its leadership, including Osama bin Laden, is still unaccounted for at the time of writing. Indeed, some of the leaders captured were snared not by war but by civil police in Pakistan. The Taliban government was overthrown as a side-effect, even an after-thought, of the anti-terror campaign because the United States and its allies needed Northern Alliance ground troops to fight al Queda, and the price of that was taking their side in the civil war. No-one can mourn the removal of the Taliban fanatics from power, but the consequences of their overthrow are still very uncertain in terms of Afghanistan's future and the stability of the region. Indeed, the present state of Afghanistan is not only one of disorder and tribal strife, but the Taliban is still a powerful force and al Queda's reach seems largely unaffected. Then there is Iraq. There can be little doubt that the invasion of Iraq has increased, rather than diminished the dangers of terrorism. This ill-motivated war has had a devastating effect upon the people of Iraq and has compounded many of the grievances (real and imagined) that help to underpin the Islamic terrorist cause. Saddam Hussein was a despicable secular despot, but his secularism made him an enemy of al Queda and that organisation now has more influence in Iraq than ever before. One positive side effect of the extraordinary mess in Iraq is that talk of extending the war against terrorism to those other members of the "axis of evil", North Korea and Iran is no longer heard in the corridors of Washington. The North Korean leaders are what used to be called 'godless communists' who are trying at last to forge closer links with the democratic South and even with the USA. Iran is a different case, but its gradual development into a serious democracy seems to offer more hope for the diminution of terrorism than external military attack. More generally, anti-terrorist measures to produce short-term remedies or satisfy the urge to strike out are foolish and counter-productive if they sow the seeds of greater terrorism in the longer term.

It is relevant to both the conditions of last resort and prospect of success that we need to avoid an obsession with purely military means for combating terrorism. The use of military force is very rarely sufficient to solve terrorist problems. It didn't work with the IRA and the Protestant terrorists in Northern Ireland, it didn't work with the Tamil Tigers in Sri Lanka, and it doesn't seem to be working in Israel. In certain circumstances, the military can provide useful, even necessary, support for terrorist counter-measures, but what is principally needed is a political strategy. This must include regional co-operation, adequate intelligence, focused civil policing, and careful understanding of terrorist grievances. Sometimes this understanding will yield the conviction that the grievances are fantastic, as seems to have been the case with the Baader Meinhof gang in Germany and the Red Brigades in Italy. But even this understanding can aid in forging campaigns to resist terror. Sometimes, however, the grievances are real, or partly real, and signify the suffering of injustices or at least perceived wrongs that must be attended to. Indeed, attending to them may be a precondition for defeating the terrorist campaign, and ignoring them may contribute to increasing the terrorist threat. In such circumstances, the slogan "no negotiating with terrorists" may be an impediment to progress. Even where one cannot agree with the claims of grievance, there may be enough room for compromise, adjustment and imaginative concessions to alleviate the situation and achieve a rational end to the underlying conflict. Of course, terrorists tend to be enemies of compromise, but so, quite often, do entrenched governmental interests. What is depressing about so much political violence, including international war, is the way that negotiations enter the picture after years of proclaiming them impossible. In the meantime, death and destruction are allowed to run their course. It may be replied that this approach is all very well for "ordinary" terrorists, but the al Queda terrorists have no interest whatever in compromise political settlements to such problems as the Palestine-Israel conflict. This is no doubt true, but much of the sympathy their terrorism receives in the Arabic world is sustained by continuing Western support for long-standing intransigent Israeli policies.

Finally, and more generally, massive aerial bombardments to aid the military overthrow of ugly regimes or outright wars against those regimes are likely to be politically and morally inadequate as responses to terrorism. The paradigm of state against state warfare is ill-adapted to the threat of terrorists like al Queda since such terrorists are not primarily state-based, are relatively independent of the host nations they infest, and breed on the oppression and injustice in the international order that remain unaddressed by campaigns of violence. Hence, such campaigns are always in danger of violating the proportionality requirement of the JIB, especially where, as in the case of Iraq, the state in question has little or no connection with the terrorist attacks to which the bombardment purports to be a response. The violation of this requirement would mean that the killing and maiming of thousands of "enemy" troops was gravely immoral. In addition, bombing campaigns like that in Afghanistan and during the invasion stage of the war in Iraq inevitably produce alarmingly high numbers of non-combatant casualties and damage to civilian infrastructure. Even where these are not directly intended, their scale can betray that immoral indifference to innocent life earlier remarked upon.

Dealing with terrorism will require vigilance and some changes to our free-wheeling democratic life style, but we mustn't respond to terror by abandoning those liberties and democratic rights that the murderers in New York, Washington and Bali hate so much. We should also continue to criticise those autocratic state regimes that seek to extend repressive measures against largely innocent minorities under the cloak of fighting terrorism. In the search for united action against terrorism, it will be tempting to turn a blind eye to these offences, but the temptation should be resisted. Apart from anything else, enlisting tyrants in one's camp will inevitably cloud the legitimacy of one's efforts. With the partial exception of the Carter years, the United States has a dismal record (along with many other nations) of supporting tyrannical regimes as long as they are "on our side". This was often justified by the claims that ordinary tyrants were not as bad as totalitarian tyrants and were more susceptible of liberalisation than the alternative totalitarian regimes that might take their place without outside support for the incumbent authoritarians.[17] Both arguments were based on dubious facts (and sit awkwardly with the moral loathing currently expressed towards the crimes of the non-totalitarian dictator Saddam Hussein) but, in any case, the tendency of this line of thought is to devalue the expression and significance of deep human and Western values. The Western political tradition has long struggled against arbitrary arrest and detention, extreme police powers, and despotic government. This is no time to abandon the struggle either at home or abroad. Anti-terrorist legislation in the West has already gone some way towards betraying that struggle at home, and the rise of draconian imprisonment measures, most notably at Guantanamo Bay, and the apparent official authorisation of the torture of detained suspects in Iraq takes the betrayal even further. It would be a striking victory for the terrorist cause if they managed to drive the infidel representatives of liberal modernity into abandoning their liberal heritage in order to combat its enemies.

NOTES

[1] This chapter is a much developed and altered version of an earlier paper published as "Terrorism, Just War and Supreme Emergency", in: *Terrorism and Justice: Moral Argument in a Threatened World*, eds. Tony Coady and Michael O'Keefe, Melbourne University Press, 2002.

[2] Schmid, Alex Peter, *Political Terrorism: A Research Guide to Concepts, Theories, Data Bases, and Literature*, North-Holland, Amsterdam,1983, pp. 119-58, cited in: Walter Laqueur, *The Age of Terrorism*, Boston, Little, Brown, 1987, p. 143.

[3] Terrorism Research Centre Inc., http://www.terrorism.com/terrorism/def.shtml.

[4] Yasser Arafat, 'The Palestinian Vision of Peace', *The New York Times*, 3 February 2002, p. 15.

[5] Quoted in Robert Taber, *The War of the Flea*, London: Paladin, 1972, p. 106

[6] A. J. Coates, *The Ethics of War*, Manchester University Press, Manchester, 1997, Ch. 5, pp. 123-145.

[7] Chuck Yeager, *Yeager: An Autobiography*, edited by Leo Janos, New York, Bantam, 1986, pp. 89-90.

[8] John Locke, *Second Treatise of Civil Government*, edited and introduced by J. W. Gough. Oxford, Blackwell, 1946, p. 435.

[9] Francisco De Vitoria, *Political Writings*, pp. 314-15. This emphasis is very strong in the major just war theorists, but it is easy to lose sight of it when they are discussing international law. Grotius, for instance, lists various awful things, including killing the innocent that are done by "right of war" when they can be done "with impunity". But later he "retraces" his steps to make it clear that most of these are unjust according to reason and natural law.

[10] The issues canvassed in this section are much more fully developed in C. A. J. Coady, "Terrorism and Innocence", *Journal of Ethics*, 8, 2004, pp. 37-58.

[11] See Robert Holmes, *On War and Morality*, Princeton, Princeton University Press, 1989, especially pages 193-203.

[12] G. E. M. Anscombe, "War and Murder", in: G. E. M. Anscombe, *The Collected Philosophical Papers of G. E. M. Anscombe,* Vol III, "Ethics, Religion and Politics", Basil Blackwell, Oxford, 1981, p. 58.

[13] The figures are cited in John Stremlau, *People in Peril: Human Rights, Humanitarian Action, and Preventing Deadly Conflict, A Report to the Carnegie Commission on Preventing Deadly Conflict*, Carnegie Corporation of New York, New York, 1998, p. 25.

[14] Michael Walzer, *Just and Unjust Wars: A Moral Argument with Historical Illustrations*, New York, Basic Books, 1977, Chapter 16, and John Rawls, *A Theory of Justice*, Oxford, Oxford University Press, 1999.

[15] I leave aside here consideration of another interesting response which consists in adjusting the definition of lying in a more evaluative direction. Instead of defining lying as (something like) "saying what is believed (by the speaker) to be false with the intention of deceiving an audience" some of the later scholastics added the clause "where the audience has a right to the truth". This would mean that the counter-example would no longer be a case of lying (since the pursuer presumably has no moral right to the truth about the victim's whereabouts) and absolutism is preserved. It would be possible to go down this path, but there are many costs, chief amongst which is the way the definition fails to fit ordinary usage.

[16] See C. A. J. Coady, "Terrorism, Morality and Supreme Emergency", *Ethics*, 2004. This article explores the issues briefly raised in this section in much more detail and depth.

[17] The classical statement of this position was Jeane Kirkpatrick's in her 'Dictators and Double Standards', *Commentary*, 1979.

JANNA THOMPSON

TERRORISM, MORALITY AND RIGHT AUTHORITY[1]

One of the requirements of *jus ad bellum* is that those who make war must have 'legitimate authority'. They must have the right to wage war. Having this right is not the same as having a just cause. A legitimate authority can wage an unjust war. If, for example, states generally have legitimate authority (as many writers on just war theory assume), then their wars, just or unjust, do at least satisfy the requirement of being waged by agents with a right to war. On the other hand, if an agent does not have legitimate authority then it cannot fight a just war, no matter what its cause. Its actions are just as illegitimate as the actions of a citizen who takes the law into his own hands in order to avenge what he regards as an injustice.

A. J. Coates argues that the requirement of legitimate authority should play a central role in our understanding of what terrorism is. A definition of terrorism which focuses on conduct – the killing of non-combatants or innocents – makes "an enormous, and almost always unwarranted, moral concession, since the distinction between combatants and non-combatants (or 'guilty' and 'innocent') is one that applies only to a state of war".[2] For a state of war to exist, he insists, combatants must be able to claim legitimate authority to wage war. If they lack this authority, then the permissions of just war theory do not apply to them.

Coates does not provide a definition of terrorism, but a characterisation that seems compatible with the emphasis he places on having a right to war is as follows.

> *Terrorism consists of violent attacks on people or property carried out by those who are motivated by political objectives but lack legitimate authority to wage war.*

This understanding of terrorism has implications that are contrary to the views of some of those who have entered into discussions about how terrorism should be defined and why it should be condemned.

The first implication is that violent acts of those who have a right to war are never terrorist-though they may be war crimes. The bombing of Dresden, however unjustifiable, was not a terrorist act. So long as states are legitimate authorities they are not terrorist organizations, though their acts may be seriously unjust. The second is that an attack does not have to be directed at the 'innocent' in order to be terrorist. Attacks on police, military officials and installations count as terrorist if they are committed by people who do not have the right to war. If an agent does not have this right then none of its violent acts can be justified as legitimate acts of war. So if a group lacking legitimate authority takes care to attack only property, government officials or military targets, this does not mean that its acts are not terrorism. Indeed, as Coates points out, killing a policeman or public official is generally regarded as a worse criminal offence than killing an ordinary person.[3] It also follows that terrorists

Meggle (ed.), Ethics of Terrorism & Counter-Terrorism, 151-160.
© 2005 Ontos, Heusenstamm.

are not combatants and cannot claim the rights of combatants: for example, the rights of prisoners of war. The definition thus seems to support the view of state officials who are inclined to regard and treat terrorists as criminals rather than combatants, and who refuse as a matter of principle to negotiate with organizations that they regard as terrorist. To negotiate with a group implies that it has legitimacy, and this is what these governments deny.

Nevertheless, it does not follow that terrorism is always morally wrong. An act can be technically criminal and yet morally justifiable. Laws can be oppressive or discriminatory; governments can be vicious and corrupt. People with no right to war may nevertheless be justified in using violence in self-defence or for the defence of others. Terrorist acts might be regarded as violent and extreme forms of civil disobedience or protest, and the moral debate would then centre on whether and when such responses to injustice can be justified. Most definitions of terrorism have the implication that justified acts of terrorism are logically possible but extremely unlikely. If, for example, terrorism is as Primoratz says, "the deliberate use of violence, or threat of its use, against innocent people with the aim of intimidating them, or other people, into a course of action they otherwise would not take",[4] then any moral position that condemns attacks on the innocent will have to condemn terrorism. The definition offered above seems to make it more likely that some terrorist acts could be morally justified as acts of self-defence against unjust government officials or for some equally weighty reason.

A definition of terrorism which makes legitimate authority central is in some respects closer to the popular meaning of the term than are the definitions of many philosophers. Most people assume that terrorist organizations lack legitimacy and that terrorist acts are criminal. On the other hand, it does not support the common idea that terrorism by its nature is unjust. Whether the definition can nevertheless play a useful role in moral judgment depends on why legitimate authority is so important and how we determine what organizations can count as legitimate.

An account which makes legitimate authority central to the understanding of terrorism has to find a way of avoiding the following problems. If we take it that states are the legitimate authorities of international society (as is common in just war literature) then it seems that nothing a state can do will count as terrorist. The definition, so understood, seems to support the questionable idea that only non-state organisations, and never states, engage in terrorist acts. On the other hand, if we insist that an agent has a right to war only if it acts justly (and thus allow that agents of the state can be terrorists) then it seems to follow that an agent engaged in an unjust war has no 'right to war' and that all of its violent acts – even those directed against enemy soldiers – are terrorist. This too seems implausible. What is needed is an account of 'legitimate authority' that can avoid these problems.

LEGITIMATE AUTHORITY

The requirement of legitimate authority in classical just war theory was meant to ban private or 'unofficial' uses of war-like violence. The purpose of this ban was to bring war under control: to make it more likely that decisions to start or continue a war would be made by accountable public officials in control of the means of violence.

The possibility of just war depends on agents having this control. In modern times, the legitimate authorities are generally assumed to be states as organizations which can act as agents in the international world and have (in Weber's words) "a monopoly on the use of force within their territories". But to suppose that all and only states are legitimate authorities would be contrary to basic ideas about justice. It would amount to an unjustified support of a status quo which can be seriously unjust, and it would give legitimate authority to the worst of states.

Most discussions of the right to war insist that 'legitimacy' has a moral, and not merely a political, content. A state's or international institution's right to war, says Coppieters, derives "from its commitment , as part of the international community, to the common good and the rule of law".[5] To be a legitimate party to a war, Coates insists, it is not enough that a group be organized and in control of acts done in its name. A legitimate authority, he believes, is a good international citizen, one that properly represents its people and acts according to law. "A state's right to war derives not from its de facto or 'coercive sovereignty [...] but from its membership of an international community to the common good of which the state is ordered and to the law of which it is subject."[6]

There are several problems with this understanding of legitimate authority. One is that it presupposes the existence and legitimacy of international law and the values that this law is supposed to uphold. But if the laws and associated values are embodied by practices and agreements which now order the international world, then it seems that some groups of people (particularly non-state groups and impoverished nations) can legitimately claim, not only that this international order is unjust, but that they are not adequately represented by it: that it is a regime whose nature is determined and governed by the powerful. Why should right to war depend on accepting the legitimacy of something that many people regard as unjust? If the law referred to is something ideal–not necessarily what now exists, but something the belongs to a just world order–then it is likely that the people of the world will have many different ideas about what that should be. This disagreement could itself be a motivation for conflict and war.

The second problem is encapsulated in the ambiguous term 'right to war'. Coates claims that states are authoritative in so far as their actions "can be convincingly construed as a defence of the international order and a securing of the common international good", and he compares the state that has recourse to war with a citizen exercising the right of self defence or making a citizen's arrest.[7] States have legitimate authority, according to him, only if they are acting in defence of law. But this requirement threatens to collapse the distinction between having a just cause and being a legitimate authority. For the implication of his idea is that states and organizations that are deemed to be fighting an unjust war – that is, violating the 'law' – have no legitimate authority, and presumably all their attacks on persons and property, military or non-military, count as criminal, and, would be, according to the above definition, terrorist. Those who have the law on their side would have to be conceived as conducting a police action against a party that is engaged in criminal behaviour. By making obedience to the law a necessary condition of having legitimate authority, Coates seems to have turned just war theory into a 'just policing theory' for international society, with all of the problems and dangers that this entails. However, this interpretation is not in accordance with the purpose of just war theory, as Coates and others generally understand it.[8]

How can we give 'legitimate authority' a moral content without falling into these difficulties? The solution to this problem, I think, lies in a proper appreciation of just war theory as a moral doctrine for an imperfect world: an appreciation that requires an understanding of the political environment to which it is supposed to apply. The political world to which just war theory is meant to apply is not a Hobbesian state of nature. Moral restrictions on behaviour are possible. The international world is not a lawless state of nature. On the other hand, there is no universal agreement on how the conventions and laws of this world should be interpreted and applied. Agents have different ideas about what should be recognised as law, and no agent has the authority, moral or political, to impose its interpretation on the rest of the world. Moreover, the interests and values of these agents will sometimes tempt them to overstep the limits of law, as this is usually understood, or to make an exception for the sake of what they regard as a greater good. Every agent interprets the law in its own way; and each has a tendency to use it in a way that serves its interests.

Just war theory presupposes that agents (generally) aspire to, and can achieve, peaceful, law abiding relations, but recognises that a state of affairs in which each agent is entitled to interpret the law for itself and in which there is sometimes a good reason for disobeying existing conventions, is not conducive to perpetual peace. War will occur and since interpretations of justice differ and few states act entirely justly, most belligerents will be able to make a case for saying that their cause is just. Even when they are wrong, it is usually not difficult to understand why they, viewing the world from their national standpoint, could persuade themselves of the justice of their cause.

Just war theory has to take into account the fact that the justice of a war is often difficult to establish and that there will usually be no consensus on the matter. But it insists that wars, whether just or not, should be waged with the expectation of making a peace in which former belligerents can establish relations of mutual respect and trust, making the compromises and concessions that are required for the maintenance of such relations, keeping the agreements that arise from this settlement, making reparation for any injustices they have done in war, or at least taking steps to ensure that these injustices will not re-occur. Just war theory tells us how belligerents who respect both each other's entitlement to exist and important human values should behave in war so that respectful relations can be maintained and peace eventually negotiated and maintained. It presupposes the willingness of belligerents to accept this end and the moral restrictions that make its achievement possible.

This understanding of just war theory allows us to make the crucial distinction between being a legitimate authority – that is an agent predisposed to respect other agents and to live in peace with them – and being an agent that acts justly in a particular circumstance. An agent can be a legitimate authority and yet do unjust acts: for example, by engaging in an unjust war or committing unjust acts in war. And it is also possible for an agent to act justly and yet not be a legitimate authority.

CONDITIONS FOR LEGITIMACY

In the context of just war theory, so understood, it is reasonable to insist that a belligerent must satisfy three conditions in order to count as a legitimate authority. First of all, it must be an organization accountable for the violence of its members; it must be able and willing to enforce obedience to the restrictions of just war theory, to negotiate a peace and to keep it. Secondly, it must recognise (even if it does not always live up to) the restrictions of just war theory, the rights of other parties and the framework and institutions which make it possible for agreements to be made and kept and for there to be an enduring (if not 'perpetual') peace. To this extent organizations that count as legitimate authorities have to regard themselves as subject to law, though they may have disagreements about the nature of this law and may not on all occasions be law abiding. These two conditions are clearly related to the function of just war theory in a political environment where war is always possible but peace is achievable. But there is a third condition which also seems important. The leaders of the state or organization should be acting as the agents of its people. "The private appropriation of power by the government of a state undermines its legitimacy", says Coates.[9] War cannot be waged on the whim of leaders, however powerful their states. This third condition not only enables us to insist that some states are not legitimate authorities. It also allows that non-state organizations can be. If a revolutionary organization fighting against a tyrannical government manages to command the support of most of the people, it has a far better claim to be a legitimate authority than does their state.

We are now in a better position to understand and apply a definition of terrorism which focuses on legitimate authority. A group will count as terrorist if it fails to meet at least one of the three conditions for legitimacy: if it either fails to be an organization accountable for the violence of its members, or it refuses to recognise the restraints of just war theory and international law, or it is not the agent of the people in whose name or for whose sake it claims to act. Let us consider more closely how these criteria should be applied and interpreted in cases of political violence.

The purpose of the first condition is obvious. If violence is uncontrolled, or if it is being controlled in a clandestine way, then making and keeping the peace becomes extremely difficult. The violence will not necessarily come to an end when leaders agree to end it. No authority can or will answer for it. Sometimes the condition will not be met because there is no authority capable of controlling the political violence. The suicide bombings now being committed by Palestinians probably come into this category. It seems doubtful that these acts were ever in the control of Yasser Arafat's government, and Israel will probably not be able to bring them to an end just by negotiating with Arafat. There are a number of groups that claim at various time to be responsible for the bombings, but even if these acts are always in the control of one group or another (which is probably not so), the fact that these organizations act independently means that the violence as a whole is out of any authority's control. Sometimes the condition will fail because control is exercised in way that does not allow responsibility to be admitted or taken. The violent attacks on the East Timorese people and their property after they voted for independence from Indonesia was blamed at the time on lawless bands of militia. Now it is widely believed that these attacks were orchestrated by the Indonesian military. Either way they count as terrorism. Even if the Indonesian military were entirely in control of what was done, the way it exercised its control was designed to ensure that neither it nor the Indonesian government would have to answer for the violence. CIA sponsored and directed acts of political violence in Central and South America are further examples of failure to take responsibility for control.

The second condition, that the belligerent must be willing to respect other parties, take seriously the restrictions of just war theory, and accept the institutions and agreements that enable enduring peace to be negotiated, does not require that the belligerent's actions be just. Nevertheless, it can be used to label some organizations as terrorist. The al Qaeda network, with its apocalyptic view of a world struggle between Moslems and the West, does not appear to be an organization prepared to negotiate, compromise and make a peace that respects other parties.

States can fail to satisfy this condition. Germany under the Nazis was uncompromising in its struggle for the domination of Europe and the enslavement or destruction of those deemed to be of an inferior race. It was not prepared to accept any peace or abide by any agreement that did not meet its terms or to respect the existence of other nations or peoples. Its lack of legitimate authority was reflected in the way it was treated by the Allies. They did not regard the Nazi government as a body that had a right to negotiate a peace. They not only insisted on removing it. They subjected its leaders to criminal proceedings; they investigated its officials for Nazi sympathies; and, even if not directly guilty of crimes, Nazi officials were supposed to be punished by being removed from their posts and forced to go through a period of de-nazification (though for pragmatic reasons this often did not happen). In other words, the Nazi government was (most think, rightly) regarded as a criminal organization.

However, a state or authority which is lawless in some of its affairs may be law abiding in respect to others. By and large, Germany treated its Allied prisoners of war according to the requirements of the Geneva Convention and German commanders were often at least as scrupulous in satisfying *jus in bello* requirements as Allied generals. This suggests not only that the Allies were right in many cases to behave as if the Germans were respectable belligerents, but that it would be a mistake to label all of Germany's acts of violence as terrorist. We can distinguish between the violence their armies committed against populations and soldiers in the Soviet Union, which showed no respect for the laws of war and were thus clearly terrorist, and acts which demonstrated this respect. In any case, judgments about whether a state is committing acts of terrorism should be kept separate from whether we think its cause is just. A state which unjustly invades the territory of another isn't necessarily committing acts of terror by attacking and killing those who oppose it. Its aims may be limited; it may have no desire to overturn the international order or behave in a lawless way toward all who oppose it. It may even think that its cause is just or at least that its vital interests require the use of force. Nor should a state be accused of terrorism just because it sometimes violates *jus in bello* restrictions. Those who fight an unjust war or violate restrictions on war deserve condemnation. But the term 'terrorist' should be reserved for those whose actions or ideological commitments show that they are truly outside of the law – at least in respect to some of their policies and actions – and have no intention of recognising reasonable restrictions.

However, if a state only has to respect the law, at least most of the time, in order to count as a legitimate authority then this requirement seems too narrow. The term 'terrorist' has come to be used more and more to label gross acts of injustice which some leaders commit against their citizens: mass slaughter, torture, violent attacks on ethnic or tribal groups. A definition of terrorism which focuses on international relations and ignores relations between state officials and citizens seems inadequate. However, this limitation is not a necessary feature of my definition. Human rights are recognised in international law and thus respect for the law includes a respect for human rights. However, even in respect to human rights, there is reason to distinguish the acts of a government that are merely unjust, or are so judged by others, from acts that count as terrorist. There is, after all, a considerable amount of disagreement about human rights: which should be recognised and how they should be interpreted. Moreover, states can be generally respectful of human rights and still believe that they are sometimes justified in violating them. It seems mistaken to call such actions 'terrorist' even if we believe them to be unjust. A state that commits acts of terror against part of its population is one that has no respect for their rights and is not willing to put any restrictions on its behaviour. It systematically aims to kill them, subjugate them, terrify them, or drive them away.

A state that subjugates its population is also likely to fail to satisfy the third condition for being a legitimate authority. Its officials would not count as agents of its people. The reason for including this as a requirement is obvious. The al Qaeda claims to be acting on behalf of Moslems, and it is in fact supported by some Moslems, but it does not in any real sense represent them. The Baader Meinhof gang that attacked military installations in Germany and the Red Brigade of Italy did not represent the people on whose behalf they claimed to be acting, and this seems sufficient reason for regarding the violent actions of these groups as terrorist-even in those cases where the violence was directed against military property or officials. To be an agent of a people the organization has to be in some way accountable to them, and the people must be in the position to take some responsibility for the actions it does.

However, explaining what the condition means encounters some obvious difficulties. It would be too permissive if it allowed any leadership that controls the levers of power in a society to count as having legitimate authority. On the other hand, the criterion would be too narrow if it insisted that a state or group is a legitimate authority only if its leaders are democratically elected by those it claims to represent. Non-democratic leaders can have widespread popular support, and even if some people in the country oppose their rule, they may still be regarded by most citizens as being the rightful representatives of the state in international affairs. So it seems best to give the criterion a fairly conservative interpretation. A group is not a legitimate authority if it has no control over those it is supposed to represent or if those over whom it exercises power have no way of influencing its decisions. On the other hand, we can in most cases presume that leaders are legitimate authorities if people who are supposed to be represented by them are generally willing to obey their directives without continual and extreme uses of force.

An organization can be a legitimate authority in respect to some acts or at some periods of time and not at others. Stalin was an unscrupulous dictator and did not, in general, act as an agent of his people. But nevertheless it could be argued that his government became such an agent in the war against German invasion.

An organisation is a legitimate authority if and only if it satisfies all three of the conditions in respect to an act or a series of acts. If it does not, then these acts, if violent, count as terror. One of the complaints that might be made against the definition of terrorism that I have elaborated is that these conditions can be satisfied a lot easier by states than they can be by resistance fighters, revolutionary organizations, or secessionists. Those who rebel against their state often have to organize in secret; they are in no position to demonstrate that they truly represent the people on whose behalf they are fighting. On the other hand, if the uprising is a mass action, then the deeds committed by the revolutionaries will probably not be under the control of any political authority and will not satisfy the first condition. Moreover, revolutionary organizations are more likely to have serious objections to the international status quo and thus likely to be less respectful of the ideas of right that are supposed to govern it.

There are two replies to this objection. One is to point out that it is inevitable that just war theory in its application will have a conservative bias. It favours conditions that enable peace to be made and agents that have already proved that they are capable of satisfying these conditions. So those who operate in its framework will tend to fall back on existing laws, established practices and political frameworks. However, the distinction between acts of war and terrorism does not favour states because they are states. It allows that states can commit terrorist acts against their own population or against outsiders. On the other hand, some revolutionary organizations have been able to demonstrate that they satisfy the condition for being legitimate authorities when they are given a chance to do so. The fact that Bobby Sands, an IRA leader serving a sentence in the Maze Prison, won a by-election as a Northern Ireland representative in the Westminster Parliament, is an indication that many Northern Irish regarded the Sinn Fein, the political wing of the IRA, as representing them. The Front de Libération Nationale in Algeria demonstrated on a number of occasions that it had immense popular support. Its guerrilla actions directed against the French Algerian population can be condemned for violating *jus in bello* requirements, but since there is reason to believe that the FLN was a legitimate authority, these acts do not count as terrorist according to the definition I am defending.

The second reply is to return to a point made earlier. An account of terrorism that focuses on legitimate authority does not imply that terrorist acts are always morally wrong. Terrorism might be justified, for example, as an act of self-defence. Those who believe that violence against the innocent is always wrong will not necessarily have reason to condemn all of the acts, which according to my definition, count as terrorist. For these acts may be directed against non-innocents – for example, politicians responsible for unjust policies. If a definition of terrorism is wanted that can be used to judge that terrorist acts are always immoral, then justifiable exceptions (like violence used in self-defence) can be built in. An act could be said to be terrorist if it is committed by an organization that lacks legitimate authority and cannot be justified as self-defence, etc. But this move strikes me as *ad hoc*.

LAW AND WORLD ORDER

Distinguishing terrorist acts from acts of war highlights a morally important distinction between violent acts of organizations whose members are able and willing to respect each other in a framework that makes peace possible and those whose actions are, for one reason or another, lawless. It has to be admitted that this distinction rests on a view of the political environment that can be contested. It assumes that there is an international order which political actors ought to maintain. But it also assumes that international society is not like domestic society: it has laws but their interpretation, even their validity, is open to question, and there is no cosmopolitan power or government that has the authority to make, interpret, or enforce this law.

These assumptions can be contested in two main ways. They will be rejected, first of all, by those who think that the international order is profoundly unjust and can only be changed by violent revolution. According to my definition of terrorism, revolutionary violence against the framework of law which makes world order possible would be terrorist, and so would the uncoordinated violence of the oppressed. But terrorism is not necessarily wrong. My definition doesn't prevent us from arguing that a campaign of terror directed against the perpetrators of injustice might be justified, at least if the oppressed have exhausted non-violent strategies for obtaining justice. Similarly, if revolutionaries who believe that the present world order is drastically unjust and cannot be changed by peaceful means could establish that revolutionary violence outside the law would have a good chance of making the world much more just, then perhaps they would have a case for terrorism. But making this case would be difficult.

The second reason for opposing assumptions made by just war theory will be held by those who think that recent developments have changed the international world into a society of laws and institutions for enforcing them – something that resembles domestic societies – and that acts of organized violence count as a violation of this law and deserve to be punished as criminal by those who act on behalf of international institutions. According to this view, contemporary wars are really police actions in which the United Nations or the United States and its allies subdue and punish those guilty of breaking the law. This idea of what international society has become amounts to a rejection of the world view that informs just war theory.

However, there is good reason to think that this rejection is, to say the least, premature. International society remains very much unlike domestic societies. There are no reliable institutions in world society for enforcing laws, for trying or punishing law-breakers. The United Nations plays a role in law enforcement in international society, but its attempts at doing so have been sporadic and not always effective. And its decision-making procedures are far from impartial. The United States and its allies have often undertaken the role of law enforcers with or without United Nations approval, but these actions are motivated by their own security needs and not necessary by an impartial respect for law and order. There is no reliable way in which an appeal made by those accused of unlawful behaviour can be heard, and there is no real protection for those who face the prospect of being punished as outlaws by those they have reason to regard as their enemies. The 'punishment' inflicted might well take the form of revenge and go far beyond anything that they deserve for their unjust acts. As Locke points out, a situation where agents are the judges in their own cause and are likely to be motivated by ill-nature, passion, and revenge in their exaction of punishment will tend to generate confusion, disorder, and perpetual conflict.[10]

The policing analogy encourages the idea that law and order must prevail. Defeating an outlaw state is bound to be regarded by those who take on this task as an important, even imperative, objective which can justify extreme measures. Since nothing less than total defeat of an outlaw is acceptable, those who fight against it will regard it as justified to do what is necessary to achieve this aim. The stage is set for protracted and bitter conflicts – wars that will have a tendency to overstep the limitations which just war theory tries to impose on conduct in war. In other words, the 'policing analogy' is incompatible with the spirit of just war theory.

These considerations do not stop us from regarding some wars as being like police actions. However, those who believe that they are engaged in such an action should try to avoid trading on a conceptual confusion. If leaders of the United States regard themselves as conducting a police action against al Qaeda, then they should favour trying those suspected of terrorism as criminals according to the laws and requirements of criminal justice. There may be reasons in an emergency to suspend some of the provisions which protect those accused of crimes. What can't be justified is to claim that terrorists and their supporters are criminals and then to treat suspected terrorists as prisoners of war: to lock them up without recourse to law or to try them in special military courts as suspected perpetrators of an unjust war. This policy illicitly borrows justifications from a discourse that has been explicitly rejected by labelling the acts of the terrorists as crimes. In practice it amount to a highly questionable violation of the rights of individuals. It affords them neither the civil protections that are supposed to be given to those accused of crimes nor the rights of prisoners of war.

NOTES

[1] This chapter draws on material in 'Terrorism and the Right to Wage War' which appeared in C. A. J. Coady and M. O'Keefe (eds.), *Terrorism and Justice* (Melbourne: Melbourne University Press, 2002).
[2] A. J. Coates, *Ethics of War* (Manchester, New York: Manchester University Press, 1997), p. 124.
[3] Coates, *Ethics of War*, p. 123
[4] Igor Primoratz, 'What is Terrorism?', *Journal of Applied Philosophy*, 7 (1990), p. 129.
[5] B. Coppieters, 'Legitimate Authority', B. Coppieters and N. Fotion (eds.), *Moral Constraints on War: Principles and Causes* (Boulder, New York: Lexington Books, 2002), p. 42.
[6] Coates, *Ethics of War*, p. 127.
[7] Coates, *Ethics of War*, p. 127.
[8] For example, in Coates, *Ethics of War*, Chapter 6.
[9] Coates, *The Ethics of War*, p. 129.
[10] J. Locke, *Two Treatises of Government*, II, 2, ¶13, is describing the state of nature where everyone is entitled to be a law enforcer.

GEORG MEGGLE

TERROR & COUNTER-TERROR:
INITIAL ETHICAL REFLECTIONS*

In memory of Georg Meggle (1900–1963),
my father.

What is terrorism? What does someone have to do or plan in order to be justly considered a terrorist? Can terrorist actions be understood? Or are those acting thus per se irrational? What is it about terrorist acts which makes them so reprehensible to, as they say, "every single one of us"? Is terrorism intrinsically evil? Or do at least theoretical cases exist in which terrorist activity would be justified? And finally: Is everything permissible in the struggle against terrorism? Even counter-terror? Or what about wars?

These are questions we need to analyse. However, I shall have to ask for your patience. Merely the first question – "What is terrorism?" – will need much care and time, as you will shortly see. Political rhetoric may be swifter, but its aim is persuasion; mine is clarity. And one of the best ways to achieve clarity is to follow the advice of an Arab philosopher, who said: "The wise man possesses abstraction." In times of war, this may also mean: The wise man keeps his distance.

PART I

1. WHAT IS TERRORISM?

1.1 I often think back to the first few hours of my philosophy studies, when the practical relevance of definitions of terms became apparent to me from the following example:

> The local council decides that order needs to be restored to the seriously overgrown municipal parks. The instructions are as follows: *All rank growth bushes are to be removed.*
> But what's a bush? And what exactly is a rank growth bush? This is an area where gardeners disagree. Some believe the new campaign will result in too much greenery being removed; for others too little. So they call in the experts – theoreticians from biology specializing in dendrology complete with their textbooks, as well as the practical specialists who have written manuals for municipal gardening. Yet the

G. Meggle (ed.), Ethics of Terrorism & Counter-Terrorism, 161-175.

experts cannot agree. According to one school of thought, all bushes imported from China – irrespective of whether they grow wild – should be regarded as high-grade plants; the other school believes a bush's origin is totally irrelevant to the campaign against rank growth bushes.

Hence what counts as a rank growth bush depends on the definition adopted by the gardeners. Equally, what counts as terrorism depends on how it's defined by those in charge of hunting down those behind it.

Yet there's obviously a difference between the terms 'rank growth bush' and 'terrorism'. The term 'rank growth bush' is neutral. The prejudice that everything which is a rank growth bush needs to be removed is not harboured in the expression 'rank growth bush'. With terrorism it's a different kettle of fish. Those who are regarded as terrorists have already been condemned. 'Rank growth bush' is a classificatory term; 'terrorist' is currently (once again) a branding iron. Heaven help those to whom it's applied!

1.2 However, we shall have to leave the value component of the term 'terrorism' to one side, at least for the present. This is vital if we are to use it with maximum accuracy rather than blindly. This in turn entails drawing a sharp distinction between the following questions: 1) *The semantic question*: What do the terms 'terrorism', 'terrorist' and 'terrorist acts' etc. mean? 2) *The verification question*: How can we tell (when we know what the terms 'terrorism', 'terrorist' and 'terrorist acts' etc. mean) whether something or somebody is terrorism, a terrorist or a terrorist act, etc.? 3) *The evaluation question*: How is terrorism etc. to be morally judged?

1.3 Of the trinity of *T-terms*:

- Terrorism
- Terrorist
- Terrorist Action or Terrorist Act

the third is the fundamental one. It can be used to define the other two, but not the other way round. Not everything that terrorists do is terrorist; just in the same way that not everything sexists or racists do is sexist or racist. Terrorists, put very roughly, are people who accomplish, prepare or plan terrorist acts, or who are deliberately involved in them in some other way. And *terrorism* refers to the broad field of terrorist actions.

To make it easier for us to abandon our prejudice in connection with terrorist acts, I will resort to a trick. From now on, terrorist acts will be referred to simply as *T-acts*. T-acts are hence *terrorist acts minus their evaluation*.

1.4 When is an act a T-act?
Let's have a look at the following example:

> X, a separatist from a certain province, activates the timing mechanism of a bomb hidden in his briefcase in a room next door to a marketplace café in the capital city of his country with the intention of blowing up

dozens of people in the café in order to make the government release his imprisoned secessionist comrades.

This is the first level of the example. It is supervened by a second:

> X expects or hopes that the government's decision to release his comrades will be prompted by the horror generated among the population by his T-act.

The first layer contains the *violence calculus*. X assumes that his acts of violence will pay off by leading to the release of his comrades. The second level contains the corresponding *terror calculus*: X assumes he will achieve his aim by means of the terror caused by his act of violence, i.e. that by using terror he will be able to make the government do something it would not otherwise do were it not for this terror. In other words, the terror calculus says: X expects that the horror induced by his terror will cause things to happen which would not have happened without this horror. The terror calculus is based on the expected *horror function*. In T-acts both calculus – the violence calculus and the terror calculus – are closely interlinked. In X's view, the violence calculus works precisely because the terror calculus works.

The T-act concerned – in this case activating the time bomb together with the related intentions – is so far merely an *attempt*. To make it *successful*, X would also have to actually achieve the intentions mentioned in the first layer, and his expectation mentioned in the second layer would also have to be fulfilled. This means the following would have to hold:

Success in the first layer:

> X's bomb blew up dozens of café customers and thus caused his comrades to be released.

And success in the second layer:

> It really was the terror impact on the population which caused the government to decide to release his comrades.

Thus T-acts are successful if both the violence calculus and the terror calculus actually work – the former with the help of the latter. Every T-act aims at this successful connection between the two calculus. It is precisely this double calculus link which differentiates T-acts from non-T-acts.

Let's put this all into plain English:

> D1:   T-acts are acts in which purposes are (attempted to be) brought about by means of terror

More precisely:

> D2:   T-acts are acts in which purposes are (attempted to be) brought about by means of terror induced by violence

1.5 T-acts may vary enormously. Let's list the elements we have mentioned so far.

Elements:	In our example:
Act/Action a	Activation of the bomb
Actor X	Provincial separatist
Violence addressee Y	Café customers
Terror addressee Z	The general public
Ultimate addressee U	The government
Intended effect R	Release of prisoners

Let's try and detach ourselves from the example. Stop looking at the right-hand column; just concentrate on the left and recall a few things.

- The *T-act a* itself: Apart from placing a bomb in a briefcase, this could be a thousand and one other things: anthrax powder in the mail; poisoning the water supply; deploying computer viruses; atomic, biological or chemical weapons; threatening the use of torture; deliberate false alarms which create panic; etc., etc. The arsenal with which humans can create hell on earth for other people is inexhaustible.

- *Actor X* needn't be acting alone. Actors may also be groups and collectives, organizations, institutions and their networks; even states or coalitions of states.

- The same goes for the *addressees.*

- *X* may even be *an element of Y, the target group of* the violence – just think of suicide bombers.

- *Violence and terror addressees* may be *identical* – and of course the ultimate target group U (or parts thereof) may also be the addressee of the violence and terror.

- *X* may even be a *member of U*, in which case the T-act would be targeted at his own group. And ultimately:

- The range of all the possible *reactions or effects R* as ultimate or other aims of T-acts for T-actors is just as limitless as the arsenal of possible T-act methods. Given everything humans believe to be worth striving for, everything is possible. The attempt to classify T-acts in terms of their aims as political, religious, merely criminal, etc., is an initial attempt to structure this huge class. Interest is currently focused on political T-acts.

1.6 So far I've missed out one important point. T-acts can also be directed at uninvolved outsiders who happen to be in the wrong place at the wrong time – or, as we often say, against "innocent victims".

At least, this was the case in our café example. The direct victims of the bomb attack came from all over the world. They had nothing to do with the suppression of the province whose secession was desired by the T-actor (a native of the province);

moreover they couldn't do anything about his comrades being in prison. None of them were hired mercenaries, or overt or covert agents of the regime X is fighting.

Does the same apply by definition to all T-acts? Does our definition need to be made stronger as follows?

> D3: T-acts are acts in which purposes are (attempted to be) brought about by means of terror induced by violence committed against indiscriminate innocents

Or can acts count as T-acts if they only affect "non-innocent victims" in the sense relevant here, e.g. the leaders of the oppressive regime itself? This is one of the most contentious issues, and I won't be able to settle it here.

The reason why innocent victims – and usually totally indiscriminately at that – are the favourite target of T-actions is obvious. This is the way to most efficiently maximize the horror function. This is for two reasons: (i) The more unpredictable terror is, the more effective it is. This unpredictability means that everyone has to somehow expect being among the next victims. (ii) The more visible the horror scenarios caused by terror are for as many people as possible, the more effective they are. One important multiplication factor for terror is its *media quality* – the supreme example being September 11. Reports or even *pictures of innocent victims*, of burnt children for example, are *ideal for the horror function* (although this 'optimization' was prevented by our media regarding the victims of the September 11 attacks).

Whether this focus on innocent parties or indiscriminate victims is necessarily part of T-acts is something I shall leave undecided. But one thing is certain: *The worst T-acts are of this type.* This is a fact – and simultaneously a tangible value judgment. This brings to an end our introductory digression into the semantics of terror. Now let's turn to its ethics.

2. THE ETHICS OF VIOLENCE AND WAR

The ethics of terror is a special case of the *ethics of violence and war*.

Therefore, let's first ask the following general question: What is the maximum justifiable violence? And here I ask in particular: Is the *violence* exercised in the period *following September 11*, in particular the war against Afghanistan, still within this maxim?

2.1 I subscribe to the classical theory of the justifiability of violence. According to this theory, violence is allowed in cases of self-defence and emergency aid – and is allowed for both individuals and collectives. As far as collectives are concerned (and only they are of interest to us here), this justification approach leads directly to the criteria *for justified war*. These criteria regulate two things: when war may be waged in the first place (*ius ad bellum*) and how such a permitted war is to be waged (*ius in bello*). They may be formulated for violence in general as follows:

(AD) *ius ad vim/ad bellum*
> (1) Reason which justifies violence/war (*causa iusta*)
> [(2) intentio recta]

(3) Correct decision authority (*auctoritas principis*)

[(4) open declaration]

(5) No alternative (ultima ratio)

(6) Success likely

(7) Injustice can be removed by violence/peace can be achieved with war

(8) Macro-proportionality

(IN) *ius in vi/in bello*

The following must apply to the way in which violence is committed/war is waged:

(1) It is required and conducive for the aim of violence/war

(2) It is not directed against uninvolved outsiders (innocent victims), i.e.:

(2.1) Not directly

(2.2) There is no strongly reprehensible collateral damage

As little harm as possible is caused:

(3) To your own side

(4) To the enemy

(5) No "mala in se" methods/weapons are used

2.2 As far as wars are concerned, the *causae iustae* include – in accordance with self-defence – large armed attacks. Hence *wars of self-defence* are permitted, and other parties may join in, i.e. the formation of coalitions is also allowed. Moreover, corresponding to self-defence, *causa iusta* also includes very severe and systematic violations of human rights. Hence *wars of humanitarian intervention* are also allowed.

2.3 The condition of *macro-proportionality* demands that before war starts, the action's anticipated overall gain (excluding any additional gain going beyond the achievement of the war's aim) must be compared with the anticipated overall harm caused by the war. The gain must be 'worth' the damage.

2.4 Of the ad bellum criteria, the most important one after the *causa iusta* (AD.1) is that of *necessity* (AD.5). Entering a war is only permitted as the ultima ratio. By contrast, the in bello criterion IN.1 refers to the type of warfare – which must be a means which is both required and suitable for achieving the war's aims.

2.5 *"Mala in se" methods* include for example ethnic expulsions, mass rape, using nuclear weapons or carpet bombing.

2.6 One *example* of the permissible entering of a war would be the Allies' declaration of war against the Axis powers, particularly Germany, in World War II. The fact that this does not sanction the type of warfare is shown by the same example: According to IN.2&5 both the atom bombs on Hiroshima and Nagasaki and the bombing of Dresden were war crimes.

2.7 *International law* has hitherto mainly only been tailored to classic wars of self-defence. By the time of the Kosovo War it became apparent it lacked clear guidelines for weighing up state sovereignty against intervention rights in the event of severe violations of human rights. As strange as it might sound, the criteria for just wars developed in the Middle Ages still provide the better moral arguments in some cases. This is not an argument against international law, but rather one in favour of improving it.

This goes in particular for cases concerning armed uprisings or civil wars and wars of secession. And it goes even more so for various forms of terrorist violence and various forms of combating terror. The criteria of just war are also relevant to the assessment of terror and counter-terror.

2.8 These *criteria* are *double-edged*: in addition to providing *reasons for justification*, i.e. reasons why violence, war and perhaps also terror and counter-terror are allowed (owing to certain criteria being met), they also provide reasons for their condemnation, i.e. reasons why violence, war, terror and counter-terror are not allowed (owing to certain criteria not being met), or in other words forbidden.

The application problem of what happens if one criterion leans in one direction and another in another direction can't be solved without further appraisal. However, this discussion really needs to be carried out separately for different types of violence. The either/or nature of the deontological criteria AD.1-5 and IN.2&5 usually gives way anyway to a more flexible more-or-less scale. Just how far this flexibility can go is *the* main bone of contention in the "application discourse". In order to focus discussion on the more important aspects, regarding the application of these criteria I shall express myself apodictically in a carefully considered manner; we are dealing here with "initial ethical reflections", not the "last word".

3. THE ETHICS OF TERROR

3.1 *Can T-acts be morally allowed?* Can they be justifiable in accordance with the criteria of just war?

This all depends on the type of T-act concerned.

Recall that under our strongest T-term, the actor's violence is directed against indiscriminate innocent victims. This is a clear violation of criterion IN.2 (innocent victims may not be the direct target; hence T-acts which have innocent victims as the direct target are morally forbidden) – isn't it?

3.2 IN.2.1 says: Direct violence against innocent victims is forbidden. Does this mean that indirect violence is allowed? This brings us to the topic of *collateral damage*, something we ought to look at in more detail.

X's violence being directed against Y (as an uninvolved outsider) can mean various things:

(D)   The actor X deliberately directs his violence against Y, knowing full well that Y is innocent.

In this case of direct violence against innocent parties, it is thus assumed that Y is an individual or a group of individuals who are not 'guilty' with respect to the political etc. intentions of X. X's violence against or even killing of 'innocent victims' cannot of course be counted as collateral damage (CD). With Y and Z representing different groups, the following can be said about collateral damage:

(CD)   X's violence, which is directed deliberately against Z, also affects innocent parties from Y.

As far as (CD) is concerned, we would have to distinguish between the following cases:

(CD.1)   X knew his violence against Z might also affect innocent parties from Y, but this didn't worry X in the slightest.

(CD.2)   X knew his violence against Z might also affect innocent parties from Y, but took this into the bargain.

(CD.3)   X didn't realize his violence against Z might also affect Y – but could have known this if he'd done his homework beforehand.

(CD.4)   X knew his violence against Z might also affect innocent parties from Y, and so tried – albeit unsuccessfully – to prevent this from happening.

(CD.5)   X simply couldn't know his violence against Z would also affect innocent parties from Y.

3.3 All cases under (CD) are cases of collateral damage. Case (D) is not, because here the actor's violence is directed with full intent against Y. This is reprehensible. So is the case when the actor (as in CD.1) doesn't worry at all about whether his violence will strike innocent or guilty parties. And it is no less reprehensible when (as in CD.2) innocent victims are simply taken into the bargain or (as in CD.3) the actor makes insufficient effort to find out whether innocent parties can be completely ruled out as victims (although whether anyone can really be accused of this in the heat of battle is admittedly a moot point; then again it must be pointed out that most such attacks are planned long in advance). The only excusable case would be CD.5. By contrast, in CD.4 a great deal more would have to be known about the exact circumstances involved. How great was the danger of innocent victims being affected? Just how serious and of what quality were the attempts at prevention? Etc.

In other words, the more reprehensible the collateral damage covered by (CD), the closer T-acts are to case (D) in which direct violence is committed with full intent against innocent parties, and hence the worse they are. ((D) and collateral damage cases CD.1–3 are strongly reprehensible, and hence blameworthy.)

3.4 Let's sum up what we have found so far. If T-acts are at all justifiable in accordance with the criteria of just war, they are so only iff they are neither T-acts which are directed with full intent against innocent parties nor T-acts which involve strongly reprehensible collateral damage (SRCD).

I shall refer to T-acts whose violence and terror are addressed either directly against uninvolved outsiders (innocent parties) (case D) or whose violence or terror cause SRCD among uninvolved outsiders (cases CD.1 and CD.2/3) simply as *strong T-acts*. Accordingly I shall use the term *strong terrorism* to refer to terrorism which is based on *strong T-acts*; by contrast, weak terrorism is a terrorism which excludes strong T. Note that the words 'strong' and 'weak' only refer to the criterion of the strong reprehensibility of violence against uninvolved outsiders; they don't say anything about the intensity of this violence.

I left unanswered the question of whether T-acts should by definition be counted among these strong reprehensibilities. But one thing is now clear: if T-acts in general were already to be defined as strong T-acts, T-acts would not be justifiable. This would stem directly from their definition plus the strict in bello criterion (IN.2).

Hence the question concerning justifiability is only still open if it is based on a weaker concept of T-acts. But there this question certainly is open!

3.5 Hence *if* violence-induced terror against a criminal regime really were the only way to halt serious violations of human rights against one's own group (AD.1&5), *if* this strategy seemed promising given the support for the guerillas among one's own people (AD.6), and *if* in the event of the guerrillas winning, something approaching peace would return to the province after decades of oppression (AD.7), *if* the whole struggle ultimately proved worthwhile (Ad.8), and *if all the in bello criteria* were met – well, what then?

In this case, *this particular guerrilla struggle* would be a *special case of just war*. In fact, no less so than the above-mentioned intervention by the Allies in World War II; in fact even more clear cut since, unlike the Americans and the Britons, the guerrillas would also ex hypothesi meet the criteria of ius in bello. By the way, the fact that such groups *can* also exist in our world was the basic postulate of the liberation theology mostly based on the special circumstances in South America.

Hence, T-acts (in the weak sense) *may* also be morally allowed.

4. THE ETHICS OF ANTI-TERROR

What does this mean for the struggle *against* terror?

4.1 If a war is just – and for us this means nothing more than justifiable or permitted – the opponent or enemy must be in the wrong. It cannot be possible for a war to be simultaneously permitted in the same respect for both sides. The same also goes for T-actions. But this means that if a T-action is permitted, fighting it is forbidden. To remain by the above example, anybody who oppresses a justified guerrilla struggle must be in the wrong.

We can thus summarize the results achieved so far as follows. In accordance with the criteria for just war:

- Strong terrorism is forbidden.
- Weak terrorism may be permitted.

4.2 What does this mean for the present? In particular, what does this mean for the current general rallying cry GRC?

GRC: Terrorism must be combated worldwide!!!

Assuming that only forbidden terrorism may be combated (which in other contexts would be trivial), this evidently means various things. If the rallying cry refers to *strong terrorism, it is absolutely correct. Strong terrorism* is forbidden not only always but also everywhere.

On the other hand, if the rallying cry also refers to *weak terrorism*, it would be:

1)   poorly substantiated
2)   possibly wrong

and whenever this rallying cry encouraged severe crimes

3)   its implementation would have to be *resisted.*

4.3 I have another objection to this rallying cry. And that is that I simply can't buy it from Bush and the others; I simply can't imagine they take this rallying cry seriously. Otherwise, they themselves and their own countries would quickly get into hot water. The USA, for example, is probably involved in actions which are clear cases of T-acts in several parts of the world, especially in South America – and many of them are most probably cases which cannot be morally justified. And the same goes for a whole number of other members of the grand anti-terror coalition.

But that's merely by the by. Political rhetoric always overdoes things. Of course, what the general rallying cry GRC really means is currently combating the *terrorism of others*, especially that of the terrorist network which (probably) was at least co-responsible for the attacks on September 11.

4.4 As far as the causa iusta criterion is concerned, there is no question that the struggle against this *terrorism* is legitimate. The *causa iusta* for permissible defence could hardly be clearer. But does this automatically mean that the war against Afghanistan has been a just war?

This is the end of Part I – the part in which mainly analytical, philosophical reflections predominate. The following Part II increasingly contains my own personal views. The important thing is that even if (contrary to expectations) you have accepted everything so far, you may nevertheless and with perhaps better reasons be of a completely different opinion from me as far as the moral assessment of current world events is concerned.

PART II

5. IS THE WAR IN AFGHANISTAN A JUSTIFIED WAR?

Do the attacks of September 11 justify the war against Afghanistan?

AD BELLUM

5.1 Let's start with the first ad bellum criterion: the *causa iusta*. As we stated above, this exists. The attacks on the World Trade Center clearly violated IN.2. Therefore, even if the attacks were, contra rem, to be regarded as acts of war, this wouldn't change anything regarding the classification of these acts as crimes against humanity. Even if the USA had been at a state of war with the attackers, the attacks on the World Trade Center would still have been a clear case of war crimes.

Yet did they provide a reason for war? At first it was uncertain whether the attacks came from outside in the first place. After certainty had been declared, there was no state which could be regarded as the attacker: there was 'only' the al-Qa'eda network spread throughout several countries with Bin Laden at its centre. The conditions for a war of self-defence in the classic sense under international law were thus not met – and hence neither were the conditions the NATO pact had originally envisaged as justifying assistance among the allies.

5.2 In this grey area between war and non-war there were 2 x 2 alternatives:

Alternative A: The decision-making authority regarding counter-reactions is either (i) the USA or (ii) an international authority. (See also the auctoritas principis = (AD.3))

Alternative B: Either (i) *classification of the attacks* as *equivalent to war* and thus as the potential trigger for a national *war of self-defence* or (ii) *classification as a crime* and thus the transfer of the case (including responsibility for punishment) to a national or international investigative body and then a national or international *court of justice*.

In both cases the first option was chosen – and the decision was taken solely by the USA.

Re: Alternative A: In the first few days after September 11, it was constantly emphasized that the attacks were an attack on the entire international community of states (and sometimes "on the entire civilized world"). Nevertheless, it wasn't its representation in the form of the United Nations but rather solely the USA which was to be responsible for deciding on an appropriate response. Consequently, the media in the USA now nearly always just refer to an "attack on America".

Re: Alternative B: The decision on Alternative A automatically decided Alternative B. The *attack on America* was turned into *America at war*. And the responsible authority since then under the President has been the Pentagon.

5.3 Note that these two alternatives are completely independent of the third decision:

Alternative C: Should military force be deployed or not?

Even if you agree with me that after September 11 the destruction of the al-Qa'eda network's training camps by for example pinpoint air strikes was perhaps inevitable and morally justified, this doesn't nail you down to either of the options under A and B.

The use of military force can also be ordered by an international court. Supreme command authority could be delegated to a special anti-terror Security Council (in which none of the countries directly affected should be involved in current decisions). Missions would then be undertaken by the national armed forces of the nations (or coalitions) represented in the UN.

5.4 "*Utopian!*" you will cry. Certainly, after the decisions which have since been taken. But definitely not as impossible *before* these decisions.

Apart from the chance of achieving with options (A.i) and (B.i) within a few days what the USA (not just according to its enemies) mainly wanted to achieve, namely simply achieving a position approximating to world domination – what actually argued *against* the unchosen options (A.ii) and (B.ii)? Was it because the UN or a world court of justice set up under its auspices couldn't work? Neither legally nor militarily?

This argument convinces many, but it's too weak. After all, what's the main cause of the UN's weakness? The blockades imposed by the USA. And the USA would easily have been in a position in concert with other countries to make the UN as strong as it needs to be so that it is better able to cope with such responsibilities.

5.5 In this context, the argument is repeatedly voiced that no power on earth – and especially not a superpower like the USA – can be expected to cede important decisions concerning its own welfare to the UN. This may be true. But if a power has the possibility to cede important decisions concerning its welfare to the UN, not taking recourse to this possibility reflects in the moral judgement of what it does. It boils down to morality, not just what's best from the viewpoints of power.

Just imagine if between September 12 and 14 the Secondary-General of the United Nations had taken the initiative, declared a state of world emergency, acting on his own authority summoned the International Court of Justice (which was already being prepared), and then on the basis of the majority vote to be anticipated in this case by the General Assembly appealed to every state in the world (including the USA) to regard the United Nations as the supreme decision-making authority in the event of international terror acts of the scale?

Yes, I know. This is a Utopian vision, whose accomplishment by Kofi Annan or anybody else for that matter would be (almost) superhuman. But supposing he could have relied on the complete support of the heads of government of some of the most important countries, including perhaps some of the USA's main friends? In other words, what would have happened if we had suddenly discovered that the current heads of government included people like Willy Brandt, Olaf Palme, Mikhail Gorbachev or even Mahatmi Gandhi? What then?

5.6 I fear that since October 7 – since the USA and the UK began waging war against Afghanistan – perhaps not the war against Afghanistan but instead the *great war against terror has already been lost.* Millions of people probably regard this anti-terror war as simply further proof of the imperialism of the West, especially the USA. Note that you need not necessarily share this view in order to be convinced of its enormous validity. After all, a conviction need not be true in order to be effective.

This assessment does not change in the slightest even if we take into account that so far the USA has based its actions in the war Afghanistan on a broad anti-terror coalition. I'm talking about people and nations, not governments. Who really believes that the grand anti-terror coalition – even if it only exists at governmental level – is voluntary? Or that the anti-terror component really is the primary motive behind the coalition? This coalition – like others before it – is based on all sorts of things: on the possibility of reshuffling the deck; the anticipation of being able to grab larger slices of the cakes which can be baked in the fire of the anti-terror war; the pride of being the ones to congratulate their own people on 'growing up' by means of their decision to enter the war; as well as on how the coalition came about in the first place – blackmail, cowardice and fear.

5.7 Why am I against this war?

Allow me to leave aside all the subtleties regarding the further ad bellum criteria. My rejection of this war does not result from the mere fact that arms have been taken up. Precise strikes destroying al-Qa'eda's training camps may well have been justifiable.

My main objection is twofold. *Firstly*, the fact that instead of such a limited intervention against carefully selected targets, the whole of Afghanistan has been and is being consumed by war. And *secondly*, the way in which this war is being fought.

5.8 Overrunning Afghanistan with a broadly organized and initially unlimited war – what does this option mean? And what does the announcement (made in early October) that this option will shortly be carried out mean?

Let's have a look at the following report given to the world by the international aid organizations working in the border area between Afghanistan and Pakistan in late September/early October.

> "Currently about 3–5 million people – and if the situation deteriorates perhaps as many as 7–8 million people – face death by starvation in Afghanistan owing to the effects of war in the past few decades and the failed harvests of recent years. This danger is extremely exacerbated by the upcoming winter. In winter, numerous valleys will be cut off from our supply convoys. In order to save these people, it is essential that within 14 days at the latest international humanitarian aid intervention be launched. Afterwards, even if peace prevails, any assistance will be too late for the suffering population cut off in the valleys. If the border with Pakistan is closed, even the current, totally inadequate aid transports will no longer reach their destinations in time. Under the conditions of war, all aid organizations would have to cease their activities. We appeal to the conscience of the world ... ", etc., etc. (This is a mixture of statements from the Websites of WHO, UNICEF, OXFAM and Conscience International.)

Hence there was a clear alternative. The decision taken is known. Now the conscience of the world knows what giving highest priority to the fight against terror means. As was to be expected, the mere *announcement* of war led to the border is being closed, rendering the necessary international rescue campaigns impossible.

We don't know how many deaths are to blame on the mere *announcement* of war. Nor can we say how many of the 3–4 million or in the meantime even 7–8 million people threatened by starvation can now be counted as indirect victims of the war since it began on October 7, 2001. Does anybody really care? Of course, the estimates vary enormously. The indirect consequences of the announcement of war are estimated to be on average around 5.000; the indirect consequences of the war itself to be so far at least 10 or 20 times higher. The *Süddeutsche Zeitung* (November 22, 2001) mentioned a figure of some 400.000.

Let me ask a simple question: How many deaths would be acceptable given the importance of the anti-terror campaign? To put it another way: How many innocent corpses is the corpse of a terrorist worth?

5.9 The argument always produced in defence is that all these deaths are just collateral damage. No American or Briton did anything to hurt a single one of these poor people. Terribly sorry: collateral damage.

The aim of my paper was to achieve clarity. In other words, spoken by a terrorist, this "terribly sorry" wouldn't wash with us – not if the collateral damage was strongly reprehensible collateral damage. But the numbers of dead I cite here certainly are. It all boils down to special case CD.2.: The actor knew his violence could also affect innocent victims – but consciously took this into the bargain.

We cannot simultaneously regard reasons which in our eyes make terrorism reprehensible as an excuse for ourselves. Hence to sum up:

Both the announcement of war and the opening and continuation of the war in Afghanistan violated the in bello criterion (2), which forbids violence against uninvolved outsiders in the sense of strongly reprehensible collateral damage. We are thus dealing with a case in which merely the announcement and start of hostilities constitute a war crime.

5.10 Moreover, the way in which the war is being fought also violates this criterion. Fragmentation bombs and carpet bombing in areas where it is impossible to distinguish between soldiers and the civilian population are again clear (CD.2) – i.e. strongly reprehensible collateral damage, and hence are forbidden by criterion (2). This type of war crime is nothing new; we have come across it (of course not personally) in Vietnam and the Russian war in Chechnya, as well as in a host of other wars.

Fragmentation bombs, they say, are sometimes the best way to maximize success when hunting an enemy. This may be true. But what would we think of hunters who, in order to kill a herd of deer, carpeted their escape route with fragmentation bombs, knowing that plenty of other game would be blown up in the process? Why do we think this is unsuitable when hunting for deer – but not when hunting for terrorists in Afghanistan?

5.11 Now we would have to discuss things such as the in bello criterion (1), in particular whether this type of war is required given its aim, and moreover whether it is expedient. One problem is that we ought not to know anything about the exact aims of the war, they say, in order for them to be achieved.

So we'll have to make do without them. But *one* aim of the war is not secret. The supreme sense and purpose of this war is to maximize the security of our own (American, British, Germany, etc.) populations against further terror attacks. For this purpose, the elimination of T-networks may well be necessary and, assuming actions are restricted to their elimination, perhaps even expedient – but not if this elimination has to be bought at the expense of the death and increased misery of uninvolved outsiders at a ratio of 1:10 or even 1:20. In my view, the war in Afghanistan (or to be more accurate its first phase until the victory by the Northern Alliance) also violates criterion AD.1.

5.12 Wars which aren't allowed, i.e. which are not just wars, are – given the nature of war – a crime against humanity. The war in Afghanistan is and was not a just war.

5.13 Therefore, since one cannot be obliged to take part in crimes, we are under no obligation to participate in the campaign against terror by fighting in Afghanistan. As this war is a crime against humanity, it is instead everybody's moral duty not to take part in it.

So what's the next step? Have a think about it!

NOTES

[*] This is the paper I presented at a number of German universities in November/December 2001. As is especially apparent from Part II, the paper was written during the first phase of the war in Afghanistan. You might think that following the victory of the USA, the UK and the Northern Alliance, I ought to have updated my personal viewpoint from that time (and recorded here) to take the new circumstances into account. For many reasons I decided against this option.

Once again, many thinkers helped me out with both aid and criticism: above all Christoph Fehige, Franz von Kutschera, Wolfgang Lenzen, Herwig Lewy, Weyma Luebbe, Daniel Messelken, Richard Raatzsch, Kazem Sadegh-Zadeh, Katinka Schulte-Ostermann, Eckhard Schulz, Rudolf Schuessler, Thomas Spitzley, Ulla Wessels, Harald Wohlrapp and Georg Henrik von Wright. To make matters clear, philosophical aid doesn't automatically mean subscribing to the results. Moreover, I couldn't adopt every improvement offered; nor did I want to. Therefore if, as some listeners thought they had to warn me afterwards over a beer, this paper really does drive anyone to suggest someone is at fault, that someone should only be me.

The valuable objections and suggestions received when presenting this paper are too numerous to name all those behind them. I will address the main objections in the planned ex post reflections.

Thanks to Beatrice Kobow and Daniel Friedrich who helped me in transforming the original German version of this paper into a non-bavarian sort of English. For the German version, see "Terror & Gegenterror. Erste Ethische Reflexionen, *Deutsche Zeitschrift für Philosophie* 50 (2002), pp 149-162; reprinted in: Georg Meggle (ed.), *Terror & Der Krieg gegen ihn. Öffentliche Reflexionen*, mentis, Paderborn 2003, pp. 31-43.

HAIG KHATCHADOURIAN

COUNTER-TERRORISM: TORTURE AND ASSASSINATION

In "On Terrorism And Political Assassination" Kai Nielsen considers the question whether political assassinations are ever morally justified, and argues that "there are circumstances in which they are justified and that this is generally recognized".[1] Later I shall examine his reasons for this claim; but what needs to be noted at this point is that, unlike Nielsen, who is concerned with assassinations committed *by* terrorists among others, one of the two themes of this paper concerns the ethics of the assassination *of* suspected terrorists, as a form of or element in counterterrorism, by the military forces of a country that is attacked by presumed terrorists. I have in mind, of course, Israel's "targeted killing" of Palestinian militants in the ongoing al-Aqsa intifada. As far as I know, that is an entirely new putative form of counterterrorism, not witnessed prior to the *intifada*.

The second main theme of this paper is the ethics of a country's use of torture of suspected terrorists in custody, as a further way of combating terrorism.

PART I: ASSASSINATION AND COUNTER-TERRORISM

In "Is Political Terrorism Ever Morally Justified?"[2] I argued that the answer to the question posed by the article's title is a categorical No; that political assassination is never morally justified in principle, not just in practice.[3] In this section I shall defend the more general claim that assassination in general, not only for political reasons, is never morally justified in principle, consequently also in practice. Since some moral philosophers as well as perhaps many non-philosophers claim that terrorism is morally justified in certain circumstances, I shall (1) provide my reasons for that general claim, and (2) criticize some main arguments – particularly by James Rachel in the *Assassination* volume, who also claims, though for different reasons than Nielsen, that assassination is sometimes morally justifiable.

Section II will attempt to evaluate arguments for and against the "targeted killing" of Palestinian militants suspected of planning terrorist acts, or individuals believed to be preparing to commit such acts, against Israel. That section will conclude with a discussion of the proposal debated in the American media in the wake of the September 11, 2001, as to whether the current prohibition of assassinations by American law ought to be changed with respect to international terrorism. Since, as I said, I believe that terrorism in general is always morally wrong, I shall argue that "state" assassinations of suspected – or even actual – international terrorists does not constitute a morally justifiable exception, and so is also always wrong.

G. Meggle (ed.), Ethics of Terrorism & Counter-Terrorism, 177-196.

Finally, in Part II I shall inquire whether the torture of suspected terrorists to extract information that may lead to the prevention of future terrorist acts is ever morally justifiable.

IS ASSASSINATION IN GENERAL EVER MORALLY JUSTIFIED?

Assassination and the Human Right to Life

In *IPAMJ* I claimed that political assassination is never morally justified

"even when the assassin's motives and (2) the overall consequences of the action are good, whether actual or probable, and (3) the victim's political activities *are* a threat to his country or the world, because it violates the victim's human right to life."[4]

My basic argument was that

"it is wrong in any circumstances to inflict avoidable or unnecessary pain or suffering on human beings and animals, i.e., that physical and mental cruelty is morally wrong. This itself is part of the more general principle that it is prima facie wrong to harm human beings and animals, in any manner or degree. The latter can be grounded on the celebrated principle that human beings have the right to life and the pursuit of happiness, though it can also be maintained, I think, as a separate human right."[5]

Concentrating on rights, I argued that

"in all cases of political assassination the victim's right to life is (i) forcibly abrogated, necessarily without his consent, and (ii) without due process of law, thereby denying him the opportunity to defend himself against the charges brought against him. Finally, (iii) the termination of the victim's life is brought about by the assassin's taking the law into his own hands, turning himself into a judge of the victim's deeds or misdeeds, and arrogating to himself the 'right' to mete out punishment – and 'capital punishment' at that!"[6]

In his Introduction to *Assassination* the editor, Harold Zellner supposes that my claim is that "people have certain rights which cannot morally be over-ridden, *not even on the basis of the better consequences of doing so*".[7] He immediately adds that:

"It may be that these rights are 'inalienable' ...; they cannot be given up or taken away or lost. ... Even Hitler was a human being, and presumably had certain rights (at least at one time); Professor Khatchadourian seems to be arguing that assassination is all but impossible to justify on this sort of ground."[8]

That is quite close to what I claimed. In saying that assassination violates the victim's right to life (in addition to other moral rights) I was claiming that, as a *human* right, the right of life cannot be either *taken away* from a person or *forfeited* by him or her as long as he or she lives, as he or she continues to be a person, because of his or her committing heinous acts. Nor can that right (and the other human rights) be *voluntarily given up* by him or her, *or be lost.*[9]

In his contribution to *Assassination* entitled "Political Assassination", James Rachels takes issue with my position. In Zellner's words,

> "while admitting that some rights are inviolable, [Rachels] takes the somewhat more lenient position that such rights can be forfeited; Hitler lost his right to life when he violated the rights of so many others."[10]

The following summarizes Rachels' reason(s) for his view that in certain extreme circumstances, within certain limits, a person's rights can be overridden, justifying his or her assassination. He writes:

> "While it may be permissible for us to override our victim's rights if it were necessary to eliminate great suffering, it would not be permissible to override his rights merely to increase the happiness of an already minimally contented population even though the net gain, according to some sort of utilitarian calculus, is the same in both cases."[11]

Concerning the "relation between human rights and social utility", he adds:

> "The achievement of a minimally decent society, where human suffering and pain has been reduced to a tolerable level, is such an important business that it may justify overriding people's rights. Respecting people's rights is not more important than bringing about this minimally decent sort of society. However, once this has been achieved, it is no longer permissible to flout people's rights simply to make things still better. ... Thus, while it may be all right for a revolutionary temporarily to set aside the rule against killing in order to eliminate a great evil from a society, after the revolution the rule must be restored to its full force."[12]

As this passage shows, Rachels gives a consequentialist rationale for the permissibility of forfeiture of a person's (human) rights in certain extreme societal kinds of cases.

Rachels' consequentialist view is considerably more textured and complex than the straightforward act-utilitarian position such as Kai Nielsen's; inasmuch as it assigns an important role to human rights as well as to certain kinds of consequences; albeit, as we saw, these rights can be forfeited, hence overridden by certain consequences. According to Rachels these conditions are: (a) that the results of the assassination must be "good enough to outweigh the evil involved in destroying a human life"; (b) "assassination must be the only, or least objectionable, means of achieving these results"; and (c) "of all the possible actions available in the situation", it must be the "best overall balance of maximizing good and minimizing evil".[13] If these conditions, together with a rule regarding human rights, are seen as rules regulating and evaluating any societal policy or practice of assassination, Rachels' theory can be profitably viewed as a form of rule-utilitarianism.

However we may classify Rachels' theory, what matters for our discussion of assassination is whether an individual's human rights *can* be forfeited, hence overridden, by the kinds of consequences just described, or by any other kinds of consequences. To this question I shall now turn.

In my recent *Community and Communitarianism*[14] I claimed, as William Blackstone cogently argues in "Human Rights and Human Dignity",[15] that

> "human rights are not *prima facie* entitlements, hence open to forfeiture. Only the entitlement to their exercise is a *prima facie* entitlement. One attraction of the view that human rights are *prima facie* entitlements is that it provides an attractive moral justification for legal punishment by incarceration or execution, and for the political assassination of dictators and others who commit heinous crimes. But Blackstone correctly argues that human rights are 'inalienable' and consequently not *prima facie* rights."

As he writes:

> "What could it mean to renounce, transfer, or waive one's right to be treated as a person, for example? Such renouncement seems to make no sense as long as one *exists* as a person [i.e., as a human being]. [And with respect to renouncement or transfer of one's human rights, he adds:] If being respected as a person means that one's preferences, needs, choices, and actions are to be respected, surely it is nonsensical to speak of *someone else* having or being given my right to have my preferences, needs, choices and actions respected."[16]

> "Similarly, it makes no sense to speak of the forfeiture of one's right to be treated as a person "as long as one exists as a person". Blackstone's argument against the claim that human rights are prima facie rests on his rejection of the view that persons are "open to forfeiture of all rights. This ... amounts to allowing the conceptual possibility of viewing persons as *things*",[17] as not worthy of respect. Blackstone's argument is cogent if by "all rights" we understand "all human rights", not necessarily also civil or (some?)[18] legal rights."[19]

I should add that, besides arguing for the "inalienability" of human rights in the sense described above, I also argued in the same book that, with one fundamental exception, these rights – including the rights to life, to be free (both positive and negative), to privacy, and so on – are not absolute but form a set of interrelated rights that limit – and sometimes conflict with – one another. If this is correct it follows that these, non-absolute rights, such as the right to life, can be *overridden* by stronger moral claims, if such claims can and do exist. The only absolute human right, the only right not open to being overridden in principle is the foundational human right: the right to be treated as a moral being; to be treated with respect and consideration as a *person,* not to be treated as a "thing" or an "object".[20] That right is the logical-*cum*-moral foundation on which all non-absolute rights are grounded, which these rights presuppose.

It might be thought that if, notwithstanding the non-absolute character of the human right to life, it cannot be ever forfeited (e.g., as a result of one's committing heinous crimes), (a) it would follow that *no* stronger moral claim(s) that can override it exist; or that if (b) it *can be* overridden, it would follow that assassination *is* sometimes justified: that is, whenever a stronger moral claim exists. My response is No to both (a) and (b): the right to life *can* be overridden; but No, it does *not* follow that assassination is sometimes justified.

The reason for my negative reply to (a) is that the right to life can be overridden by at least one stronger moral claim; viz., the claim of criminal justice. I have murderers in mind, persons who deprive their victims[21] of their right to life (and, as a result, of all their other human rights) by ending their life, or persons who commit other heinous crimes, such as oppressing others or subjecting them to their evil wills. But – and this pertains to (b) – the criminal's right to life can only be overridden, in principle and in practice, only if and when the demands of criminal justice are fully satisfied. For – and this is extremely important – *the right to life* – and, by implication, the right to be treated as a moral person – *entitles one to defend that right, i.e., one's life, against evidence intended to override that right; so that right can only be overridden by sufficient evidence against the individual in a fair and just trial.* That is, provided that (i) the criminal's violation of the victim's/victims' right to life, or other human rights, is proved beyond a shadow of a doubt in a fair trial, in which the defendant's moral and legal defenses and rights are fully respected (e.g., in the U.S. in accordance with the Constitution and the Bill of Rights); and provided that (ii) no extenuating circumstances that serve to mitigate his or her just sentence can be found. This means that the demands of criminal justice may require that an individual who has been justly shown in a court of law to have, say, committed murder, may be justly put to death if countervailing moral claims – such as the claim that capital punishment fails to deter potential murderer, or other countervailing consequentialist claims – do not render the death penalty itself morally wrong. The phrase "has been shown in a court of law" is crucial. In its absence – and this point will be reiterated in the rest of this section and the next – the killing, including the assassination of someone who is only *suspected* of having committed acts of terrorism, would itself be murder.[22]

I said that the demands of criminal justice may require the overriding of an individual's right to life. But can that right not be also overridden if doing so serves to enlarge or expand *others'* human right to life, etc. – in short, the human right to be treated as a person – particularly, of a large number of persons? For instance, assassinating a dictator in order to enable his people to enjoy their human rights, including the freedoms to which, as moral persons, they are entitled? For are not the human rights of the many of greater worth than a single individual's human rights?

It is granted that the answer to the last question is Yes – but! For by the very nature of assassination, the victim is denied the opportunity to defend himself or herself, either physically or in a court of law, before his or her life, hence all that his or her life entails, for ever forcibly taken away.[23]

Again, the ability of as many individuals as possible – ideally, of all human beings on earth – freely to exercise their human rights so as to achieve self-fulfilment and therefore happiness is indeed a great good. If a powerful individual or group of individuals prevents others from exercising their human rights, stopping him or them from continuing to do so would be morally justified, particularly if achieved by a minimal *restriction* of their human rights. But depriving them of their very capacity to exercise their rights once and for all by killing them is, in my view, quite another matter.

Assassination and Consequentialism

Act-Utilitarianism and Assassination

On act-utilitarian grounds assassination is justified whenever the assassination's bad consequences are outweighed by its good consequences. But act-utilitarianism suffers from certain well-known difficulties in addition to those involving, e.g., the application of the concept of consequences of actions to actual or possible cases difficulties that face rule-utilitarianism as well. The problem of the comparative weighing of such goods as pleasure and pain, happiness and unhappiness, or of liberty,[24] is a serious theoretical problem faced by consequentialism in general,[25] while the problem of predicting the actual or even the probable consequences of actions – particularly the long-range, often widespread consequences of important actions by political leaders that affect the lives of large numbers of people, often for long periods of time[26] – is a further serious practical problem for consequentialism. Another familiar theoretical problem is whether the probable or the actual consequences should be weighed when trying to assess the overall goodness or badness of particular actions or classes of actions; or whether the agent's having "good reason to believe that ... [the] act will produce good results"[27] should be considered the criterion of right action.

I shall now point out certain central difficulties with act-utilitarianism that vitiate it as a way of justifying assassination in certain circumstances. Some of these difficulties also vitiate "pure" rule-utilitarianism. In the next sub-section and especially in Section II I shall discuss some special difficulties facing rule-utilitarian attempts to justify the assassination of suspected terrorists.

A central problem with both act- and rule-utilitarianism is the absence of *independent* deontological side-constraints, such as the constraints of human rights and the principles of justice, thus allowing acts or kinds of acts that violate these principles. For rights as well as the principles of justice are subordinated by both to the (general) good; as we saw for example in Rachels' case.[28] The problem of "telishment" – which permits the "punishment" of innocent persons whenever doing so serves the "general good", has "good consequences on the whole", notwithstanding its blatant violation of the victim's human rights as well as the principles of criminal justice[29] – illustrates this central difficulty well.

Another, perhaps less known difficulty with "pure", traditional utilitarianism/consequentialism[30] stems from the consequentialist's duty to maximize the "general good". As Bernard Williams argues, that saddles the utilitarian/consequentialist with what Williams calls the "strong doctrine of negative responsibility".[31] Since the difficulty is discussed at some length in *Community and Communitarianism* (pages 95 ff.), I shall only give the gist of that central difficulty here.

According to Williams "the strong doctrine of negative responsibility flows directly from consequentialism's assignment of ultimate (intrinsic) value to states of affairs". In *Ethics and the Limits of Philosophy* he states the matter thus:

> "There are states of affairs I can affect with respect to welfare which, because I can do so, turn out to be my concern when, on nonutilitarian assumptions, they would be someone else's concern."[32]

In *Utilitarianism For and Against* he gives two examples to show what is wrong with the strong doctrine of negative responsibility. The first example concerns George, a chemist with heavy family responsibilities who is faced with the dilemma of whether to accept, against his moral principles, a job "in a certain laboratory which pursues research into chemical and biological warfare".[33]

If he refuses the position his family will be in financial difficulty and the position

> "will certainly go to a [chemist] who is ... likely ... to push along the research with greater zeal than George would."[34]

The second example finds Jim, an American traveler on a botanical expedition, "in the central square of a small South American town" where the captain in charge has rounded up a random group of Indians who,

> "after recent acts of protest against the government, are just about to be killed to remind other possible protestors of the advantages of not protesting".[35] "The captain tells Jim that if he kills one of the Indians he will let the other Indians go free."[36]

William thinks that the utilitarian resolution of the dilemmas would be,

> "in the first case, that George should accept the job, and in the second, that Jim should kill the Indian"[37] (Cf. "telishment".)

Williams argues that

> "in its strong doctrine of negative responsibility, utilitarianism [consequentialism] 'cuts out' the fact 'that each of us is specially responsible for what *he* does, rather than for what other people do'."[38]

For Williams 'this is an idea connected with the value of integrity', a value he thinks utilitarianism makes 'more or less unintelligible'.[39]

> "Integrity as Williams understands it involves 'the relation between a man's projects and his actions'.[40] The idea of integrity essentially arises in relation to a person's projects, which Williams calls 'commitments, those with which one is more deeply and extensively involved and identified'."[41]

Rule-Utilitarianism and Assassination

The basic question for the rule-utilitarian would be whether a state or societal *policy* or *practice* of assassination of terrorist suspects would have greater benefits than bad consequences for the particular country or society (or even for human society in general). For instance, whether it would deter and so prevent future acts of terrorism. The belief that it does do so is perhaps the rationale for e.g., the Israeli government's practicing targeted killing of suspected Palestinian militants or terrorists during the ongoing al-Aqsa *intifada*; although, in point of fact, these assassinations have definitely failed as a deterrent. Prevention or deterrence is also unlikely to happen so long as people are willing and ready to die for what they consider to be a great cause – in this particular case, liberation from Israeli rule. That is above all true if the militants consider death in the cause of liberation as a religious *jihad*, and thus both consider themselves and are considered by their compatriots as martyrs, in the event of their death.

The danger that the people would lose faith in their system of justice is another main reason why a consistent rule-utilitarian country or society would not adopt an *overt, public* political-legal *policy* or *practice*[42] of assassination of the "enemies of the people" and/or of the state. Instead, it would adopt a *public* policy or practice that includes (in the latter case, would include a "regulative") moral/legal rule[43] that prohibits all assassinations in principle. A government or society that adopted assassination, even if, theoretically, only against suspected terrorists, is likely to be considered by its own people as undermining, or on its way to undermining, the rule of law in general indeed, of the very idea of due process – by violating the principle that a person is innocent until proven guilty. In short, the people would tend to believe that a slippery slope effect will gradually take effect. In fact, once the government comes to believe that the assassination of suspected terrorists deters terrorist violence, it may be tempted to think it desirable to deter ordinary murders, rapes, kidnaping and other garden variety felonies too by the "taking out" of individuals suspected of having committed one of more of these crimes.

It might be thought that a *covert* policy or practice of assassination of perceived enemies such as suspected terrorists or heads of enemy or terrorist states by the state's intelligence agencies (e.g., the FBI or CIA in the case of the U.S.A.) would avoid the preceding difficulties. But that is not really so; since it is always possible that the covert policy would be exposed by the domestic or foreign media, particularly whenever the assassination attempts fail. Such revelations are likely to result in a domestic and international outcry and condemnation; not least by the particular country's enemies if one or more of their political leaders happen to be the targets of the assassination or assassination attempts.[44]

Another reason why an *overt or* a *covert* practice or policy permitting the assassination of a country's real or perceived enemies would tend to be counterproductive is that hostile states would be encouraged to pay that country with its own coin, targeting its own agents and/or political leaders, perhaps even its head of state. (I shall return to these points later, in Section III, in relation to debates in the American media following September 11, 2001, as to whether the U.S. prohibition against assassination, which has been in effect for some time, should be lifted in relation to terrorists.)

A public, governmental institution or practice *IP* that adopts a given policy *P* in order to help realize the state's particular goals *G* would spell out or define *G* by, among other things, stipulating a rule that enjoins certain methods of realizing *G*, and, thereby, furthering *IP's* broader national and international goals. For *P* to be properly executed, *IP* would include, among its regulative rules, a regulative rule that (a) regulates and periodically evaluates *P's* implementation; determining when and how its personnel should implement *P*; and (b) enables the particular agency or branch of government periodically to evaluate the (degree of) success or failure of *P's*, hence *PI's*, implementation.

In the case of an (e.g., a covert) institution/practice *IP* whose objective is to protect the country by, among other things, gathering sensitive political, military and strategic, and, perhaps, economic intelligence or information, and even aims hence has a policy *P* to destabilize or overthrow hostile regimes through political assassinations, would indicate the nature and aims of that policy *P* by, among other things, issuing a directive that permits, even encourages "well-timed", "well-executed" political assassinations. In addition, *IP* would include in its regulative rules a rule that (a) regulates and (b) periodically evaluates *P's* implementation. In this case it would determine, and evaluate, the appropriateness and effectiveness of the assassinations planned or implemented in a given period of time, hence the extent to which they are or have been serving *P's*, and so *IP's*, and – with it – the state's or country's goals.

The same would be true, *mutatis mutandis*, of a state policy prohibiting political assassinations except perhaps in wartime; insofar as state assassinations would hurt – or would hurt more than advance – the particular state's or country's political, military-strategic or other goals. (As we shall see later, the same kinds of argument would show that a rule-utilitarian would prohibit or condemn a societal or state practice or policy of torture of suspected terrorists or indicted alleged terrorists in custody.)

State-sponsored assassinations and national self-defense

I now turn to the question whether state assassinations are morally and legally justified in time of defensive war.

It is common knowledge that the Israeli government of Prime Minister Ariel Sharon claims to be fighting a "defensive war" against Palestinian terrorism during the ongoing Aqsa *intifada*, and that, consequently, is justified in destroying what it calls "the infrastructure of terrorism" in the Palestinian territories. Although that declaration came some time after Israel had all but stopped targeted killing of suspected terrorists (possibly after legal restrictions were placed on targeted killings by the Israeli government)[45] during its recent massive military incursions into the West Bank and Gaza, I shall now turn to the claim that (a) the wartime assassination of enemy military and political leaders would be morally justified on act-utilitarian grounds; that is, whenever it helps the country perpetrating the assassination to win the war.[46] It might even be thought that (b) a policy of assassination of enemy leaders in wartime can also be justified on *rule-utilitarian* grounds. For it might be claimed that a policy that includes a regulative rule permitting such assassinations whenever it is likely to advance the *just* party's war efforts, can be justified on rule-utilitarian grounds.

In light of our earlier discussion of act-utilitarianism, claim (a) would undoubtedly be true. But it is otherwise with claim (b), for reasons similar to those I gave against assassination as a state policy in general. I mean that a warring party's policy of that nature would encourage the enemy to pay it back with the same coin; although it is granted that that may not be possible in a particular case. For example, the Japanese did not assassinate any American military leader in retaliation for the assassination of a Japanese Admiral in the Pacific Theater during World War II. But the real possibility of a pay-back cannot be excluded.

Even if we leave aside our earlier general criticism of "pure" act- and rule-utilitarianism, it would still remain that claims (a) and (b) are inapplicable to Israel's assassination of Palestinian militant leaders such as Abu Ali Mustafa, "the leader of the Popular Front for the Liberation of Palestine", and the Hamas leader, Mahmoud Abu Hanoud.[47] The perfectly obvious reason is that war consists in actual belligerence between states: something which is not the case with the current Palestinian-Israeli conflict; although the rhetoric of "war against Palestinian terrorism" has enabled Israel to extract considerable psychological-rhetorical advantage during especially when its army

185

"made lengthy, repeated incursions" into the West Bank and Gaza strip. Similarly President Bush's 'war' in 'war on terrorism' applies to the al-Qa'ida and other international terrorist organizations (as opposed to the Taliban Afghan regime) only in an extended, *metaphorical* sense. While deterrence is obviously not a realistic goal of wartime assassinations, deterrence (together with the desire for retaliation if not revenge) is clearly the Israeli government's goal in assassinating suspected terrorists.

It is worth noting here the Israeli writer David Grossman's criticism of the Israeli assassination of Abu Ali Mustafa, the leader of the Popular Front for the Liberation of Palestine, which he calls

> "foolish and dangerous even within this tangled context. It was an act of revenge meant, first and foremost, to bolster Israeli deterrence. It was also aimed at dealing a blow to Palestinian morale, one that would force the Palestinian Authority to talk with Israel."

He significantly adds:

> "Neither of these goals was achieved. It seems to me that it shouldn't have been difficult to guess that the action would achieve the precise opposite and only make matters worse."

But Grossman goes beyond the assassination of Abu Ali Mustafa, and rightly equating assassination with murder, he adds:

> "Apparently, we have all become so callous, have become so accustomed to the unbearable lightness of death in our region, *that we need to remember that to murder a human being, whether Israeli or Palestinian, is blatantly to cross a red line.*"[48]

Amos Oz, another well-known Israeli writer, defends the opposite position.[49] Pleading that Israel is

> "entitled to defend itself, though not by hurting or killing innocent civilians, not by killing politicians, ideologists or even dreadful inciters and agitators. [Although] with a heavy heart",

he justifies the

> "killing of Palestinian fighters, uniformed or not, but of no one else. The term assassination is a very misleading one. Killing unarmed civilians is assassination; killing fighting Palestinians or active terrorists is self-defense, and I justify it."

> "Israel deserves very serious criticism when it kills civilians. It does not deserve criticism when in a state of war [note the use of the word] it kills fighting enemies. In principle, when a country is attacked, it can choose among three ways: it can indiscriminately kill the 'others', it can turn the other cheek to its enemies, or it can fight back against those who carry weapons. I prefer not to fight at all, but if there is a war I definitely prefer the last way."[50]

Like Oz, Grossman maintains that

"Israel has every right to defend itself. If official spokesmen for the Palestinians declare that they intend to send dozens of suicide bombers to Israeli city centers, they should hardly be surprised that Israel responds with a lopsided display of force aimed at foiling such deeds and impeding their perpetrators. When Palestinian leaders declare that Israel has 'crossed a red line' they sound disingenuous. After all, it is they who have encouraged acts of indiscriminate mass murder of innocent citizens, children and infants within the borders of the state of Israel."[51]

In conclusion, Grossman, like Oz, eloquently pleads for a peaceful resolution of the conflict:

"in the current circumstances, Israel and the Palestinians must show less 'creativity' in killing and attacking each other and more in seeking a resolution of the conflict. But parties must resume negotiations unconditionally. Without negotiation we will all be helplessly caught in a spiral of murder and revenge. Without hope, we will all be doomed to be battered time and again by the deadly symptoms of our *disease until, perhaps very soon, we will find ourselves powerless to treat the illness itself.*"[52]

To this I can only say "Amen".[53]

It remains that genuine, morally justified Israeli self-defense against Palestinian militants – terrorists and non-terrorists – who attack Israeli civilians and soldiers, must be distinguished from the assassination of suspected terrorists, which, I have argued, is nothing short of murder, hence morally wrong, as well as a violation of international law.

Moral/Juridical Arguments against State Assassination of Suspected Militants or Terrorists, as a Form of Counter Terrorism

As will be recalled I have maintained that (1) human rights, with the exception of the right to be treated as a (moral) person are not absolute and can be overridden by stronger moral claims, (2) a human person cannot possibly forfeit his or her human rights, nor can they be taken away from him or her as long as he or she lives, and (3) a person's human right to life can be morally overridden by the demands of criminal justice, if or when he or she commits heinous crimes. From (1) and (3) it may seem that a person's right to life can be overridden if (a) he or she commits acts of terrorism or other serious crimes, whenever it is impossible or practically impossible for the authorities to arrest him or her and bring him or her to justice; or perhaps even (b) preemptively, whenever convincing evidence exists that an individual (who has hitherto not committed acts of terrorism, and the like) is actively engaged in planning to commit acts of terrorism. In either case, (a) or (b), it might be held that the individual's assassination would be morally justified, satisfying the demands of criminal justice. The advocate of assassination under conditions (a) or (b) may exempt juveniles engaged in or planning acts of terrorism.

The defender of assassination in the case of both (a) and (b) may additionally argue that terrorist acts are more evil and more felonious than "ordinary", garden variety acts of murder, rape, kidnaping, and other morally and juridically wrong acts; indeed, as specially heinous acts, they are *sui generis*, in a class by themselves as evil acts. Hence (i) a terrorist's targeted killing would be a lesser evil than the evil he or she perpetrates by his terrorist acts. Moreover, (ii) refraining from killing a terrorist may well enable him or her to strike again. Assassinating a terrorist would therefore be justified as a preemptive or preventive act. Thus a terrorist's assassination would be justified on act-utilitarian grounds. It would be added that in the case of (a) above the assassinations would also be morally and juridically justified as acts of national self-defense; while they would be justified as acts of national self-protection in the case of (b).

My response to (a) and (b) is as follows:

With regard to (a) let us assume for the same of argument that terrorist acts are morally or juridically *sui generis*: that they are essentially different in kind from ordinary kidnaping, killing of innocents, and other morally evil acts;[54] and let us also assume that overriding a terrorist's right to life is morally justified. It would remain that that justification cannot justly apply either in relation to merely *suspected* terrorists or to individuals who *plan* to commit terrorist acts; but only in relation to *actual, bona fide* terrorists, who have been to be legally guilty of terrorism in a fair and just court of law. To assassinate alleged, suspected militants or terrorists is to act "extra-judicially as judge, jury, and executioner", as Professor Shibley Telhami[55] recently observed in criticism of Israeli targeted killings; especially when, as he added, Israel is able to arrest Palestinian militants and bring them to justice – as it has in fact been recently doing during repeated massive incursions into Palestinian territories – as well as applying great pressure on the Palestinian Authority to arrest suspected terrorists.[56]

The ethical issues concerning the ethics of terrorism and counter terrorism are complicated by the widespread confusions about what terrorism is: not surprisingly given that vague and loose conventional concept. But the problem goes well beyond unintended confusion or misunderstanding. For instance, crucial distinction or differences between "terrorism" and "freedom fighting" in general and therefore between acts of terrorism and acts of freedom fighting, have been practically obliterated, particularly by governments intent on preserving the status quo against bona fide liberation movements.[57] Since September 11, 2001 in particular, many governments as well as the media have been exploiting the term's ill-defined character, arbitrarily redefining or stretching the word in different directions to further their own political-military agendas.

As I argued in "Terrorism and Morality" and *The Morality of Terrorism, terrorism* is an essentially "bifocal" concept. I mean the crucial distinction between (a) the "immediate victims", the individuals who are the immediate targets of terrorism, and (b) "the victimized", those who are the indirect but real targets of terrorist acts. Normally the latter are individual governments or countries or certain groups of governments or countries, or specific institutions or groups within a given country. The ultimate targets may also be certain social, economic or political systems or regimes which the terrorists dislike and hope to change or destroy by their terrorist activities.[58] The indiscriminate harming killing, wounding, hostage taking, etc. of innocent civilians, which is most widely thought to constitute terrorism, neither defines nor distinguishes it from other forms of violence. In terrorist violence, the discriminate or indiscriminate *violence* is motivated by certain political, military, economic, moralistic/religious or other ends, and is but a *means* to the "real", political, economic, military, moralistic/religious or other *objective(s)* of terrorist acts. Additionally as Mark Juergensmeyer shows,[59] especially significant terrorist acts and their immediate targets (such as the September 11, 2001 attacks in the U.S.) are symbolic acts. And by their very nature, symbols in general, including symbolic acts, are "bifocal" in the sense that they refer to or represent something beyond themselves, the object(ive) symbolized.

Moral Evaluation of the Palestinian al-Aqsa intifada and Israel's military response to it

Neither the Palestinian *intifada* nor Israel's military response to it, *as a whole*, satisfy all conditions of a morally justified military struggle. The *intifada* does have just cause, insofar as it is a liberation movement, but violates the principle of discrimination by frequently targeted innocent Israeli civilians, whether by acts of terrorism which are always morally wrong, wrong in all possible circumstances,[60] or by non-terrorist acts of vengeance or retaliation against innocent civilians. The *intifada* is, also, far from a last resort. Yasser Arafat could and should have accepted the Clinton-Barak plan with respect to the West Bank and Gaza Strip, with the proviso that the future of the Old City of Jerusalem and the Palestinian refugees whose homes were originally in what is now Israel would have to be later negotiated, for example, when the precise borders of the Palestinian state are agreed upon.[61] Arafat's rejection of the Clinton proposals is the absolutely worst mistake an Arab leader has made since the Palestinian and other Arab leaders rejected the U. N. Partition Plan fifty-four years ago.

Israel's military response to the *intifada* also violates several conditions of morally justified self-defense. The most obvious are: its gross violation of the principle of proportionality as a *jus ad bellum* and as a *jus in bello* principle, by its use of excessive military force against Palestinians, and its violation of the principle of discrimination, involving the death or wounding of a hitherto unknown but nonetheless large number of innocent civilians its forces killed or wounded during the *intifada* as a whole, and massive destruction of dwellings and homes, especially during its repeated military incursions into Palestinian territories; in particular, the Palestinian refugee camp in Jenin, which led the Human Rights Watch and Amnesty International to condemn Israel's human rights violations.[62]

To these we must add the moral wrongness of Israel's targeted assassinations of suspected terrorists and other militants, which we discussed at some length. Fortunately, Israel has recently switched from targeted killings to arresting suspected militants – possibly as a result of recent legal advice against targeted killing it has come, as I mentioned, at a terrible price to innocent Palestinian civilians during the Israeli military incursions.

Israel has just cause in responding with military force against members of Hamas and Palestinian Islamic Jihad, who attack its military forces and/or civilian population – since their long-range aim is to destroy Israel – and against other militants who kill or wound innocent Israeli civilians. Still Israel's self-defense morally only extends to those who actually commit acts of violence, including terrorism, against Israeli citizens. Its self-defense also justifiably includes – whenever it does not unnecessarily place innocent civilians in harm's way – the arrest and trial of suspected militants, either by its own forces or by the Palestinian Authority under pressure from it.

Finally, if the condition of "just peace" is to be even partially met once a Palestinian state alongside Israel has been created, Palestinians and Israel must pay restitution for the lives and property destroyed by both sides as a result of the latest Palestinian-Israeli conflict.

PART II: TORTURE AND COUNTER-TERRORISM

Our next question is whether torture, whether psychological or physical, is ever morally justifiable in general; consequently, as a counterterrorist measure.

Part I, Article I of the U.N. General Assembly RES 39/46, Annex[63] defines 'torture' as follows:

> "1. For the purposes of this Convention, torture means any act by which severe pain or suffering, whether physical or mental, is intentionally inflicted on a person for such purposes as obtaining from him or a third person information or a confession, punishing him for an act he or third person has committed or is suspected of having committed, or intimidating or coercing him or a third person, or for any reason based on discrimination of any kind, when such pain or suffering is inflicted by or at the instigation of or with the consent or acquiescence of a public official or other person acting in an official capacity. It does not include pain or suffering arising only from, inherent in or incidental to lawful sanctions."[64]

Following the recent changes in American law respecting suspected foreign terrorists after September 11, 2001, effected under President George W. Bush and the attorney general John Ashcroft, some members of the American media have debated whether the torture of suspected terrorists should now be allowed. For instance, in "Time To Think About Torture",[65] Jonathan Alter suggested that the psychological torture of terrorists should be legalized. In a readers letter in the November 19, 2001 issue of *Newsweek*, he responded to readers who took issue with his suggestion in an earlier issue of the magazine by observing that he "opposes legalizing physical torture ... It is contrary to American values and doesn't generally work well." His reasons were that:

> "I placed psychological torture in a different moral category. At a minimum, the problem of extracting critical information that could save thousands or even millions of lives should not be off-limits for public discussion."[66]

(1) William F. Schulz, Executive Director, Amnesty International USA, in a readers letter in the same issue as Alter's response, states a number of cogent reasons against the use of torture against suspected terrorists. He writes:

> "Alter fails to understand that not only is the use of torture illegal and immoral: it could also place Americans' lives in danger by increasing hostility toward the United States. Moreover, nothing would alienate the international community, whose support the United States desperately needs, more than the abandonment of the most widely agreed-upon human right, the prohibition against torture. The 1984 Convention Against Torture states: "No exceptional circumstances whatsoever, whether a state of war or a threat of war, internal political instability or any other public

emergency, may be invoked as a justification for torture." Few other prohibitions under international law are so absolute. Although banned by Israel's Supreme Court in 1999, the use of torture is not uncommon there. It has not brought the country peace or security, nor will it in the United States. On both moral and practical terms, torture is dead wrong."[67]

(2) Jean-Francois Benard, President of ACAT- (Action of Christians for the Abolition of Torture) France, responds to Jonathan Alter's statement that "we can't legalize physical torture because 'it's contrary to American values'" and concludes that 'We'll have to think about transferring some suspects to our less squeamish allies, even if that's hypocritical.' "In fact", Benard counters,

> "this would be more than hypocritical – any authority that made such a transfer would be a direct accomplice to the foreign torturers to whom the suspects would be turned over. All over the world, free citizens dedicated to the rights and duties that underpin this civilization are supporting the fight against terrorism. They sincerely hope that this struggle will not be diminished by inhuman practices like torture, which would negate the values on which this civilization is founded. Torture is a crime under international law, and ACAT ... is fully confident that U.S. citizens will resist the dubious arguments made in an attempt to justify its use, whether practiced in their own country or, by virtue of a skewed delegation of power, by barely scrupulous allies."[68]

(3) Besides violating international law, as Benard states, torture can violate municipal (domestic) law, given the fact, noted earlier, that 'terrorism' is unfortunately being constantly stretched in many countries around the world in all sorts of ways to suit their political interests and goals, is made to cover kinds of violations of municipal law very different from bona fide terrorism. This laxity and vagueness in the term's employment can lead to the torture and/or execution of individuals who commit *non*-terrorist capital crimes for which the punishment prescribed by law is life imprisonment or a lesser prison term.[69] The torture and conviction of "suspected terrorists" in the name of counterterrorism, may even result in the conviction and execution of perfectly innocent persons.

(4) It is an empirical fact that psychological and not only physical torture is quite unreliable as a means of extracting reliable information designed to preempt or prevent acts of violence. It does not work. because, as Arthur Koestler writes in *Darkness at Noon*, in his powerful portrayal of Stalin's use of torture against his political victims in 1936-37, which culminated in the notorious Moscow Trials,

> "human beings able to resist any amount of physical pressure do not exist. I have never seen one. Experience shows me that the resistance of the human nerve system is limited by Nature."[70]

Under prolonged torture even the most determined and resistant victims will eventually crack and confess to any crimes their torturers want them to confess. Koestler graphically shows that in relation to the novel's central character, Rubashov (a fictional composite of several leading communist party members, including Trotsky and Bukharin). The mainly mental-psychological torture and humiliation Rubashov endures, coupled with his own political convictions as an Old Bolshevik, lead him at the end to confess to all the trumped-up crimes of which his torturers accuse him.

In "And they all confessed ...",[71] Gudrun Persson writes as follows about the Moscow Trials:

> "There is no doubt that torture was used to force confessions. Though by no means uncommon earlier, torture only became an approved method of examination during the investigations leading up to the first Moscow trial. On 29 July, 1936, an official, albeit secret, document was drawn up, sanctioning the use of "all means" to extract confessions.[72] Krostinsky's submission was clearly the result of a night of brutal torture. Naturally, psychological torture in the form of threats to relatives and the rest of the family members also played their part in the confessions."[73]

(5) Given these and similar facts about the results of torture, even an act-utilitarian would be hard pressed to justify torture in practice; while any rule-utilitarian view worth its salt would expressly prohibit psychological and physical torture *in principle,* for essentially the same sorts of reasons that, I argued earlier, would lead a country to prohibit a policy or practice of assassination. Unfortunately, as noted earlier, unethical governments continue to practice torture with impunity, in the absence of any international force ready and able and to stop or penalize them, even when they are repeatedly exposed by Amnesty International or other human rights watches. These governments act not on act- or rule-utilitarian grounds but on the dangerous and immoral "principle" that the "end" – here, the state's alleged interests – justifies the "means".

(6) In light of the preceding, it is not surprising that the principle of "double effect" cannot justify torture, notwithstanding the fact that the evil of the pain and suffering inflicted would be intended to help realize a putative greater good,[74] and the torturer may claim (as the Spanish Inquisitors claimed) that they only intended the good, not (or not also) the torture's evil consequences. For as Elizabeth Anscombe has cogently argued, one cannot validly detach the intention from the act performed, with (as we say) "that intention".[75] Moreover, the principle of double effect proscribes certain acts, such as murder, as inherently immoral.

(7) In the passage quoted earlier, Schulz rightly speaks of the prohibition against torture as a human right. For to torture a human being is to treat him not as a moral person, possessing dignity and deserving of respect, but as a tool, an "object", nothing but an instrument for the torturer's ends, even when these ends happen to be moral ones. In fact, torture is not unlike rape in its physical aspect; while psychological torture is not dissimilar to the emotional and mental aspects of rape. In both types of cases the victim selfhood is violated; and as I earlier maintained, the fundamental, Ur-right to be treated as a moral person is *absolute*, and so, cannot be overridden by any putative superior moral claim or claims.

NOTES

[1] *Assassination*, Harold M. Zellner, ed. (Cambridge, MA, 1974), p. 97. The same is true of the other contributors to that volume who share Nielsen's view of the justifiability of political assassination in certain circumstances.

[2] Ibid., pp. 41-55. Hereafter referred to as *IPAMJ*. See also "Responses to Terrorism", in my *The Morality of Terrorism* (New York, 1998), Chapter 6, pp. 113-135.

[3] To use a distinction Zellner makes in his Introduction. See later.

[4] Ibid., p. 49. Italics in original.

[5] Ibid., p. 50.

[6] Ibid., p. 51. Thus in the Introduction, p. 6, Zellner misconstrues my position by stating that "all of the philosophers writing herein agree, ... that there are circumstances in which assassination could be justified", since I argued that there are *no* [theoretical or practical] circumstances in which assassination could be justified; although a little later he states that "at least Professor Khatchadourian seems to take the other view".

[7] Introduction, p. 7.

[8] Ibid.

[9] Ibid. However, in certain circumstances, one can freely and voluntarily *refrain from exercising* his or her right to life; for example, in order to allow another person morally to terminate his or her life, or to assist him or her to do so, out of compassion and caring.

[10] Ibid., p. 7.

[11] Rachels, op cit., pp. 15-16.

[12] Ibid., p. 16.

[13] Rachels, op cit., p. 13.

[14] New York, 1999.

[15] *Philosophical Forum*, vol. 9, March 1971, pp. 3-38.

[16] Op cit., p. 6. Italics in original.

[17] Blackstone, op cit., p. 7. Italics in original.

[18] "I say *some*? because it can be plausibly argued that a society's stripping a criminal of *all* of his or her legal rights "amounts to treating him or her as a thing: an argument that may have some force against capital punishment." (*Community and Communitarianism*, note 36, p. 134. Italics in original.)

[19] Ibid., p. 122.

[20] Op cit., Chapters 6, pp. 115 ff.

[21] That is, at least in the case of a multiple or mass murderer: above all, in the case of someone who commits genocide or crimes against humanity. With regard to the latter, see "Humanitarian Military Intervention: Justice vs. Rights", in this volume.

[22] At the beginning of his contribution to *Assassination*, titled "Assassination, Responsibility And Retribution", Douglas Lackey states that murder is the "deliberate killing of the *innocent*, and given this definition, we know that murder is always wrong" (ibid., p. 57). True, murder is always wrong, but not because, by definition, it is the killing of "the innocent", unless by 'the innocent' we mean "the legally innocent"; e.g., persons in custody who have not yet been tried and so are *legally* innocent before the law, or persons who are at large and are not suspects in any crime. Lackey's definition would be incorrect if by 'the innocent' we mean "the morally innocent": those who are innocent of any at least of any serious – *moral* wrong. Killing another and we must add the proviso, "if not done in self-defense" – constitutes murder whether the victim is morally innocent or no. (Indeed, how many human beings are innocent of any, including any serious, moral wrong?)

[23] The fundamental concept of self-defense is also crucial to the concept of a just war. See, for example, my "Self-Defense and the Just War". In the relevant papers on war in this volume I concurred with the theoretical possibility of just wars on consequentialist-*cum*-deontological grounds (the latter, e.g., with respect to the discrimination rule). But can any conception of human rights e.g., the conception of human rights I expressed in *Community and Communitarianism* and in this paper – allow for the theoretical possibility of just war? Drawing on the concept of self-defense, my answer is Yes. In terms of human rights, a just war would be, *inter*

alia, a war whose goal is to defend – to preserve or to enhance – the human rights, or these rights among other values, of a country or people.

[24] This pertains to e.g., Douglas Lackey's view that "an act is justified if the person who performs it has good reason to believe that it will produce good results". He defines 'good results' as "an increase in the amount of happiness and liberty, in the world, provided that this increase in happiness and freedom is fairly distributed". In the case of terrorism, he adds: "that is, that it is enjoyed by nearly everyone, not just the friends, associates, or favored groups of the assassin." (Assassination, Responsibility And Retribution, *Assassination,* p. 57.)

[25] Except an ethic of caring (or of care), which is a very special form of "consequentialist" ethic. See *Community and Communitarianism,* Part 2.

[26] The assassination of the head of a government is a particularly good example.

[27] Douglas Lackey, op cit., p. 62.

[28] For an extended discussion of this see *Community and Communitarianism.*

[29] It can be shown that the general principle of utility results in a similar kind of injustice with respect to distributive justice. But I am not concerned with that here.

[30] The special, feminist form of consequentialism known as the ethic of care or of caring, is a noteworthy exception. For this the interested reader is referred to *Community and Communitarianism.*

[31] "A Critique of Utilitarianism", *Utilitarianism For and Against,* Bernard Williams and J. J. Smart, editors (Cambridge, 1973), p. 95 ff.

[32] *Community and Communitarianism,* p. 96; Williams, op cit., p. 77.

[33] Ibid., p. 98.

[34] Ibid. Quoted from *Community and Communitarianism,* p. 96.

[35] Williams, and Smart, ibid.

[36] *Community and Communitarianism,* p. 96.

[37] Williams, and Smart, op cit, p. 99. *Community and Communitarianism,* p. 96.

[38] Ibid. Italics in original.

[39] Ibid. *Community and Communitarianism,* pp. 96-97.

[40] Ibid., p. 100.

[41] Williams, and Smart, op cit., p. 116. *C and C,* p. 97.

[42] In the semi-technical use of the word defined by John Searle in e.g., *Speech Acts.*

[43] A practice's (or an institution's) "regulative rules or principles", as distinguished from its "constitutive rules", which set up or define the practice or institution, regulate and evaluate the practice or institution as a whole.

[44] We will have to wait to see whether this kind of fallout will actually occur in the wake of President Bush's latest (June 17, 2002) dangerous directive to the FBI and CIA to try to covertly oust Saddam Hussein, and if need be kill him, "in [*sic.*]self-defense".

[45] I say "all but stopped targeted killings" because, after a considerable lull, the Israeli forces, on June 17, 2002, BBC reported that a prominent member of Hamas. Was pulled out of a car and shot dead point blank by Israeli soldiers, hours after a Hamas suicide bomber killed 19 and wounded dozens more Israelis civilians.

[46] Note Michael Walzer's remarks on World War II in Europe: "Now it may be the case I am more than open to this suggestion that the German army in France had attacked civilians in ways that justified the assassination of individual soldiers, just as it may be the case that the public official or party leader is a brutal tyrant who deserves to die. But assassins cannot claim the protection of the rules of war; they are engaged in a different activity." (*Just and Unjust Wars,* p. 183.) Walzer does not say on what ethical grounds assassination can be justified in wartime.

[47] "'No Choice' in killing Hamas figure, defiant Israel says", *Milwaukee Journal Sentinel,* November 25, 2001, p. 3A. "Abu Hanoud, 34, was killed late Friday when an Israeli helicopter fired missiles into a car near the West Bank village of Kfar Farah. Also killed were an aide identified as Mahmoun Rashid Hashaika, and his brother Ahmed." Israel's Foreign Minister Shimon Peres defended Hanoud's killing, "calling ... [him] 'a professional terrorist' who was planning more attacks". "We had no choice", Peres said. "Israeli officials described Hanoud as a key figure in the Izzedine al Qassam Brigades, Hamas' military wing."

[48] "Does Israel Have a Right to Assassinate Leaders of the Palestinian *Intifadeh*?", *Time,* September 10, 2001, p. 41.

[49] Ibid., p. 40.

[50] Ibid.

[51] Ibid., p. 41.

[52] Ibid.

[53] In this connection, see my *The Quest for Peace between Israel and the Palestinians* (New York, 2000), which, in its author's view, is even more urgently relevant now than before the start of the latest Palestinian *intifada*.

[54] I say "most" since it can hardly be claimed that they are as serious as massacres, pogroms, and, above all, unjust wars, genocides or other crimes against humanity.

[55] Professor Telhami is Chair of the University of Maryland's Peace and Development Center. The words I quoted were part of his talk, "US Policy in the Middle East", presented at the Middle East Institute meeting, October 19, 2001.

[56] Particularly regarding the assassination of Israel's minister of tourism. Under great Israeli pressure, Yasser Arafat finally arrested five suspects of the murder.

[57] For important differences between "freedom fighting" and terrorism, see my *The Morality of Terrorism* (New York, 1998), Chapters 5.

[58] Ibid., p. 6.

[59] *Terror in the mind of God: the global rise of religious violence* (Berkeley, CA, c.2000).

[60] See my "Terrorism and Morality", in: War, Terrorism, Genocide, and the Quest for Peace: Contemporary Problems in Political Ethics (Lewiston, 2003), S. 123-145. The violation of the discrimination rule is but one reason among several why all terrorist acts are always morally wrong.

[61] See in this connection my *The Quest for Peace between Israel and the Palestinians* (New York, 2000), *passim*.

[62] For example, in "Amnesty report raps post-Sept 11 policies" (CNN.com, May 29, 2002), William F. Schulz, executive director of Amnesty International, U.S.A., criticized the United States "for failing to push Israel to stop human rights abuses against Palestinians during incursions into the West Bank".

[63] *Convention Against Torture And Other Cruel, Inhuman or Degrading Treatment or Punishment.*

[64] Ibid., p. 1.

[65] *Newsweek*, November 5, 2001.

[66] Degrees of Coercion. "Jonathan Alter Responds", p. 19. It may be wondered why psychological torture is supposed to be different in that respect. Does it cause less (albeit mental, not physical) suffering, less agony than physical torture? In the case of physical torture there are limits to the physical pain that a person can endure before he or she mercifully loses consciousness, while, in the case of psychological torture no such limits exist.

The interested reader is referred to other readers letters in the "Degrees of Coercion" section of that issue, some of which agree with Alter while others disagree with him. For instance, one reader states: "Jonathan Alter makes the assumption that coercion of a terrorist suspect by means of "torture" is considered by most Americans to be a human-rights violation. But can we really consider people *human* if their whole concept of the value of life is tainted by hate? ... We must rationalize their being brought to justice in a way that strongly takes into consideration the inhumanity of their acts. It is eerily ironic that some of these monsters are now being protected by the very system that they hope to destroy." (ibid., pp. 19-20)

This is a good example of the dehumanization or objectification of "suspected terrorists" discussed in this section, which is supposed to justify not protecting them by the "system of justice that they hope to destroy".

[67] Ibid. Schulz's quotation is the text of Article 2 of the Convention. Among the countries that have been mentioned in the media as practicing torture are Egypt and Pakistan. Thus, concerning these two countries, in its June 24, 2002 issue, "War and Terror", *Newsweek* speaks of "a shadow war [that followed the war against Al Qaeda in Afghanistan] that is equal parts Tom Clancy and John le Carre, with a little Torquemada thrown in, as U.S. allies like Pakistan and Egypt apply their own harsh interrogation techniques. The bounds of morality are unclear and it may not be known until decades from how, when the histories are written, just how far America was willing to go to rid itself of this [terrorism's] scourge." For Israel's torture of Palestinian inmates in Al-Arish jail in the Negev, see, for example, Judith Miller, *God has Ninety-Nine Names* (New York, 1996), and my *The Morality of Terrorism*, Chapter 6, and *The Quest for Peace between Israel and the Palestinians* (New York, 2000), p. 76. The Palestinian authority has also used torture (in some instances, resulting in death) of incarcerated suspects or convicted terrorists.

[68] Readers Letter, *Newsweek*, December 10, 2001.

[69] If, say, the Wisconsin lawmakers who want to restore the death penalty in the State for the express purpose of executing convicted terrorists, have their way.

[70] Ibid., pp. 101-102.

[71] *The Art Bin*, Articles and Essays, translated from the Swedish. (On *The Art Bin* website)

[72] Conquest, Robert, *The Great Terror: A Reassesment* (Oxford, 1990), pp. 121-122.

[73] Ibid. She adds: "But important though it was, torture was not the whole explanation. Many of the accused were hardened revolutionaries. Prosecuted and punished by the Czar's courts, they were themselves advocates of hard methods. Here lies an important part of the explanation: ideological loyalty." Since the torture victims of Stalin's torture machine were all high level communist party members, it created a special type of situation absent from other cases of torture. See also Robert Conquest, op cit.; especially Chapters 4-7, and Appendix A.

[74] I say "putative good" since the prevention of violence against a given country is a good only if the latter is fighting a just fight against the violence. If an authoritarian or dictatorial regime tortures its suspected opponents to prevent future acts of violence against it, the desired end cannot be considered as a good if those using force against it as part of a just liberation movement.

[75] "War and Murder", *War and Morality*, Richard A. Wasserstrom, ed. (Belmont, CA, 1979), pp. 51 ff.

PETER SIMPSON

THE WAR ON TERRORISM: ITS JUSTIFICATION AND LIMITS

The first thing to say about terrorism is that it is an evil and a crime.[1] I say this because there has been a tendency in some parts of the media and among some commentators to excuse the terrorists who launched the attacks of September 11th, 2001, on the grounds that the US brought these attacks on itself by its own policies, especially in the Middle East. But however plausible these claims may be, we should not let them blind us to manifest truths. The attacks on the US were evil and those who planned and carried them out were also evil. To doubt this is to betray a certain confusion if not corruption of mind. We all know, and we have all known from our earliest youth, that two wrongs do not make a right. Let it be that the terrorists had grievances, even legitimate grievances, against the US. These grievances could never justify their deeds. An evil deed can never be justified. An evil deed is precisely that, an evil deed. No grievance or pretext, however strong, can ever make it to be a good deed.

I do not mean by these remarks that we should pay no attention to the alleged grievances of terrorists. Nor do I mean that, because the evil of their deeds is so obvious, we should not discuss or explain the evil or say in what it consists. What I mean is that, whatever else we say or discuss, at no point should we say, or allow others to say without challenge, that terrorist attacks are not evil. If we are to have any hope of understanding the phenomenon of terrorism or of how to deal with it, we must all start with the fact that it is evil. Thankfully, this is not a point on which our political leaders have any doubt. For them it is clear that terrorism is an evil. Commentators in the media and some philosophers may hesitate and even doubt this truth, but our leaders at least have not lost their grip on common sense. As evidence I can do no better in the present context than quote the words of the Chinese permanent representative to the United Nations: "Terrorism, which endangers innocent lives, causes losses of social wealth and jeopardizes state security, constitutes a serious challenge to human civilization and dignity as well as a serious threat to international peace and security." (*China Daily*, Friday, October 5, 2001.)

But grasping this truth, vital though it be, is only the beginning. We must, for the sake of clarity of understanding, carry our reflections further. The first step to take in this regard would seem to be to lay down some general account of what we mean by terrorism, so that we know in general terms, and not just in a particular case, what it is we are talking about. One point that immediately arises here concerns what has been called state terrorism. Those who use this term typically have in mind acts of violence used by governments and government forces against parts of their own people or against other peoples. The attacks by Israeli forces, for instance, against segments of

G. Meggle (ed.), Ethics of Terrorism & Counter-Terrorism, 197-205.

the Palestinian population have sometimes been described as state terrorism, and so have some of the actions of the US in Central and South America. Indeed the Taliban themselves, at the beginning of the recent hostilities in Afghanistan, described US and British bombing attacks on terrorist camps and government buildings as acts of terrorism. I will not comment on the justice or injustice of any of these attacks. I will only say that, if one wishes to condemn them as wrong, one should, at least in the present context, refrain from using the word terrorism to do so. It would be better, I think, to use other words to describe the unjust assaults of governments, such as tyranny, despotism, imperialist aggression, police brutality, and the like. I say this because terrorism in its primary use today,[2] and especially in its use in the phrase "the war on terrorism", refers to acts of private individuals or groups of private individuals and not to governments, even if these individuals receive support and succor from governments. After all, the phenomenon which is now mainly under consideration and which prompts the present reflections is what happened on September 11th, 2001, and that was clearly private acts, not government acts. Once this phenomenon of private acts of violence has been adequately grasped, we can then return, if we wish, to the question of the violent acts of governments and ask how far the word terrorism may usefully be applied to them as well.

I think we should also distinguish terrorism in this its primary sense from the acts, often destructive and sometimes evil too, of rebels and revolutionaries against existing governments and peoples. By rebels and revolutionaries we mean typically people who belong to the country whose government they are attacking and whose aim is to overthrow that government and to replace it with another. As such rebels and revolutionaries are not so much a grouping of private individuals as a rival government in waiting. But terrorists as typically understood are not a rival government in waiting nor are they seeking to overthrow the existing government, even if they would not be sorry if that happened. The terrorists who attacked the US on September 11th, for instance, were not Americans seeking to overthrow the US government and replace it with another.

There is something else that also needs to be noted about terrorism if we are to be clear about what it is. The violence of terrorists is typically directed at civilians and civilian institutions, albeit civilians of the country against which the terrorists have a grievance, and is meant to be indiscriminate. It is from this feature, indeed, that terrorism would seem to get its name. For such indiscriminate and violent acts are designed to cause terror among the people at large, and it is by means of such terror that terrorists seek to attain their goals and force the hand of governments. Such indiscriminate violence can also be a feature of the acts of certain government officials and of certain rebel groups. Members of the police force in some parts of the world engage in random acts of violence against the civilian population as part of a policy of terrorizing the people into subservience. I think in particular of Guatemala. Again, some rebel groups, devoted to overthrowing the existing government, may also engage in similar acts of random violence against the civilian population. I think here of the Basque group ETA and the IRA. Such groups have also, of course, engaged in attacks on military installations and personnel, including assassination. I would nevertheless want to call these acts of police force and rebels acts of terrorism. The members of police forces who engage in random acts of violence are doing so clandestinely and when off duty, as it were, even if with the connivance and encouragement of their superiors. Were they to do so openly and in their capacity as police officers I would say their acts were acts of tyranny and government oppression. Again, in the case of ETA and the IRA, I would say that their attacks on military installations and government agencies could be acts of rebellion (though they need not be) while their attacks on civilians would have to be acts of terrorism. This is because attacks on civilians cannot be construed as attacks on the existing government so as to overthrow it, and hence cannot be construed as attacks by a would-be rival government in its capacity as a would-be rival government. They can only be construed as attacks by certain persons, who may indeed belong to a group that wishes to overthrow the government, but who in this case are operating as individuals to sow terror among the population at large. And I would say the same was true of attacks on military personnel if the aim here too was to sow terror and was not part of an act of defense against or of an attack on an armed force that was hostile and threatening (so the attack, for instance, on the USS Cole in Yemen some years ago would be terrorism and not rebellion or revolution).

But perhaps I need not insist on all these distinctions for my present purposes. Let it be sufficient if, in the light of what has been said, we characterize terrorism as *acts of violence committed by private individuals or groups of individuals who have as such no political authority, and directed indiscriminately against civilian or at least non-hostile populations and institutions, so as to spread fear and terror there in order to achieve some limited goal short of the immediate overthrow of the existing government.* This definition may need some further clarification and correction, and it is, one should note, different from other definitions that have been offered.[3] It differs, nevertheless, more by way of addition than of subtraction. The reason for this is my desire to isolate as clearly as possible the phenomenon in question, I mean the phenomenon of terrorism as we ordinarily speak of terrorism and as we are certainly speaking of it in the present context of the war on terrorism. Other phenomena, which may be close to it but are not really part of it, such as rebellion or revolution or acts of violence by governments, can thus be set aside – not indeed so as to be ignored, but so as to be dealt with more clearly in their own place and in their own terms. I should perhaps add, though, that this definition could readily be made to fit acts of violence by governments, and so could be made to accommodate the phrase 'state terrorism', if reference to governments is added to that of private individuals and groups, and if the goal to be achieved is expanded to include such things as retention or strengthening of the power and control of the existing rulers. But, as I said, I am reluctant to change the definition to make this accommodation, at least in the present context. For the present context is that of understanding terrorism as it is now most in our minds, and that is terrorism of the sort that was displayed on September 11th, 2001.

At all events, armed with this definition of terrorism, we can see at once why terrorism is and must be evil and unjust. Note first that the evil and injustice of terrorism is not part of the definition of terrorism. I have not defined terrorism as *unjust* or *evil* acts of violence.[4] I have defined it by reference to certain acts of violence, to be sure, but without mention of good or bad. The injustice of terrorism does, nevertheless, immediately follow from this definition when we add to it the further proposition that deliberate and intentional attacks on the innocent are unjust.

That it is unjust to attack the innocent is something of a self-evident proposition. Justice is fundamentally a matter of giving each their due, but the deliberate infliction of harm or injury is not due to the innocent who, precisely as innocent, are owed peace and protection, not violence. That civilian populations and also non-hostile military personnel, who are the objects of terrorist attacks, are innocent in this sense is also obvious. However, to avoid misunderstanding, it is important to note that innocence here must be taken in a strict or even formal sense.[5] To say that the objects of terrorist attacks are innocent is not to say that they are guilty of no crime or misdeed whatever. Some might very well happen to be wrongdoers. But it is to say that they are innocent in the precise respect in which they are attacked. For they are attacked simply in their capacity as civilians or non-hostile military going about their ordinary, peaceful tasks (a warship in a friendly port, for instance, is not a hostile presence about to inflict injury or death, nor is a thief walking down the street such a presence – even if he is on his way to commit a robbery). Such tasks are not attacks or threats against anyone, least of all against the terrorists. They cannot, taken precisely as such, be construed as in any way deserving of injury or death (and even if, in some larger context, they might be deserving of punishment, it is not the terrorists whose duty it is to judge or inflict that punishment). These tasks are innocent tasks. But it is against people engaged in such innocent tasks that terrorists launch their attacks. Terrorist attacks are therefore attacks on innocents and so cannot be anything but evil and unjust.

It matters not here what grievances the terrorists may have or what accusations they level against those countries whose people they attack. An evil deed is, as I said at the beginning, an evil deed and nothing can make it to be a good deed. Not even religion, not even the Muslim religion, can make it to be a good deed. Those who say it can, or who claim the support of Islam for their terrorist attacks, are abusing religion and Islam. Do not take my word for this. Take rather the words of one of the Taliban themselves, namely the Taliban ambassador to Pakistan, who said of the attack on the US: "This action is terrorist action. We know this was not Islamic and was a very dangerous action, and we condemn that." (*China Daily*, Thursday, October 4, 2001.) Mr. Bin Laden, of course, along with his followers in Al Qaeda, said the exact opposite. They praised the attacks on the US and on civilians, and said that Islam expressly requires Muslims to engage in such attacks. But if even the Taliban have denied that this is what Islam teaches, one wonders what sort of Islam Al Qaeda is following. At all events decent Muslims have good reason to repudiate the Islam preached by Al Qaeda. We can be grateful, therefore, to those Islamic countries and authorities that have openly done so.

Terrorism then is an evil and indeed, because of its indiscriminate nature, an evil of a particularly cruel sort. Those countries, therefore, which love peace and care for the good of mankind must do something to rid the world of this evil. Not to do so would be a dereliction of duty. It is everyone's duty to do good (pursuing good and avoiding evil is an elementary injunction of reason), and among the good things to be done is the removal of evils, especially grave evils – to the extent, at any rate, that this is possible. Here, however, we must be careful, for in opposing evil it is all too easy to fall into evil oneself. We are doubtless all aware of how easy it is, when someone has injured or insulted us, to respond with hatred and to inflict, or try to inflict, worse injury than we first suffered. We may in this way satisfy our lust for revenge but we do not in this way remove evil or make the world a better place. On the contrary we simply add to the evil in the world, for we add our own evil to the evil of the other. One cannot defeat evil with evil. That is contradictory. To use evil against evil is not to defeat evil but to be defeated by it and to become evil in one's own turn.

Now it is a striking fact that in all the build-up to the war on terrorism after September 11th, 2001, and in the subsequent prosecution of that war in Afghanistan and its possible continuation into other countries, there have been repeated and persistent calls from all sides that the war should be conducted with great prudence, that it should only target the guilty, that clear evidence of guilt or threat should be forthcoming, that any military action undertaken should not result in collateral damage or as little such damage as possible, that the UN be properly informed and consulted, and so forth. These calls came first from the US Government itself. They have been repeated by almost all countries round the world, whether friendly or hostile to the US. The hostile countries made these calls with a certain indignation and even with fear (springing, perhaps, from secret guilt). But it is something of a tribute to the US that they made these claims at all. The claims were an admission that it made some sense to appeal to justice when talking to the US; that one could expect the US to have a certain sensitivity to the claims of justice and to the opinions and judgment of the international community, and in particular the UN, when deciding what to do; that one had some hope, indeed, of getting the US to change its mind if its policies could clearly be shown not to accord with justice. I do not mean to imply by this that the US always acts with justice, that none of its policies is unjust, or that none of its officers behaves unjustly. That would be too much to expect of any country or government. We are human, all too human. We make mistakes, sometimes deliberately. We regret only after the event and not before. But at least we can regret; at least we can acknowledge the claims of justice against us; at least we can be restrained by appeals to what is good. Certainly the world thought that was true of the US, for otherwise why make appeals to justice?

But consider the contrast here. Has the world thought it worth appealing to justice with Al Qaeda? Has the world beaten a path to Al Qaeda's door appealing to them to follow justice and prudence or the counsels of the international community and the UN in their decisions of whom and what to attack? Has the world appealed to them, in the name of justice, to give themselves up, or at least Mr. Bin Laden, to a court of law to prove their innocence or to admit their guilt? Or again, to change focus, has the world appealed in the name of justice to Mr. Saddam Hussein (or to other despots of the same ilk) to stop the tyranny and oppression of his people, to abide by UN resolutions, to apologize and make reparation for his aggression against Kuwait? This has not happened, or at least not on the same scale as appeals to justice have been made in the case of the US and the war on terrorism. And if Mr. Saddam Hussein seems, as of this writing, ready, though grudgingly, to accept some UN resolutions and to make some gesture of apology to Kuwait, it is patent that he is doing so only because he has coalition troops breathing down his neck and not because of any sense of remorse or desire for reform. His continuing oppression of his own people is proof enough of that. But why this difference in the way the world makes appeals of justice to the US but not to Al Qaeda and Mr. Saddam Hussein? Surely because no one believes that the latter have a sufficient sense of justice or of responsibility to world opinion to make such appeals worthwhile. Only force could bring home to them the error of their ways, and there could be no guarantee of success even then.

Be that as it may, however. Let it at least be agreed that we must resist evil and resist it with good. How then are we to resist the evil of terrorism with good? The short answer is that we should resist it with all the good at our command. In all our actions, in all our lives, we should be doing the most good we can and encouraging our neighbors to do the same. For the evil of terrorism springs from many sources, and in particular it springs from the injustices, real or apparent, committed by others against what the terrorists hold dear. Such injustices give no excuse, of course, to the evil deeds of terrorists as I have already remarked, but if we can, each in our own way and in our own place, reduce the injustice around us, we will be doing our part to reduce the emergence of more terrorists in the future, as well as making the world a better place in general. But such an answer, while vital and in need of frequent repetition, is not enough. Our concern is the more specific question of whether force, in particular the force of war, is a just response to terrorism. If it is not we ought not to engage in it; but if it is we need to know what sort of force, under what conditions, subject to what limits, and so forth.

The first thing to note here is that force is a neutral term. It does not by itself connote something either good or bad. The same is true, for instance, of tolerance. That too connotes something neither good nor bad in itself. Everything depends on what is tolerated and why. Tolerating the murder of infants would clearly be bad; tolerating the expression of different opinions in the course of philosophical debate would clearly be good. That is why those who praise tolerance as a virtue are speaking too simply. Tolerance as such is not a virtue, nor is intolerance as such a vice. We need to know tolerance or intolerance of what, by whom, when, how. That is also why those who condemn force as a vice, such as pacifists, are speaking too simply as well. Is all use of force always and everywhere wrong? Is the force used by parents to discipline children wrong? Is the force used to arrest criminals wrong? Is the force used to defend oneself against attackers wrong? It seems patent that to answer yes to all these questions is absurd. Some uses of force are clearly right and just. The only interesting question to ask is which uses are so.

Since force is in itself neutral, it can only be just or unjust according to the way it is used, that is to say for what goals or ends, in what amount or kind, against and by whom, when and where, with what likely consequences, and so forth. Of these several features, the goal or end of force would seem to be the first and most important. No amount of force, used by anyone on any occasion, could be just if the end aimed at were not just. So what are the just aims for which force may be used? Well ultimately, since we are talking of the use of force by men against men, the goals must be the good of men. Only if force has as its goal the promotion of the human good could it be good. The human good is clearly a complex whole consisting of many parts, from material and physical goods, to external goods, to cultural, educational, and spiritual goods. There is no need to spell these out in detail or explain their connections and relative subordination to each other. It is enough to note them in their general outline. For our concern is less about what the human good is than about what uses of force are justified with respect to it. In particular, since the war on terrorism is directed to resisting an evil, the evil of attacks on innocent life and limb, on habitations and property, on economic and social structures, the question is what determines the legitimate use of force in resistance to evil.

The operative idea here is that of self-defense. Since the human good is the object of pursuit, whatever attacks that good or hinders that pursuit may be resisted and repulsed sufficiently to make the pursuit of the good possible again. It seems manifest, therefore, that in some cases physical force must be just, for in some cases it is the only, or only reasonable, way to pursue the human good. The fact that war typically causes much damage – and to one's own people and country as well as to those of the enemy – is not a decisive objection. Not every just act has to be such that it involve no abandonment of lesser goods for the sake of greater ones. We regularly forego immediate pleasures for the sake of bodily, mental, and spiritual health. Moreover, we consider it right to amputate a diseased limb to save the whole body or to cast overboard precious cargo to save the ship from sinking. Such acts are, of course, acts of last resort. One must look at the war on terrorism in the same way. Regrettable though the loss of other goods might be, yet in this case the use of force is the only sensible way forward.

Force, then, is necessary for the protection and pursuit of the human good, but only as a last resort and only as long as force is necessary. As soon as it becomes possible to pursue the good again without recourse to the use of force we should do so. Now in the case of the current war against terrorism the US and its allies have hitherto been following the logic of this argument. Before any force was used in Afghanistan appeals were made through many channels to get the Taliban to give up the terrorists within their midst and to close down the camps where these terrorists trained. The Taliban refused, or at any rate delayed and prevaricated sufficiently to make the exercise of further patience in their regard imprudent. The terrorists also refused to give themselves up voluntarily. Hence both groups effectively declared themselves at war with the civilized world – for any part of the civilized world was a potential object of their attacks. The civilized world, therefore, was driven by them into the last resort of using force against them. The same is happening (as of this writing) in the case of force against Iraq. While the threat of force has been real and has been backed up with clear and concrete preparations, considerable efforts have also been made by the international community, especially through the UN, to get the Iraqi government to forestall the actual use of force by voluntarily abiding by its obligations and coming clean about its support for terrorism and its possession of nuclear, chemical, or biological weapons. These efforts may be paying off, and as long as they continue to do so the need for force will be removed. Al Qaeda, which has not abandoned its terrorist acts or intentions, must still be pursued, of course, and countries that aid or abet them must still be required to desist, and by force if need be.

Judging how best to do this and calculating the consequences, whether good or bad, of different policies and actions are hard matters, requiring much knowledge, good sense, and good will. Still these are the sort of matters that we expect our military and political leaders to decide and to be qualified to decide. The rest of us must, perforce, leave these matters to them. We can nevertheless all intervene in insisting that, whatever decisions are made, they are made within the limits of justice. For these limits are general enough, and accessible enough, that those not involved in concrete decision making can still know them and can still judge how far they have been or are being observed.[6] These limits have been touched on above, and are in essence twofold: first, that if a decision is made to use armed force against terrorist groups and their supporters, there be sufficient and compelling reason (in particular that no other options are plausible or available);[7] and, second, that, in the prosecution of such use of force, the force be proportionate to the goal aimed at and, in particular, that it not target innocents, civilian or otherwise, and that any unintended and collateral damage to innocents be reduced to a minimum (otherwise one would sink to the same level as the terrorists themselves and defeat the very point of opposing terrorism).[8]

There is little more that I think I can usefully add at this stage to the discussion of these questions. So I leave such discussion to others better qualified and informed in these respects than I. There is, however, another issue that I would like to end by raising, for it has become particularly compelling and worrisome in recent months. I mean the denial of freedom and civil rights that several governments have deliberately, and even cynically, got involved in since September 11th, 2001.[9] Here I find myself obliged to criticize the domestic anti-terrorism policy of my own US government, in marked contrast with my relatively favorable opinion – as of this writing at least – of its foreign anti-terrorist policy. Citizens, legal residents, and visitors in the US, especially of an Arabic or Muslim background, have been subjected to arbitrary arrest and detention, to threats or acts of deportation, and to other abuses of a like nature. Such acts have been encouraged, if not entirely justified, by the Patriot Act, passed by the US Congress barely a month after September 11th, 2001. This act has dangerously extended the power of the policing agencies to invade personal privacy. The justification given for such behavior by the US government is that it is necessary to protect the American people from further terrorist attack. But this justification is as self-contradictory as the behavior itself is counter-productive. How can the US proclaim its goal in the war on terrorism to be defense of the free and civilized world if its own domestic acts are denials of freedom and civilization?

Indeed if, contrary to my strictures at the beginning, I am to allow some use of the term 'state terrorism', I would allow it here. For here it has a certain rhetorical force – to make clear, even in the very words, the contradiction of which I am speaking. To use terrorism (state terrorism, that is) against terrorism, is to promote terrorism, not to defeat it. If we must choose, therefore, let us, as true heirs of our civilized heritage, choose freedom with terrorism rather than slavery without it. But we do not in fact face such a choice, and we should not let governments or their agents trick us into believing that we do. After all, no policing or investigative power is going to be proof against every possible terrorist attack, and the attacks that we can reasonably expect to prevent should not require us to deny ourselves in the process the rights that make living worthwhile. Free peoples of the world must be as alert against attacks on freedom by home governments as against attacks on life by alien terrorists. It may well be less the adventurism of foreign armies in Iraq or elsewhere than the tyranny of domestic policing at home that should give us most cause for fear – and for vigilance.

NOTES

[1] This point was forcefully made by Rüdiger Bittner and Ivan Vukovic in their contributions to the conference – though Uwe Steinhoff did explore, in the spirit of philosophic provocation, what reasons there might be for doubting it.

[2] But not, apparently, in its first historical use. As Laurence Lustgarten reminded us, the word 'terrorism' was first used to describe acts of state terrorism, namely the Reign of Terror unleashed during the French Revolution.

[3] Tony Coady pointed out in his paper that there are over 100 definitions of terrorism already in the scholarly literature. Definitions, of a partial if not always of a comprehensive sort, were offered by Coady himself and also by Per Bauhn, Haig Khatchadourian, Georg Meggle, Seumas Miller, Walter Pfannkuche, Igor Primoratz, Ralf Stoecker, Uwe Steinhoff, and Ivan Vukovic. The differences between these definitions seemed to be more ones of emphasis than of substance.

[4] The desirability of not defining terrorism as wrong or unjust was pointed out in particular by Georg Meggle and Uwe Steinhoff.

[5] How precisely to understand innocence was a topic of some dispute at the conference.

[6] Judging the success and morality of the war on terrorism also provoked much debate at the conference.

[7] Some of the complications here were explored in interesting ways by Janna Thompson.

[8] The difficult question of how to measure the just limits of collateral damage was a subject taken up in particular by Ulrich Steinvorth.

[9] Laurence Lustgarten and Ralf Groetker are especially to be thanked for making this question an express topic at the conference.

RÜDIGER BITTNER

MORALS IN TERRORIST TIMES

This is a volume without actual subject-matter. That is not the editor's fault: when the volume was being planned, it seemed to have a topic, and an important one, too. This turned out to be an illusion. The subject was to be the ethics of terrorism and counter-terrorism. As for the ethics of terrorism, I confess I would have doubted right from the start that this is a live subject, since there is nothing worth asking here. It is wrong, and obviously wrong, to kill third parties, or with the common but misleading term, to kill innocent people, for political aims without political authority. Not that it is right with political authority to kill third parties for political aims. Perhaps it is, perhaps it is not, that is not obvious. Terrorism, by contrast, is a matter as clear as can be. At least real terrorism is. Maybe philosophers could come up with tricky scenarios that would be hard to judge in moral terms. Actual cases of terrorism, cases we heard about in the news, never present any moral problem. The ethics of terrorism is a subject as interesting as the ethics of murder.

The ethics of counter-terrorism is not a suitable topic of inquiry for a different reason. Let us first be clear about the concept. "Counter-terrorism" could be taken to refer to a fight against terrorism conducted itself by terrorist means. This is not how I will use the expression, for that turns the ethics of counter-terrorism immediately into the same non-subject as the ethics of terrorism is. Moreover, it is only state agencies that are currently fighting, or pretending to fight, terrorism, and states do not use terrorist means – mind you, not thanks to their virtue, but thanks to their concept: state terrorism is, on my understanding of the words, a square circle. This concept of counter-terrorism would be empty, then, and uninterestingly so. Instead I shall take "counter-terrorism" to mean "measures by state agencies designed to combat terrorism". Now with respect to counter-terrorism so defined important questions could have emerged regarding the moral grounds and the moral limits of such measures. In fact, however, these questions are moot. In the sense defined, there is no counter-terrorism to speak of. The concept is practically empty again, though this time more interestingly so. There is no war against terrorism being waged or being prepared for waging. What we have been witnessing since 2001 and what we are going to witness in the near future are not wars against terrorism, but wars, period.

True, there have been bits and pieces of counter-terrorism. In various countries police measures have been taken with the aim, first, of bringing to court persons responsible for preparing the terrorist attacks of September 2001, and second, of preventing further activities of terrorist organisations in these countries. True also, some of these measures raise difficult political and legal issues, for instance what evidence authorities need to have, and to produce publicly, to justify taking these

G. Meggle (ed.), Ethics of Terrorism & Counter-Terrorism, 207-213.

measures, and what kind and degree of danger individuals or groups must present to be justly hindered in their activities. However, such problems are not specific to terrorism, they come up in ordinary police law as well: where is the line between legitimate prevention of crime and illegitimate abridgment of individual freedom? Yet police measures of this kind have not formed the center of states' activities in terrorist times. Hence our topic was rather to be the employment of military, as opposed to police, means to combat terrorism. However, military means are actually not being employed to combat terrorism. So the topic is moot.

It will be asked: if terrorism is not the target of current military activities, what is? and also: if terrorism is not the *target* of current military activities, what is it? As for the first question, the considerations put forward by the governments of the United States and the United Kingdom to show that an attack on Iraq is called for, indicate that such an attack is aimed at a state whose government pursues a political course not in accordance with the objectives of the United States government; whose government is, in particular, building up, or capable of building up, a military power which, from the point of view of the objectives of the United States government, it should not have. And Iraq is going to be an exemplary case only, politically exemplary, I mean: recent declarations on the part of the United States government indicate that it is now their general strategy to put down deviant governments by force; though one might expect that other governments, on seeing the fate of Iraq, will surrender without resistance. Just to have a handy term, and without endorsing a particular theory of international relations, let us say that the wars currently waged or prepared by the United States and their allies are imperialist wars. True, the United States' Empire differs in important respects from other empires, like the British or the Roman Empire. What nevertheless justifies the common term is this feature they share, the erection of a formation of rule extending far beyond the boundaries of the respective central state.

The second question was what terrorism has got to do with current military activities, if it is not, contrary to what representatives of the United States and the British government claim, their target. The answer, I should think, is evident: terrorism is the pretended reason for undertaking these activities and therefore the real reason for which a large number of people, in the United States and elsewhere, support them. The terrorist attacks of September 2001 formed a window of opportunity for a number of governments, above all for the United States government, and they have been using to the full the political leverage thereby afforded. The sense of vulnerability that has spread in the United States population, the sense of humiliation at seeing the symbols of United States' superiority felled, the urge for taking revenge, these reactions made war, any war, undertaken with whatever intention and directed against whatever opponent, wonderfully easy to sell to the United States' citizens. It just needed to be called a war against terrorism, and the broadest support was ensured. Other governments like those of Israel and Russia followed suit in the armed conflicts in which they are involved. Other governments again, like the German and the British one, presently having no armed conflict on their hands, used the so-called war against terrorism for cutting down civil liberties.

Thus, "terrorism" has actually become the name of whatever enemy governments wish to be supported in attacking, with the special advantage that both exterior and interior opponents can plausibly be brought under this label.

It may be said: Fine, there is no such thing as counter-terrorism at present. So let us put quotation marks round the word "counter-terrorism", and we can proceed then to discuss the ethics of terrorism and so-called counter-terrorism. – Not with me, for I fail to see an interesting issue here. The ethics of imperialist war, whether you name the latter "counter-terrorism" or "so-called counter-terrorism", is as much a non-subject as the ethics of terrorism is. Imperialist wars are morally unacceptable, and that is the end of it. Nor does it take a radical pacifism to say that. It is the standard view of the just war tradition, from Augustine on, that wars not aimed at restoring a state of right are morally prohibited, and the prominent example of a war not so aimed is, classically, the imperialist war, i.e. the war aimed at extending some state's sphere of domination.

What I have said so far is not likely to go uncontested, and I would have to defend these claims in suitable detail. That is not, however, what I should like to do here. Frankly, if you do think that the military activities currently underway are indeed intended to combat terrorism, and are not merely called so to gain public acceptance for them, you strike me as believing in Santa Claus; and while I am confident of the power of my arguments to prove your belief wrong, the present occasion can surely be used more profitably.

Let us rather turn the question around. There is the practice of moral judgment on terrorism, alleged counter-terrorism and war. That is the direction of inquiry I have been pursuing so far, with little success, or in a way with too much success, everything of interest here being clear. There is, conversely, the employment of moral notions by those who practice terrorism, alleged counter-terrorism and war: that is what I propose to consider now. That is to say, I am inviting you to leave the moral point of view which subjects the political landscape to moral judgment, and to take up a political point of view instead which subjects the practice of moral judgment, among other things, to political judgment. The truth or falsity of moral judgments is then irrelevant. The point is to understand what they are good for. However, knowing too little about the role of moral notions in the thoughts of terrorists, I shall restrict my topic further and consider only so-called counter-terrorism, asking how it is served by moral notions. "Morals in terrorist times" allows two readings: let us now turn from what morals say to what they do in terrorist times.

The salient fact is that morals in terrorist times have become a tool in the preparation of war. Perhaps not an indispensable tool, such things are hard to judge. But it does seem to be a central element now in the orchestration of warfare in the technologically and economically advanced states. The Hutu may have slaughtered hundreds of thousands of Tutsi just because of their ethnic difference. This could not happen here. Our governments only kill masses of people for the sake of the good.

You may object that this is not a recent development. In all ages the enemy was described in derogatory terms, both to give our troops a feeling of superiority and to diminish any misgivings they might feel about killing large numbers of people on the other side. Still, what does seem to be a recent development is the re-casting of such contrasts in chiefly or even exclusively moral terms. People going to war used to imagine themselves superior in all sorts of ways, in their technology, military valour, political institutions, or even in their biological makeup. It seems to be only now that they insist on being good and fighting evil. And the moral distinction does not merely wrap up a political or economic one, as was still the case in the rhetoric of the Vietnam war. There we were good and they were evil because we defended freedom and they fought for communism. Nowadays it is no longer their cause that makes them evil. They just are evil, and that is why it is right for us to fight them.

Why this change? One thing that may explain the significance of moral distinctions in the current rhetoric of war is the enhanced sensitivity of people to war's moral questionability. This again, it would seem, is a relatively recent development. Not being a professional historian, I can only judge on the basis of the experiences that happened to come my way, but a watershed in this respect does seem to lie between World War II and Vietnam. Both Germany's waging war in World War II and the United States' waging war in Vietnam were morally reprehensible, I take it, but while the German population by and large did not consider World War II a moral issue at the time, a sizeable part of the United States population came so to consider Vietnam. The students singing in front of the White House: "LBJ, how many babies did you kill today?", heralded the arrival of moral judgment on a field hitherto the exclusive domain of Realpolitik. It was an important change, not least by contributing to the eventual withdrawal of the United States forces. A war in conflict with the moral convictions of a considerable part of the population, it turned out, is difficult to sustain in states answerable, or pretending to be answerable, to independent and reflective individuals.

The fact has not been lost on war-planners that war, in contrast to the progress in military technology that makes killing and destruction smooth, clean, and easy, has become considerably more difficult to sell. They drew several lessons, the one of interest here being the imperative to occupy the moral high ground before starting any actual killing. So this is the first thing the moral distinction of good and evil does for you in terrorist times, it helps to stabilize the home front. You won't have defections, scepticism or outright moral indignation as you had in the Vietnam war, or at least you will have much less of that, if it is settled beforehand that the enemy embodies evil. Morals are good for morale: killing large numbers of people is alright, or at any rate not seriously objectionable, once these people are seen as serving evil.

Here is a second explanation, related to the first, for the significance of moral interpretations in current preparations of war. Holding the moral high ground may help you to escape the demands of law, international or domestic. For everybody agrees that law is not the last arbiter on what we are to do. We know that law is sometimes not just, and its claims on our compliance are sometimes overridden by moral considerations. Accordingly, once our opponent is not this country or that political system, but evil plain and simple, we seem to have an argument for no longer obeying laws that would otherwise restrict our military activities. No holds are barred in a battle against evil objectified.

The phrase "evil objectified" is taken from Michael Walzer's discussion of "supreme emergency" in "Just and Unjust Wars",[1] and a closer look at his text may help to see how the argument works. Walzer is concerned in that book to exhibit what he calls "the war convention", the set of moral, legal or professional norms governing our judgments of conduct in and around war; and perhaps the most important strand of the war convention is the prohibition against killing non-combatants. What about the British bombing of German cities between 1940 and 1942, then: was it morally objectionable? No, says Walzer, arguing as follows: "we see it [i.e. Nazism] – and I don't use the phrase lightly – as evil objectified in the world",[2] the threat of its victory therefore constituting a supreme emergency, which justifies overriding the war convention. (And because that threat receded after 1942, the later bombings, which killed far more people, were not justified.) So there are bigger evils and smaller evils, Walzer thinks, none of them justifying a breach of the traditional norms of war conduct, but then there is, in a different order and beyond comparison, evil itself having become an object in the world, and in the face of that the norms of war conduct yield.

What we are offered here is a kind of inverted incarnation story: as for Christians God became flesh in Jesus, so for Walzer evil itself appeared in the world as Nazism. And just as Christian warriors, authorized by God through his worldly representatives, were free to do what otherwise would have been morally impermissible, so on Walzer's view those who fight, not evils, but evil itself, are no longer subject to the moral laws governing war. Which is excellent advice for war-planners: by all means, take the very high moral ground, present yourself, not as pursuing lowly goods like oil, power, or even freedom, but as just fighting the forces of evil, and you will be off any hook whatever.

This is not to suggest that Walzer wrote his text to open a gate for governments, or indeed for the United States government, to evade the strictures of the war convention. It is merely to suggest that he did open such a gate. His insistence that genuine cases of supreme emergency need to be distinguished from merely pretended ones does not prove otherwise: anyone using the gate he opened is likely to insist that nearly everybody else must not do so, and in this way the path becomes a busy highway. And this is also to suggest that Walzer used illicit means, theoretically speaking, in opening it. Evil objectified is as mythical as the God incarnate.

There is a discrepancy, then, between what morals say and what they do in terrorist times. Morals reject, at least on my understanding, both terrorism and war waged under the pretense of fighting terrorism. In effect, however, morals serve the efforts of war, both in fending off doubts about one's own cause and in lifting, if needs be, the restrictions to which warfare, by law or by custom, is subject. This discrepancy should not cause too much surprise. Given how much power moral considerations still have in directing people's steps, it is only to be expected that political leaders bend them to serve their purposes. The interesting reflection, once again, is the political one: what are the political consequences of moral distinctions being harnessed to political service? The modern state was not conceived for fighting evil, nor was it traditionally accused of doing evil, except by a handful of anarchists: what will it become on turning into a moral player?

It may be that nothing much will change, because moral talk in the political realm is mere varnish covering political interests and political actions continuing as before. The moral vocabulary, it is true, may wear out in the process, the way, say, a harmless word like "exciting" was worn out by thousands of ads, and we may just get bored by people pretending to fight evil. In political substance, though, there would be no change.

Or it may be that states will pursue a moral mission in earnest. Hobbes had told states to leave behind all moral intentions and to restrict themselves to the one aim of securing peace within and abroad. It may be that with an agenda as modest, resources sufficient for contemporary warfare can no longer be marshalled; and so states, as masters of war, find themselves bound to rally citizens behind a moral agenda. States, the idea is, cannot continue in business unless diversifying their products. Peace alone won't do. So they go into fighting evil. And in that respect terrorism again comes handy, for here there is evil aplenty, and evil whose political sources easily go undetected, which again helps the moral rallying call.

If that is what is happening, citizens are soon going to be assembled not as free and equal human beings, but as good ones, with divergent views about goodness being ironed out by repression; and they are going to select at the behest of their leaders those evil people who need to be killed next. In an international context and on a larger scale, we will thus in effect re-install 'la terreur' (using the French expression to prevent confusion with 'terror' which, remember, states cannot engage in), where the good maintain their power and at the same time continuously prove their goodness by killing ever new groups of allegedly evil human beings.

Then again, if citizens do warm to the idea of gathering behind a moral flag, this may be a victory that governments will learn to regret. Once going, people are likely to find other causes worth dying and worth killing for, not to mention worth paying, than those determined by political authorities, and so Hobbes' historical compromise will break apart. If governments kill for the sake of the good, it is natural to ask, why should not we do the same off our own bat, especially when governments are falling behind in serving the good? Thus the level of inner-state violence can be expected to rise in consequence of governments' killing abroad for moral reasons.

With people taking what they consider the good into their own hands we are back with terrorism, or at least a close relative of it. Thus the political use of morals and terrorism go together. Terrorist attacks of unheard of dimensions called forth a military build-up and military action justified in moral terms. Military action undertaken for moral purposes in turn sets the stage for terrorism. Sets the stage: whether or not it triggers or provokes it, the point is that terror forms a response in kind to a public killing in the name of the good, and a response that is predictable. Terror makes sense in moralist times. That is what the game is now, and it may change the states we knew.

These states were by their charter committed to seek peace, external peace at least as a modus vivendi, internal peace as founded on law; and peace was deemed, if not natural, at least feasible for humans. It may be that the kind of state being formed before our eyes is no longer committed to peace. It no longer considers peace possible, and so is committed to fighting it out by any means, whatever "it" is. In the end that may be an especially important function to which morals are put in terrorist times, namely to lead us to acquiesce in that change. For who would dream of a fight against evil coming to an end?

NOTES

[1] Walzer, Michael (1977, ²1992): *Just and Unjust Wars*. Chap. 16. Basic.
[2] Ibid. p. 253.

UWE STEINHOFF

THE ETHICS OF TERRORISM[*]

Georg Meggle's essay on "Terror and Counter-Terror: First ethical reflections" is probably the most important philosophical contribution made thus far in the German-language discussion of the problems of terrorism and counter-terrorism since September 11th.[1] Meggle approaches the topic systematically and wins his argument with analytical acumen and by means of the unambiguous manner in which he makes his political position explicit. His contribution is a piece of politically engaged philosophy in the best sense of the word. Despite these merits, it is nevertheless to be criticized that Meggle does not take his analysis far enough. On the one hand, Meggle comes to the conclusion that terrorism in the "strong" sense, i.e. terrorism directed against innocents, is always morally reprehensible and never to be morally condoned (in fact, according to a widely-held interpretation of the term "terrorism" which I too endorse, one can only speak of "terrorism" in the case that is directed against innocents). Nevertheless, Meggle is complacent to found this conclusion (that terrorism is morally reprehensible and to be forbidden) by invoking just-war theory. Yet, under secular conditions, a reference to the moral theories of medieval church fathers will not do. These theories are bound to theological and metaphysical suppositions which became dubious during the Enlightenment, at the latest – a fact which many modern theorists of just war who seek authority in the Catholic tradition tend to ignore.[2] We must therefore place the question once more, and with emphasis: Could terrorism be justified under certain circumstances after all?

Nowadays, whoever seriously poses this question runs a good chance of being excommunicated from the so-called discourse community, and of not even being listened to in the first place. This explains why several pre-existing philosophical analyses of the phenomenon of terrorism, some of which well antedate September 11th, are paid practically no attention at all in the current public debate. The reason they are ignored is this: these philosophical investigations have as their goal the critique and questioning of socially promoted modes of discussion and prejudices, *not*: their docile acceptance.

In the following I will attempt to defend such analyses and bring out that which is valid in them – for they are valid, and useful as well. To this end one can appeal both to a sense of justice, as well as to reason. The appeal to reason may be made with the simple remark that abstinence from reflection surely cannot be an appropriate method for solving problems. The appeal to a sense of justice may be made with reference to, for example, public opinion in the United States, which denounces terrorism as unjustifiable on the one hand, but, when it comes to the moral questions surrounding the dropping of the Atomic bomb on Nagasaki and Hiroshima, sees the matter quite differently. When, therefore, certain analysts in the United States are given ample

215

G. Meggle (ed.), Ethics of Terrorism & Counter-Terrorism, 215-224.
© 2005 Ontos, Heusenstamm.

opportunity in the serious press to develop alternative views to a moral condemnation of the directed mass-killing of civilians in Hiroshima and Nagasaki, or when in Germany ample space is provided to explain why the United States should be given unconditional solidarity in its so-called "War against Terror", though it shows no mercy to civilians – positions for which good arguments might speak and which one cannot at all reject out of hand –: if, then, those who hold these positions are given ample opportunity to be heard, one should not be wroth to grant a similar freedom of speech and opportunity to speak also to those philosophers who seek to approach the phenomenon of terrorism as soberly as possible, even when it happens to be directed against the West.

But can we really make this comparison; was the dropping of the Atomic bomb really an act of terrorism? In posing this question we already find ourselves in the midst of the discussion and have arrived at a second philosophical question which – as Meggle himself emphasizes – must be handled before this first one, to wit: What is terrorism? According to the definition given by the U.S. State Department – a definition apparently shared by the better part of the Western press in the current debate – acts of terror can only be committed by sub-national or underground organizations.[3] The Nazi regime would not have been, according to this definition, a regime of terror. But such a conclusion hardly corresponds to our linguistic and moral intuitions. Therefore we must reject as inadequate such a definition of terrorism which gives states the right to apply a double standard. Whether an act is one of terrorism or not, is a question to be decided by the act itself, and not with reference to the perpetrator. Here we may cite Bruce Hoffman, whose view is representative of that of others as well, and who enjoins that such a position plays "into the hands of terrorists and their apologists who would argue that there is no difference between the 'low-tech' terrorist pipe-bomb placed in the rubbish bin at a crowded market … and the 'high-tech' precision-guided ordnance dropped by air force fighter-bombers from a height of 20.000 feet or more that achieves the same wanton and indiscriminate effect on the crowded market-place far below."[4] But in fact, whoever does not apply a double standard plays only into the hands of objectivity and universalism, whereas Hoffman himself plays into the hands of partisanship and state terrorism. This partisan attitude is manifest in his distorting comparisons. Thus he explains that, although armies too have attacked civilians, oftentimes legal steps were taken in order that the delinquents might be made responsible for their actions. "By comparison, one of the fundamental *raisons d'être* of international terrorism is a refusal to be bound by such rules of warfare and codes of conduct."[5] Firstly, we also notice such a refusal in the handling of the Taliban prisoners by the United States, as well as in the extreme hostility on the part of this state towards the international criminal court. Secondly, Hoffman is comparing apples and oranges when he seeks to compare legal possibilities with the disposition of perpetrators. If we avoid this skewed view, we will have no difficulty in recognizing that not just crimes of war, but also sub-national acts of terror are pursued legally (the latter even more frequently). We will also see clearly that there are instances *both* of armies *as well as* of sub-national groups which accept certain rules waging war and applying force. (In fact, Hoffman himself stresses the fact that ethno-nationalistic and separatist groups and, in particular, left-winged terrorists are also subject to certain ethical constraints in their choice of targets.)[6]

Hence it remains the case that terrorism is to be defined as a method. C. A. J. Coady offers a classical definition. Under "terrorist act" he understands:

> "A political act, ordinarily committed by an organized group, which involves the intentional killing or other severe harming of non-combatants or the threat of the same or intentional severe damage to the property of non-combatants or the threat of the same."[7] (Coady's further remarks suggest that he does not mean just any political acts, but rather acts of *violence*.)

This definition did not escape criticism, even outside of objections in the style of Hoffman. Thus Virginia Held warns that, according to Coady's definition, the 1983 bombing of US Marine barracks in Lebanon in which 241 people died, most of them US soldiers, would not be an act of terrorism. But this, so Held, would be arbitrary.[8] In fact it is really consistent. If American attacks on military targets in which primarily soldiers are killed are celebrated in the media as "surgical operations", then we cannot suddenly speak of terrorism when the situation is simply reversed. Held is thus rather alone in her criticism. Things stand differently with the wide-spread objection that the intention of spreading *terror*, i.e. fear and panic, is not to be found in Coady's definition as a necessary component of terrorism. Coady's procedure is nevertheless justified. As Thomas C. Schelling or Annette C. Baier (among others) remark, the motivation behind terrorist acts such as attacks on civilian sky-scrapers or airplanes can lie for example therein, that these acts strengthen the enduring will of a group or direct the attention of the world on a certain problem by means of shock.[9] Nevertheless, we still usually assume that, at least in the *paradigmatic* case of terrorism, the intention of intimidation and the targeting of innocents are defining characteristics; and it suggests itself to begin the ethical analysis of terrorism with such paradigmatic cases of terrorist acts. Meggle calls them terrorist acts in the "strong sense" and defines them as "acts in which an effecting of ends is attempted by means of terror-inducing violence against certain innocents".[10] In contrast to Coady's definition, here violence against innocents includes not only that violence which chooses innocents as a direct target, but also such violence which takes the harming of innocents into account and accepts the possibility of making them victims. In this context, Meggle speaks of "Highly Imputable Collateral Damage".[11]

Can terrorism thus defined ever be justified? Meggle denies this, which leads him to condemn both the attack on the World Trade Center, as well as the "Counter-Terror" measures of the United States in Afghanistan. What eludes him, however, is this: According to his own definition of terrorism, those legislators who employ a system of justice with penal and process law in order that they may punish criminals and *deter* delinquents from committing crimes, commit thereby themselves a terrorist act in the strong sense. For even if they take precautions to minimize the danger of killing innocents by their acts, they know very well that this danger can never be completely removed, and what is more: they know that innocents will ever and again be affected. This risk – the risk of "conscious collateral damage in a strong sense", to

217

use Meggle's own terms – is one which such legislators clearly take. The applicability of Meggle's definition to a system of criminal justice does not at all show that this definition is faulty, however. As Agnes Heller has ascertained: "Terror does not originate in totalitarianism. Rather, it has its origin in the principal of deterrence ..., which has also been introduced in the legal procedures of democracies."[12] But since it is counter-intuitive to deem such acts of positing penal law as *per se* morally contemptible, Meggle's thesis on the categorical illegitimacy of ("strong") terrorism remains unconvincing.

To the contrary: The analogy with a system of criminal law for punishment and deterrence rather opens a line of argument for the justification of terrorism, where possible. Let us suppose, for example, that the attack on the World Trade Center was an act of punishment for the policy of Israel and the United States toward the Palestinians. (In the United States there recently appeared a collection of essays from American dissidents; on the cover of the book the remains of the World Trade Center are pictured, and in the foreground we read: "A Just Response".) Human rights organizations such as Human Rights Watch have made reference to the fact that civilians have been (and continue to be) targeted in diverse Israeli military actions. In this sense, we are indeed dealing with Israeli state terrorism, which is also supported by the United States, and to which we may add the non-state terrorism of Israeli settlers. This Israeli-American terrorism has caused more casualties than all the Arab strikes of retaliation taken together. But would this justify a retaliatory strike on the World Trade Center, assuming that the attack really was such a strike? Even if one were to assign many of the victims a partial responsibility for American policy in the Middle East – the United States is, after all, a democracy –, their responsibility could hardly be large enough to warrant the death penalty. Nevertheless, one could argue – in the sense of Meggle's definition of terrorism – that the victims of the attack on the World Trade Center are meant only as a kind of means: to punish either all American and Europeans, or at least as many as possible, namely by means of a growing feeling of fear and uncertainty. Surely innocents were also affected (for example people who were engaged in the struggle for the rights of the Palestinians) or guilty parties were punished too severely, but this is a risk which one also takes in a system of penal and criminal law with the principle of deterrence. The difference between the two would no longer be one of principle, but would rather lie in the dimensions and appropriateness of the attack. And if, as certain Israeli and US governments have believed and continue to believe, those so-called acts of retaliation by the Israeli army which terrorized the entire Palestinian population are justified; or if Clinton's strike against Sudan – which, according to the report of the German ambassador there, caused thousands of deaths – was justified; or even if the sanctions against Iraq are justified, though they have caused some half million civilian deaths, of which half have been those of children: if all these acts are justified, then it is not at all clear why the attack on the World Trade Center should not be justified, if it is in fact understood as an act of retaliation as well.

Here one might object that both Israeli and Arab terrorism are illegitimate and that both are very well to be distinguished in principle from criminal and penal law, to the degree that the latter does not *intend* to affect innocent victims, but rather only *takes them into account.* This distinction, which goes back to Thomas of Aquinas' theory of double effect, strengthens Coady's definition against Meggle's. But, first of all, we are also accountable for the collateral damages we cause. For whether one employs the death of civilians as a means to attain certain ends, or only as a coincidental result, in both cases one pursues one's goals in walking over the corpses of innocents. Admittedly: according to Kant, one should never use anyone exclusively as means, but also see the person in question as an end. Yet it is not quite clear to what degree one deems another as an end in itself when one accepts the death of that other as a secondary effect, i.e. as an acceptable result which one effects in the pursuit of one's own goals. Secondly, the moral relevance of the distinction between intention and the conscious acceptance of risk is interpreted incorrectly as soon as one claims that this distinction corresponds to that between means-ends deliberation on the one hand and secondary effects on the other. As for Thomas of Aquinas, in his well-known remarks on the right to self-protection (ST II-II, 64.7) he himself allows that one may intend something bad (in this case, the death of people, namely the attacker) in order to achieve something good (namely one's own survival). (He expressly permits this to officials in public service, and seems at least not to forbid private persons from intending and causing the death of an attacker in order to protect an innocent third party.) When, however, a court servant secures his own survival by intentionally killing another person, then this act of killing is clearly the *means* by which his own survival was achieved.[13] All that Thomas actually forbids is only that defenders let themselves be determined by "personal passions".[14] Thus he does not distinguish sinful actions from those which are without sin by the question as to whether the specific intentions and expectations were directed towards something bad as a means, or only as a secondary effect. Those actions which are without sin because they aim for a good, though they achieve it by means of an ill, are rather distinguished by the emotional tenor of the intentions and expectations behind them. And in fact it is *this* distinction which corresponds to the one between intention and the conscious acceptance of risk. For someone who employs as means the death of innocents, but finds this bad and does so only after much deliberation and as a last possibility for the accomplishment of her goals, can be said to have only accepted an evil; inversely, someone who sees certain inevitable consequences as a pleasing surplus can be said to actually intend them. In other words, the morally relevant difference does not lie in the question as to whether someone employs the death of innocents as a means to his ends or foresees it as a consequence, but rather whether the person in question welcomes the death of the innocents or regrets it. But this is not a difference between terrorists on the one hand and legislators on the other; it is rather one between different kinds of legislators and/or terrorists.

Coady's definition of terrorism must therefore be revised accordingly. For an act is not then non-terrorist when the death of innocents is only accepted as a risk. This can be easily illustrated with many appropriate examples. It is, for example, often emphasized that the attackers on September 11th chose the World Trade Center because of its symbolic character. It may, however, be the case that their *intention* was directed toward the collapse of the *buildings*, and that they simply accepted that those working within them would die. Admittedly: according to Coady's definition, such an attack would still be terrorist in nature, since the building, as one could say, belonged to innocent civilians. But if we were to discover that the building was in fact in the possession of the Pentagon, although only as an object of financial speculation and without any military use whatsoever, would we classify the attack as non-terroristic in retrospect? Probably not. Or, to mention a further example, would we call that attack non-terroristic which would be directed against a building which coincidentally belonged to the Pentagon, and in which a kindergarten was located, if the attack had as its primary objective the destruction of the physical building, and only accepted the foreseen death of those inside? Most certainly we would not call such an attack non-terroristic. Hence: the attempt to construe a categorical difference between the punishing and deterring violence of penal law and similar violence in certain terroristic acts, and hence to block the outlined legitimization strategy for terroristic acts, fails when this attempt is made with reference to the presence or absence of a direct intention to violently harm innocents.

Another possible legitimization of terrorism is given by Virginia Held.

> "It seems reasonable, I think, that on grounds of justice, it is better to equalize rights violations in a transition to bring an end to rights violations than it is to subject a given group that has already suffered extensive rights violations to continued such violations, if the degree of severity of the two violations is similar. ... If we must have rights violations, a more equitable distribution of such violations is better than a less equitable distribution."[15]

The attack on non-combatants would be legitimized here by means of reference to *groups* as recipients of a supposedly just distribution of rights violations. Since Held explicitly understands this strategy of legitimization as based on rights and not on utility, a question from the logical point of view suggests itself right away: How can one have recourse to rights in order to legitimize their infraction? This is a difficulty which Held could solve simply by giving a more carefully worded version of her argument. But perhaps it is also appropriate, especially in light of certain extreme situations, to re-think the logic of rights. Be that as it may, one may readily assume that a position such as Held represents would not be unattractive for many members of groups which fall victim to oppression and rights violations. The concept of "poetic justice" plays a certain role here. The ethnologist James C. Scott reports the reaction of many black people to the sinking of the *Titanic*:

> "The drowning of large numbers of wealthy and powerful whites ... in their finery aboard a ship that was said to be unsinkable seemed like a stroke of poetic justice to many blacks. ... 'Official' songs about the loss of the *Titanic* were sung ironically ('It was *saaad* when the great ship went down')."[16]

Naturally, similar reactions could be seen in wake of the destruction of the World Trade Center – and in fact, such reactions are indeed natural. In reaction to them certain persons, especially in the German and American press, pointed the moral finger and condemned the lack of compassion on the part of many in the Arab world (the level of compassion in a significant portion of the Latin-American population was not much greater, but this the established press chose to keep silent about). Herein is another injustice to be found: the oppressed not only have to bear an unequal distribution of rights violations, one also demands of them more compassion for those who profit from this unequal distribution than the privileged are required to show for the oppressed. Thus Ron Hirschbein remarks on public opinion in the United States during the second Gulf War: "There was no public outcry, for example, when the popular press cited the conclusion of a Harvard Medical School study: 75.000 Iraqi children would die due to the destruction of the Iraqi infrastructure. The civic celebration continued as Bush's popularity soared."[17] And yet, though such a lack of compassion in the public opinion of the United States was manifest, moral fingers were pointed neither there, nor in Germany. Apparently Americans who do not let the death of 75.000 children rain on the parade for their bombs are more acceptable than Arabs who, in view of 3.000 American casualties, are glad that misfortune hit the other side for a change. Such discrepancies understandably increase the willingness of oppressed peoples to see whole groups as enemies and thus to have recourse to an argumentative strategy such as Held's.

A further strategy for the legitimization of terrorism may be developed from considerations forwarded by Michael Walzer, though very much against his intentions. He thinks that sub-national terrorism is neither to be legitimated, nor to be excused. In accordance with this position is the manifesto signed by 58 scholars in the United States, in which we read that "no appeal to the merits or demerits of specific foreign policies can ever justify … the mass slaughter of innocent persons."[18] And yet, in his book on *Just and Unjust Wars*, he considers the mistakes committed by the German government as sufficient justification for the terror bombing of German cities (Walzer himself uses this term). Supposedly, German policy threatened the survival and freedom of the political community of Britain in such a way as to justify this use of the only potent offensive weapon which the British possessed in the years 1940 and 1941.[19] "But why is it", asks Andrew Valls, who criticizes Walzer's double moral standard, "that the territorial integrity and political independence of, say, Britain, justify the resort to … violence that targets civilians – but the right of self-determination of a stateless nation never does? "[20] Apparently there is no reason for this, especially since Walzer explicitly deduces the rights of states from those of communities, and the rights of these from those of individuals.[21]

Whoever seeks to legitimize certain *particular* acts of terrorism carries the burden of proof, for the protection of innocents is indeed an extraordinarily precious right and legal good. To outweigh this right in any particular situation there must be very good and very carefully examined reasons. On the other hand, whoever claims that terrorism can *never* be justified also carries the burden of proof, as shown by the fundamental disposability of such legitimization strategies as the ones just outlined. This claim – that terrorism is never justified – would only be valid under the ethical premise that direct attack on civilians in acceptance of risking the lives of innocent victims is *absolutely* forbidden. Sorry to say, such a premise is hardly plausible in the context of an ethics of responsibility; and this premise is also rejected by the great

221

majority of those who now loudly denounce terrorism as absolutely evil and bad. For when such persons want to justify the terrorism which they think is good, they often have recourse to one or the other of the patterns of argumentation described above, often in combination. Of course they do not call it terrorism – they may call it a "war against terror", as in the case of the massive bombing in Afghanistan or Clinton's rocket strike in Sudan, or they may also call it a "war-shortening measure", as in the case of the dropping of the Atomic bomb on Hiroshima and Nagasaki.

A first result of these considerations is that the inference from the terroristic character of an attack to its illegitimacy is not valid. At best, the inference of the probability of the act's illegitimacy would be valid. But this in turn means that, according to the criteria of just war, if a state falls victim to a terrorist attack, it must first examine the reasons motivating the attack and can certainly not out of hand dismiss the question of motivation as irrelevant, before it has the right to take a bellicose counter-measure. And even if this examination is brought to the conclusion that the attack was illegitimate, it still opens the possibility to recognize that the perpetrators did not act out of purely evil intentions, but rather more probably out of desperation – a desperation for which the victim is perhaps not completely unaccountable. And this recognition could possibly lead to a certain amount of moderation in the application of counter-measures. Herein lies precisely the purpose and meaning of a theory of just war (or at least, it should do so today): to limit war – and not to promote self-justice and open warrants to destroy.

A second, substantial conclusion of these considerations results from the nature of the patterns of justification outlined. As previously mentioned, these are also used by the apologists for state terrorism. However, these patterns do not fail to recognize the validity of proportionality or just measure and of the probability of success as criteria in the judgment of the justification of an act of violence. It is not only, but also for this reason that the constraints of these schemes are not just difficult to fulfill, but in fact: they are *more difficult for strong parties to fulfill than for weak ones*. Let us take the pattern of argument borrowed from Walzer as an example. The freedom of the political community of the Palestinians is not only threatened by Israel, but has in effect been prevented for some decades, and the creation of a Palestinian state or even an autonomous region has been foiled. The Palestinians are not standing with their backs to the wall: they are being smashed against the wall. But has the existence of Israel ever been threatened by the Intifada or by the Palestinian Autonomy Authority, or would the existence of Israel be threatened by a Palestinian state? In consideration of the military might of Israel and its American ally, such a thought seems absolutely absurd. The idea that al-Quaida or the Taliban could threaten the existence or freedom of the United States is just as absurd. A similar asymmetry is to be found in other patterns of argumentation, as could easily be shown. Nevertheless, most "serious" commentators tend to excuse the violence committed by the stronger party. (One could consider the mild, even positive reactions to the American bombing of Tripoli in 1986 and of a pharmaceutical factory in 1998; the frequent retaliation measures directed against civilians in Palestine; or the continuing sanctions against Iraq which, as previously mentioned, have already cost the lives of hundreds of thousands of civilians, of which half were of children. At least recent reactions to

Israel's youngest attacks against the Palestinians give occasion for some glimmer of hope.) This is not only immoral and hypocritical, it defies all logic.

Terrorism is not at all the instrument of the weak, as is often claimed, but rather the routinely employed instrument of the strong, and usually only the final resort for the weak. (This is true for secular terrorism, not for that kind of terrorism which is motivated by apocalyptic visions such as may be found in the Aum sect, certain racist militias in the USA and partially also in al-Quaida.) As such a final instrument terrorism is, to cite Baier, "a demonstration of this power to make resentment at exclusion felt".[22] We may add: resentment at exclusion from justice and freedom. Even if the United States were to succeed in their so-called "War against Terrorism" and were to annihilate all such terrorism which is neither promoted, supported or approved of by them, and thus were to remove the last resort of those who are excluded to put up some resistance – even then there would be only a little less violence in the world. There would certainly not be more justice. This "War against Terrorism" – waged by state terrorists and with terrorist means – does not have as its object universal values, but rather the undisputed power.

If strong states really want to fight terrorism, then there are only three legitimate and recommendable means at their disposal: the rejection of a double moral standard, focused persecution of crimes (insofar as the committing of a punishable crime – and not of an act of justifiable resistance – may be demonstrated) and, finally, the inclusion of the excluded.

NOTES

* Translated by Colin King.
[1] Georg Meggle, "Terror & Gegenterror. Erste Ethische Reflexionen", *Deutsche Zeitschrift für Philosophie* 50 (2002), pp. 149-162.
[2] Cf. Laurie Calhoun, "Violence and Hypocrisy", *Dissent* (Winter 2001), pp. 79-85, esp. pp. 81 f.
[3] U.S. Department of State, *Patterns of Global Terrorism 1997*, Washington D.C., 1998, p. vi.
[4] Bruce Hoffman, *Inside Terrorism*, Columbia University Press, New York 1998, p. 33.
[5] *Ibid.*, p. 35.
[6] *Ibid.*, pp. 158 ff.
[7] C. A. J. Coady, "The Morality of Terrorism", *Philosophy* 60 (1985), pp. 47-70, here p. 52.
[8] Virginia Held, "Terrorism, rights, and political goals", in: R. G. Frey, Christopher W. Morris (eds.), *Violence, Terrorism, and Justice*, Cambridge University Press, Cambridge 1991, pp. 58-85, here p. 62.
[9] Thomas C. Schelling, "What purposes can 'international terrorism' serve?", in: Frey and Morris, *op. cit.*, pp. 18-32, here p. 23. Annette C. Baier, "Violent Demonstrations", *ibid.*, pp. 33-58.
[10] Meggle, *op. cit.*, p. 153.
[11] *Ibid.*, p. 156.
[12] *Freitag*, February 22, 2002, p. 17.
[13] Cf. Gareth B. Matthews, "Saint Thomas and the Principle of Double Effect", in: Scott MacDonald, Eleonore Stump (eds.), *Aquinas's Moral Theory: Essays in Honor of Norman Kretzmann*, Cornell University Press, Ithaca and London 1999, pp. 63-78, here p. 68.
[14] Thomas of Aquinas, *Summa Theologiae* (Die Deutsche Thomas-Ausgabe, Bd. 18. Edited by the Albertus-Magnus-Akademie Walberberg bei Köln), Heidelberg und Graz 1953, p. 175.
[15] Virginia Held, "Terrorism, rights, and political goals", in: Frey and Morris, *op. cit.*, pp. 58-85, here pp. 77 ff.

[16] James C. Scott, "Domination, Acting, and Fantasy", in: Carolyn Nordstrom and Jo-Ann Martin (eds.), *The Paths to Domination, Resistance, and Terror*, University of California Press, Berkeley 1992, pp. 55-84, here p. 67.

[17] Ron Hirschbein, "A World Without Enemies (Bush's Brush with Morality)", in: Deane C. Curtin and Robert Litke (eds.), *Institutional Violence*, Rodopi, Amsterdam and Atlanta 1999, pp. 343-352, here p. 344.

[18] "What We're Fighting For", electronic resource, cited February 2, 2002 under: www.propositionsonline.com/Fighting_For/fighting_for/html.

[19] Michael Walzer, *Just and Unjust Wars: A Moral Argument With Historical Illustrations*, Basic Books, New York 2000, pp. 255-263.

[20] Andrew Valls, "Can Terrorism be Justified?", in: idem (ed.), *Ethics in International Affairs: Theories and Cases*, Rowman and Littlefield, Lanham et cet. 2000, pp. 65-79, here p. 73.

[21] Michael Walzer, *Just and Unjust Wars: A Moral Argument With Historical Illustrations*, op.cit., pp. 53-55, p. 254.

[22] Baier, "Violent demonstrations", *op. cit.*, p. 54.

III

TERRORISM & COUNTER-TERRORISM

LAW AND POLITICS

CAROLIN EMCKE

WAR ON TERRORISM AND THE CRISES OF THE POLITICAL

Since September 11th there were distorted images, scraps of language, wreckaged systems of belief, broken templets of political thought or ideology. Language, words, opinions were weighed, over and over again, and considered too light. Pieces of knowledge were too big, too small, unfit for the new puzzle of reality.

Speechlessness, it seemed, was at the heart of the order violence seeks to produce.

Maybe this had to do with the shock with which such events paralyse the witness and those affected by it.[1]

Most of my friends and colleagues, though, had turned suddenly into Islam experts, Central Asia experts, terrorism experts, anthrax experts. As if all gender studies and multiculturalism theorists in academia and all bio-ethics and cloning specialists in the media were reprogrammed on 9/12, quasi over night, as Islam specialists.

I, instead, was mostly speechless. There wasn't a single reasonable thought or analyses in months. The analytical tools to give appropriate accounts of what had happened, where it rooted, and whether it changed anything, seemed useless.

Quite soon, the war on terrorism began its mission, and the attempt to analyse the actual events and to trace their geneaology was overwritten, covered with the "right" answer, the "right" interpretation, and the rhetorics of the righteous. And it became more and more difficult to search for an understanding of the events.

In this respect, it is an archeological project to seek to decipher a description that renarrates the events – those actions which triggered and provoked the response we call "counter-terrorism". A preliminary description, in any case, that does not assume or claim to be authoritative or objective or all-encompassing.

Politics consists in giving meaning to the social world and our actions in it, it consists in shaping the world, it reacts to natural, social, political, scientific events and individual or collective desires – and it interpretes those events and desires and integrates them into a dynamic symbolic, cultural system of meaning which constructs a new social reality. So, already before the political materializes those identifications or significations of meanings in social practices or political institutions, is the social reality digested and constructed in processes of interpretation and narration.[2]

> "We cannot understand a society outside of a unifying factor that provides a signified content and weaves it with the symbolic structures. The factor is not simply "reality"; every society has constituted *its* reality."[3]

G. Meggle (ed.), Ethics of Terrorism & Counter-Terrorism, 227-243.
© 2005 Ontos, Heusenstamm.

The spectrum of political action and debate ranges according to and consists in the various significations we assign to "reality", to "mere facts", to the metanarrative with which politics reproduces and creates itself.

The political forum is a vivid, porous, flexible, moving sphere in which discourses of self-understanding and discourses on the meaning of events, form and shape the tasks of political debate and action. Usually, in democratic societies fundamental political freedom also always roots in our ability to nurture the heterogeneity, the vitality, the ambiguity, the richness of competing narratives, significations, meanings of how to understand our social world, and answer the questions it poses to us.

One of the main strategic objectives of the Bush administration has been to design the presentation of the attacks of 9/11 as if they already implied a certain objective, as if they could decide on the meaning, intentionality, scope of the attack, and – more importantly – as if there was only one adequate way, only one possible way to respond to it. The response of counter-terrorism was supported by a form of aestheticisation of both: the complexity of a speechless violent act and the wordiness of the political violence of the state responding to it.[4]

The Bush administration's attempt to dominate the interpretation of the events was so exclusive that it suppressed practically all discourse about the meaning of the attacks.

In this paper, I will first of all return to a renarration of the attacks themselves, and will see what a variety of interpretations of symbolic signification and political meaning they could offer.

I will try to argue that the response of the war on terrorism was founded on one very particular interpretation, one that was not inevitable.

My claim will be, that the American government decided to interpret the attacks in such a way that it would justify their claim to power, an understanding of hegemomic power freed of all conventional norms and human or civil rights which usually restrict the sovereign in democratic states. I will argue that the understanding of the political in the response to the terrorist attacks has been reduced to a pre-democratic, authoritarian conception.

Societies tend to "erase calamity quickly from its memory in order to keep its worldview unharmed", is what Wolfgang Sofsky suggests,[5] but interestingly enough the American administration and media opted for the opposite: in an almost neurotic manner, they stuck to the disaster, to the injury,[6] and repeated and memorized its image over and over again, as if the image of being attacked would only *prove* (and not, as would seem more reasonable after such an attack, *call into question*) their system of values and belief. Instead of searching for reasons (which is not to say justifications!) for their attracting such violent criminal energy, instead of self-critical reconsideration of their policies abroad, or at least a reevaluation of the perception of their policies abroad, the administration used the attack as a proof of the quality and morality or civility of their practices and values.

In the course of the response to the attack with all rhetorical, political, and military means, the permanent visual or discursive repetition of the traumatic events slowly parted from the frugal facts, and more and more included assigned, constructed features which served the purposes of a powerful counter-terrorism freed of all restrictions of conventional laws and norms.

I. WHAT HAPPENED?

Four groups of men, none of them nationals of the United States, kidnapped four commercial airplanes filled with civilian passengers and flew them into the World Trade Centre and The Pentagon – thereby killing more than 3000 men and women. Only a small portion of the victims were employed by a government agency, the Pentagon, and an even smaller segment of that last group were members of the military. The perpetrators died with the victims in the attack. No declaration was issued by the actors themselves, neither in letter nor in film. There was no previous warning, no declaration of war, there were no soldiers involved. The victims were all non-combatants.

Was this an act of terrorism?

You may say that it is self-evident that we call these acts terrorist. Clearly, one could – in absense of a declaration of the perpetrators claiming political motives for their deed – also consider calling the attack on innocent civilians simply that: a criminal act, murder, mass murder.

And yet, we all tend to call this an act of "terrorism".

Why?

Even though the actors differ from most European terrorists of the 70ies and 80ies in their not seeking the attention of the public sphere by issuing political statements, even though we are lacking an explanation for their crime – why do we call it "terrorist"?

It seems, it is the choice of *targets* that we read as a statement on the political aspirations of the perpetrators. First, the group chose to attack a government building: the Pentagon, and second, the World Trade Centre seems to have acquired a symbolic status as the imago of global capitalism.

Nevertheless, whatever good indications there are for the "political" motives behind the choice of the targets, it is still *us* assigning an intention to attack "the state", "the nation", "us".

The act in itself seems first of all nothing but intentional kidnapping and murder of innocent civilians.

This is *not* to say that there was no criminal act, this is *not* to say that the people attacking the World Trade Centre and killing thousands of innocent people did not commit a horrendous, senseless mass murder. Clearly, al Qaeda is not a phantom, it is not merely a ghost, or a rhetorical conspiracy. Indeed, there is a real, concrete threat resulting from certain terrorist networks around the globe. And it needs a reaction.

Any response to terrorist acts, though, should include the acknowledgement that there never will be and there never can be complete safety of any society. Sadly enough, no individual, whether prime-minister, military commander or normal civilian can be totally protected against terrorist attacks.[7]

In the following, I will analyse the response to the terrorist attacks of 9/11. I will focus on the discourse and rhetorics of counter-terrorism as expressed in statements, speeches, laws, decrees issued in the aftermath of the attacks.[8] I will seek to illustrate the constructions of the "us" versus "them", the enemy and friend antagonism, and a language which permanently restages the battle between "good" and "evil", thereby discursively producing a permanent state of threat, a condition of perpetual war and not peace.

I will argue that the Bush administration staged and fought a war not even declared to them – and in the course of it reduced its own legitimacy and the political freedom of its citizens.

Via an engagement with the writings of Carl Schmitt I will argue that the central concern of the Bush government has not been the protection of its citizens, or the punishment of the perpetrators but the performance of sovereign power. Interestingly enough at the moment when that power was called into question. Its main effort has been to restage its power as the ability to not only react but act, its main concern has been to reclaim its shattered subjectivity by reclaiming its right to act, to declare war, to actually declare all military aggression as justified acts of self-defense.

The texts of Carl Schmitt serve only as a metaphor for the deconstruction of the rhetorics of the Bush administration. Comparing Schmitt's political theology with the Bush administration's rhetorics and actions allows to delineate the decline of the political in times of counter-terrorism.

II. SCHMITT'S POLITICAL THEOLOGY AND THE DETERMINATION OF THE ENEMY AFTER 9/11

"Sovereign is he who decides the exception" Carl Schmitt states,[9] and the war on terrorism justifies its extra-legal actions, its transgression of laws and human or civil rights by declaring a state of emergency. Parallel, Schmitt introduces a concept of the political which situates the friend-enemy distinction as its prime objective. The friend-enemy distinction is the matrix along which politics creates its own purpose. "The high points of politics are simultaneously the moments in which the enemy is, in concrete clarity, recognized as the enemy." In this respect, the friend-enemy distinction and politics constitute one another. The enemy in its almost ontological difference is perceived as a threat to the general order, and insofar always functions as an occasion for a reenactment of sovereign power. The concept of the political, for Schmitt, almost *depends* on the enemy, because only in recognizing the enemy as an enemy does politics appear. And only when responding to the threat the enemy poses, can politics stage and present itself as sovereign power – able to suspend law. The paradoxical Schmittian logic of self-protection suggests that when the order is under attack, the order can be lifted. When the norms are under threat, the norms can be transgressed.

> "The concepts of friend and enemy", Schmitt explains, "receive their real meaning precisely because they refer to the real possibility of physical killing. War follows from enmity. War is the existential negation of the enemy."[10]

The defining criteria for political groups, whether collectives or states, is that they attain their political stature precisely in their ability to recognize a shared foe:

> "For as long as people exist in the political sphere, this people must, even if only in the most extreme case determine by itself the distinction of friend of enemy. Therein resides the essence of political existence."[11]

For Schmitt, groups transform into political groups, whether they otherwise unite according to geography, religion, ethnicity or economic commonalities, once the antagonism to an enemy is strong enough a motivation to unite the group.

The reference to Schmittian theory allows to read the Bush administration's understanding of counter-terrorism critically.

It becomes clearer why it is relevant to trace the genesis of the judgment to call these attacks "terrorist". It seems crucial, because *in that act*, in the judgment rests such a decision, the decision to consider the situation on and after 9/11 a "critical" situation, to consider the criminal acts "acts of terrorism" (later also often coined as "acts of barbarism"), and to perceive them as an attack "on the state".

From very early on, the administration decided to convey that the perpetrators not only attacked innocent civilians *of* the United States, but that they attacked *the* United States and their values. In almost each of its statements or comments on the attacks, the administration not only focussed on presenting information about the police work, about the investigation in the history, background, logistics of the crime, or the profile of the perpetrators, but the Bush administration officials always discursively reproduced the attacks and in the course of the narrative transformed the target, later the enemy. What began as an attack on an office building turned into an attack on civilisation, as a Holy War which needed to be answered, in Bush words, by a "Crusade".

Donald Rumsfeld presented the new enemy on the 16th of September:

> "The terrorists don't have targets of high value. They don't have armies and navies and air forces that one can go battle against. They don't have capital cities with high-value assets that they're reluctant to lose. (...) They work in the shadows. They operate in safe houses and apartments. And they use weapons that are distinctively different – plastic knives, our own aircraft in this case – to bring about the damage. And they're trying to strike directly at the way of life of free people of the United States of America. (...) The network that did this does not have things to blow up as such. They're in apartments, and they're using laptops, and they're using cell phones. And they are functioning in the shadows, not out in front."[12]

Rumsfeld first identification of the enemy begins with a stunning contradiction which relates to the confusion about whom the administration wants to fight, and who the actual perpetrators were: on one hand, the terrorists don't have armies, navies or capitals, and they don't have high value targets, on the other they seem to lead a life of high values with cell-phones, laptops and apartments. Whereas the actual perpetrators of the attacks, indeed, resembled the latter type of terrorists, the first depiction already refers to completely different men or groups, namely the Taliban in Afghanistan ("without high value targets").

It is important to remember that it was not that easy, at first, to "fight the enemy", since actually the enemy was *dead*. The problem of counter-terrorism's first weeks was that there was no evident form of dealing with the public and collective desire for punishment for those outrageous crimes – since the perpetrators had died in the attacks themselves.

Whom to fight? Who to punish for such deeds? How to satisfy one's nation's desire for revenge? How to cope with the feeling of vulnerability, of paralysation?

The media's permanent re-vision of the images of the attacks of New York somehow fixed the public to the shock of the unimaginable. But the images of the collapsing towers conjured not only the trauma of one's unexpected vulnerability, but the repetition of the same pictures prevented any political or emotional dynamic. The moving pictures were only a sign of a state of paralysation not only related to the subjective sentiment of inability to understand, but also to the objective problem of inability to do something since the perpetrators were "unpunishable", were gone. Surprisingly enough, *the* media-crime of the new millenium was not too visual, but actually in a specific sense not visual enough – it was lacking both: the victims and the perpetrators. Both remained, at least in the scene of the crime, *faceless*.

Repetition includes the possibility of failure,[13] in the memorizing of the events of 9/11 a slow process of transformation took place, the image of the enemy more and more lost a connection to the original perpetrator. It served, whether intentionally or not, the purpose of constructing an enemy whom one could identify, whom one could visualize, even personalize (in the figure of Osama bin Laden), and whom one could actually *fight*.

This kind of minimal but slowly growing disruption between the actual perpetrator and the new enemy might stem from the disconnection between the past and the present, symptomatic for the phenomena of haunting events:

> "Haunting is also unsettling to the very degree that a past remark of event or figure hovers over the present. To be haunted often entails being touched or suffused by something that one cannot quite recall, feeling the importance of something that one has laid aside or tried to forget (...) So haunting takes place between history and memory; it is simultaneously an achievement of memory and a failure of memory with regard to some significant historical effect. As an achievement, haunting keeps the phenomenon alive and potent; as a failure, it indicates or points toward a history that it cannot fully conjure or command."[14]

This is what the Bush administration has done: to keep the phenomenon alive and potent, trying to instrumentalize it for a restatement of its power as sovereign and unharmed from such a threat, and therein only reproduces the trauma which ties them to the experience of their unexpected and disturbing vulnerability.

If American counter-terrorism calls for a war against its enemy, and stages a war against not only Osama bin Laden and al-Qaeda, but also the Taliban in Afghanistan, and Saddam Hussein in Iraq, it is not only but also because it is *possible* to fight them.[15]

In another statement, a few days later, Rumsfeld says:

> "Our adversaries are not one or two terrorist leaders, even a single terrorist organisation or network. It's a broad network of individuals

and organisations that are determined to terrorize, and in so doing deny
us the very essence of what we are – free people."

Rumsfeld combines a description of the enemy with a reassertion of America's own
identity, from very early on the identification of the enemy is connected to a self-
explanatory discourse. Whereas it would be bad or disturbing or saddening or
upsetting or criminal enough to be *killed* by terrorists or murders – it is not only their
killing, their taking our lives, but it is their *denying what and who we are* that annoys
Rumsfeld: "free people". Rumsfeld makes it sound as if it were a greater crime to
negate our freedom than to take our lives. Ideologically and rhetorically, this implicit
sacrificial logic of appreciating values higher than life sounds amazingly similar to
the religious discourse of the Islamic fundamentalists praising suicide for a "greater
cause".

For Schmitt, groups attain a political stature precisely in their ability to recognize
a shared foe, and it is this what Rumsfeld seeks to do from very early on: to define the
enemy, and to create a political unity, a new political identity – one preferably
broader than the United States – that recognizes a shared foe.

The human grouping which organizes and pursues political enmity is, for Schmitt,
the state whose sovereignty and political character are evidenced precisely by its
ability to unite collective enmity against a political enemy. It is not only a responsive
dynamic, it is not only a reactive process which describes the state's attitude towards
its enemies. It is a *decision*, an active move in which both occur: the political
grouping declares its enemy, and in that process unites and constitutes itself as a
particular, sovereign political entity. "The ever present possibility of a friend-enemy
grouping suffices to forge a decisive entity which transcends the mere societal-
associational groupings."[16] As such, the state owns the possibility to decide at any
moment, in any concrete situation upon the enemy "and the ability to fight him with
the power emanating from the entity."[17]

It is this (pre-democratic) conception of an inherent connection between the state's
existence as a political entity, and its ability to decisively declare the enemy ("at a
time of our chosing", as Bush and its military spokesmen have come to call those
stagings of their sovereignty) that sheds light on the Bush administration's immediate
response to the attacks of 9/11.

III. THE ADMINISTRATION'S FRIEND-ENEMY DISTINCTION

"Sovereign is he who decides the exception", as Schmitt begins his Political
Theology. In his political understanding it is the exceptional case, not norms or laws,
that display the sovereign subjectivity of power.[18] The regular political order may be
dominated by the constitution and legal codices, but the exceptional case always
trumps. The exception may require suspension of rules and procedures that in peace
structure political and social order.

In the following (III) I would like to analyse the ways in which the Bush
administration's rhetorics and arguments in their "war on terrorism" display exactly
those features of the political as the sole dispositiv for offering criteria to decide
between enemy and friend. In a second step (IV) I would like to discern the

233

administration's attempt to reassure themselves and the disturbed and wounded nation about its sovereignty by exercising the one crucial power assigned to someone sovereign, namely, the ability to declare the state of exception.

> "Some worry that it is somehow undiplomatic or impolite to speak the language of right or wrong", Bush said in his commencement adress at West Point on the 1st of june 2002, "I disagree. Different circumstances require different methods, but not different moralities. Moral truth is the same in every culture, in every time, in every place (...) We are in a conflict between good and evil, and America will call evil by its name. By confronting evil and lawless regimes, we do not create a problem. We reveal a problem. And we will lead the world in opposing it."[19]

In times of a national crises (and this is how the attacks of 9/11 were interpreted from the start: as a national threat), in times of fears of dissolution, the enemy works to secure identity and sovereignty.

For Bush, the enemy did not simply attack civilians, the enemy attacked our entire being, and the enemy did not declare a war on us, we declare war on all "evil-doers", and they thereby help us to show our moral or military strength – as the leader of the world. At the moment, when the world's superpower had just been attacked by a group of 19 men, armed with *carpet knives*, the United States restates its claim to leadership in the world.

For Schmitt the state is the entity that organises its members and its opposition along the matrix of the friend and enemy, it is the state whose sovereignty and political character are evidenced precisely by its ability to channel collective enmity against another group.

In Bush's words:

> "More and more civilized nations find ourselves on the same side, united by common dangers of terrorist violence and chaos. There can be no peace in the world where differences and grievances become an excuse to target the innocent for murder. Against such an enemy, there is no immunity, and there can be no neutrality (...) I will not relent in this struggle for the freedom and security of my country and the civilized world (...) Terrorism must be stopped. No nation can negotiate with terrorists, for there is no way to make peace with those whose only goal is death ... since september 11th I've delivered the same message: Everyone must chose. You're either with the civilized world, or you're with the terrorists."[20]

With a strategically brilliant move, the Bush administration interpreted the attacks not only as an attack on the United States (and even less so as a – criminal and unjustifiable – response to their questionable policies in countries outside the US – as Susan Sontag suggested), but as an attack on civilisation sui generis.

By calling the terrorists opposed to "civilisation", Bush constructed an antagonism between terrorism and civilisation which implied that there could not be an immanent connection between modernity and terrorism. Instead, terrorists were cast as outside civilisation, as an Other to modernity and the civilized world. They are constructed as "barbarians", as "evil", "uncivilized" – a depiction which clearly contradicts the profile of the 19 perpetrators of 9/11. These were *products* of the civilized world of the West: students at Western universities, well-educated men with a middle-class chance, well-acquainted with the values of Bush's free world, men qualified for a Green Card in each of the countries of the West who close their borders to unwanted immigrants. It was not men who had not encountered the advantages of a life in the "free world". As Rumsfeld himself pointed out, these terrorists had "cell phones", and "apartments", and "computer laptops".

But with the interpretation of the attack as an attack on civilisation, the Bush administration not only externalizes terrorism from civilisation (and thereby oppresses all questions or doubts about the origin of the hatred of the terrorists, about the motivation for the crime), but it also identifies an either-or opposition which casts everyone opposed to the US as opposed to civilisation.

In his book on "The Conquest of America", Tzvetan Todorov writes about the efficiency of colonialism, and the various ways in which differences in not only technical developments but also communication and knowledge formed and decided the cultural conflict between the Spaniards and the Indians. Todorov suggests that the relation between knowledge, understanding and communication of the two cultural identities predisposed the use of violence as the dominant means of influence.

> "It is possible to establish an ethical criterion to judge the form of influences: the essential thing, I should say, is to know whether they are imposed or proposed (...) A civilisation may have features we can say are superior or inferior; but this does not justify their being imposed on others. Even more, to impose one's will on others implies that one does not concede to that other the same humanity one grants to oneself, an implication which precisely characterizes lower civilisation."[21]

What is interesting about Todorov's argument for this – certainly different – context is the way in which the communication precluded any understanding of the other, the way in which a particular discourse, perspective was established as an authoritative one, and how the asymmetrical communication suppressed other views and symbolic meanings. Violence appears when influence is not merely proposed but imposed Todorov claims, and the dominant discourse of counter-terrorism after 9/11 produced similar features of violent repression of the "inferior", the "other", the "uncivilized".

With the move that constructed the enemy as uncivilised, the war on terrorism was designed not only as a battle of the United States against their enemies, but as civilisation against "barbarism", thereby forcing other nations to declare themselves as either allies – or uncivilized, barbaric countries. The war on terrorism hereby declares its claim for global hegemony in which the terrorists could not find any state or territory anymore that would protect them:

> "Every terrorist must be made to live as an international fugitive."[22]

Charges of terrorism have often included the topos of "barbarism" committed by those with "no conscience and no soul". "Good" and "evil" fit into the moral rhetoric of those who narrate the conflict. The friend-enemy distinction situated in the international context is structured – according to President Bush – in terms of "the great divide of our time (...) not between religions and cultures, but between civilisation and barbarism".

Quite surprisingly, the discourse of the war on terrorism introduced also allegations of "totalitarianism". Whereas on one hand, the counter-terrorism analysts depicted al Qaeda as decentralised, independently operating networks of cells, harbored by a regime without the infrastructure or institutions of a nation state – on the other hand they were considered "totalitarian", an ideological and political phenomena which is historically rooted at the beginning in the 20th century and which is characterised by an all encompassing state.[23] Nonetheless, Bush compares the rather post-modern, post-nationstate phenomena of 21st century terrorism on the 20th of September to the totalitarian regimes of the states of the 20th: they are

> "the heirs of all murderous ideologies of the 20th century. By sacrificing human life to serve their radical visions, by abandoning every value but the will to power, they follow in the path of Fascism, Nazism, and Totalitarianism."

But Bush's association of the new threat posed by terrorist networks like al Qaeda with the old phenomena of totalitarianism is misleading. Whereas the rise of totalitarianism is immanently connected to the rise of nation states and their methods of consolidating their power with the means of an omnipotent state apparatus, the genuinely distinctive nature of modern terrorism is ignored in such characterisation. Clearly, the vagueness of the phenomena "terrorism", and the disgusting quality of its murderous acts, facilitates such instrumentalisation.

IV. BUSH'S STATE OF EXCEPTION

Let me now look at the ways in which the response by the Bush administration displays an exercise of its sovereign power not only in deciding to declare the enemy, but also in declaring the state of exception.

The vanishing point of my argument here is that the exercise of sovereign power as holding the defining monopoly, reduces the political to an enemy-friend matrix, along which the scapegoating or detention of all kinds of foreigners becomes justified, along which the suspension of civil and human rights can be legitimized, along which all our non-political actions, all our military actions are justifiable as acts of "self-defence".

Giorgio Agamben offers in his "Homo Sacer" the following interpretation of the state of exception:

> "The state of exception is not chaos that precedes order but rather the situation that results from its suspension (...) The situation created in the exception has the peculiar characteristic that it cannot be defined either as a situation of fact, or as a situation of right, but instead institutes a paradoxical threshold of indistinction between the two. It is not a fact, since it is only created through the suspension of the rule."[24]

Let us see how this paradox unfolded in the aftermath of 9/11. There are two contexts in which it is possible to analyse the reduction of the political, the suspension of norms and laws by recurring, by referring to the discourse and the logic of the state of exception. First, in the national context and the issue of the prisoners inside the US, second, the international context, and the issue of other sovereign states and the alleged threat they pose.

On September 16th in an interview with Fox News, Rumsfeld already announced the departure from former understandings of politics or defense against terrorist threats:

> "It's a new kind of war. The old rhetoric, the old words aren't going to work quite right for this problem. We're going to have to reorder our priorities. We're going to (...) be resolute and patient. It has to be very broadly based. It will be political, economic, diplomatic, military. It will be unconventional, what we do."[25]

1.) The strategically most important move by the Bush administration was to create the term "unlawful combatants", and thereby avoid all the existing rules, laws, and conventions regarding prisoners of war, or other prisoners. The invention of a legally new category freed the US-administration of all concerns for human or civil rights which would have restricted their ability to imprison, interrogate, prosecute or torture those arrested. By detaining those men captured during the war on terrorism on Guantanamo Base, Cuba, and declaring them "unlawful combatants", they prevented that their enemies could be protected by the Geneva Convention.

This is an interesting change of terminology and policy: during the first phase of the war on terrorism, right after the attacks of 9/11, when the administration needed a justification for declaring war against the Taliban regime, they called the terrorist attacks against the World Trade Centre and the Pentagon a "declaration of war". And so they could answer to a *war* they had not begun. But when they capture soldiers *of* this war, fighters of this war who could possibly be benefactors of procedural protection by the Geneva Convention – the administration needs to redefine the concept of the combat.

First, a "terrorist attack" was redesigned as a "declaration of war". Then, the soldiers of the war who are captured are not "prisoners of war" but "unlawful combatants". So suddenly what was begun as a war has turned again into mere terrorism.

It is the announced state of exception that gives the government the right to define the status of those captured, to declare before the intervention of any courts or trials, the category of the crimes and the status of those detained – thereby introducing a legal order of its own that precedes the existing rules, norms, laws, and procedural safeguards.

2.) The second context is the international context. In August 2002 Donald Rumsfeld cautioned:

> "Life seems to be returning almost to normal but that we must not do."[26]

Rumsfeld does not want the population to continue with life, he does not want normalcy to return, he does not want a linear continuation of time, he wants the events of 9/11 not to repeat themselves, but to permanently disrupt, he wants the trauma to be upheld, he actually instrumentalizes the haunting of the traumatic events.

In "Spectral Evidence" Ulrich Baer writes about the connection between the experience of trauma and the photographic image:

> "Trauma blocks routine mental processes from converting an experience into memory or forgetting, it parallels the defining structure of photography, which also traps an event during its occurrence while blocking its transformation into memory."[27]

The discursive strategy of the secretary of defense intended even more: not only did Rumsfeld want to prevent the traumatic experience to be overcome, to allow the public to forget the events that had haunted them for such a long time, but he wanted on one hand to "trap the event during its occurrence", blocking its transformation, and he wanted to control the viewers' perception of the image (and deliver already the interpretation of what they saw).

Rumsfeld wanted 9/11 to remain the disrupting event which justifies the permanent disrupture of norms and laws, because it justifies the permanent state of emergency.

> "Life seems to be returning almost to normal but that we must not do."

In other words, the state of exception must be extended, the population must be reminded, so Rumsfeld suggests, that it is at war.

> "Our enemies are sharpening their swords", he added.

The distinction between a state of war and a state of peace is eroded in the public's mind, and Rumsfeld uses the moment to reclaim the phase of peacefulness as one still within the condition of the state of war, still within the state of exception. The declaration of the state of exception, the repetition of that declaration, the intentional prolongment of its duration by the administration itself, keeps the exceptional powers of the sovereign state as one not bound by normal laws, rules and conventions, but one driven by the laws of self-defined needs in times of threat. More and more, Rumsfeld's warning of the threat becomes threatening itself. He conjures and invokes and stimulates fear. It is fear which should dominate public-political discourse, because through fear, as Hannah Arendt argued, the public can be transformed into "accomplices of tyrannical regimes".[28]

In the National Security Strategy of the United States, as of September 2002,[29] the White House explains its new foreign policy in the following words:

> "We will disrupt and destroy terrorist organisations by defending the United States, the American people, and our interests at home and abroad by identifying and destroying the threat before it reaches our borders."[30] And: "The United States can no longer solely rely on a reactive posture as we have in the past."[31]

Not only does the White House break with the international convention of the Anti-First-Strike policy, but also does the Bush administration quite frankly declare that they will not only protect the lives and safety of its people, but also defend its *interest* abroad. Whether the interest is political, economic, or hegemonic is not further qualified. As if interest in itself were a legitimate political category in international relations. Rather, it seems, that the United States features a concept of international relations which are none, or at least none which could be understood in the conventional sense of symmetrical relations according to the same standards of norms, laws and convention, applying to all states equally.

> "While the United States will constantly strive to enlist the support of the international community, we will not hesitate to act alone, if necessary to exercise our right of self-defense by acting preemptively against such terrorists, to prevent them from doing harm against our people and our country."[32]

Whereas in normal times, a threat can be distinguished as one of potentiality and one that constitutes an imminent danger, a direct and concrete threat – it is the state itself, the state as holding the defining monopoly, who has the sovereignty to decide on those distinctions.

In his address at West Point, George W. Bush states:

> "If we wait for the threats to fully materialize, we will have waited too long."[33]

So, before a threat actually becomes, before it materializes as a threat, before the threat can be threatening, a threat can be taken as an attack – and hence allows and justifies a counter-attack.

It has been the Bush administration's aim to blur the distinction between an *eventual* or possible and a *real* threat. A potential threat according to the new official doctrine can be weighed and measured as a real aggression, and thereby justifies a pre-emptive strike.

As Condoleezza Rice, the National Security Advisor, framed it in an interview:

> "It really means early action of some kind. There are times", she goes on, "when you can't wait to be attacked to respond."[34]

The pre-emptive logic reframes not only the logic of causality, but also of materiality.

Basically, what Bush and Rice are saying suggests that before a threat materializes, so when it is still in the morphological condition of an idea, a thought, an imagination is it to be considered a threat. In this new order of thoughts and materiality a projection is, by definition, indistinguishable from reality, there need not be any correspondence between imagination and an object in the world.[35]

Rice' semantics seem to have lost track with the speed and contradictory logic of this new policy when she still calls a pre-emptive strike a "response" even after she herself just said that it should be an action, not a reaction.

According to this logic a pre-emptive strike isn't even a pre-emptive strike – it has become an act of self-defense.

It is the perfect example of an analogy of Schmitt's description of the monopoly of decision which unfolds here on the international level.

The regular political order may be dictated by founding documents and is positivised in norms and legislations, but the exceptional case always trumps, always suspends those norms, always exceeds the legal codices. What suffices in peace has no meaning nor validity in exceptional circumstances.

As could be seen in the early months of 2003, it is exactly this discourse of a state of exception which lies at the root of the Bush administration's justification-strategy for its war against Iraq, a state which could not be connected in any way neither to al Qaeda[36] nor the World Trade Centre attack, by reference to the rhetorics and morals of self-defense.

At the time of this writing,[37] no weapons of mass destruction have been found in Iraq. The country was attacked, defeated, occupied – and *retroactively* the search for the material reason for the aggressive war has begun.

Whereas the political discourse and the war on terrorism began with the actual, concrete crimes and the perpetrators and the networks behind them, it quickly developed a dynamic of its own and expanded more and more into the imaginary domain. In the beginning, the US administration wanted to bring al Qaeda and Osama bin Laden "to justice". When that proved to be more difficult than expected, the war on terrorism included the fight against the Taliban. And when it became evident that the war in Afghanistan would not achieve its prime objective, namely the arrest of Osama bin Laden, the target and goal was redefined yet again, and so it suddenly looked as if it had been all about the liberation of women.

The transformation of the justification of the war against Iraq was even more irritating:[38]

Whereas first of all the US government claimed that Iraq supported al Qaeda, after a while they accused the Iraqi regime to have developed weapons of mass destruction and promised to prove these allegations. When they later noticed that they could not bring any material to support their claims, and when the Iraqi government not only said that they did not have any weapons of mass destruction anymore but also invited the weapons' inspectors in, the US reversed the burden of proof and now demanded that Saddam Hussein should prove that he had destroyed his weapons.[39]

Despite the lack of any signs or indications of even the *possibility* of a threat, the US administration argued that there was no evidence of the destruction of the conditions of the possibility of a threat – and thereby there was enough imminent danger to justify the abandonment of the article condemning the use of force of international law, and allowing an aggressive war disguised as an act of self-defense.

How did President Bush put it?

> "Different circumstances require different methods, but not different moralities. Moral truth is the same in every culture, in every time, in every place."[40]

But with the decline of the political to a predemocratic version (similar to Carl Schmitt's political thought of 1932), the Bush administration's policy of the state of exception has called their own self-understanding as one of moral universalism into question.

> "Moral truth is the same in every culture, in every time, in every place."

Well, clearly, the moral truth has not been the same on Guantanamo Bay, Cuba, or in any other detention centre inside the United States or in Iraq.

The "moral and legal truth" of post 9/11 has unfortunately proven to be an issue of momentary, arbitrary decisionism of a sovereign power, able and willing to suspend norms and laws at its will.

In a response all too mimetic to the distorted image the terrorists had assigned to us, we transformed more and more into such authoritarian societies or states, governed by an administration which claims, stages and performs its sovereign power with and through acts of arbitrary decisionism.

Politics as a public process which forms and challenges social practices and meanings, which produces discourses of self-understanding that call into question dominant or established views and values and stabilizes others, politics as a collective effort to defend and expand private and public freedom has been more and more mutilated. Militarization has penetrated political thinking and practice, the theme of security has contaminated all social and political life and slowly suffocated all other issues, concerns and space.

All those ethical and political achievements and values of freedom and democracy which, indeed, we should appreciate, are slowly, almost invisibly given up, undermined by *ourselves*. It is us attacking civilisation ourselves, allowing fear more and more to destroy those norms and conventions which defend individual and collective freedoms against violence or arbitrary decisionism.

The political discourse has more and more adapted the rhetorics of a religious quest: the values of modernity are praised and defended with an archaic language and Christian metaphoric. The political practice, on the national and the international level, has excavated those laws and norms which made our societies worth defending.

This is the real terrorist threat, maybe one more dangerous and long-lasting than the sad losses of all those innocent civilian lives, namely, that the terrorists might have achieved to shake us so fundamentally in our own self-understanding that we are provoked to react without all those civilisational restrictions and norms which were thought to distinguish "us" from "them".

But this is a threat which has to be met and fought *inside* our societies – not outside.

NOTES

[1] Due to a combination of completely contingent circumstances, I happened to be on a street in downtown Manhattan, close to the World Trade Centre, on the morning of September 11th. Even though only on vacation (and thereby off duty) in New York on the day of the terrorist attack, I became both: a potential victim and a witness who had to comment. Someone who could have lost her life, and someone who was asked to analyse the events. The conservative theoretical and political debate often suggests that the perspective of the person affected differs substantially from the perspective of the bystander. It is assumed that the distant commentator refuses solidarity or support of the war on terrorism because of a lack of understanding, a lack of empathy, due to an ignorant perspective on fear, suffering and despair of those who had become victims of the attacks. The critique of the war on terrorism is easily fended off with such a claim that binds authoritative critique to an idea of authentic victimhood. I reject the concept that only those affected by actions or events can grasp their meaning. I reject that suggestion already for epistemological reasons. The human species differs from, say, vegetables because of its ability to feel empathy for others, to change perspective, to imagine the experiences of others. Other than spinach, for

example, we can imagine and make sense out of the feelings and thoughts of others. So, even if I had been nothing but a distant commentator I could criticize the war on terrorism. And yet, it is in particular this knowledge of the weight of the events that informs and nurtures my critique of the inappropriate response to the attacks of 9/11.

[2] See also: Ernesto Laclau, *The Making of Political Identities*, London/New York 1994, p. 4.

[3] Cornelius Castoriadis, *The Imaginary Institution of Society*, Cambridge 1998, p. 160.

[4] On the visual paradigms in the prosecution of political warfare and its culture of representation, see: Allen Feldman, "Prosthetics and Aesthetics of Terror", in: Veena Das, Arthur Kleinman, Mamphela Ramphele, Pamela Reynolds (ed.), *Violence and Subjectivity*, Berkeley/Los Angeles 2000, pp. 46-79.

[5] Wolfgang Sofsky, *Zeiten des Schreckens. Amok, Terror, Krieg*, Frankfurt 2002, p. 64.

[6] See also: Wendy Brown's analyses of "wounded attachments", in: Wendy Brown, *States of Injury. Power and Freedom in Late Modernity*, Princeton 1995, pp. 52-77.

[7] In the following I will refer to the "war on terrorism" and not to the "war on terror" as it is usually called, since "terror" has also quite a distinct field of associations and meaning, namely also pointing to the sentiment of trauma felt by those affected by acts of violence. "War on terror" seems, therefore, slightly misguided.

[8] The analyses of the discourse and rhetorics of the Bush administration in this text is founded on an theoretical understanding of language which is not limited to "a system of abstract grammatical categories, but as *ideologically filled* language". See Michail Bachtin, "Das Wort im Roman", in: Bachtin, *Die Aesthetik des Wortes*, Frankfurt 1979, p. 164.

[9] Carl Schmitt, *Political Theology*, Cambridge 1988, p. 5.

[10] Carl Schmitt, *The Concept of the Political*, Chicago: University of Chicago Press, 1996, p. 33.

[11] Schmitt, *Concept of the Political*, p. 49.

[12] http://www.defenselink.mil/news/Sep2001/t09162001_t0916ts.html.

[13] For the possibility of unintentional failure as rooted in the necessity of (linguistic) repetition, and therefore as a source for subversion see: Judith Butler, *Excitable Speech. A Politics of the Performative*, New York/London 1997, pp. 1-42.

[14] Wendy Brown, *Politics out of History*, Princeton/Oxford 2001, p. 153.

[15] If the government had been really serious in their declaration to fight not only terrorists but also those states and regions that "harbored them", my hometown Hamburg, in particular the neighbourhood Hamburg-Harburg where Mohammed Attah lived and studied, would be in ruins today.

[16] Schmitt, *Concept of the Political*, p. 45.

[17] Schmitt, *Concept of the Political*, p. 46.

[18] Carl Schmitt, *Political Theology*, Cambridge 1988, p. 5.

[19] http://www.whitehouse.gov/news/releases/2002/06/20020601-3.html.

[20] http://www.firstcoastnews.com/news/2002-06-01/usw_bush.asp.

[21] Tzvetan Todorov, *The Conquest of America*, New York 1984, p. 179.

[22] Bush in his new warning on terrorism, 11th of March 2002.

[23] Lon Troyer also comments on this totalitarianism charge in his wonderful article: Lon Troyer, "Counterterrorism. Sovereignty, Law, Subjectivity", in: *Critical Asian Studies*, 35:2 (2003), p. 165.

[24] Giorgio Agamben, *Homo Sacer*, Stanford 1998, p.18.

[25] http://www.defenselink.mil/news/Sep2001/t09162001_t0916ts.html.

[26] http://www.defenselink.mil/news/Aug2002/briefings.html.

[27] Ulrich Baer, *Spectral Evidence. The Photography of Trauma*, Cambridge/London 2002, p. 9.

[28] Hannah Arendt, *Elemente und Urspruenge totaler Herrschaft*, Muenchen 1986, p. 725.

[29] National Security Strategy, http://usinfo.state.gov/topical/pol/terror/secstrat.htm.

[30] National Security Strategy, p. 6.

[31] National Security Strategy, p. 15.

[32] National Security Strategy, p. 6.

[33] http://www.whitehouse.gov/news/releases/2002/06/20020601-3.html.

[34] http://www.commondreams.org/headlines02/0617-04.htm.

[35] The pathological in this is not simply the projective attitude as such but the breakdown of all reflective reasoning. See for the paranoic who perceives the world around him just as it serves his "blind purposes": Max Horkheimer/Theodor Wiesengrund Adorno, *Dialektik der Aufklärung*, Frankfurt 1988, p. 199.

[36] The only group with connections to al Qaeda is Answar-al-Islam. But they were located in Kurdish Northern Iraq, opposed to both: the Iraq regime in Baghdad and the Kurdish regional government in Suleimania and Arbil. And they received their support from Iran, and not from Saddam Hussein.

[37] End of April 2003.

[38] The critique of the arguments for a pre-emptive war against Iraq does not negate the truth that Saddam Hussein, indeed, is/was one of the most brutal and abominable dictators of our times. His aggressive war against Iran and, most of all, his Anfal campaigns of "Arabisation" against the Kurds in Northern Iraq (their deportation, expulsion, and mass murder) are among the worst crimes against humanity. The criticism of a war without legitimation of the United Nations does not preclude criticism of the Iraqi dictator.

[39] An absurd strategy almost comparable to a person x claiming to be able to prove that person y has an affair. And when y denies, person x does not come up with any evidence, but now argues that y should prove that he has no affair.

[40] www.ibb.gov/editorials/09932.htm.

ALEKSANDAR PAVKOVIĆ

TERRORISM AS AN INSTRUMENT OF LIBERATION: A LIBERATION IDEOLOGY PERSPECTIVE[1]

WHY LIBERATION IDEOLOGIES?

Liberation ideologies are a set of political beliefs, value judgements and exhortations to action which call for and attempt to justify the liberation of a group of oppressed people from oppression and their oppressors. In this essay I shall examine only one kind of liberation ideology – the kind that justifies the use of indiscriminate or undifferentiated violence against the oppressors. A liberation ideology of this violent kind would consider any act of violence against the oppressors justified, provided – and this is an important proviso – that this act does indeed contribute to the liberation of the oppressed. Liberation ideologies of a non-violent kind do not attempt to justify any kind of violence against oppressors (except in the self-defence of individuals); and there are also liberation ideologies which would only attempt to justify violence against particular agents of oppression or officials of oppressive organisations.

For the purposes of the present essay, it is assumed that *some forms of* terrorism involve using violence against persons who in their everyday occupation do not coerce anyone, or do not help anyone to do so (or who are not capable of doing so). For example, most waiters, shop assistants, street sweepers, academics, nurses do not coerce anyone in their daily occupation while small children, the infirm and the old are not capable of doing so. Policemen and women, military personnel and debt collectors are trained to coerce, and do so as part of their primary occupation. In the present essay the discussion of terrorist violence will be restricted to the kind directed against any member of the 'enemy' group, regardless whether he or she engages in coercion or not. As Robert Young points out, this is not the only kind of violence that terrorists use and, and, therefore, this kind of violence cannot (or should not) be used to define terrorism.[2] In describing terrorist violence in this rather vague way, I only want to distinguish one type of victim of terrorism – those whose work or activity does not present a threat of coercion to anyone – from another type of victim of those acts, that is, those whose work or activity does present such a threat. Under a very broad definition of self-defence, one could argue that violence against those who present a threat of coercion or violence may constitute an act of defence. Since the former – those whose work does not involve coercion or who are incapable of it – do not threaten anyone with coercion, violence against them would not normally considered an act of self-defence.

Yet under the specific circumstances of a liberation struggle the ideology of liberation to be discussed here does attempt to justify this kind of violence. As we

Meggle (ed.), Ethics of Terrorism & Counter-Terrorism, 245-260.

shall see, in order to do this, this ideology construes the very existence of oppressors (including those who are not engaged or not capable of engaging in coercion) within a system of oppression as constituting a threat to those who are oppressed. This aspect of its attempted justification of terrorism may appear be too abstract and hence rather artificial and specious, and for this reason it may not attract too much scholarly or non-scholarly interest. In spite of this, liberation ideologies of the violent kind are of interest to anyone trying to understand both what motivates some of the terrorists and how they (or their leaders) would like to justify their acts of terrorism; in particular, I think that exploring attempts at justification of terrorism of this kind may help us understand how Osama bin Laden, the leader of Al-Qaeda group, attempted to justify the terrorist acts perpetrated in 2001 by his organisation.

In this essay I would like first to outline an attempted justification of terrorism offered within a liberation ideology of the violent kind and then to consider how the proponents of this ideology defend their endorsement of terrorism against those objections arising from a familiar ethical view which I shall call universal humanism. The essay thus explores the framework of justification of terrorism offered by a liberation ideology in order to identify the major points of difference between such a justification and a widespread ethical view which condemns violence against non-threatening and unarmed civilians. The primary aim of the essay is to point out the differences in ethical principles and values between the two views; for this purpose it is not necessary to examine, in a systematic way, the theoretical framework and historical origins of either of the two.

The principal source of the ideology of liberation to be discussed here is the essay 'Concerning Violence' by the psychiatrist, political theorist and anti-colonial activist Frantz Fanon published in 1961 in his collection *The Wretched of the Earth*.[3] In order to understand Fanon's justification of the use of violence and of terrorism, it is necessary to examine the key concepts of his ideology: that of the oppressed, of the oppression and of the liberation. As we shall see, in the messages videotaped and broadcast in 2001, Osama bin Laden used similar concepts in his justification of terrorist violence. Fanon's essay has been translated into Persian by the influential Islamic thinker Ali Shariati who appears to have used concepts similar to Fanon's in his own works. While Osama bin Laden's ideology originates in a religious worldview similar to Shariati's but quite different from (and often incompatible with) Fanon's Marxist worldview, the similarity between his key concepts and Fanon's is quite striking and possibly instructive.

THE OPPRESSED VERSUS THE OPPRESSORS: KEY CONCEPTS OF AN IDEOLOGY OF LIBERATION

The *oppressed* were, in the context of Fanon's writing, usually colonised peoples, defined by their race – non-European – and by their status of being colonised or controlled by another race, the Europeans. But the oppressed could also be defined not only by their race but also by their class, their profession or the lack of it, their nationality and, of course, their religion. However defined, the oppressed group is in some tangible sense politically unequal to another group which exerts a degree of unwanted or undesirable control over them and in doing so humiliates or denigrates them. According to Fanon, both political control and humiliation are necessary aspects of oppression. In a system of oppression, the oppressors believe that the oppressed are neither culturally nor cognitively equal to them and therefore deserve to be controlled and oppressed; they attempt to justify their oppression by the latter's inferiority. Thus the oppressed are humiliated not only because they are controlled but because in being controlled they are presented as incapable of the autonomy characteristic of other human beings. This strips them of their human dignity. Therefore, in being controlled in the way they are, the oppressed are denied the status of being equal and autonomous human beings. While some members of the oppressed group – those, for example, who collaborate with the oppressors, or share some of their values – are perhaps less subject to the oppressors' control or less open to their abuse, they are equally humiliated because they are viewed as honorary human beings: their being human is conditional on their collaboration with the oppressors. Even if the extent of control over members of the oppressed group is varied, the humiliation inflicted on all members of the group is equal. The oppressed are thus members of a group – defined by its race, nationality, religion or some other salient feature – which is, as a group, controlled and humiliated.

The *oppressors* are the controllers – those who possess the means of control and who participate in controlling the oppressed. In Fanon's writings, they are defined again by their race – the Europeans – and their social and political role – that of colonisers. But the oppressors could also be defined by their profession, class, nationality or religion and not only by their race. In fact, the oppressors are not only those who in effect do the controlling – say, government officials, corporation employees or bosses – but any member of the group who in any way participates in the system of oppression. Thus if the French are the oppressors of the native population of Algiers (as Fanon sees them in his writings), any French person involved in any way in the system of oppression belongs to the group of oppressors. 'Being involved in the system of oppression' is, intentionally, a very broad and rather undefined category. In Fanon's writings this meant every French person who resided in Algiers (and some who did not) and who benefited from the system of oppression there.

A wide and collective definition of the oppressors was clearly needed to establish a parallel with the previous definition of the oppressed: each member of the oppressed group (for example, a colonised people) is subject to oppression and, by analogy, each member of the oppressor group shares in the oppression. A person is an oppressor not in virtue of any specific act of oppression but in virtue of belonging to the group which collectively does the oppressing. This type of collective definition of the oppressors by analogy with the group of oppressed ensures there are no 'innocents' among the oppressors as there are no 'non-oppressed' among the oppressed.

According to Fanon, in paradigmatic cases of oppression, those of colonised peoples, oppression involves the use of physical violence against the oppressed, although not necessarily against all, or even the majority of them. Apart from targeting those who oppose them, colonisers often use violence in a random and arbitrary way against any member of the oppressed group so as to assert their authority and to spread fear and terror.

Osama bin Laden's October 2001 message suggests that, like Fanon, he believed that the violence suffered by the oppressed and their ensuing humiliation justifies their acts of terrorist violence against their (alleged) oppressors:

"Our nation (the Islamic world) has been tasting this humiliation and this degradation for more than 80 years. Its sons are killed, its blood is shed, its sanctuaries are attacked, and no one hears and no one heeds.

When God blessed one of the groups of Islam, vanguards of Islam, they destroyed America. I pray to God to elevate their status and bless them. Millions of innocent children are being killed as I speak. They are being killed in Iraq without committing any sins, and we don't hear condemnation or a fatwa (religious decree) from the rulers. In these days, Israeli tanks infest Palestine – in Jenin, Ramallah, Rafah, Beit Jalla, and other places in the land of Islam, and we don't hear anyone raising his voice or moving a limb …

When the sword comes down (on America), after 80 years, hypocrisy rears its ugly head. They deplore and they lament for those killers, who have abused the blood, honour and sanctuaries of Muslims. The least that can be said about those people is that they are debauched. They have followed injustice. They supported the butcher over the victim, the oppressor over the innocent child. May God show them His wrath and give them what they deserve. […]

These events have divided the whole world into two sides. The side of believers and the side of infidels, may God keep you away from them. Every Muslim has to rush to make his religion victorious. The winds of faith have come. The winds of change have come to eradicate oppression from the island of Muhammad, peace be upon him."[4]

According to Osama bin Laden, the oppressed and their oppressors are each defined by their religion: the oppressed are the Muslims or the Islamic nation and the oppressors are non-Muslim or infidel. The former have been exposed to indiscriminate killing, including that of children, to disrespect of their religion and its sanctuaries, and, as a result of this, to a continuous humiliation and degradation. The oppressors have either committed these hostile and unjust acts against the Muslims or have, in some undefined sense, supported them. This makes them morally depraved or morally inferior to the oppressed. All this, Osama bin Laden believed, justifies violent revenge or retribution against the oppressors. Whether a construction of the two opposed groups and of their mutual relations in this way has any truth value or not, is not explored any further in this essay. I shall only examine the role this kind of distinction plays in a justification of terrorist violence.

Liberation from oppression. It is the superior technology and superior command over the instruments of oppression that enable oppressors to control, at least temporarily, the oppressed. In paradigmatic cases, according to Fanon, the oppressors possessed superior military hardware – for example, guns – as well as much more efficient military and state organisation than the oppressed. The oppressed, therefore, cannot compete with them on the level of technological and military organisation. However, the oppressor's use of violence is subject to some constraint both from inside and outside their own (oppressors') community. First, the oppressors are constrained by the cost of their oppression and their use of violence; if this is resisted, the cost of overcoming resistance may be greater to them than the benefits to be gained from the use of violence or from the oppression itself. Second, they are constrained by domestic public opinion and by public opinion in other states which do not participate in that oppression. In the post-1945 era, public opinion in West European and North American states has grown rather squeamish when confronted with the media images of large-scale violence against civilians and this has provided a significant constraint on the deployment of such violence. How significant or effective such a constraint is, is subject to a continuing dispute: in Osama bin Laden's view, as evidenced by his invectives against Western or 'infidel' hypocrisy, public opinion in non-Muslim countries offers no effective constraint on violence against the oppressed.

In Fanon's view, the principal resource the oppressed have against oppression is their moral superiority, in particular, their moral virtues resulting in their readiness to sacrifice their own lives for their liberation. In praying for the blessing (or for the elevation to Paradise) of those who sacrificed their lives in terrorist actions against the oppressors, Osama bin Laden appears to be praising the same virtue. The oppressors are, as mentioned above, constrained by the cost of their oppression. They do not want to pay – nor could they pay more – than the oppression is worth to them. They often consider it not to be worth the loss of too many lives of their own people. If a large number of them or a large number of sufficiently important people are to be killed in the effort to maintain control over the oppressed, they may see the operation as too costly. In short, usually the oppressors are not as ready to sacrifice their lives to maintain oppression as the oppressed are to sacrifice theirs to free themselves from it.[5] This is the main advantage of the oppressed over the oppressors.

In view of this, the only way for the oppressed to liberate themselves from oppression is to make oppression too costly for the oppressors. Terrorist violence is one of the ways to achieve exactly this. In a situation in which the oppressed group has neither organisational framework nor military hardware required to fight the oppressors' armed force, terrorism may be the only way of achieving this. In other situations, in which the oppressed have a fighting force capable of waging guerilla warfare against the oppressors' armed forces, terrorism may be viewed as the most effective way of increasing the cost of oppression for the oppressors beyond a level acceptable to them. For example, while the oppressors often regard the lives of their mercenary soldiers as expendable – they are paid to kill and to be killed – this is not the case with the lives of their non-combatants, for example, the wives and children of their officials. The death of those members of the oppressors' group and the continued threat of more being killed may turn out to be too high a price for maintaining oppression. Whether this is the case or not, terrorism is viewed here as one way – or one aspect – of waging the struggle for the liberation from oppression. The ultimate goal of the oppressed – liberation from oppression – provides grounds for attempts to justify terrorism or the use of violence against those who are not engaged in coercion. What kind of justification is this?

ALEKSANDAR PAVKOVIĆ

WHY TERRORISM IS JUSTIFIED: FROM THE POINT OF VIEW OF A LIBERATION IDEOLOGY

The liberation ideology outlined above appears to offer two quite different patterns of normative justification for terrorism – the first appeals to the alleged right of group retribution and the second to a means/end justification.

The right of (group) retribution. Since oppression, in the cases considered here, involves the use of random or undifferentiated violence against the oppressed, this justifies a response in kind – terrorist violence against the oppressors. This type of justification appeals to the (alleged) right of group revenge or of group retribution: If members of one group indiscriminately kill members of another group, then the latter is (allegedly) justified in indiscriminately killing members of the former in the same way.

The collective definitions of the oppressed/oppressors appear to be specifically designed for the purposes of this type of justification: if all members of a particular group (for example, 'infidels') are considered to be oppressors or supportive of oppression, then this alleged right justifies terrorist killing of any members of the oppressor group, regardless of whether they have actually committed (or were capable of committing) any acts against the oppressed. Thus in his statements, Osama bin Laden praises terrorist acts as acts of revenge against the infidels who, as a group, subjected the believers (the oppressed) to oppression.

There are two major problems facing attempts at justification of this kind. First, setting up two parallel groups, of the oppressed and the oppressors, does not demonstrate that all members of the oppressor group are equally responsible or are responsible at all for the oppression. Thus, even if one grants that all of the oppressed are equally humiliated by the oppression, it does not follow that all of the oppressors are equally responsible for that humiliation. Some people belonging to this group, such as the infirm and minors, are not capable of being responsible for any of those acts which lead to humiliation or oppression. This justification either requires a concept of responsibility which makes minors or other individuals responsible for acts which they cannot even comprehend, let alone commit, or, alternatively, it implies that one is justified in exacting revenge or retribution even against those who are in no way responsible for the oppression. In the latter, alternative case, retribution ceases to be a punishment for a wrongdoing: those who are subject to retribution are no longer those who are responsible for it.

This leads to the second problem concerning the ethical status of this alleged right. While some religious or ethical teachings propound the right of individual retribution – the eye for an eye principle – as a principle of punishment for individuals for certain crimes of violence, it does not follow that a similar principle holds for the punishment of groups. The individual retribution is meted out as punishment to the individual who committed a particular act. But groups or individuals randomly selected from a group are not responsible (at least not in this way) for particular acts committed by specific individuals. Therefore, even if one accepts the principle of individual retribution as an ethical principle, one has no reason to accept an analogous principle of group retribution as a principle of the same kind.

However, some religious and ideological doctrines endorse a view of collective responsibility which would allow for group retribution. Some Islamic *shariat* teachings regard groups – usually kinship groups – responsible for acts of its members, whereas some Marxist doctrines hold the socio-economic classes – in particular, the propertied classes – responsible for actions of some of its members. Their adherents probably constitute a receptive audience for attempts at justification of terrorism or political violence by way of group retribution. But the need to appeal to esoteric teachings such as these only shows that the right of group retribution, as outlined above, is not generally accepted either as a right or as an ethical principle. Hence, it is highly doubtful that the group retribution provides an ethical justification of terrorist violence.

The means/end justification. Terrorism is in some situations the only, and in others the most effective, way to make the cost of oppression unbearable to the oppressors and thus to liberate the oppressed. Since liberation from oppression is the only way of restoring human dignity to the oppressed, this goal justifies the only, or the most effective, way of achieving it. The end (telos) – the restoration of human dignity to some – justifies using the lives of others merely as a means towards that end.

In addition to this rather general teleological justification, the above liberation ideology offers four more specific justifications which follow a similar pattern but do not, explicitly, mention the ultimate end of terrorism.

1. *Terrorism as a means of attacking the system of oppression.* In spite of posing no threat to the oppressed, family members of the agents of oppression (the actual perpetrators of coercion) are part of the system of oppression and receive its benefits. In attacking family members, the oppressed are attacking the system and raising the cost of maintaining it: had the family members not been part of the system, the attacks on them would not have increased the costs of maintaining the system of oppression. In short, an attack on any part of the system is justified, if it will hasten or contribute to liberation.

2. *Terrorism as a means of equalising the conditions of combat.* The oppressed are not in a position to compete with their oppressors in the field of military technology and organisation; therefore, to require them to target only their military and police is to expect them to accept their combat inequality and to remain oppressed. This is obviously unfair as well as unrealistic. The fairness of combat requires that they be allowed to use those means in which they have an advantage over the enemy and this may include targeting those members of the oppressors' group who are not engaged in any coercive activity.

3. *Terrorism as a means of mobilising public opinion for the liberation from oppression.* Whereas attacks against the military and police force can easily be hidden from the media, when terrorist acts are committed in public spaces, primarily against civilians, the media of the oppressors state can hardly ignore them. Media attention to the opposition to oppression puts the whole issue of oppression and its cost under the scrutiny of both domestic and international public opinion. If the public realises how costly and how unjust continued oppression is, this may bring about its early demise. By hastening liberation, terrorism may reduce the over-all cost that the liberation struggle incurs in human lives.

4. *Terrorism as a means of restoring dignity to the oppressed.* When oppressed fail to respond to the oppressor's violence and oppression that failure can be taken to indicate their lack of human dignity. By responding to oppression by unleashing undifferentiated violence (which has also been used against them), the oppressed are throwing off this burden of humiliation and showing themselves to be equal in dignity to their oppressors. These violent acts would help them overcome the persistent feeling of humiliation. As Fanon puts it:

> "At the level of individuals, violence is a cleansing force. It frees the native from his inferiority complex and from his despair and inaction; it makes him fearless and restores his self-respect."[6]

All of the above attempts at teleological justifications assume that the ultimate value, at least for the oppressed, is the liberation from oppression and the restoration of their human dignity. Liberation from oppression should enable those who have been prevented from enjoying liberty and dignity to enjoy them as other human beings do. It is because Fanon believed in the value of human liberty and dignity that he urged those who enjoy neither to fight to liberate themselves from the control of their oppressors and from the resulting humiliation. The ethical conception according to which the ultimate value is the restoration of human dignity of the oppressed through liberation may be called *liberation humanism.* Terrorism, in Fanon's view, is presented as a practical means of securing humanist values in the world in which some groups and their members are denied both liberty and dignity.

Teleological justifications of this kind are open to variety of criticisms, some of which are explored by Robert Young.[7] Here I shall only discuss one test of a teleological justification, namely, as to whether the values which define the end (*telos*) are compatible with the proposed means towards that end. The end is here defined in terms of the dignity and liberty which are be restored to the oppressed. But the means, terrorist violence, denies not only the dignity and liberty of the victims of terrorism but also their lives. To avoid the obvious incompatibility between the means and the values through which the end is defined, the liberation humanist is forced to fall back on the oppressed/oppressors distinction. As long as their oppression continues, the oppressors' lives, their liberty and dignity has no equal standing to those of the oppressed. In other words, in virtue of their (alleged) responsibility for the oppression, the oppressors have lost the right to their lives, dignity and liberty which the oppressed have; once their oppression ceases this right is restored to them. Therefore, killing the oppressors for the sake of restoring liberty and dignity to the oppressed is not the denial of the oppressors' rights – as oppressors, they are not entitled to these rights. Since, on this argument, terrorist violence does not deny the dignity and liberty of the oppressors, it is compatible with the values which define the end towards which this violence is a means.

By divesting the oppressors of their rights to life, dignity and liberty, liberation humanism partially (and perhaps temporarily) divests the oppressors of their humanity and thus considers them as ethically unequal to the oppressed. The oppressors, according to Fanon, deprive the oppressed of the very same aspects of their humanity. It appears then that the oppressed in this way attempt to do to the oppressors the same as the latter do to them! This may be yet another form of group retribution: as the oppressors allegedly deprive the oppressed of their human dignity and liberty, so liberation humanism in turn deprives the oppressors of the same. Whether this is a form of group retribution or not, there is no reason to accept either such an ethical degradation of the oppressors or the teleological justifications of violence against the oppressors based on the assumption of their moral inferiority. Why this is so may become clearer if we contrast liberation humanism with humanism of another kind which rejects ethical inequalities among human beings.

WHY TERRORIST VIOLENCE IS NOT JUSTIFIABLE: UNIVERSAL HUMANISM

Most of us are familiar with an ethical conception which asserts the intrinsic and equal value of each and every human life. Christianity and other universal religions incorporate an ethical vision of this kind, and its most elaborate secular version is probably to be found in the works of the 18th century German philosopher Immanuel Kant. This conception asserts that:

a) All human lives are of equal and paramount value;

From this postulate one can further infer[8] that:

b) The intentional killing of another human being is permitted only in self-defence or in the defence of those who cannot defend themselves.

c) For the purposes of the above, one can defend oneself or others only against those who are threatening to use physical violence or those who enable them to do so by supplying them with or maintaining their weapons.

In contrast to liberation humanism, the ethical conception based on assertions (a) to (c), postulates the value of human life as a universal value of paramount importance. Hence I will call it *universal humanism.*

Universal humanism endorses or incorporates the ultimate values of liberation humanism: liberty and dignity of the oppressed, to which the latter is committed, is also a high ranking (although not the highest ranking) value of universal humanism. Those who endorse universal humanism can, without any inconsistency, endorse the goal of liberation humanism – the liberation of the oppressed from oppression. Further, universal humanism can also justify the use of violence (including killing) against those who kill, threaten to kill, or aid the killing of the oppressed: violence of this kind qualifies as self-defence or defence under (c) above. But universal humanism prohibits killing another human being – regardless of the group she or he belongs to – in pursuit of any other objective except self-defence or defence as defined in (c). This rules out as impermissible terrorist violence as described in the beginning of this essay.

Thus universal humanism rules out only one particular means towards the liberation of the oppressed: that of violence against those who are not engaged in any coercive activity. The reason for this is found in its conception of the ultimate value or, in other words, in its ranking of values. For universal humanism the ultimate value is the life of *every* human being. Liberation humanism, as we have seen, does not rank the life of every human being as highly as that: in its view, the liberation of the oppressed is the ultimate value which overrides that of the life of every human being.

To put it very crudely, liberation humanism holds that the lives of the oppressors are of less value than the achievement of liberation for the oppressed.

Liberation humanism thus rejects the first premise (a) – that each and every human life is of equal and paramount value – which universal humanism shares with a number of religious and secular ethical conceptions. Instead, liberation humanism assumes that some human lives (those of the oppressors) have less value than others and claims that those of less value can be used as instruments, or means, towards its preferred end – the liberation of the oppressed. Consequently, on this view one is allowed to take the lives of the oppressors – one is allowed to kill them – if this is to lead to the attainment of that liberation.

In assessing the value of human lives, liberation humanism appeals to overtly political and, in a sense, accidental criteria. An individual belongs to a group of oppressors only by virtue of circumstances which are not necessarily within his or her control. Nevertheless according to liberation humanism, just being a citizen of a particular state – for example, the USA or France – qualifies an individual as an oppressor. Belonging to this group makes the life of an individual less valuable than the life of another individual who belongs to a group which, according to the liberation humanist criteria, is oppressed – for example, the Palestinian nation. It is highly doubtful whether such criteria can offer any assessment of the value of human lives. Under the cloak of ethical values, these criteria appear to express political preferences as well as a determination to use these political preferences as a justification for indiscriminate use of violence against the less preferred group of people.

Universal humanism rejects any attempt to rank the value of lives of different individuals and denies that there is any ethically tenable ranking of this kind. While universal humanism generates a variety of conceptual and ethical problems, it effectively prevents the use of political criteria in assessing the value of human lives and rules out any ethical justification of killing based on such criteria. As we shall see in the next section, universal humanism is not an ethical conception which is designed to serve or to defend the pursuit of any particular political or social ends. To see this let us consider the objections to universal humanism advanced by Fanon and his interpreter and supporter, the French philosopher Jean-Paul Sartre.

LIBERATION HUMANISM AGAINST UNIVERSAL HUMANISM

Liberation humanism counters the above claims of universal humanism in two complementary ways. First, Fanon and Sartre argue that in practice universal humanism sides with the oppressors by blocking attempts by the oppressed to liberate themselves from oppression and, second, they expand the concept of self-defence to include defence against the system of oppression and thus against anyone involved with that system in any way. The first strategy is foreshadowed in justification (2) which demands that the conditions of combat be equalised. Against universal humanism, liberation ideologues point out that the oppressors have already willingly abandoned universal humanism by engaging in oppression. Under these circumstances universal humanism denies to the oppressed the only, or the most effective, means of liberation that they themselves have. Therefore, universal humanism denies to the oppressed control over the means of their own liberation and demands that if they cannot liberate themselves in the manner acceptable to universal humanism (which their oppressors actually reject), they abandon, at least temporarily, their quest for liberation. If the paramount aim of the oppressed is to liberate themselves from oppression by the most effective means they have, it would not be rational of them to deny themselves the only or the most effective means of liberation: from that point of view, the prescriptions of universal humanism appear irrational.

The second strategy, foreshadowed in justification (1) above, consists in widening the conception of self-defence. According to liberation humanism, any system of oppression continuously violates the human dignity of those oppressed and also presents a continued threat of physical violence against them. These violations and the threats of physical violence are equal in gravity to the threats of actual physical violence against their persons. Since it is the system of oppression and not only particular individuals within the system that poses these threats, the oppressed are justified in using violence against the system itself. If violence against the system requires – as indicated in instrumental justifications (1)-(4) – that those who are not engaged in coercive activities be attacked, then self-defence against this system also justifies terrorist violence.

The advocates of liberation humanism argue, in very broad terms, that universal humanism ignores the very injustice of oppression and the highly unequal distribution of power and resources between the oppressed and the oppressors and consequently ignores the gravity of the threats to the oppressed. How could universal humanism respond to these arguments?

Perhaps universal humanism need not respond to the accusation that it fails to back up the oppressed and their struggle for liberation. Unlike liberation humanism, universal humanism does not aim to prescribe or attempt to justify a particular type of means for achieving any social or political ends, such as that of the liberation from oppression. Therefore, its failure to justify the actions which supposedly lead to the liberation of the oppressed is not a defect of that ethical conception or an objection against it. Admittedly universal humanism does not offer such useful guidance to political action as that offered by a liberation ideology or any other political ideology specifically designed to do just that.

In spite of this, one can still evaluate a particular political action or a type of action by reference to the ethical prescriptions of universal humanism. If a particular type of action – such as terrorist violence – does not accord with its ethical prescriptions, one faces a choice between the prescriptions of universal humanism and that of the liberation ideology which does. In such a case, the choice is not between two rival or incompatible political visions or ideologies, but rather between a political ideology and an ethical conception or vision. As we have seen, the universal humanist ethical conception endorses the values which define the goal of the liberation ideology but rejects only one particular means towards that goal. This does not imply that this ethical conception should be able to propose an equally effective means towards that particular goal.

Ethical conceptions, such as universal humanism, can and do constrain political as well as individual actions: they rule out as impermissible certain actions, and rank, in terms of ethical values other permissible actions. In contrast, liberation humanism appears designed to license a certain type of political action which other ethical conceptions prohibit. In view of this, one may suspect that liberation humanism is an ethical view specifically designed to serve a particular political ideology; if so, one could argue that it offers no judgment or evaluation of political actions independent of that ideology.

As we have seen above, its adherents retort that all ethical conceptions – including universal humanism – are in one way or another tied to a political ideology or doctrine which they are then used to defend. Universal humanism, they suggest, is used to defend non-resistance to oppression and thus serves the needs of oppressors' political ideologies.

To rebut this charge, it is not sufficient, I think, to point out that universal humanism, as outlined in (a)-(c) – imports no political criteria or political goals in its evaluative apparatus. It would also be necessary to show that universal humanism is impartial in its treatment of political actions which cause the deaths of innocent people. In other words, it would be necessary to show that universal humanism does not permit actions, carried out by technologically superior states or political groups, which cause the same kind of harm as is caused by terrorist violence. For example, the imposition of UN sanctions on Iraq in 1993, which were initiated and policed by the US and its allies have, probably, resulted in the death of a large number of children in Iraq (to which Osama bin Laden is referring in his statement). While this is not a case of intentional killing, had the UN sanctions not been imposed in the way they were, many Iraqi infants and children would not have died. In view of postulate (a) of universal humanism, causing death of innocent people in this way is as unacceptable as is killing them by terrorist action. This suggests that universal humanism needs to broaden its prohibition of killing innocent people to the cases of causing death of innocent people by means other than actual physical violence.

While it is possible to refine the evaluative framework of universal humanism to yield an explicit prohibition of actions of this kind, it is not possible to regulate the use of the tenets of universal humanism in political debate. For example, its prohibition on intentional killing of innocents has been used selectively to condemn terrorist violence while various types of state-sponsored violence leading to the death of innocents are, on purpose, exempt from such condemnation. As it offers no practical guidance to political action in pursuit of various political goals, universal humanism offers no recipe for the abolition of hypocrisy or the use of double standards.

More importantly, universal humanism, as any other ethical conception, cannot determine whether or how its prohibitions are to be enforced. One could certainly argue that the current instruments of enforcement – the sovereign states and their international organizations such as the United Nations – are neither impartial nor effective instruments for enforcing prohibitions on political acts leading to the death of innocents. One can argue, further, that a sovereign state as a political organization operates within a framework of constraints and interests which are often incompatible with the tenets of universal humanism. For example, most if not all sovereign states are ready to pursue any action leading to the death of innocent citizens of other states if they consider such an action necessary. Under the conditions in which the tenets of universal humanism are only imperfectly and randomly enforced, potential victims of indiscriminate violence or death-causing actions would quite naturally seek to protect themselves by alternative means or instruments which do not, necessarily, follow these tenets. In other words, in a situation in which keeping to the tenets of universal humanism would offer no protection, it would be rational, as Robert Young points out in his essay, to seek protection by means which would do so, including those of terrorist violence.

If seeking other means of protection would be rational in those circumstances, the question is whether, in some situations, the constraints imposed by universal humanism would go against the interests of those who are not protected from random violence and who naturally seek protection from it. Consider the following situation in which a group does not enjoy the protection from random and lawless violence of the kind that is normally provided by North American and West European states. Group A, defined by the religious or national characteristics of its members, is exposed to a random and lawless violence by armed members of group B; the latter are armed and supported by a politically and militarily dominant power C. Without the latter support, members of group B would not have been in position to use this kind of violence against group A. Because of the overwhelming superiority in military hardware, training and numbers of both B and C, members of group A is not in position to protect themselves and their group against this type of violence either by attacking the perpetrators of violence from group B or those in the dominant state C who arm and support them. The only instrument of self-defence, in the view of many members of group A, is terrorist violence against the members of group B and C who are not, through their occupation, responsible for the violence against group A. Those members of group A who approve of and engage in terrorist violence, also believe that these acts of terrorism may deter further violence against their group as the cost of violence and oppression to either group B or C (or both) may become too high. In other words, they believe that these are the only effective instruments of self-defence that they have at their disposal. Their belief may, indeed, be wrong or only partially true. To show the latter one could argue while they may not have any other instruments of self-defence (except, allegedly, terrorism) which they could use to respond to acts of random violence instantly, but there may be other, non-violent, instruments of self-defence which are effective in the long term but of which members of group A are ignorant or which they regard too humiliating or demeaning.

The present question, however, is not whether their belief in the effectiveness of terrorism as an instrument of self-defence is true or false. The present question is only whether – given their belief in its effectiveness and their lack of any means by which they can immediately respond to acts of random and lawless violence – the constraints introduced by universal humanism on the targets of self-defence (as articulated in (c) above) are contrary to the interests of their self-defence. In a situation of the above kind, universal humanism still prohibits intentional killings of those who are not responsible for the violence to which these victims are exposed. In this way, universal humanism would deny to the victims of the violence an instrument which they may regard as an effective or the only weapon of self-defence. These victims may, in a situation of the kind described above, regard this denial as contrary to the interests of their self-defence.

Universal humanism, as we have seen above, is not concerned with providing guidance to the effective instruments of self-defence. In view of this, the victims of such violence may, in some situations, be justified in believing that its constraints are contrary to the interests of their self-defence. In situations of the kind described above, the only way to show that they are not so justified would be to show that in their particular situation terrorism is not the only effective instrument of self-defence Such an argument would aim to show that there are other instruments of self-defence that are equally or more effective than terrorism. This would be then an argument about the facts of their situation and about the instruments for self-defence which they have at their disposal. For example, one could argue that the UN or other international organisations offer to victims of random violence less violent instruments for self-defence which are more effective – at least in the long term – than terrorism; these would consist of the political pressure, economic sanctions or even targeted military intervention by the UN against the perpetrators of this violence. But an argument would not show that universal humanism would in all such situations of random violence provide for a choice of adequate instruments of self-defence. At most an argument of this kind would establish that in some situations of random violence there are effective instruments of self-defence for the victims of such violence which are compatible with universal humanism. It could not establish that in every such situation so compatible instruments would be available and that, therefore, victims of random violence always have at their disposal instruments of self-defence compatible with the constraints of universal humanism. In short, such an argument would hardly establish the preferability, for the victims of random violence of this kind, of universal humanism to any other ethical doctrine; to the powerless victims of violence this arguments offers no overriding reason for preferring universal to liberation humanism.

Indeed, it is difficult to see how one could show to the politically powerless victims of random violence that universal humanism always offers constraints on their actions which will serve the interests of their self-defence. Any such argument would need to assume that the interests of those who are exposed to random and lawless violence and of those who are not (but may be) exposed to it, are of equal value and that, therefore, the defence of the former has no priority over the defence of the latter. Victims of random violence would, on this assumption, be required to agree that they should give up their only effective defence against further random violence in order to prevent the use of equally random violence against other innocent people (who happen to be members of the oppressor group). This assumption implies that the current victims have to prefer the interests of other innocent people, unknown to them, to their own interests and the interests of their family or friends. To expect of the victims of random and lawless violence to accept this assumption and its implication would require a degree of altruism if not self-sacrifice which appears not only unrealistic but also unreasonable.

While altruistic such a preference for the defence of the interests of other innocent people is not, of course, irrational. It is not irrational to refuse to kill or to condone killing of innocent people even when one believes that such killing may protect oneself against violence. It is not irrational to prefer the continuing risk of being killed (say, by one's known oppressors) to participating in or condoning the killing of innocent people (from the oppressors' group). Therefore, it would not be irrational of those victims (in a situation described above) to endorse and live up to the tenets of universal humanism. Yet they would have no reason to regard the interests of these innocent people, who are potential victims of random violence through terrorism, as overriding their own interests as actual victims of random violence. That is why it would be unreasonable to expect them, when faced with continuing random violence against themselves, to endorse universal humanism

Of course, the constraints of universal humanism do not specifically target the means of self-defence of the politically powerless victims of random violence. The same constraints apply to the politically motivated violence perpetrated by their opponents, that is, their oppressors. In this sense, universal humanism, contrary to Sartre's and Fanon's suggestions, is indeed impartial: it rejects, equally and impartially, any violence against innocent people, whether perpetrated in the course of oppression or in self-defence, whether perpetrated by the oppressors or by those who resist oppression. But one may still argue that this very impartiality disadvantages the politically powerless victims of random violence. The impartiality of universal humanism, such an argument claims, simply ignores the plight of these victims arising from the very unequal distribution of power and of instruments of violence. In prohibiting, impartially, random and lawless violence both by the oppressors and by the oppressed, the argument concludes, universal humanism may deny to the victims, the oppressed, the only weapon of self-defence that they have. In such a situation, it would not be in the interest of those victims (at least not in the interest of their self-defence) to endorse universal humanism; these victims would understandably prefer an ethical doctrine which would not deny them the only reliable instruments of self-defence they may possess. Liberation humanism is, as we have seen, one such doctrine: it justifies the use of terrorist violence as an instrument of self-defence.

While showing its limitations as a guide for action in some situations of random and lawless violence, this argument does not question the validity or consistency of universal humanism as an ethical doctrine; it only questions the claim that it is in the interest of every human being to follow its tenets regardless of his or her particular circumstances. In doing so, it not only presents a significant challenge to universal humanism as a guide to practical political choice but it also explains why, in some circumstances, victims of random and lawless violence may prefer other ethical views to that of universal humanism.

NOTES

[1] An earlier and shorter version of this paper was published under the title 'Towards Liberation: Terrorism from a Liberation Ideology Perspective', in Tony Coady and Michael O'Keefe (eds), *Terrorism and Justice: Moral Argument in a Threatened World*, Melbourne, Melbourne University Press, 2002, pp. 58-71.
[2] See Robert Young 'Political Terrorism as a Weapon of the Politically Powerless', in Tony Coady and Michael O'Keefe (eds), *Terrorism and Justice: Moral Argument in a Threatened World*, Melbourne, Melbourne University Press, 2002, pp. 22-30.
[3] Harmondsworth, Middlesex: Penguin books, 1967 (1963). Translated from the French original *Les damnées de la terre* (1961) by Constance Farrington. Jean Paul Sartre has a provided a rather succinct but useful commentary on the essay in the preface he wrote to this edition.

[4] Osama bin Laden video-taped statement of October 7, 2001, Associated Press translation from Arabic. Accessed at: http://users.skynet.be/terrorism/html/laden_statement.htm, on April 3, 2002. The BBC translation differs from the above at a few important points. Here are the BBC variants: 'I ask God Almighty to elevate their status and grant them Paradise ... One million Iraqi children have thus far died in Iraq although they did not do anything wrong ... The least that one can describe these people is that they are morally depraved ... These incidents divided the entire world into two regions – one of faith where there is no hypocrisy and another of infidelity, from which we hope God will protect us ... The winds of faith and change have blown to remove falsehood from the [Arabian] peninsula of Prophet Mohammed, may God's prayers be upon him.'
Accessed at /news.bbc.co.uk/hi/english/world/south_asia/newsid_1585000/1585636.stm on April 3, 2002.

[5] Al-Qaeda spokesman seems to refer to this difference in his statement that: '[T]here are thousands of the Islamic nation's youths who are eager to die just as the Americans are eager to live.' From 'In full: Al-Qaeda statement' accessed at http://news.bbc.co.uk/hi/e.../middle_east/newsid_1590000/1590350.stm on April 3, 2002.

[6] *The Wretched of the Earth*, p. 74

[7] In his 'Political Terrorism as a Weapon of the Politically Powerless' (see note 2) Young examines this type of justification as a form of consequentialist justification of terrorism.

[8] To validate this inference one needs to introduce further premises or assumptions which are not of central interest for our present inquiry. Of course, not all of those who accept (a) are ready to make the inference to (b) and (c).

LAURENCE LUSTGARTEN

NATIONAL SECURITY, TERRORISM, AND CONSTITUTIONAL BALANCE[1]

Protection against threats to the fundamental order and institutions of a society is the most elementary function of the state and its rulers. Thomas Hobbes is perhaps the most celebrated exponent of this view in English political thinking; it led to his (then) radical conclusion that failure to provide such protection would justify refusal to accept the continued rule of the Sovereign. In a Conference held in Germany, it hardly needs pointing out that the same theme was echoed nearly three centuries later by Carl Schmitt, in what – to judge from conversations with legal academics – must be the best-known phrase in modern German constitutional jurisprudence: 'Souverän ist, wer über den Ausnahmezustand entscheidet', conventionally translated into English as 'sovereign is he who defines the exception'.[2] The 'exception' of course is the state of emergency, or whatever one wishes to call the state of affairs where the normal constraints of rule-bound government and debate-based politics must be suspended because the existence of the institutions which constitute it are in dire peril.

For both Hobbes and Schmitt it seemed obvious that the organ of government most suited, indeed the only one suited, to this protective function was, in contemporary terms, the executive power. Indeed early in his career Schmitt harked back to Roman times and its institution of dictatorship, although that institution was in fact hedged about with restrictions on the appointment and continuation in office of the dictator.[3] However, in a democratic state, and in particular 21st century democratic states which have proclaimed a permanent commitment to legally-guaranteed human rights, that allocation of power is radically open to challenge. In parliamentary systems – the norm in Europe, France alone being a partial exception – the legislature as the forum of the directly-elected representatives of the people has *prima facie* a greater legitimacy to take decisions of such grave consequences. Certainly on one conception, the parliamentary executive functions as the agent of the legislature, which is in turn composed of 'deputies'. This title clearly implies subordination – in this case to the electorate, in whom ultimate sovereignty rests. Moreover, to move human rights from the realm of political rhetoric and moral discourse into legal norms necessarily implies that the courts will be granted powers to enforce them. When those legal rights conflict with measures taken to further other aims or protect other interests, a conflict of norms arises which becomes a matter for the judiciary. How they define their role in such cases is discussed below, but clearly the notion of unrestricted executive discretionary power is no longer sustainable.

In this paper I will address the issue of constitutional balance – though it may be that 'interaction' is a more accurate term – among executive, legislature and judiciary in the context of measures taken to protect national security and/or to counter

Meggle (ed.), Ethics of Terrorism & Counter-Terrorism, 261-280.
© 2005 Ontos, Heusenstamm.

terrorism. I will restrict myself largely to the United Kingdom (UK), but I hope the discussion will be relevant to other states which have in common certain key features of the European model of parliamentary democracy, notably the fusion of legislative and executive personnel and therefore at least indirectly of power. The UK is unique in some respects, notably in governing itself through an unwritten constitution (or in not possessing a written one) but that characteristic, though important, does not mean that no useful comparisons or analogies can be made. Indeed there are many states, such as Canada and Australia, where British constitutional norms have survived and been transposed in various ways into a complex document and praxis.

Conversely, I do not even attempt to address the issue in the context of a constitutional order which lays down a formal separation of powers between executive and legislature, with an explicit textual commitment of certain powers, notably that of declaring war, to the legislature. The paradigm case here is of course the United States of America, and the disputes between executive and legislative branches over the extent of their relative powers have been a consistent theme in American constitutional history almost from its inception.[4] It is perhaps not surprising that a constitutional system committed to an unusually strict version of separation of powers produces persistent conflicts, but the converse does not follow: the parliamentary executive model produces distinct problems of its own.

THE EXECUTIVE AND THE LEGISLATURE

Montesquieu was perhaps the first, and certainly in the English-speaking world is the best-known, writer to point out the dangers of fusion of power between executive and legislature. As is well-known, he misunderstood what he saw in England during his visit in the late 1720s, and imagined that the King (the executive) and the Parliament enjoyed sharply differentiated powers and served as counterweights to one another. This misunderstanding was then fed into the American constitution via James Madison's analysis in the Federalist Papers, drawing on Montesquieu's *Spirit of the Laws* (1748), of the necessity for what has become known as 'checks and balances' to maintain a free and democratic government.[5] Its widespread acceptance as a fundamental constitutional principle throughout the world of democratic states is attested by an examination of those constitutions, which may embody the same values in different institutional forms.[6]

It is worth considering why the principle is considered to be of such high importance. It is not primarily for reasons of competence, though that may be relevant, but for its role as a brake on tyranny. One fear is if those making the laws were also able to enforce them, they could draft them in openly self-interested or partisan terms, as weapons against their enemies, whether of a class, religious, ethnic, ideological or party-political character. Much more important, however, has been the reverse problem: preventing those charged with the execution of the laws from gaining the power to formulate them. Concern with this danger grew out of specific political history, in which the hereditary monarch, controlling the armed forces and detached from civil society, often sought to engage in wars, spend money, punish opponents, and suspend the operation of particular laws he found inconvenient to his purposes. This created great opposition among powerful political and economic interests among the small property-owning elite, which were sometimes overlaid with religious disagreements engaging larger numbers of the population. Yet what were at times parochial conflicts among interest groups had major constitutional fallout. They eventually produced in west European states a role for the independent legislature as a countervailing power. In the space between Monarch and Legislature, liberty could begin to flourish. England, in which these conflicts occupied most of the 17th century, was the first major state to undergo this evolution.

Liberty may have flourished, but not democracy. That came much later, and (in terms of the proportion of the population eligible to vote), later in England than almost everywhere else.[7] 'Democracy' or 'democrat' was a political swearword in early nineteenth century England, rather like 'subversive' and almost (though not quite) like 'terrorist' today. Its advent however reinforces the importance of separation of legislative and executive powers, and redefines the difference in functions, in a fundamental way. Citizens in a parliamentary democracy vote for their representatives or deputies in the legislature. They have no choice in selecting those who wield executive power. In theory this affront to democratic principle is overcome by making the executive 'accountable' or 'responsible' to the legislature, in an extreme case, to use the English parliamentary parlance, the executive forfeits (by vote) the 'confidence' of the House of Commons and can no longer remain in office. Thus this element of indirect or attenuated democracy (as contrasted with direct election of the President in France or the USA) is prevented from becoming an instrument of oppression because ultimately those directly elected by the people determine who remains in office.

This theory actually reflected the reality of Victorian Britain. Administrations fell as they 'lost the confidence of the House' and were followed by new administrations composed of a mix of those who had held office in the fallen regime and previous outsiders. This was notably true of the conduct of war and foreign relations, the primary activity of government in the days before the Welfare and Regulatory States. Written immediately after the country's greatest military disaster of the century, Lord Tennyson's celebrated poem 'The Charge of the Light Brigade' with its famous line 'Some one had blunder'd' is renowned throughout the English-speaking world; much less well-known is that fact that the Government fell in reaction to the incompetence of the military authorities on a battlefield a thousand miles distant. The suggestion that matters of foreign relations or military affairs should not be debated in Parliament, or were matters exclusively or largely for the Executive, would have been greeted with horror by the Victorians. They would have viewed it as an assault of the English constitution and the liberty it protected – nothing less than a revival of the attitudes of the Stuarts, twice overthrown in the 17th century.

The great irony is that the coming of democracy has brought with it the quiescence of Parliament in the highest matters of state, in a manner of which the Stuarts would have approved. Issues of defence and foreign relations, which in the mid-20th century were subsumed under the general rubric of 'national security'[8] are the areas on which Parliament receives the least information, and debates with diminished frequency and – even more strikingly – competence. It is in this realm too that Parliament is most readily ignored when the Executive wishes to move with determination. As I write this exactly a year after the attacks on New York, in the midst of an intensive political and public relations offensive orchestrated by the American and British governments to generate support for an invasion of Iraq, Parliament remains in recess. Only a sustained campaign by MPs from all parties, plus growing opposition from trade unions which are an important support of the Labour Party has led the Prime Minister to agree to recall (i.e. convene early) Parliament – it remained a matter entirely within his gift. At the same time, however, it has been decided that MPs will not be given an opportunity to vote directly on whether to support any such invasion. The most effective forum, in the sense of one which may sway the Prime Minister, will remain newspapers and public opinion polls.

The short-circuiting of Parliament is not simply a reaction to the greater speed of decision-making that modern technology sometimes requires: matters such as the sending of troops to the Gulf War, Kosovo – or Iraq – are not decided within hours. It is partly a habit of deference to Executive power that reflects the demands of two World Wars, carried over unthinkingly into the Cold War – although Ministers, civil servants and military leaders have certainly done their best to cultivate the habit. It also reflects two other factors:

1) the wide consensus on national security issues among political elites since 1945, which has meant that only a few figures on the fringes of both ends of the political spectrum sought seriously to challenge key policies, and

2) an obsession with secrecy, going far beyond what was rationally required to protect military effectiveness.

The latter in particular is self-reinforcing, for the more that legislators are kept in ignorance and acquiesce in that allegedly blissful state, the less intelligently can they question or criticise. Hence of course the less attention that needs to be paid to their views by the Executive and the 'experts' who serve it, and the less credibly can they present an alternative set of policies to the wider public.

The constitutional pillar on which the Executive's power rests is known in UK public law as the Royal Prerogative. This is conventionally defined as the legally-recognised powers of the Monarch which require no statutory authority for their exercise. They are emphatically not extra-legal, but are recognised and defined (in the sense of that limits are imposed) by the courts. The legacy and residuum of the days when the Monarch conducted affairs of state personally, they are now exercised by the Prime Minister and Cabinet in the Monarch's name.[9] Two well-recognised facets or applications of this power concern the conduct of foreign affairs and defence, though bitter historical experience in the 17th century of the dangers to freedom presented by armed forces under the control of the Executive led to a prohibition imposed by the Bill of Rights against maintenance of a peacetime army without consent of Parliament. Thus where royal power under the Prerogative had been abused, the legislature has long been able to assert its powers to combat it. Nonetheless the Executive starts from a position of primacy in these areas, but this too is a legacy, not merely of pre-democratic times, but of an era when the monarch's power greatly exceeded that of the legislature and was ideologically buttressed by notions of the Divine Right of Kings to rule. In a sense the law badly lagged behind the evolution of constitutional practice as it evolved into the 19th century when, as noted earlier, foreign and military affairs were subject to regular and severe parliamentary scrutiny. This legislative assertiveness did not require, nor did it bring in its train, any legal alteration; and the stasis of the law served to assist the executive when in the age of total war and mass democracy beginning around the First World War, it reasserted its grip on these vital matters. Any serious attempt at genuine democratisation of British political life must include drastic pruning of the Royal Prerogative in these (and some other unrelated) areas, though it must be said that the American attempt to do so has, at any rate as interpreted in the 20th century, been less than an outstanding success.[10] It is notable too that neither Canada nor Australia, whose constitutions were drafted more than a century ago, have never tried to define or delimit executive power, even as they delineated legislative powers in infinite detail. To take the former example, only nine sections in a document containing 147 sections are devoted to Executive Power, and insofar as they address significant issues at all, are content simply to vest those powers, including the power of commanding all military forces, in the Queen.[11] I have yet to find a good working constitutional model of executive-legislative power sharing in these fields.

The approach to measures devoted to countering 'terrorism' has been shaped by these wider trends and developments. 'Terrorism' has been subsumed under the national security rubric – mostly obviously and directly in relation to deportation, where alleged terrorists have been expelled from the country under the longstanding catch-all category that their presence is not 'conducive to the public good', being detrimental to the 'interests of national security'.[12] As a result, decisions about the deployment of soldiers overseas with the clear risk of loss of life, and the mobilisation of ships and planes at great extra expense, are taken by the Prime Minister and a few hand-picked reliable members of the Cabinet and simply announced to Parliament. It would be impossible to contend, for example, that the dispatch of British soldiers to Afghanistan in autumn 2001 was adequately debated there.

Even more secretive are the actions of security agencies, whose response to terrorism in the past years has included the extension of surveillance to increased numbers of people and to places (e.g. mosques) that had previously been regarded as off-limits. This is not to suggest that the Security Service should publish a list of their surveillance targets; rather that significant changes of policy at a general level should be announced in advance and require parliamentary debate and approval in principle. For example, during the long guerrilla war with the IRA, Roman Catholic churches were not targets for infiltration by security agencies, despite the sectarian nature of the conflict and, in a few well-known cases, the involvement of priests in paramilitary activities. It seems that mosques are now being treated with less restraint. This issue of apparent discrimination is important,[13] not least because it could feed the hostility of the Muslim community towards the institutions of government and British society in general. Failure to discuss the issue openly could mean that only one set of considerations – those relating to immediate security concerns – would shape policy, without adequate awareness of long-term implications. Of course it may be argued that such open debate carries with it the risk of inflammatory statements and emergence of strong majority sentiment hostile to the religious liberty of a minority portrayed as suspect. To this there are two responses. One is that it is important to point out to advocates of ethnic or religious intolerance that the approach is short-sighted and may have long-range consequences they themselves would not welcome. The second is that, regardless of the outcome, states which proclaim themselves to be democratic (and preach the superiority of their system to poorer nations round the world) thereby place themselves under a duty to discuss such issues of principle openly and civilly if they wish to earn and retain the right to the title. And though the legislature is only one forum for discussion, it is the only forum in which a decision which can claim the legitimacy of democratic representation may be taken.

The Executive does not merely make policies and direct the armed forces and ancillary bodies. It also frames legislation which when enacted may have severe and pervasive impact on the freedom of individuals and the well-being of communities. Most obviously in relation to terrorism, successive British governments have introduced measures granting enhanced coercive powers to the police; restricting access to courts; permitting long-term detention of people without trial; and altering rules of evidence and other aspects of court procedure to make conviction of suspects easier.[14] Equally important, and particularly relevant to acts justified by the purported need to combat terrorism, it may introduce regulations to restrict the scope of human rights instruments, or to give effect to measures agreed with other states, either within the framework of the European Union or more globally.[15] This is of the highest importance in Britain, because such measures are introduced under special procedures. Briefly, they do not require primary legislation (i.e. an Act of Parliament), but only subordinate legislation. The practical importance of the distinction is that the normal legislative process is not required, meaning that the time allocated to the measure is greatly reduced and sometimes minimal, and – most vitally – no amendment to the proposal is permitted. It must either be accepted or rejected in full, which almost invariably results in approval, often at speed.

As a matter of technical drafting, many of these instruments are lengthy and complex; often they are obscurely phrased due to the haste with which they were conceived. In other circumstances, where adequate time is granted, the quality of legislation has been measurably improved by careful scrutiny. Conversely, governments have used the emotional revulsion after some atrocity as a political opportunity, as sort of Trojan horse. As part of a large package of legislative proposals heavily advertised as a response to 'terrorism' they have included measures only tangentially related to that end. In the words of a former Home Secretary during the Debates on the most recent anti-terrorism law, some of these provisions were 'hanging around in the Home Office for a long time' awaiting a suitable legislative opportunity.[16] Even more insidiously, they have used the same window of opportunity to enact proposals that had previously been defeated after extended debate, relying on the alleged need for speed to curtail further discussion and in effect steamroller them through.[17]

One of the most effective means by which the Executive has usurped legislative powers is through its control of the Parliamentary timetable. In theory – a theory which long precedes democracy – the legislative chamber is the site at which proposals for new laws are subject to intense debate over matters of principle, as well as detailed scrutiny as to whether the specifics of any proposal are well-suited to its intended purpose, and, in a technical sense, well-crafted as a legal instrument. That is not the reality of political life in contemporary Britain. The Government, through its majority, controls the amount of time any particular measure will receive on the floor of the House of Commons.[18] The result is that the Blair Government's legislative response to the suicide attacks on the USA – the Anti-Terrorism, Crime and Security Act 2001 [ATCSA], a statute of 129 sections and 8 Schedules running well over one hundred pages in length, received precisely 16 hours consideration by MPs. The special Parliamentary Joint Committee on Human Rights protested this limitation (along with the inclusion of material outside the main purpose of the statute), but to no effect.[19] This near-contemptuous treatment of elected representatives in my view strains the democratic legitimacy of the outcome virtually to breaking point.

Ironically, it is the House of Lords, the legislative chamber comprised entirely of hereditary and appointed members[20] and thus possessing little obvious democratic legitimacy, which has been the only effective forum of scrutiny, mature consideration and principled opposition. This is partly due to its composition: it numbers amongst its members some of the nation's most distinguished and experienced lawyers, as well as a significant number of former holders of public office and persons of great distinction in various walks of life. This membership also means that the Government often does not command a majority within it. Equally important is the tradition of independence that animates it as a corporate entity. The result is that for the past 15 years the House of Lords has been the main source of thoughtful and critical debate concerning a large number of Bills introduced by successive governments of both parties. Many of these have concerned criminal justice, another emotionally supercharged issue, but the contrast with its performance and that of the House of Commons in connection with the three pieces of anti-terrorist legislation[21] introduced by the Blair Government has been particularly striking. Had protection of human rights (or in traditional English terminology, civil liberties) been left solely to elected representatives, they could have disappeared, not with a bang, but with a whimper. The Lords were not able to scupper many of the provisions it opposed, due to its clearly-understood subordinate place in the constitutional hierarchy compared with the elected first chamber. Yet their ability to chivvy the Government; to force it defend certain controversial proposals and to take a second look at some which in the clear light of debate were exposed as ill-conceived or badly-expressed; to raise public awareness of certain matters which were then picked up in the media; and in some instances to force concessions by putting pressure on the legislative timetable, were the only effective expression of the parliamentary function as traditionally understood. That the site of this expression was found in its pre-democratic element is ironic but perhaps not altogether surprising. The values safeguarded and nourished by separation of powers predate democracy, and indeed are antithetical to one influential conception of it, that of simple majoritarianism. The treatment accorded anti-terrorism legislation is but an extreme case of the pathology of contemporary majoritarian democracy, in which the Executive exercises a tight grip over members of the legislature through the system of party discipline. The tradition of the independent legislator, exercising their own judgement and not serving merely as the mouthpiece of those who elected (or initially selected) them, identified pre-eminently with Edmund Burke,[22] is deeply ingrained in British political mythology. It is now nearly extinct or at any rate effectively suppressed and – yet another irony – is actually more honoured elsewhere. A notable example is Germany, where the Basic Law specifically mandates in Art. 38(1) that deputies to the Bundestag 'shall be representatives of the whole people, not bound by orders and instructions, and shall be subject only to their conscience'. It would be well worth exploring empirically the extent of the influence of this conception in German political practice.

One mechanism through which even a tame legislature can force some accountability upon the Executive is through so-called sunset clauses. Normally a statute remains in force until explicitly repealed by another statute. A sunset clause inserts into legislation an expiry date, for the Act as a whole or for one particularly controversial portion of it. The underlying idea is to force the Government to rethink the necessity of the law, or (a sometimes unspoken aim) to hope that a different government in office at the later date with a different view of the matter would simply let the measure lapse, a much quicker, easier and less controversial way of ending it than introducing repealing legislation. The Blair Government felt constrained to accept such clauses in its most recent anti-terrorist legislation. The most controversial provisions are those which authorise detention without trial of those purportedly involved or even 'linked' to terrorist activities, whom the authorities choose not to prosecute but are unable to deport because European Convention jurisprudence bars deportation to states where torture or inhuman treatment awaits the person expelled. The people affected are held in one of England's worst prisons in what their solicitor called 'concrete coffins', with no knowledge of what they are supposed to be guilty of. Indeed 'guilt' is perhaps the wrong word, because they will never have the opportunity of defending themselves in legal proceedings and having a verdict or guilt, or of innocence, pronounced upon them. The Government was able to force this measure through Parliament, but with the concession that authorising legislation is to expire within fifteen months. However, the relevant Minister may instantly revive it repeatedly with the approval of Parliament[23] for up to five years until November 2006, when *that* power lapses and new legislation is required.[24] There is also an allied requirement of review by a high-powered committee[25] of the Act as a whole, to be undertaken within two years.[26]

These all sound like valuable safeguards, but long experience with the operation of similar provisions makes one very doubtful. For one thing, those undertaking the reviews are appointed by the government, thus ensuring that they are 'reliable'. Secondly, the Executive will be sure to exercise firm control over votes on extension of the legislation. It is inconceivable that it will be allowed to expire without the Prime Minister's approval. The paradigm here is the so-called Prevention of Terrorism (Temporary Provisions) Act 1974. Passed at breakneck speed after the IRA bombing atrocity in Birmingham, the Home Secretary Roy Jenkins, who genuinely cared about civil liberties, mollified critics by insisting that the law would initially last for only six months, and would lapse when it was no longer needed. Jenkins soon moved on (to the Presidency of the European Commission) and out (of the Labour Party) and the Act was in fact renewed continuously, at first yearly then every five years, for a quarter of a century. Numerous reviews were undertaken, but they never offered a fundamental reconsideration, concerning themselves with suggesting marginal changes. The last comprehensive review, by a judge sitting in the House of Lords, recommended that the pretence of contingency be abandoned. The law was to be put on a permanent basis, with an even wider definition of 'terrorism' to be incorporated. (Some forms of control, notably exclusion orders, were eliminated.) This was carried out in 2000, with the statute enacted after the attacks on the USA superimposed on that massive piece of legislation the following year. Britain now has the most comprehensive, and in some respects most draconian, legislation directed against 'terrorism' anywhere in the world, and certainly in Europe. It is difficult to see how the review and renewal process has provided, or will provide, much protection for personal and political freedoms.

With the legislative track record largely one of complaisance and timidity, the sole recourse available to anyone caught up in the maw of the state machine is to the courts. Yet, as I will attempt to show, that route is extremely problematic.

THE ROLE OF THE COURTS

Contemporary Western democracies have in the last two decades acquired a new and notable characteristic element. Virtually all[27] have some form of legally-guaranteed human rights. Many have entrenched these rights in their constitutions, thereby according them superior legal status to ordinary legislation, as in Germany, Canada, USA and all the former Soviet bloc states. Others have either absorbed them through the position of international law in their legal system (e.g. the Netherlands and France in relation to the European Convention on Human Rights) or enacted them domestically in some form (Norway, Sweden, and the UK). Whatever the legal form, the expectation of citizens in an increasingly 'rights conscious' era is that individuals will enjoy protections against abuse of fundamental rights by state authorities, and that these protections will be enforceable in the courts. This is a fundamental change, for it raises more directly and inescapably than was possible under the constitutional relationships formerly prevailing, the role of the judicial branch of government[28] in connection with the issues of power and freedom created by anti-terrorism measures. Thus the structure of separation of powers is now more appropriately represented by a triangle; and its dynamic is more complex.

The UK judicial system has certain characteristics which reflect its historical role as the progenitor of the common law, and also its place in the nation's fluid constitution. Unlike most civilian legal systems, there is only one High Court of general jurisdiction, and obviously there is (nor can be) no Constitutional Court. Many legal issues concerning terrorism will arise in the context of criminal prosecutions, which will be heard by judges who may not even be full-time members of the judiciary, and who may very well not be criminal specialists. This is by no means necessarily a disadvantage in assuring fair proceedings and proper application of the law, but it does mean that issues of procedure, evidence and application of human rights norms will all be decided at the same time by the same judge(s), at first instance and on appeal. Thus issues that elsewhere would involve interpretation of a specific article of the Constitution (and would be transferred for separate decision to a Constitutional Court if one existed), and which might even be regarded as of constitutional significance by the British judges, will be decided by the ordinary courts along with all other legal issues raised by the particular case.

However some of the most contentious applications of anti-terrorism legislation concerns deportation and detention without trial. These cases have been channelled into an unusual specialist body known as the Special Immigration Appeals Commission, or SIAC. This was established after the UK lost a major decision in

European Court of Human Rights in the case of *Chahal v. UK*,[29] which held that persons detained pending deportation on grounds of national security did not have access to a proper court to determine their appeal. This body is a court-equivalent, or court-substitute, and its most striking characteristic is that it hears evidence in secret proceedings at which the Appellant and his lawyer is excluded. However, following a suggestion by the European Court in the *Chahal* judgment, the Appellant's interests are looked after by a Special Counsel, who has full access to all secret material and is tasked with putting forward the strongest possible case on his behalf. The Special Counsel is modelled on a similar system operating in Canada[30] and is designed to allow the government to introduce secret material – e.g. the names and activities of informers and the results of telephone intercepts which in the UK are not permitted to be used as evidence in court – whilst allowing security-vetted lawyers to present the strongest possible case for an appellant. SIAC is chaired by a Judge of the High Court, but its two other members are not necessarily of that rank (though they can be), nor indeed be legally-trained; one member can be a person with experience in security matters. Critical issues arising under the latest anti-terrorism statute, including the legality of the UK's derogation from Art. 5 ECHR so as to permit indefinite detention of terrorist 'suspects' who cannot lawfully be deported, will come before this body.

Indeed the courts in the UK play a lesser role in controlling the executive's use of intrusive and coercive powers than is the case in most other countries, whether common law or civil law jurisdictions. Neither telephone tapping nor 'bugging' – the more advanced form of technological surveillance – require prior judicial authorisation.[31] How this can meet the standards of the ECHR, and its recent incorporation into UK domestic law in the form of the Human Rights Act 1998, remains rather mysterious. The result is to leave an enormous amount of discretion to ministers, police and civil servants. To say this is not to imply that they are ever-eager to abuse their powers, nor that they act capriciously. They are mandated to comply with statutory standards before authorising tapping or bugging,[32] and among the 43 chief constables in England and Wales there is considerable variation in attitude and willingness to authorise intrusive measures. In practice, perhaps the most effective constraint on the extent of these intrusions is financial: extended surveillance, including the transcription of the material gathered, most of which is entirely irrelevant to the investigation, is expensive and the costs must be met from the budget of the organisation requesting the operation. It remains an open and genuine question whether, taken as a whole, these non-legal controls are less effective than those which operate in legal systems requiring judicial authorisation but in which other restrains are less important. It remains true that the relatively limited role of the UK courts in this process is, from a comparative perspective, quite striking.

The primary means by which the legality of administrative action (which includes the exercise of a discretionary power under statute or the Royal Prerogative) may be challenged in the civil courts is through a process known as judicial review. In the traditional approach, this has involved a relatively weak standard of review known as 'irrationality', which meant that any discretionary decision which was not clearly based on extraneous considerations, or appearing virtually inexplicable (often a matter of deduction, since giving reasons for administrative decisions has never been required) was upheld. This is to be contrasted with the more demanding German approach, which has been adopted in EU administrative law and European Convention law as well, which demands 'proportionality' between the aim or policy and the means chosen. However, the incorporation of the ECHR into UK domestic law has meant that where a recognised Convention right is in issue, the proportionality standard must be applied. How this will be interpreted by the English courts is very unclear at this point, with diverse decisions pointing in different directions.[33]

However, over and above general principles of judicial review (which also include the overseeing the administration's interpretation of statutes granting it various powers, and insistence upon observance of fair procedures) the courts have developed doctrines of judicial deference in certain areas of decision-making. One of these, broadly, is the realm of socio-economic regulation. Another concerns matters coming under the broad heading of national security. This was illustrated forcefully in a ruling of the House of Lords last year, written before the attacks on New York and Washington though delivered afterwards.[34] A Kashmiri Muslim who had at least indirectly supported militant action against what he regarded as Indian conquest of his homeland was served with a order for deportation in 1998, on the grounds of his 'involvement with an Islamic terrorist organisation' made him a danger to national security. He appealed to SIAC, which ruled that the case against him was not, on the facts, established to a sufficiently high standard of proof. It also rejected the extremely wide definition of 'national security' used by the government, under which Britain's need for assistance from India to counter the 'world-wide terrorist threat' meant that a threat to Indian national security would be considered a threat to UK national security. The House of Lords reversed on both grounds. It held that the question of whether someone's involvement in terrorism made him a risk required a 'global approach' which could be decided by taking into account the 'executive's policy', not a matter of fact to be determined by judicial standards.[35] It further held that the executive is entitled to use any definition of 'national security' it considered appropriate. This ruling was buttressed by extended analysis of one of the judges, Lord Hoffmann, who insisted that the doctrine of separation of powers requires judicial deference to the executive in this field.[36] The result is to give security agencies and the police – who provide the factual basis for the Home Secretary's decision to deport in any particular case – a remarkable degree of power over individuals' lives. It also allows the political executive virtually unrestricted power to use immigration control and the admission of refugees as an instrument of foreign policy. And for the reasons argued earlier in relation to the decline of Parliament, these powers are exercised with very little political accountability. By withdrawing from the field, the judiciary have left the executive with literally ir-responsible power – effectively responsible to no one. In these circumstances, I would suggest that the principle of separation of powers, with its ultimate rationale lying in the need to prevent arbitrary power, justifies the courts taking a more active role in protecting the interests of people faced with a devastating sanction and little capability (and in some cases no right) to protect their interests through participation in the political process.

In terms of the tripartite constitutional dynamic, the questions concerning the proper role of the judiciary may be posed as follows:

When should the courts overrule decisions taken by the executive acting under i) prerogative powers or ii) statutory powers to uphold individuals' rights based on 1) common law 2) statute or 3) the Convention rights enacted by the Human Rights Act, which may be regarded as 'superstatutory'? Before addressing those questions in the specific context of terrorism and national security, a number of general points, some constitutional and some matters of positive jurisprudence, must be considered.

1) There is no proper role for the UK courts in the absence of some sort of rights recognised in positive law. This may sound obvious, but it has one important implication: it leaves no scope for the sort of case that went to the German Constitutional Court, challenging the use of troops outside German territory. As I understand it, this case involved a dispute about the relative powers of the executive and legislature, with the *Bundesverfassungsgericht* interpreting the relevant provisions of the Basic Law which allocate the powers of the two branches.[37] As such adjudication is not possible in Britain, the result is to leave the balance of powers between them, and the locus of decision, entirely to the political process, with the consequences discussed earlier in this paper.[38]

2) Principles of common law are always subordinate in the legal hierarchy to provisions of statute. Therefore any rights an individual may have enjoyed as a matter of common law can always be taken away by Parliament. However, in the interpretation of statutes, there is supposed to be a presumption against loss of common law rights, i.e. where there is an ambiguity the statute should be read so as to preserve such rights. However, in practice this presumption tends to be ignored nowadays, with courts more willing to effectuate what they see as the aim of the legislation even if it curbs traditional rights. The present context is one of those in which this modern practice is most clearly manifest.

3) The HRA is a very peculiar statute in the way in which it fits into the legal structure. An important corollary of the *Grundnorm* of parliamentary sovereignty is that where there is a conflict between two statutory provisions, the later one governs, as being presumptively the most recent expression of the will of Parliament.[39] Putting legislation concerning UK membership in the EU to one side, the HRA is unique in that it explicitly requires the courts to interpret all legislation, *whenever enacted*, 'in a way which is compatible with Convention rights'.[40] Thus regardless of the date of any statutory restriction on a Convention right (but *not* on a right conferred by an earlier statute, let alone a right based on common law), that restriction must be read in light of, and in some way harmonised with or accommodated to, any applicable Convention right. This is why I described such rights earlier as 'superstatutory'.

4) Convention rights are of three sorts:

a) *absolute*, admitting of no qualifications whatever. Two examples are the right to be free from torture and 'inhuman or degrading treatment' (Art. 3);

b) *qualified*, which admit of only those restrictions spelled out within the text of the right itself. A primary example is right to 'liberty and security' in Art. 5, which is then subject six prescribed exceptions which are meant to be definitive and exclusive;

c) *conditional*, where the right is subject to restrictions based on a wide range of aims recognised as legitimate, and which must be 'necessary in a democratic society'. The right to privacy (Art. 8) and to freedom of expression (Art. 10) are the best known examples.

The judicial role in relation to these three types of rights is quite different. In the first two, the real task – by no means a simple one – is to determine whether the right is engaged or whether the prescribed exception applies to the facts of the case. Thus once a court decides that certain conduct constitutes torture, or that a person was lawfully detained with a view to his deportation (one of the specified exceptions in Art. 5), the litigant wins or loses the case on that relatively precise point. Where conditional rights are engaged, however, the scope for judgements of morality is very much greater, as is the almost unavoidable necessity of venturing into the territory of highly contested issues of public policy.

5) The *Grundnorm* of parliamentary sovereignty requires the courts to accept the validity of any Act of Parliament. To put the point conversely, no statute can be annulled by the courts on grounds that it violates some human right or other constitutional guarantee.[41] This avoids any direct conflict between legislature and judiciary. However, statutes concerning terrorism and national security are almost invariably structured so as to confer very wide discretion on ministers or administrative officials, including police and immigration authorities. The issue for the courts – and it is on this apparently technical level that the true effectiveness of legal protections is tested – is whether to imply any limitations on the breadth of that discretion. This can be done in several ways – by reading in a requirement of 'reasonableness' before a minister's 'belief' or 'suspicion' that someone is a terrorist or a danger to national security can be acted upon; by requiring a factual demonstration to a high standard of proof of the basis of such suspicion or belief; by implying procedural protections for the person subject to special powers if none, or none sufficient, has been created by statute. In the mythology that has grown up over centuries exalting the common law and its judges as protectors of liberty, such interpretative practices would be the normal response to open-ended grants of executive discretion that abridge personal freedoms. However, since the First World War, the judges have fallen in behind the executive, applying what a distinguished legal historian has called 'the Reading presumption of executive innocence'[42] – Lord Reading being the Lord Chief Justice who delivered a series of rulings in favour of the executive in internment cases, in one of which he stated: 'It is of course always to be assumed that the executive will act honestly and that its powers will be reasonably exercised.'[43]

This presumption is nothing less than a betrayal of judicial responsibility. Judges above all others should have an instinctive scepticism of untested factual assertions, born of awareness of the dangers of factual inaccuracies, and of prejudice replacing proof. It is to avoid these dangers that criminal accusations must satisfy a high standard of proof and must be tested by a forensic procedure which allows the accused person the opportunity to subject the case against him to rigorous interrogation. The repeated history of mistakes and dragnet operations sweeping up the totally innocent in various wartime and 'emergency' internments in the UK alone[44] should provide a stark warning against a lax approach. Yet instead the courts in national security and wartime internment cases have developed a series of practices that might be called 'games judges play' – informal and subtle ways of lightening the difficulty for the Government in supporting its case, whilst imposing extra burdens of persuasion on those challenging executive decisions – that make effective challenge

273

to those decisions virtually impossible.[45] This is not justified by obedience to the will of Parliament, for the statutes in question seldom explicitly command the action challenge, and in instances where the power in question derives from the Royal Prerogative, Parliament has not spoken at all.

6) The effect of the jurisprudence of the Strasbourg Court is ambiguous. For one thing, that Court operates a doctrine known as the 'margin of appreciation', under which deference is granted to national authorities, including national courts, as best placed for various reasons to make judgments about what measures are required to combat particular evils. This is an extremely controversial doctrine, as inspection of any treatise or textbook on the Convention will quickly show,[46] as it runs the risk of abdicating the Court's functions to the very national bodies whose restrictions on Convention rights are supposed to be challengeable in Strasbourg, at any rate as a last resort. Without going too deeply into its complexities, which would require a extensive paper of itself, it may be said that the application of this doctrine seems to vary depending upon which rights are at stake. In particular, it seems to operate more generously with some of the conditional rights than with the qualified rights.[47] Notably in relation to the procedural rights in Art. 5 and Art. 6 (which governs fair trial), the Court seems less willing to leave matters to national variation, subject however to the very important qualification that it has repeatedly held that Art. 6 does not mandate adoption of any particular rules of evidence.[48]

Not many cases involving anti-terrorist measures have been decided by the ECtHR, and almost all of them have arisen out of attempts by the UK or Irish authorities to curb Irish republicanism.[49] Considered collectively, the judgements send out mixed messages.[50] On the one hand, 'terrorist crime' has been said to manifest a 'special nature', and in some instances the Court has upheld the conduct of the police where it seems doubtful the same result would have been reached if the appellant had been involved in 'ordinary' crime, however serious.[51] On the other hand, the majority of cases has recognised this principle but gone on to find violations of Convention rights in relation to length of detention without judicial supervision, absence of adequate justification for arrest, and violation of the right to silence and the right against self-incrimination.[52] It seems clear, however, that the Court has up to now firmly set its face against easy acceptance of 'the need to combat terrorism' as a justification for radical erosion of Convention rights. It is doubtful, however, whether this stance will extend to cases involving conditional rights such as privacy, where countervailing public interests such as national security and public safety are given more prominence in the textual definition of the right itself. This will be of particular importance in relation to various forms of surveillance.[53]

In addition, a major test of its integrity as a judicial body may emerge in the political climate engendered by the attacks on New York and Washington last year, when it comes to consider the legislation and administrative practices adopted in several states, including the UK. However, given the glacial pace at which litigation in Strasbourg proceeds, (it takes about four years on average from the date of admissibility to the rendering of a final decision by the Court), it will be years until any such issues reach the Court, so prediction as to the outcome would be little more than speculation. Yet if a climate of fear is present at the time, there is so much ambiguity in existing precedents and principles that they could readily be interpreted and applied so as to uphold various forms of repression, whilst claiming that the jurisprudence has itself remained unchanged. A truly testing case, in all senses of the term, will be a challenge, presently working its way through the English courts, to the UK's 'derogation' (i.e. temporary withdrawal, permitted by Art.15 ECHR) from Art. 5 in respect of the internment of non-citizens suspected of involvement in terrorism who cannot be deported because they face torture or execution in their home countries. To justify the derogation the UK, as required by Art. 15, has claimed that the country in a state of 'public emergency threatening the life of the nation'. This hardly accords with the experience of daily life,[54] and it is also notable that no other member state of the Council of Europe has entered a similar derogation. The ECtHR has required that any such measure be limited to the 'extent strictly required by the exigencies of the crisis', yet it the same breath (or rather, paragraph) it has also accorded a substantial margin of appreciation to national authorities in such cases.[55] The fear is that politics rather than law will determine the outcome.

7) It often seems that something is lost in the transition (or is it translation?) from Strasbourg to the UK courts, where the ECtHR's references to the necessary 'balance' between individual rights and public interests has led – and not only in the context of terrorism – to the 'balancing away' of defendants' rights in a manner that arguably fails to comply with Convention requirements. This seems particularly marked in the sphere of criminal procedure, where the English judges' reassuring message to each other has very much been that the Convention is really what we have been doing all along, only with different words.[56] I would suggest that this is, as a matter of positive jurisprudence, quite mistaken in many cases, and the practical import is that the seductive metaphor of 'balance' can readily be used to override Convention and other protections when the public clamour is loud enough. It takes some courage to resist popular pressure, even for a judiciary which enjoys solid security of tenure.[57] The difficulty with 'balancing' is that the courts are forced to weigh incommensurables: there is no common measure, for example, between damage to privacy or freedom of expression and prevention of disorder and crime. Judges are understandably tempted to allow the political branches of government considerable latitude in their conclusions about what the public interest requires. There is a danger that they will do so by narrowing the meaning or devaluing the importance of the right in question, rather than facing up to the fact that in upholding an act of the executive they are in effect saying that a particular right, though generously conceived and of high importance, must give way to some specified public interest for certain fully-explained reasons. The stakes are high in such cases, and it is unacceptable to reach such a result by ignoring the implications or hiding behind a purportedly mechanistic process of 'balancing'. There may, in other words, be sound constitutional or policy reasons to uphold the executive in a particular case, but the result must be reached candidly.

SUMMATION

In light of the foregoing, I would offer the following suggestions as to the constitutionally appropriate role for the judiciary in terrorism and national security cases:

1) The more policy-laden a particular decision and the less it directly affects fundamental rights of individuals, the greater the degree of deference owed to the executive. A good example is a Canadian case called *Operation Dismantle v. the Queen*.[58] The applicants there argued that Government's decision to allow testing of Cruise missiles on Canadian soil undermined arms control and made nuclear attack more likely, and thus violated their rights to liberty and security under s. 7 of the Charter of Rights and Freedoms. The Supreme Court of Canada said that although the decision could be scrutinised under the Charter, the effect of the decision was too hypothetical to give rise to a violation. My own view is that such a decision involves so many considerations, short-term and long-term, of politics and strategy as to be entirely non-justiciable – i.e. not appropriate for a legal decision which should be grounded in principles, rules and precedent. Moreover the connection between the right said to have been violated and the action challenged was so speculative and tenuous that, again, there is little scope for a judge to substitute his or her view of the matter as a rule of law.

Operation Dismantle was an extreme case, however. Where statutes use open-textured terms like 'national security' or 'public safety', that seems to me to be an inescapable invitation to the courts to exercise their normal function of interpretation without deference to the executive. Hence, contrary to the House of Lords in the *Rehman* case,[59] I believe the courts should have decided that 'national security' could not properly encompass the sort of lateral extension for which the Government contended. Notwithstanding that the term is so inchoate, the dangers of permitting such a wide interpretation should have dictated a narrower reading consistent with the fundamental purpose of protecting the nation as a whole. The danger of course is that the British government has in effect incorporated the political interests (in this case, India's continued control of its conquered territory, Kashmir) into its security apparatus, and is using the might of its immigration powers to punish those who take an opposing view of their homeland's future. Since the people of Kashmir have never been offered a free choice as to their political status, the alignment of the power of British state with military conquest is an affront to the democratic values which that state claims to represent. Whether Britain should recognise India's claim to Kashmir as a matter of foreign policy and international law is a pre-eminent example of a non-justiciable issue; but that is a very different matter from saying that the power of deportation should be used against those who, in these particular circumstances, resist the claim.

The view advocated here implies that courts or tribunals would have to investigate and evaluate claims about the political situation in a given country, but that is no longer a novelty: asylum appeals regularly involve determinations of the likelihood of persecution of particular ethnic or political minorities in scores of nations round the world. This entails intensive scrutiny and extensive evidence of the political situation and attitude of governments and security agencies towards various groups.

However, whether a particular measure is necessary for safeguarding the judicially-inspired interpretation of national security is a matter on which greater deference is due. Thus a decision by the Home Secretary, based on an intelligence assessment that acts undertaken in Britain to further the aims of a particular organisation – for example, personal involvement in a political group's plans to attack opponents, or in training members in military techniques – are so serious as to be detrimental to British national security (as opposed to being a minor irritant), that evaluation should in principle be respected. However – and the importance of this qualification cannot be stressed too much – the judges have a vital role in demanding clear and convincing evidence that the person alleged to have undertaken these activities in fact did so. In abandoning this paramount role of testing factual assertions – the function for which the judicial process is pre-eminently suited – the UK courts in the *Rehman* case did a great disservice to the maintenance of the rule of law.

Finally, I would suggest that a sort of sliding scale should operate, by virtue of which the stronger the right (absolute > qualified > conditional), the more rigorous and intense judicial scrutiny is demanded. When an alleged terrorist faces extended interrogation and police detention – and *a fortiori* imprisonment, internment, or deportation – the constitutional balance of a free society demands a strict judicial control over the exercise of these executive powers. Parliament is too remote to offer any effective response, even it could break free of the shackles of party government, and public opinion is likely to be either unaware or actively hostile to those perceived as threats. But if the judges look the other way, abuse of power, calculated or casual, is sure to follow: the beast grows upon what it has fed.

CODA

In December 2004 the House of Lords, Britain's highest court, gave judgement in an appeal brought by those interned without trial under provision of the anti-terrorism legislation discussed in this article. Sitting as a panel of nine judges, itself a rarity which highlighted the historic importance of the issued involved, it found firmly, with only one dissent, against the Government's legal position. The decision has produced what some newspapers have called a 'constitutional crisis' – a key element of Government policy has been declared unlawful by the courts. For Britain this is a novelty, and the House of Lords – which reversed rulings in the lower courts in the Government's favour – displayed an admirable and, for many, unexpected fortitude in insisting upon the paramount judicial function of protecting statutory human rights.

However, the actual decision turned on a relatively narrow point. Only two judges were prepared to reject the derogation from Art. 5 of the ECHR, a position which would, at least under current conditions, have made detention without trial legally impossible. The central issue was not the legality of internment, but its limitation to non-citizens; in effect the Government had made immigration law the fulcrum of anti-terrorist measures. It was the violation of Art. 14, the non-discrimination clause of the ECHR, that was the Government's undoing. In theory at least, this means that an interment measure that swept up all suspects, citizen and alien, would satisfy the judgment. This is almost certainly politically impossible, as the judges would have been well aware. Thus whilst the decision is to be welcomed and some of the language about the constitutional position of the judiciary in relation to the executive quite encouraging, it is by no means clear whether less crass invasions of human rights in the name of 'national security' or combatting 'terrorism' would meet the same robust judicial response.

NOTES

[1] This essay was completed in the autumn of 2002. Subsequent legal and political developments confirm, in the author's view, the constitutional and policy analysis offered below. Hence no attempt has been made to discuss subsequent judicial decisions or reports of review bodies; any such discussion, if present, would have been for illustrative purposes only.

[2] C. Schmitt, *Political Theology: Four Chapters on the Theory of Sovereignty* (1922) (trans. G. Schwab) (Cambs, Mass., MIT Press, 1986), p. 5.

[3] C. Schmitt, *Die Diktatur* (*Of Dictatorship*), published in 1921. See J. P. McCormick, 'The Dilemmas of Dictatorship: Carl Schmitt and Constitutional Emergency Powers', *Can. J. L. & Jurisp.*, 10 (1) (1997), pp. 163-187.

[4] See especially L. Henkin, *Foreign Affairs and the U.S. Constitution* (2d ed. 1996) (Oxford: Clarendon Press), Part II.

[5] Federalist Papers Nos. 47 and 51 (Penguin ed. 1987).

[6] See the classic study by M. J. C. Vile, *Constitutionalism and the Separation of Powers* (1967), and the extremely useful article by E. Barendt, 'Separation of Powers and Constitutional Government', [1995] *Public Law* 599.

[7] See C. Matthew et al., 'The Franchise Factor in the Rise of the Labour Party' (1976) 93 E.H.R. 723.

[8] For a brief discussion of the origins and prevalence of the national security concept, see L. Lustgarten and I. Leigh, *In From the Cold: National Security and Parliamentary Democracy* (Oxford Univ. Press, 1994), pp. 23-26.

[9] For a good up-to-date description and discussion of the Royal Prerogative and its application to foreign affairs and military matters, see A. Bradley and K. Ewing, *Constitutional and Administrative Law* (13th ed. 2002), chs. 12, pp. 15-16.

[10] See especially the material presented in Henkin, above n. 3. See also H. Koh, *The National Security Constitution* (New Haven, Conn., 1990).

[11] Constitution Act 1867 (the Constitution of Canada), Chap III, ss. 9-16. This of course means in practice the Prime Minister and Cabinet.

[12] Immigration Act 1971, s. 3 (5), read together with s. 15 (3). These are the current form of provisions that have been part of immigration legislation for many decades.

[13] The justification for the present approach is that some imams and preachers are using mosques as places of recruitment, and it is they rather than the mosque or the congregation generally that are the target. However, this distinction is difficult if not impossible to maintain in practice, as was seen in the strikingly analogous Cold War example of the surveillance of Left-wing organisations. The Security Service has long maintained that it was concerned only to keep tabs on members of the Communist Party, and that other members of organisations in which Communists participated (trade unions, nuclear disarmament groups, etc.) came under their scrutiny only in their relations with these targeted individuals. Not only is this hard to credit, it makes little difference to someone whose telephone calls may be overheard or whose movements come under surveillance – the invasion of privacy is in no way diminished.

[14] Examples include vastly expanded powers of arrest and search of people not necessarily suspected on any particular act but of having been 'concerned in' commission or preparation of acts of terrorism; detention for extended periods which only since 2000 has been reviewable by a judge; and several special measures in Northern Ireland, including abolition of jury trials and admission of evidence of the opinions of police officers as 'experts' on the question of the accused's membership in a proscribed organisation. The detention powers in the Act of 2001 are considered later in this essay.

[15] This is of growing importance as the EU moves towards a common asylum policy and uniform extradition rules, which are implemented domestically in this manner. Derogations from the requirements of the ECHR (see below, pp. 27-28) are also enacted this way.

[16] Quoted in A. Tompkins, 'Legislating Against Terror: the ATCSA 2001', [2002] *Pub. Law* 205, 220.

[17] Two notable examples: Part XI of ATCSA had been proposed and withdrawn in the face of parliamentary opposition during the passage of the Regulation of Investigatory Powers Act 2000 the previous year; and Part III, concerning disclosure of information among government departments had been withdrawn in the same circumstances only months before (see *ibid.* at p. 209).

[18] Many important pieces of legislation receive clause by clause consideration in what are known as Standing Committees. However, legislation passed in circumstances of particular urgency, like that discussed in the text, are not considered in this way.

[19] Tompkins, *op. cit.* at 205. See also the comments of the Legal Advisor to the Parliamentary Joint Committee on Human Rights: D. Feldman, 'Parliamentary Scrutiny of Legislation and Human Rights', [2002] *Public Law* 323, p. 346.

[20] The number of the former has recently been substantially reduced but remains at 92, of a total membership of approximately 700.

[21] The Criminal Justice (Terrorism and Conspiracy) Act 1998, passed through a specially-recalled Parliament in two days in response to the worst bombing atrocity in Northern Ireland's history; the Terrorism Act 2000 (the longest of all) and ATSCA 2001.

[22] Burke was an eighteenth century MP and political philosopher, now best known for his critical *Reflections on the Revolution in France* (1790). His 'Address to the Electors of Bristol, 1774' (a small number of propertied men, as it happens) is the most famous expression of this view in English. See his *Speeches and Letters on American Affairs* (London, 1908), p. 68.

[23] Under the accelerated procedure with very limited debate described above at TAN 10.

[24] ATCSA 2001, ss. 28-29.

[25] To be composed of Privy Councillors, who have sworn a centuries-old oath regarded the secrecy of matters of state, and are regarded as particularly reliable and trustworthy. Mostly they are retired politicians or judges.

[26] ATCSA 2001, s. 122.

[27] Australia I believe remains the only significant exception.

[28] A concept which would itself be firmly rejected by many judges, particularly in England.

[29] Chahal v. UK, App. No. 22414/93, Judgment 15th November 1996.

[30] For details see Lustgarten and Leigh, op.cit., pp. 81-84, 159-160, 191-92. This material was cited to the Strasbourg judges in the written submission on behalf of Mr Chahal.

[31] Telephone taps are authorised by a Cabinet Minister, usually the Home or Northern Ireland Secretary; other forms of electronic surveillance by a very senior police officer. There is an oversight mechanism whose effectiveness must be regarded as doubtful, if only because there has never been a successful complaint about telephone tapping in nearly 20 years. The relevant legislation is now found in RIPA 2000, Pt. I and the Police Act 1997, Pt. III.

[32] RIPA ss. 5-6; the Police Act 1997, which authorises bugging, is in similar terms.

[33] See further I. Leigh, 'Taking Rights Proportionately' [2002] *Pub. Law* 265.

[34] Sec. of State for the Home Department v. Rehman, [2001] 3 W. L. R. 877.

[35] [2001] 3 W. L. R. at para. 29, per Lord Steyn approving the judgement of Lord Woolf M.R. in the Court of Appeal.

[36] *Id.*, paras. 50-54

[37] BverfGE 90, 286, Decision of 12 July 1994.

[38] It is not simply the absence of a written constitution that is dispositive, but also the ideology and practice that has grown up around it. I believe that the Canadian courts, having received the UK constitutional traditions, would construe the relevant provisions of the Constitution (above, TAN 10) so as to leave any such dispute to be decided by political actors, i.e. would refuse to entertain any challenge based on excess of executive power in similar circumstances.

[39] And also because, if the earlier one were held to govern, it would in some sense be regarded as superior to the later one, thus enabling one parliament to bind its successors – a logical negation of parliamentary sovereignty as traditionally understood.

[40] HRA 1998, s. 3.

[41] Always excepting the impact of EC/EU law which does not yet extend to the area under discussion, though that may well happen in the near future.

[42] A. Simpson, *In the Highest Degree Odious: Detention Without Trial in Wartime Britain* (Oxford, 1992), pp. 29-30.

[43] R. v. Governor of Wormwood Scrubs Prison, ex p. Foy, [1920] 2 KB 305, quoted ibid.

[44] The UK has operated internment – detention without trial – in both World Wars, the Gulf War, and now under ATCSA 2001. In addition it has operated regional internment regimes in Ireland on many occasions, including briefly in the early 1970s when it was soon abandoned as its notable effectiveness in recruiting new IRA members was recognised. Documentation of the harsh verdict expressed in the text may be found in Simpson, *op.cit., passim*; K. D. Ewing and C. A. Gearty, *The Struggle for Civil Liberties* (Oxford, 2000), chs. 2 and 7; N. Stammers, *Civil Liberties in Britain in the Second World War* (London, 1983), *passim*, and Lustgarten & Leigh *op.cit.*, ch. 7.

These abuses pale behind the wholesale roundup of all persons of Japanese ancestry, regardless of citizenship, and internment into what should be recognised were concentration camps (though of course not extermination centres) in the USA and Canada in the Second World War.

[45] For further discussion of this point, see Lustgarten & Leigh, *op.cit.*, pp. 330-334.

[46] E.g. C. Warbrick, M. O'Boyle, and D. Harris, *The Law of the European Convention on Human Rights* (London, 1995), pp. 12-15; P. van Dijk and G. van Hoof, *Theory and Practice of the European Convention on Human Rights* (The Hague, 3rd ed. 1998), pp. xx.

[47] See above p. 23 for explanation of this terminology.

[48] *Schenk v. Switzerland*, App. No. 10862/84, 12 July 1988), reaffirmed in *Khan v. UK*, App. No. 35394/97, 12 May 2000.

[49] No case involving German or Italian legislation or other measures adopted in the 1970s to deal with domestic terrorism reached the Court, though some were heard and dismissed at Commission level.

[50] For good brief review, see A. Ashworth, *Human Rights, Serious Crime and Criminal Procedure* (London, 2002) pp. 29-30, 51-55.

[51] E.g. *Margaret Murray v. UK*, App. No. 14310/88, 28 October 1994.

[52] In, respectively, *Brogan v. UK*, App. No. 11209/84, 30 May 1989; *Fox, Campbell and Hartley v. UK*, App. No. 12244/86, 30 August 1990, and *Quinn v. Ireland*, App. No. 36887/97, 21 December 2000.

[53] See also *Klass and others v. Germany*, App. No. 5029/71 (1978), a national security case with overtones of anti-terrorism. Surveillance cases fall under Art. 8.

[54] In marked contrast to the experience of Northern Ireland before the current ceasefire, in relation to which a similar derogation was understandably upheld in *Brannigan & McBride v UK*, App. No. 14553/89, 26 May 1993.

[55] *Ibid.*, para. 43, and see also *Marshall v. UK*, App. No. 41571/98, declared inadmissible on 10 July 2001.

[56] See further Ashworth, *op.cit.*, pp. 62-80.

[57] Here there are some exta-curial encouraging sings. In a public lecture delivered on 15th October 2002, the Lord Chief Justice, Lord Woolf, said that it was 'almost inevitable' that the government would infringe human rights as it tried to combat international terrorism, and that the judges, serving as a 'longstop' under the Human Rights Act would have to risk unpopularity to prevent long-term damage to democracy.

[58] (1985) 18 DLR (4th) 481.

[59] Above pp. 20-21.

THOMAS MERTENS

CRIMINAL JUSTICE AFTER 9-11: ICC OR MILITARY TRIBUNALS[*]

1. INTRODUCTION

Nowadays, widespread consensus exists that the dramatic events of September 11 2001 changed not only the country that suffered these attacks, but also the way many in the West view the world outside this exclusive circle. For quite a number, it confirmed Huntington's thesis of a clash of civilizations – a vision of a future of 'us' versus 'them'.[1] But as the attackers were being identified, it became clear that in a sense they came from among us; although technically foreign nationals all, they lived and studied inconspicuously in western, multicultural societies.[2] How are we then to deal with this enemy within? How is democracy to fight this so-called War on Terror[3] and survive? Such questions are obviously not new. Bearing De Tocqueville's assertion in mind that a long war is not needed in order to put freedom at risk in a democratic society,[4] this article, using the technique of a thought experiment, seeks to examine the increased prerogatives that governments – fearing the enemy within – have granted themselves in the realm of criminal law to deal with the perceived threat. This experiment will bring the reader, in a non-specialist way, from the criminal justice system of Germany to the possible role of an operational International Criminal Court, and from the criminal justice system of the United States to military tribunals as a means of dealing with what those in power claim is an extraordinary threat.

2. AN IMAGINARY CASE: CRIMINAL JUSTICE IN GERMANY AS 'RECHTSSTAAT'

One of the frontlines of the so-called war on terrorism is the legal one: those responsible "must be brought to justice".[5] What follows is an attempt to envisage the path this legal battle might take.[6] The main actor in this legal fantasy is Osama Bin Laden. Suppose he were to surface in Europe one of these days, say in Germany. He had managed to escape Tora Bora and the Afghan-Pakistan border long ago and, after much wandering along drug and migrant trafficking routes had ended up in Europe. He has assumed a new identity, built a new life inside the Fortress Europe, but as restrictions on the level of pressure that may be exerted on captured Al-Qaeda suspects are lifted, the intelligence agencies of the West – now co-operating like never before – gain information as to his whereabouts.[7] He is in Germany. Since the

281

Meggle (ed.), Ethics of Terrorism & Counter-Terrorism, 281-300.

Security Council has declared that the attacks of September 11 constituted a threat to international peace and security,[8] and although the German Government has not been allowed an insight into the evidence against Bin Laden, it is willing to accept that he is the mastermind behind the attacks. Germany's border control officers arrest Bin Laden as he attempts to flee the net encircling him. By doing so, Germany also fulfills its duty as a loyal member of NATO, as Article 5 of the NATO-treaty has been invoked. How could this highly implausible story continue?

According to the rule of law, the German Government could not immediately put Bin Laden on a plane to the United States – washing their hands of a most embarrassing detainee – but must hold him in custody in a safeguarded penitentiary awaiting a request for his extradition. Although there are a number of extradition treaties between the US and Germany, a request by the US Government for Bin Laden's extradition would not in fact be so simple a thing. Germany is a state party to the European Convention on Human Rights (ECHR) and to its Protocol VI, which forbids the administration of the death penalty.[9] These commitments on the part of State Parties to the ECHR played an important role in a case that took place some time ago.[10] An American NATO-serviceman stationed in The Netherlands had killed his wife in The Netherlands and had been arrested. The US requested his extradition based on the NATO-Status Treaty. That Treaty gives primary jurisdiction to the sending State for this crime.[11] To prevent his extradition to the US he successfully appealed to The Netherlands's obligations under Protocol VI, Art. 1 to the ECHR: "The death penalty shall be abolished. No-one shall be condemned to such penalty or executed." That State Parties of the ECHR cannot extradite those in their detention to trial in countries where they are likely to face torture or inhuman and degrading treatment has been a mainstay of the Council of Europe legal order since the now-famous *Soering* judgment.[12]

Bin Laden's lawyers naturally call upon this important precedent. Additionally, it is argued that it is highly unlikely that their client will face a fair trial after all that has been said about him in the media. Article 6 of the ECHR requires that: "Everyone charged with a criminal offence shall be presumed innocent until proved guilty according to law" – a stipulation, it is alleged, that the US Government could not fulfill; even outside the US it is now received opinion, endlessly repeated, that Bin Laden and Al-Qaeda planned and carried out the 9/11 attacks. Finally, his lawyers argue that since September 11 the standard of civil liberties in the US has deteriorated significantly: hundreds of people are now detained without trial (contrary to the right of *habeas corpus*)[13] and the confidentiality principle between lawyer and client – so integral to the integrity of the justice system – is no longer respected, as such conversations and correspondence are now intercepted.[14] In fact, there are a number of interesting terror related extradition cases currently underway, highlighting the difficulties regarding extradition of suspects from Germany to the US.[15]

According to the thought experiment, the German courts show themselves fairly immune to political pressure, whether from the German Government or from the European Union eager to rebuild bridges with the US. And in the light of the above, it is fair to suppose that the request by the US for the extradition of Bin Laden would be refused. The German Government cannot but obey the ruling of the court and ends up with Bin Laden in its custody. So, what next for the world's most infamous terrorist?

3. SCENARIO ONE: ICC

Let us imagine that the German Government turns to the International Criminal Court (ICC), in an attempt to see Bin Laden charged with crimes against humanity. The German authorities argue that the 9/11 attacks fit exactly the definition of Article 7 of the Rome Statute: "Crime against humanity means murder when committed as part of a widespread or systematic attack directed against any civilian population"[16] and as anticipated by Article 14 (1) of the Statute.[17] This description of the crime would fit the rhetoric of President Bush himself, that the attacks on his nation constituted an attack on civilization itself. Moreover, in his taped addresses to the world, Bin Laden has repeatedly called for an attack on all Americans without prejudice.[18] For such crimes was the ICC established.

If the German Government chose to turn Bin Laden over to the ICC, it would opt for a court that was established by the Rome Statute, signed by 120 states (now 139) in 1998 and thus reasonably representative of the international community as a whole. The treaty establishing the ICC came into force, however, only in July 2002, following ratification by 60 states (now 92). To be sure, the ICC has no retroactive force and can only try new cases. In this thought experiment, the German Government holds that the principle of *nulla poena sine lege* is nonetheless respected as although the attacks predate the establishment of the court, the statute itself had already been signed.[19]

In addition, the German Government maintains that the crimes with which Bin Laden is charged were already, prior to the Rome Statute, illegal under international law. The definition of crimes against humanity, over which the ICC now has jurisdiction, was found in existing positive law, such as treaties (the Genocide and Geneva Conventions), precedents (decisions and rules of the Nuremberg- and Tokyo-tribunals, and those of the more recent Yugoslavia- and Rwanda-tribunals), customary law and prevailing legal opinion (what some would call 'natural law'). Often, as in the Eichmann trial,[20] the issue of an international court has been raised in relation to crimes against humanity. With the high profile trial of Bin Laden the ICC would have the opportunity to establish its reputation. Germany turns over Bin Laden to the ICC in the Dutch city of The Hague, which prepares to host the first major international trial of the 21st century.[21]

The difficulties connected with an extradition to the US, such as the likely imposition of the death penalty and the near-certainty of a lack of fair trial and due process are thus resolved. But a new major problem arises. It is unclear whether the ICC has jurisdiction, since it does not have universal jurisdiction automatically. There are a number of grounds upon which the ICC can try a case (Art. 13), for example, where the Security Council demands prosecution in its powers under Chapter VII, where a State Party refers a case and where the prosecutor initiates his or her own investigation. However, admissibility is governed by the principle that the national state of the accused or the state where the crime took place has the right to investigate and try the suspect first; the ICC thus has jurisdiction only if the state of which the suspect is a national fails to prosecute[22] – being either unable or unwilling –, or if the state within whose territory the crime is committed waives its jurisdictional rights (Art. 17(1)(a)). It is unimaginable, even in this flight of fancy, that the countries involved will defer their own jurisdiction in favor of the ICC. The decision of Saudi Arabia in 1994 to strip Bin Laden of his nationality has apparently left him stateless[23] and it is unlikely that any state will claim Bin Laden as one of its nationals in order to give the ICC jurisdiction. Nor is it conceivable that the state in which the crimes were committed would waive its jurisdiction. The US, as is well known, opposes the ICC vigorously.[24] Moreover, the US veto on the Security Council ensures that this body will not make the appropriate request granting the ICC jurisdiction.

Yet, the Court can determine that a state is unwilling or unable to try a suspect and waive the principle of complimentarity, where it judges that national proceedings "were not or are not being conducted independently or impartially" (Art. 17(2)(c)). It is highly unlikely, however, although not inconceivable that the Court would, on the same grounds that gave the German courts such cause for alarm, hold that the US could not offer Bin Laden an independent or impartial trial and assert their own jurisdiction. Such boot-strapping is not unusual for international tribunals; the International Tribunal for the Former Yugoslavia (ICTY) had to face similar hurdles in *Tadic*,[25] and successfully answered the questions about its jurisdiction.

Moreover, the German Government argues that the US Government should be consistent: having supported the ICTY, it must support the ICC as well. *Prima facie*, this might seem a weak argument, but the attacks of September 11 and the continuation of horrific attacks on civilian populations around the world underline the necessity of ongoing international cooperation, not only as far as information and intelligence sharing are concerned, but also in the field of criminal law. If the Bush administration explicitly states that it considers these attacks to constitute a crime against humanity, it should, so it is argued, allow those accused of masterminding the attacks to be tried by humanity. Moreover, it is worth noting that Al-Qaeda is accused of more crimes than those committed in New York and Washington. As the whole of the international community is increasingly affected, the US cannot claim precedence over the rights of other countries to try the network's mastermind and the truly international scope of Al-Qaeda's reach means that the ICC is again the only place where justice for all their victims can be done.

Germany is determined to see that such justice be done and hands Bin Laden over to the ICC in The Hague, relying upon the Dutch Government's commitment to international law despite the difficulties this may cause them. In 2000 the US passed the so-called 'The American Servicemembers' Protection Act', designed to protect "US military personnel and other elected and appointed officials (...) against criminal prosecution by an International Criminal Court to which the US is not a party".[26] The Act authorizes the president "to use all means necessary and appropriate to bring about the release of US personnel or other parties held by the ICC" (Section 8 a). Accordingly, were the Court to claim jurisdiction on the grounds suggested above, it is not beyond the bounds of imagination to foresee a US raid on The Netherlands to free our suspect from the captivity of the ICC were the wishes of the US Government to be disregarded.[27]

4. CRIMINAL JUSTICE IN THE US POST-9/11: GENERAL SITUATION

For Bin Laden to find himself in the custody of the Americans, any number of events may have occurred. Imagine that German state officials do not respect the rule of law. Either the authorities hand Bin Laden directly over to the Americans, perhaps to the US troops stationed in Germany, or, more shockingly, decide that political and not legal arguments must prevail and put him on a plane to the States in contravention of the ruling of it's own courts.[28] Whichever route he has taken, Bin Laden is in US custody, facing trial in a criminal justice system that has changed radically over the course of the last few years.[29] The principal changes can be summarized in three categories: measures in relation to domestic security, measures concerning the treatment of suspects of terrorism – this category consisting mainly of detainees taken into captivity during the Afghan war – and finally the institutionalization of military commissions or tribunals, most likely to be charged with trying Bin Laden.

4.1 The domestic legal system

In Bush's legal war against terrorism, the most important change on the domestic front is the 'USA Patriot Act' (2001), an acronym for 'Uniting and Strengthening America by Providing Appropriate Tools Required to Intercept and Obstruct Terrorism'.[30] This act aims to enhance domestic security and does so by introducing more than 1000 provisions concerning surveillance procedures on all kinds of international money transactions, border control, criminal laws against terrorism, and information coordination.

At the core of this Act stands a broad definition of 'terrorism' targeted specifically at non-US citizens. It gives greatly enhanced powers to both domestic law enforcement and domestic and international intelligence agencies, and eliminates the checks and balances that previously gave the judiciary the opportunity to review the operation of such powers. If the attorney general has reasonable grounds for suspecting an alien of terrorism or aiding terrorism broadly defined, he may detain that person for seven days without any charge. If he then finds 'the release of the alien will threaten the national security of the United States or the safety of the community or any person', this detainee may be held in custody for a much longer period, indeed, indefinitely. As a result, newspapers report regularly upon the detainment of several hundred of people by the US Justice Department without conviction or based on minor charges unrelated to terrorism.[31] Thus, as an alien under the Patriot Act, it is suggested that Bin Laden might be subject to indefinite detention without trial, held incommunicado, at the direction of the attorney-general.

The most important argument in favor of such legislation as the Patriot Act says that the protection of individual rights, like liberty and privacy, cannot come at the cost of the safety of society as a whole. The attacks of September 11 suggested the need to find a new balance between basic rights and security, the latter being the prime objective of the leviathan. The US Constitution, along with certain rights guaranteed to all individuals,[32] should not become a suicide pact. Securing the homeland, following such reasoning, justifies the enhancement of the executive's powers and the corresponding reduction of the procedural rights of alleged criminals.

In his important series of articles examining the state of this balance post-9/11, Ronald Dworkin acknowledges the importance of security, yet argues that it is misleading to speak of finding a new balance between risks and rights, between security and liberties. The question is not where our interests lie, he writes, but what justice requires. As a principle, government must treat everyone as of equal status and with equal concern, since every human life has a distinct and equal inherent value.[33] This requires that a system of criminal law shall treat all equally in equal cases. If the system denies to one class of suspects rights that it considers essential for others, it acts unfairly. A system that nevertheless aims at doing so (as does the USA Patriot Act by specifically targeting non-US citizens) has to meet the following two requirements, so Dworkin argues. First, it must have the candor to admit that it is treating one class of suspects unjustly because of security reasons. Second, it must reduce this injustice to the absolute minimum by allowing only the smallest curtailment of traditional rights possible.[34] The new legislation does not meet these two essential conditions. It rather testifies to the Bush administration's general attitude of putting American safety first, at the expense of what Dworkin calls the international moral order that nations should respect even under threat.[35] As a threat to US security, Bin Laden would undoubtedly find himself in special custody. Arguably, however, it would not suit the Bush administration to keep Bin Laden in indefinite detention. Bush stated that the perpetrators of September 11 had to be brought to justice. What kind of justice would that be?

4.2 Foreign Nationals detained during the War on Terror

To imagine the most likely scenario of Bin Laden in US custody, it would be helpful to look at the fate of those already held in US custody. The second element of the US's legal war against terrorism concerns the treatment of those foreign nationals captured in the course of the war on terror, mainly in Afghanistan and now in Iraq. Bin Laden would surely be the most important detainee of the War on Terror, but he is not the first. From the perspective of international law, matters seem quite clear: the treatment of detainees in any armed conflict is governed by international humanitarian law.[36] The US considers itself at war and if one understands the attacks of September 11 as the occasion of that war beginning, anyone arrested (read: taken prisoner) in connection with this war must be treated in accordance with the laws laid down in the Geneva Conventions. The designation of the actions of Al-Qaeda, except where members participate alongside more conventional armed forces in, say, Afghanistan or Iraq, as constituting part of an international conflict is obviously a controversial interpretation,[37] but one which can turn to the designation by the Security Council of the events of 9/11 as a threat to international peace and security for support.[38] Moreover, the Appeals Chamber of ICTY in its *Tadic* ruling set a standard for an armed conflict protected by the Geneva Conventions as "protracted armed violence between governmental authorities and organized armed groups".[39] It can be argued that the regular terror attacks claimed by members of the Al-Qaeda network in the period before and since September 11 meets the definition of 'protracted'. Although contentious, it is thus alleged that Bin Laden has been detained in a situation of international armed conflict.

Since we are dealing with a situation of war, most relevant here are the Third and Fourth Geneva Conventions,[40] dealing with the protection and treatment of captured combatants during an international armed conflict – those entitled to Prisoner of War (POW) status – and with persons involved in an armed conflict who can not aspire to the high level of protection granted POWs, such as civilians, respectively. These two conventions aim at providing a certain status to every person involved in an armed conflict. Article 5 of the Third Convention thus reads as follows:

> "Should any doubt arise as to whether persons, having committed a belligerent act and having fallen into the hands of the enemy, belong to any of the categories enumerated in Article 4,[41] such persons shall enjoy the protection of the present Convention until such time as their status has been determined by a competent tribunal."

Thus, all those arrested or taken prison are considered POWs until determined otherwise by a 'competent tribunal', whereupon they are either confirmed as such or fall under the protection of the Fourth Convention regarding civilian persons.[42] According to the Commentary of the authoritative International Committee of the Red Cross, these articles ensure that nobody in enemy hands can fall outside the law. The category of 'unlawful combatant' is not part of the Geneva Conventions' regime.

This, of course, does not mean that those falling under these two Conventions, protecting POWs or civilians, cannot be tried by a court martial or a criminal court. The taking up of arms against the enemy during war does not in itself constitute a criminal offence. The question of *ius in bello* is not connected to the matter of *ius ad bellum* and thus the fact that hostilities were not announced by the organizers or perpetrators of the 9/11 attacks prior to them, does not affect their status once captured. Nonetheless, POW status does not protect a person from being charged with war crimes, crimes against humanity or common crimes; nor are persons granted civilian status under the Fourth Convention free from prosecution for such offenses. According to convention provisions, however, both civilians and POWs must receive a fair and regular trial and each detainee is entitled to "the essential guarantees of independence and impartiality as generally recognized".[43]

The US authorities have not followed this generally accepted interpretation of the Geneva guarantees. From the outset, Secretary of Defense Rumsfeld declared that the detainees were, as he labeled them, 'unlawful combatants' without rights under the Geneva Conventions.[44] Those taken into custody by the US Army were transferred to Guantanamo Bay, a small Cuban strip that is legally speaking not part of US territory.[45] For that reason, those detainees cannot appeal to ordinary American courts, for example, for a writ of habeas corpus, and standards guaranteeing a basic level of detention conditions are not applicable.[46] This decision has been severely criticized, and the US Government has in the meantime moderated its position by distinguishing between Taliban Government forces and Al-Qaeda fighters,[47] and by promising to treat them humanely, "in a manner that is reasonably consistent with the principles of the Third Geneva Convention, to the extent that they are appropriate".[48] Only recently, the US Supreme Court has decided to take on four terror-related cases, two of which relate to the indefinite detention of non-US citizens at Guantanamo and the two others relate to the power of the President to designate US citizens as enemy combatants. Hearings are supposed to start shortly, with a decision foreseen for this summer.[49]

While this concession to international criticism mitigates the earlier decision, there are several good reasons why the decision not to apply the standards of the Geneva Conventions is not simply unlawful, but unwise. Firstly, decisions on what status detainees should be granted must be decided by a court on an individual basis, as the US Government did during the First Gulf War, and not by way of classifying a whole group of persons; secondly, deviating from the Geneva system will work as a dangerous precedent and have adverse effects for all combatant parties including the American army;[50] thirdly, circumventing international humanitarian law in order to obtain valuable information from imprisoned 'terrorists' is of no avail, since the duty to abstain from torture and inhuman and degrading treatment does not follow from this alone, but also from other sources of legal guarantees.[51]

Thus, in conclusion, Bin Laden in US custody finds himself in a country in which the protection of domestic civil liberties for US citizens, but most especially for aliens, has been restricted to a considerable degree. He himself will be denied the protection of the Geneva Conventions. The refusal to apply the normal standards of either peacetime or war is justified by the contention that fighting terrorism is an exceptional situation, very different from both 'ordinary' situations of armed conflict and peace time, and that the rules of the legal game have to be changed accordingly. This battle against terrorism demands new instruments, of which 'military commissions' or 'military tribunals' constitute the third element of this experiment. Bin Laden would very probably have to face justice in the form of such a commission.

4.3 Scenario Two: Military Tribunals

Although some have suggested the contrary,[52] the concept of 'unlawful combatants', used for the Guantanamo detainees, cannot be found in the Geneva Conventions, neither explicitly nor, it is argued here, implicitly. The concept has a uniquely American different origin, a point that will be elaborated below.

Nothing in the war on terrorism has provoked as much criticism as Bush's 'Military order of November 13, 2001 – Detention, Treatment, and Trial of Certain Non-Citizens in the War Against Terrorism'.[53] Based on "an extraordinary, national emergency", this Presidential order declares that any individual who is not a US citizen and whom the President reasonably believes to belong to Al-Qaeda or to be engaged in acts of terrorism, must be placed under the control of the Secretary of Defense and be tried exclusively by a military commission, established by the Secretary of Defense and without application of "the principles of law and the rules of evidence generally recognized in the trial of criminal cases in the United States district courts".[54] The suspects shall be detained "humanely" by the Defense Department until their trial before a military commission, a body composed of military officers. This commission admits all evidence "as would have probative value to a reasonable person", but proceeds in a manner which is consistent with the protection of classified information. Conviction will follow upon the concurrence of two-third of the members of the commission, to be followed by a sentence that may include the death penalty. Only the President or the Secretary of Defense can review this conviction. The possibility of remedy "by any court of the United States or any State thereof, any court of any other nation or any international court" is explicitly excluded.

After fierce criticism, the Defense Department promulgated, on March 21, 2002, an order in which the most extreme provisions have been removed: it introduces the presumption of innocence until a suspect is proven guilty beyond reasonable doubt; the possibilities for legal advice are extended; a unanimity vote is required for a death penalty; some kind of appellate review is introduced although still not by any domestic or international court; under certain circumstances, any such trial would be open to journalists and the public.[55] These revisions constitute real improvement and a step in the direction of a fair trial, but reason for suspicion remains.[56]

Dworkin, for example, has argued that the public status of the trials is still dubious, since it might easily be held behind closed doors (even barring the accused himself), if classified and classifiable information is presented to the court, and any possibility of appeal to civilian courts is still lacking. Even under these new procedural rules, an accused might be tried in secret and sentenced to death "on evidence that neither he nor any other outside the military has even heard".[57] In addition, the Pentagon's chief lawyer has stated that the government might not even release accused terrorists who were acquitted by such a tribunal "if they were thought to be dangerous".[58] This renders the effectiveness of these tribunals fully dependent on the executive, and their existence seems to violate one of the corner stones of the rule of law, the separation of the executive and the judiciary. These tribunals do not arguably constitute a court at all but are merely an extension of the powers of the President, who acts either personally or through the officers he commands as prosecutor, judge, jury, and appeal judge.

It is essential to distinguish these tribunals or commissions from the institution of military courts or court-martials, which are common in many legal systems.[59] There are good reasons for having this sort of military justice. Sometimes, for example in times of war, there is a need for rapid adjudication near the battlefield, based on specialized knowledge. Even when war is not imminent, the differences between the military world and the civilian may justify the existence of specialized courts, which take seriously the demands of strict authority relationships, discipline, restricted privacy and the use of lethal weaponry. Importantly, the fact that these courts exist, does not necessarily affect the quality of the trial itself. Generally, it is held that the US military justice system respects basic principles of fairness.[60] And if it adjudicates its own soldiers in a fair way, nothing stands in the way of adjudicating by way of the same procedures foreign soldiers who are accused of committing crimes.[61]

The military commissions have their roots in American history. Military commissions are connected with the distinction between legal and illegal combatant. While legal combatants can indeed be tried before an ordinary court or a court-martial, illegal combatants may not be. These commissions have been used repeatedly by the US in times of war. They were used during the American Revolution by George Washington, during the Mexican-American War in the mid 19th century and especially during the Civil War, where there may have been as many as 4000 military commissions. This institution created the possibility of trying and convicting people who would otherwise have been released by civil courts, not because of their innocence but because of the sympathies of the jurors.[62]

During the Civil War period, the use of these commissions was contested. In '*Ex Parte Milligan*',[63] Lamdin Milligan was convicted by a commission for serious offenses, including violation of the laws of war, while aiding the Confederacy. His conviction was overturned by a unanimous Supreme Court, which argued that he, as a citizen of a non-seditious state, could not be tried by a military tribunal and that regular courts were available to hear his case, in full respect of the Fifth and Sixth Amendment. The Supreme Court said:

> "[U]ntil recently no one ever doubted that the right to trial by jury was fortified in the organic law against the power of attack. It is now assailed. [T]his right – the most valuable in a free country – is preserved to every one accused of crime who is not attached to the army, or navy, or militia in actual service."

Thus, the jurisdiction of the military could not be extended beyond those who were actually serving in the military, to the civilian world outside.[64] The Supreme Court also argued, although without unanimity, that only Congress, and not the President, could authorize detention without trial.[65]

In order to justify the recent order, however, the government relies upon a later Supreme Court decision in which the use of military commissions was upheld. This is the now well-known '*Ex Parte Quirin*' case.[66] In 1942, eight Nazi saboteurs, one of them named Richard Quirin, landed on American shores in order to commit acts of sabotage. Mainly through deliberate negligence and by supplying the FBI with information, the saboteurs, none of them committed Nazis, were arrested without having caused any damage. President Roosevelt, however, demanded that these men be tried before a military commission and refused them access to a civilian court.[67] The aim was that their trial be held quickly and in secret. Furthermore, the prestige of the FBI would be protected and the American public assured that their coastlines were well protected. The saboteurs were accordingly convicted by a military commission and sentenced to death. The men's lawyers contended before the Supreme Court that the military commission violated the US constitution and the precedent set by the *Milligan* decision, and requested a new trial. The Supreme Court, however, upheld the legitimacy of the military commission, arguing that the situation in the *Milligan* case was entirely different from that of *Quirin*. The Court held that

> "by universal agreement and practice the law of war draws a distinction between (...) those who are lawful and unlawful combatants. Lawful combatants are subject to capture and detention as prisoners of war by opposing military forces. Unlawful combatants are likewise subject to capture and detention, but in addition they are subject to trial and punishment by military tribunals for acts which render their belligerency unlawful."[68]

Today, it is '*Ex Parte Quirin*' that is cited as precedent.[69]

This decision is widely regarded, however, as unsuitable to serve as such an important precedent. It is overtly reverential to the government[70] and the then-

Supreme Court, operating in the tense period of World War II, did not have a good record on civil liberties.[71]

The most likely fate for Bin Laden were he to fall into American hands and not suffer summary execution would be trial before such a military commission, followed by the imposition of the death penalty. Following the closure of our thought experiment, the consequences of trying Bin Laden before a military commission, both in terms of practical advantage and of justice, will be considered. The Bush administration holds indeed that a category of 'illegal combatants' must be distinguished from the categories of ordinary POWs and ordinary criminals. Like the German saboteurs, terrorists are illegal combatants who sneak behind enemy lines, conceal their military affiliation and have no regard for the laws of war. Since terrorists thus violate the laws of war, they are to be tried before a special commission. Such a principled stance, it is argued, also has a number of practical advantages: in a trial by military commissioners, there is no risk of a jury being intimidated by terrorists; confidential and classified material, essential for the war on terrorism, need not be disclosed to the general audience, but is only made available for the vetted commissioners; the risk of lengthy, time consuming procedures is minimal and the trial will not provide a platform for terrorist propaganda; in sum, one should accept flexibility with regard to the characterization of a fair trial.

Many commentators do not find this principled stance or the practical advantages asserted very convincing. They argue that there seems to be no practical necessity to resort to military commissions. In the past, ordinary civil courts have successfully tried terrorism cases, such as that of Timothy McVeigh or that of the 1993 attacks on the World Trade Center. Legislation exists to successfully accommodate both the government's wish for secrecy and the requirement that the accused be able to confront the evidence against him. Likewise, legislation has served to protect the identity and security of jurors in criminal cases against organized crime.[72] An ordinary trial might indeed be more time consuming, but this is what procedural justice requires. Moreover, it is not evident that a long trial will serve propaganda purposes: does the Serbian nationalist cause benefit from Milosevic being able to tell his 'truth' in The Hague?[73] What would be the most effective way to neutralize Bin Laden? To have him tried, convicted and executed after a secret trial which would assure him of hero status in the eyes of many, or to subject him to a demystifying trial which would reveal not only the morally appalling consequences of his deeds, but also his and his organization's hypocrisies and cruelties? An ordinary criminal trial against Bin Laden would not focus on a so-called clash of civilizations, but simply on the 'mens rea' for the commission of a crime against humanity. It would reduce Bin Laden "to human stature".[74]

To the implausibility of the so-called practical advantages of military commissions many practical disadvantages can be added. Convictions reached by these commissions might easily lack sufficient credibility, especially outside the US.[75] This institution devaluates the earlier US critique of similar courts in other countries and makes any future critique look hypocritical.[76] The use of these commissions will undermine the willingness of other countries to extradite suspects[77] and aggravate the tension that already exists between the US and other countries because of the Order's neglect of international standards for due process, as embedded in Articles 14 and 4 of the International Covenant on Civil and Political Rights, and due to divergent views on the death penalty.

Whether sufficient legitimation for military commissions exists does not depend entirely on the lists of practical pros and cons. The argument in principle is decisive, and that centers on the question of whether it is legitimate to distinguish between legal and illegal combatants. If acts of illegal combatants such as terrorists differ in essence from ordinary criminal acts and from ordinary war crimes, than this distinction is valid and prosecuting them before a military commission with restricted procedures, justified. But the main flaw in this reasoning is the question of *quis judicabit*. One cannot prosecute suspects before such a military commission unless there is convincing evidence that they indeed committed the atrocious acts that would characterize them as illegal combatants. The decision to try them before a military commission effectively declares them to be illegal combatants. Yet it should precisely be the commission's task to establish whether or not they are 'illegal combatants', guilty of 'unlawful belligerency' or not. The use of military commissions violates the presumption of innocence. This flaw was apparent in '*Ex Parte Quirin*': the reason why the saboteurs were refused a trial by jury was that they were accused of being 'illegal combatants'. Despite their denial – at least two of them claimed that they were present on these missions solely to escape from Germany – they were nonetheless turned over to a military tribunal and convicted. Although their determination as illegal combatants did not necessarily entail conviction, it reduced their opportunity to prove their innocence because of the procedural restrictions applied. The institution of military commissions does not respect the principle that criminal procedural rules should be designed in such a manner that the risk of convicting someone who is innocent be as low as possible.[78]

While the proponents of military commissions might admit such flaws, they would stress that the sort of terrorism seen on 9/11 is something completely new. As it has changed the world, it must change our standards of fairness. In ordinary criminal procedures and in ordinary court-martials, it is rightly assumed that it is better to set a hundred guilty persons free than to convict one single innocent person, and to accept the risk involved in this balance.[79] With regard to terrorism, it is alleged that we simply cannot afford to take such risks. It is no longer, the proponents argue, an acceptable policy to let to the guilty go free for fear of punishing the innocent. A different balance must be found between the security needs of society and the protection of the rights of the accused.[80] In this new era, it is, regrettably, better to convict an innocent person than to let a terrorist go free.[81] Such an argument plays on understandable fears and thus seems stronger than it really is. If the argument is turned around and one asks whether it would be acceptable to convict and sacrifice a hundred innocent people in order to 'neutralize' one terrorist, the answer is less evident. If however indeed national security requires the curtailment of the rights of the accused – an argument not necessarily accepted –, the government should aim at curtailing them as little as possible, and it should publicly acknowledge that by doing so it acts unfairly.[82]

5. CONCLUSION

This piece is a thought experiment indeed. However, the likely outcome of Bin Laden in US control is clear. Yet the reason as to why the authorities would pursue a course so widely condemned, even by staunch allies[83] and US citizens,[84] and which would not necessarily bring the practical advantages claimed, remains to be examined. It would be too easy to presume on the part of the US Government an unwillingness to listen to good arguments and to attribute to the latter bad faith with regard to due process and fair trial.

The preference in the US for military commission justice arguably stems from two interconnected reasons. Firstly, there exists a basic difference in the way in which the US and Europe have traditionally regarded international law.[85] This is clearly formulated by Habermas in his assessment of US policy both in Kosovo and, recently, in the second Iraq War in identifying the dual elements of pursuing national interests and of promoting human rights at the base of US policy. With regard to actions in Kosovo, Habermas wrote that the US "conceives the international enforcement of human rights as a national mission of a world power which pursues this goal according to the premises of power politics. Most of the EU Governments see the politics of human rights as a project committed to the legalization of international relations."[86] While the EU stresses the need to embed human rights in international law, the US is rather distrustful of international law and remains committed to its own standards. In connection with the recent Iraq War, Habermas took a stronger stance and initiated the engagement of leading European intellectuals to formulate a European answer to what he understood as American unilateralism.[87]

Secondly, this division has been intensified by the way in which the attacks were and are perceived on either side of the Atlantic, and by differing views as to the best means to address this new threat. While Europeans do not deny the magnitude of the events of September 11, they are not (yet) fully convinced of a fundamental transformation in the nature of international relations. For the US it seems, the entire nature of the world they inhabit has changed; Condoleezza Rice spoke of a shifting of the tectonic plates of international politics.[88] Much of course has been written and said on the different approach of the Europeans and the Americans to international relations since 2001 and it does not need repeating here; there is however a clear connection between the different understandings of the attacks and the different approaches to criminal justice for those caught up in these new hostilities. In his now well-read article 'Power and Weakness', one of the Bush administration's house intellectuals Robert Kagan contrasted the Promethean tasks faced by the US in the real world of international anarchy with the European view of an ideal world regulated by binding international law.[89] The disagreement, according to Kagen, boils down to an opposition between Kant and Hobbes. Kagan writes:

> "It is time to stop pretending that the Europeans and Americans share a common view of the world, or even that they occupy the same world; Europe is entering a post-historical paradise of peace and relative prosperity, the realization of Kant's Perpetual Peace. The United States, meanwhile, remains mired in history, exercising power in the anarchic

Hobbesian world where international law and rules are unreliable and where true security and the defense and the promotion of a liberal order still depend on the possession and the use of military might."[90]

This would indeed, if a fair characterization, explain much of the different attitudes revealed in the thought experiment.[91]

Hobbes' political vision is not the comforting story of a government dedicated to protecting a wide range of natural rights or to promoting 'life, liberty and the pursuit of happiness', but the discomforting story of a government whose legitimacy is derived solely from its capacity to guarantee its citizens' safety and self-preservation.[92] In order to make this plausible, as we all know, Hobbes sketches a miserable picture of the state of nature, in which the life of man is solitary, poor, nasty, brutish and short. The foundation of the 'leviathan'[93] brings an end to this miserable situation, but it does so only temporarily. The world remains a dangerous place and the leviathan's safety is permanently threatened from the inside by disobedient acts, but is at risk especially from the outside, by acts that aim at destroying the bonds of the leviathan itself. There is, so to speak, always the possibility of an 'emergency situation'. The concept of 'illegal combatants' would seem to fit well into Hobbes' vocabulary: these warriors aim at destroying civil society; they live in the state of nature, where civil laws, both domestic and international, do not apply. If they are captured, leviathan does not need to grant them any rights: it may treat them humanely, but it is under no obligation to do so.

Kant never accepted so 'realistic' an interpretation of concepts such as the 'state of nature' or the 'social contract'. The latter does not give us a historical explanation of the state, but informs us of how the state ought to be, according to Kant.[94] He did not fear so much the return of the state of nature after the establishment of the leviathan, but the continuation of the state of nature between a plurality of 'leviathans' or between 'leviathans' and 'outlaws', illegal combatants or terrorists in other words. This state of nature can only be brought to an end when these sovereigns form a League of Nations in which their conflicts can be resolved peacefully; the failure to form such an association will see them and their leaders place themselves above the law. The leviathan is thus not threatened by the return of the illegal combatant, but by the absence of international law, which makes these 'leviathans' themselves illegal combatants. International law, including international criminal law, must prevent that by considering all 'individuals and states as citizens of a universal state of mankind'.[95]

Although military commissions and the ICC are juxtaposed by the differing visions of world order underpinning those that promote them, there is yet a commonality between the two individuals who have provoked this discussion. When concluding his September 20th State of the Union, President Bush expressed his confidence that God would watch over the United States of America. From the taped statements he has released, Bin Laden is apparently also fully convinced, using similar rhetoric, that Allah is on his side. Both invoke their ultimate 'Sovereigns'. Here lies the real danger, namely that in changing our societies according to the perceived needs of security, we face turning Kantian open societies into Hobbesian fortresses, and nothing will then in the end distinguish democracy from fundamentalist societies.[96] The fundamentalist Bin Laden may lose the legal battle, but he will win the political war if his opponents mirror fundamentalist values by accepting the view that this war is a clash between two equally justified leviathans.

NOTES

[*] This article was first published in the *German Law Journal* 5 (2004) 5, 545-568. I would also like to thank Aleksander Pavković and Morag Goodwin in particular.

[1] S. Huntington, 'The Clash of Civilizations', in: *Foreign Affairs* 1993 (72), 22-49; B. Tibi, *Fundamentalismus im Islam*, Darmstadt, 2000.

[2] Those who carried out and provided the logistical support for the 9/11 attacks had studied in Germany, the United States, lived in the UK etc.; similarly, those accused of the Madrid bombings have been present in the country for a number of years and were registered at universities there.

[3] According to President Bush, the 'war on terrorism' is a 'war' on many fronts: foreign governments will have to choose between supporting the war on terrorism or not; terrorists' financial networks will be dismantled; the military will be on the highest alert for a just battle; internal, domestic safety will be increased by a set of legal measures; and the perpetrators of these random killings and of the attack on civilization will be brought 'to justice'. Taken from Bush's State of the Union Address 9 days after the attacks: J. W. Edwards and L. DeRose (eds.), *United We Stand – A Message for All Americans*, Ann Arbor, MI 2001.

[4] A. de Tocqueville, *Democracy in America* (ed. and with an introd. by Harvey C. Mansfield and Delba Winthrop), Chicago UP, 2000, 621.

[5] Bush, *op. cit., supra* n. 3.

[6] When this paper was first conceived the courts had yet to provide guidance as to the course they intended to follow; the recent days of course have seen the German courts make their mark in the war on terror gratifyingly similar to the lines envisaged here. *Infra*, n. 15.

[7] J. Lelyveld, 'In Guantanamo', in *The New York Review of Books*, November 7, 2002, quoting an officer: "If we put them in the Waldorf Astoria, I don't think we could get them to talk."

[8] Security Council Resolution 1368 (2001); 12th September 2001.

[9] In his 'Unsere Erneuerung. Nach dem Krieg: Die Wiedergeburt Europas', in: *Frankfurter Allgemeine Zeitung*, May 31, 2003, Habermas cites the abolition of the death penalty as one of the defining elements of European identity.

[10] NJ 1991, 249 (Short) (Dutch Case Law).

[11] Nato Status Treaty, Art. VII (3).

[12] *Soering v. UK* (1989); available at http://hudoc.echr.coe.int/hudoc/ The *Soering* case is particularly pertinent as the applicant – a German national accused of the murder of his girlfriend's parents – faced the death penalty if convicted in the US; the Court did not conclude that the death penalty *per se* was contrary to the provisions of Article 3 but rather held that the manner in which it was imposed or executed or the conditions of detention whilst awaiting execution were two factors that may, dependent upon the circumstances of the case, constitute a breach of Article 3. The severity of the conditions in which detainees in Guantanamo Bay are kept leaves little doubt that the threshold of inhuman and degrading treatment would be met, even without the allegation that torture is a regular tool of interrogation there.

[13] Article 5 ECHR; Article 9 ICCPR, and the 5th Amendment to the US Constitution.

[14] Provisions of the Patriot Act and the changes it brought are considered in more detail below.

[15] M. Hartwig, 'The German Federal Consitutional Court and the Extradition of Allegedged Terrorists to the United States', in: 5 *German Law Journal*, no. 3 (2004). On the recent overturning of alleged terrorist convictions by the German Federal Criminal Court, see: http://www.rferl.org/featuresarticle/2004/3/ 76BF1BD9-921B-4DDB-A5BC-28CC94328693.html; news.bbc.co.uk/1/hi/world/europe/ 3592857.stm.

[16] In this respect, one can allege that the 9/11 crime falls into the same category as the assassination of 8,000 Kurdisch civilians in Halebja in 1988 or that of 7,000 Muslims in Srebrenica in 1995, to mention only couple of examples. It almost goes without saying that so far states have been far more efficient in the killing of innocents than any terrorist organisation. That Bin Laden should be tried on the charge of crimes against humanity is also suggested by G. Robertson, *Crimes against Humanity – The Struggle for Global Justice* (2nd edition) Harmondsworth 2002, 507-510.

[17] "A State Party may refer to the Prosecutor a situation in which one or more crimes within the jurisdiction of the Court apper to have been committed requesting the Prosecutor to investigate the situation ..."

[18] See e.g. Y. Bodansky, *Bin Laden – the man who declared war on America*, New York 2001(1999), 279-80. See also his Declaration on *The International Islamic Front for Jihad against Jews and Crusaders*, at February 23, 1998: '... to kill the Americans and their allies – civilian and military – is an individual duty for every Muslim ...'. See: http://www.fas.org/irp/world/para/docs/980223-fatwa.htm.

[19] A claim that places the German Government admittedly in direct contravention of Art. 11(1) of the Rome Statute.

[20] H. Arendt, *Eichmann in Jerusalem*, Harmondsworth 1994 (1963), 269, concurring with previous similar comments by K. Jaspers.

[21] A salient but often forgotten detail in this context is the fact that ideas of an international criminal court as it functioned for the first time in Nuremberg do not originate from (the context of) the Second World War and the Charter of London, but rather from the First World War. After Germany's defeat, an international tribunal was pursued, in particular to try the German emperor (under the slogan 'Hang the Kaiser', Treaty of Versailles, sec. 227-9). At that time, the Dutch Government objected. By not extraditing the German emperor, who fled to The Netherlands, and calling upon its neutrality, The Netherlands obstructed this first step towards international criminal justice. See e.g. T. Bowder, *Blind Eye to Murder*, London, 1995 (1981), 17-19; G. Robertson, *Crimes against Humanity, op. cit., supra* n. 16, 225-6.

[22] Robertson, *op. cit.*, supra n. 16, 350. This is the principle of complementarity.

[23] The story of the Saudi authorities stripping Bin Laden of his citizenship was carried by the BBC (http://news.bbc.co.uk/hi/english/world/middle_east/newsid_1599000/1599088.stm; 14th October 2001) However, an international arrest warrant for Bin Laden posted on the interpol website in 1998 lists his nationality as Saudi Arabian. http://www.interpol.int/public/Wanted/Notices/ Accessed 15th April 2004.

[24] Even though many argued that it is exactly the principle of complementarity that "offers a greater protection to American personnel than current international practice and/or status of forces agreements that uphold a sovereign nation's exclusive jurisdiction to try and punish offences committed by persons of any nationality within its borders", United Nations Association of the United States of America, http://www.unausa.org/dc/advocacy/iccfact.htm. In connection with this: this principle would render obsolete the notorious and at first secret appendix B (granting immunity to NATO personel from any form of arrest) to the unsuccessful Rambouillet-negotiations preceeding the Kosovo war.

[25] Tadic Case (*Prosecutor v. Dusko Tadic*) 1995, International Criminal Tribunal for the former Yugoslavia, The Hague, published on the internet at: http://www.un.org/icty/tadic/appeal/decision-e/51002.htm.

[26] http://www.unausa.org/dc/advocacy/iccfact.htm.

[27] Additionally, the Act forbids any cooperation with the ICC, on the level of intelligence cooperation, like handing over classified national security material (Section 6) on the level of physical extradition of suspects to the ICC (Section 4 c), and on the level of military support to countries that do recognize the ICC (Section 7 a). The US tries to circumvent the ICC's jurisdiction by means of bilateral agreements, on the basis of article 98 of the ICC Statute: "The Court may not proceed with a request for surrender or assistance which would require the requested State to act inconsistently with its obligations under international law with respect to the State or diplomatic immunity of a person or property of a third State, unless the Court can first obtain the cooperation of that third State for the waiver of the immunity."

[28] Possibly using the slogan: "Fac et excusa" (act first and justify later), as, for instance, cited by I. Kant, *Perpetual Peace – A Philosophical Sketch*, in: *Kant's Political Writings* (ed. H. Reiss), Cambridge UP, 1970, 120. Moreover, for the German government's 'disappointed' reaction to the FCC's ruling on Mounir El Motassadeq's case, see http://www.bundesregierung.de/-,413.616894/pressemitteilung/Schily-Entscheidung-ist-zu-bed.htm.

[29] See also: W. E. Scheuerman, 'Rethinking Crisis Government', in: *Constellations* 2002 (9), 492-505.

[30] New anti-terrorist legislation has also been implemented in countries like the UK, France and Germany, and in the EU as a whole. On Britain's detention camp under this legislation, see: http://observer. guardian.co.uk/waronterrorism/story/0,1373,1106664,00.html.

[31] E.g. S. Taylor Jr., 'Congress Should Investigate Ashcroft's Detentions', in: *The Atlantic Monthly*, May 28, 2002; R. Dworkin, 'The Threat to Patriotism', *New York Review of Books*, February 28, 2002. Today, such harsh detention regimes are also being applied to US citizens, like José Padilla, see e.g. R. Dworkin, 'Terror & the Attack on Civil Liberties', in: *New York Review of Books*, November 6, 2003.

[32] Supreme Court decision 2491, 2500 (2001), in 'Zadvydas v. Davis' evidences that "the Due Process Clause applies to all 'persons' within the United States". (Fifth Amendment: "no person shall be held to answer for a capital, or otherwise infamous crime, (…) without due process of law".) See also: R. Dworkin, 'The Threat to Patriotism', *ibid.*; ACLU letter to Secretary of Defence Rumsfeld, January 15, 2002: http://www.aclu.org/NationalSecurity/NationalSecurity.cfm?ID=9301&c=111.

[33] E.g. R. Dworkin, *Freedom's Law – The moral reading of the American Constitution*, Oxford 1966, 10, 25; Dworkin, 'Terror & the Attack on Civil Liberties', *op. cit., supra* n. 31.

[34] Dworkin, 'The Threat to Patriotism', *op. cit., supra* n. 31.

[35] See: Dworkin, 'Terror & the Attack on Civil Liberties', *op. cit., supra* n. 31.

[36] The question of the applicability of the Geneva Conventions in the War on Terror is controversial and has been the subject of vast amounts of print. The conflicts in Afghanistan and Iraq are clearly international armed conflicts and, as all are parties to the Geneva Convention, the conclusion suggested here is that the Geneva Conventions as well as customary international humanitarian law apply in full; as McDonald and Sullivan note, international humanitarian law must be interpreted in light of the principles thereof, such as the Martens Clause of 1899, and that such guiding principles ensure the applicability of the Geneva Conventions even in types of conflict previously unseen, such as a so-called War on Terror. McDonald and Sullivan, 'Rational Interpretation in Irrational Times: The Third Geneva Convention and the "War on Terror"' (2003) 44, *Harvard Journal of International Law*, 301. While the Bush administration clearly disagrees, they have failed to provide a legal reason upon which they base their decision, asserting instead that the Conventions are simply no longer relevant in this not-so-brave new world. See also: http://www.icrc.org/Web/Eng/siteeng0.nsf/0/C82A7582AE20DCD1C1256D34004AEA41/$File/George+A ldrich_3_final.pdf?OpenElement.

[37] According to the State Department, Al-Qaeda is "not a state party to the Geneva Convention; it is a foreign terrorist group". US Department of State Policy Document, *Status of Detainees at Guantanamo*, Feb. 7, 2002, http://www.state.gov/p/sa/rls/fs7910pf.htm.

[38] Security Council Resolution 1368 (2001); 12th September 2001, Para. 1.

[39] *Op. cit., supra* n. 25. Noëlle Quénivet, 'The "War on Terror" and International Humanitarian Law'; available at http://www.ruhr-uni-bochum.de/ifhv/news/Tashkent_Speech%20Quenivet.pdf.

[40] It is assumed, for ease, that it is accepted by all that Additional Protocols I and II have not attained the status of custom and thus do not apply (the US is not a signatory and nor are any of the parties against whom it considers its enemies). The application of the Protocols effects the definition of combatant but will not be considered here.

[41] Third Convention's Article 4 enumerates: "A. Prisoners of war are … 1. Members of the armed forces…; 2. Members of other militias and members of other volunteer corps, …, provided that … (they) … fulfil the following conditions: (a) That of being commanded by a person responsible for his subordinates; (b) That of having a fixed distinctive sign recognizable at a distance; (c) That of conducting their operations in accordance with the laws and customs of war. 3. Members of regular armed forces who profess allegiance to a government or an authority not recognized by the Detaining Power. 4. Persons who accompany the armed forces without actually being members thereof, …; 5. Members of crews (…) who do not benefit by more favourable treatment under any other provisions of international law. 6. Inhabitants of a non-occupied territory, who on the approach of the enemy spontaneously take up arms to resist the invading forces, without having had time to form themselves into regular armed units, provided they carry arms openly and respect the laws and customs of war. B. The following shall likewise be treated as prisoners of war under the present Convention: …"

[42] Or: 'protected persons', see: J. Cerone, 'Status of Detainees in International Conflict, and their Protection in the Course of Criminal Proceedings', in: *The American Society of International Law Insights*, http:// www.asil.org/insights/insigh81.htm.

[43] Fourth Convention, Article 3; see also Third Convention, Article 84.

[44] See e.g.: http://www.armed-services.senate.gov/statemnt/2001/011212wolf&rums.pdf; see also: http://www.us-mission.ch/press2002/0802detainees.htm.

[45] At the time of writing, some 650 persons from around 42 countries are being held there.

[46] In order to have the lawfulness of their detention tested by the court.

[47] This distinction might not work since some argue that Al-Qaeda was part and parcel of the Taliban Government, Robertson, *Crimes against Humanity, op. cit., supra* n. 16, 478, 480, 496. See also: Article 75 Geneva protocol I (ratified neither by the US nor by Afghanistan, but nevertheless regarded as customary

law). For a different view, see: A. Roberts, 'Counter-terrorism, Armed Force and the Laws of War', in: http://www.ssrc.org/sept 11/roberts_text_only.htm. Also published in: *Survival* 2002 (44).

[48] US Department of State Policy Document, *Status of Detainees of Guantanamo, op. cit., supra* n. 37.

[49] T. Mauro, High Court at Crossroads, in: http://www.law.com/jsp/article.jsp?id=1076428374712; D. Cole, Goodbye, Menschenrechte, in: http://www.zeit.de/2004/17/Essay_Cole.

[50] Indeed, the US Government is quick to demand the application in full of the Geneva Conventions where its personnel are involved in quasi-legal situations. The capture of Army Chief Warrant Officer Michael Durant in the course of a US operation against the Somali warlord Mohamed Farah Aideed – a non-state party to the Conventions – saw the US Government demand that his treatment be consistent with the provisions of the Third Convention. Details taken from McDonald and Sullivan, *op. cit., supra* n. 36, who note futher: "If the Geneva Conventions are binding on Somali warlords, non-state parties must be granted the same protection", 310.

[51] Despite White House legal Counsel Gonzales's leaked memo that modern terrorism 'renders obsolete strict limitation on questioning of enemy prisoners', quoted in: S. Taylor Jr., 'We Don't Need to Be Scofflaws to Attack Terror', in: *The Atlantic Online*, February 5, 2002. See not only: Third Convention, Art. 17, but also Universal Declaration of Human Rights, Art. 5; International Covenant on Civil and Political Rights, Art. 7; Convention against Torture and Other Cruel, Inhuman or Degrading Treatment or Punishment. The latter prohibits in its Art. 2 (2) the use of torture under emergency situations. Moreover, McDonald and Sullivan argue persuasively that Art 17 of the Third Convention does not prevent interrogation and suggests that the authorities could have interviewed detainees without needing to deprive them of POW guarantees. *Ibid.*

[52] S. Taylor Jr., 'We Don't Need to Be Scofflaws to Attack Terror', *ibid.*; J. Lelyveld, 'In Guantanamo', in: *The New York Review of Books*, November 7, 2002. A. Roberts, 'Counter-terrorism, Armed Force and the Laws of War'.

[53] Federal Register, Vol. 66, No. 222, 57833-57836; See also: A. Arato, 'The Bush Tribunals and the Specter of Dictatorship' (2002) 9, *Constellations*, 458-463.

[54] It could be argued that this order establishes some sort of rival to the International Criminal Court itself, since it seems to aim at anyone connected to terrorism among the more than 20 million non-citizens in the US and all others in the rest of the world, see: American Civil Liberties Union (ACLU), *Memorandum on Military Tribunals*, November 29, 2001, 4.

[55] Department of Defense, Military Commission Order No. 1, March 21, 2002.

[56] http://news.bbc.co.uk/1/hi/world/americas/3334823.stm.

[57] R. Dworkin, 'The Trouble with the Tribunals', in: *The New York Review of Books*, April 25, 2002.

[58] Dworkin, 'The Trouble with the Tribunals', *ibid.*; see also: J. Lelyveld, 'In Guantanamo', *op. cit., supra* n. 52.

[59] C. L. Eisgruber and L. G. Sager, 'Military Courts and Constitutional Justice', see: http://www.utexas.edu/laws/news/colloquium/papers/Sager-Eisgruber.doc; see also: Robertson, *Crimes against Humanity, op. cit., supra* n. 16, 502, 508.

[60] C. L. Eisgruber and L. G. Sager, 'Military Courts and Constitutional Justice', *ibid.*, 5, referring to Supreme Court's Weiss v. United States, 510 US 163 (1994); A. Neier, 'The Military Tribunals on Trial', in: *The New York Review of Books*, February 14, 2002.

[61] Article 102, Third Geneva Convention. Of course, fighting a war itself is not a criminal offense, as the important difference between a soldier and a criminal is acknowledged.

[62] J. Dean, 'Military Tribunals', see: http://writ.news.findlaw.com/dean/20011207.html, and J. Wallace, 'Military Tribunals', see: http://www.spectacle.org.

[63] 71 US (4 Wall.) 2 (1866).

[64] Statement of T. Lynch, Cato Institute, before the Senate Judiciary Committee. http://www.cato.org. It seems as if 'Milligan' allows only two kinds of justices: civil justice for civilians and military justice for those serving in the armed forces. Some argue that the critical stance of the Supreme Court in Milligan could have been prevented by better legal counsel on the part of the government, see: J. Dean, 'Military Tribunals', *ibid.*; R. G. McCloskey, *The American Supreme Court*, (3rd Edition) Chicago 2000, 71-3.

[65] This point was not unimportant as it is related to the fact that there was no official declaration of war or act of Congress on which the President could rely. US Constitution, Art. 1, Section 8, Para 11.

[66] 317 US 1 (1942). For extensive details of the case, G. Cohen, 'The Keystone Kommando's', in: *The Atlantic Monthly*, February 2002; Furthermore, the government relies upon '*Johnson v. Eisentrager*', a 1950 decision in which a *habeas corpus* petition filed by German nationals seized in China and held in a

U.S. prison in Germany was denied by a court, the justices refusing to exert jurisdiction. See: T. Mauro, 'High Court at Crossroads', in: http://www.law.com/jsp/article.jsp?id=1076428374712.

[67] Roosevelt's Proclamation of July 2, 1942: 'Denying Certain Enemies Access to the Courts of the United States', in: Federal Registrar 1942, p. 5, 103, quoted in: A. Roberts, Counter-terrorism, Armed Force and the Laws of War, *op. cit., supra* n. 47.

[68] Quoted in: J. Wallace, 'Military Tribunals', *op. cit., supra* n. 62. The Hague Convention would then protect only the former, but not the latter.

[69] See e.g. A. Neier, 'The Military Tribunals on Trial', *op. cit., supra* n. 60.

[70] See e.g. R. Dworkin, 'The Threat to Patriotism', *op. cit., supra* n. 31.

[71] Only two years later, the Supreme Court upheld the internment of Japanese Americans, in: Korematsu v. United States, 323 US 214 (1944). In the Yamashita case, 327 US 1 (1946), the Supreme Court upheld the legitimacy of the military commission trying the Japanese Commander of the Philippines Yamashita. In this case too, the court held that procedural protections were not available to enemy combatants. Two justices dissented here. Justice Murphy argued that the due process right mentioned in Fifth Amendment applies to all persons and that this was not respected in this case. Justice Rutledge argued that hearsay evidence of all type was admitted here which would have been excluded in a US court, and he complained that the universal protection of fair trial was violated. See: J. Wallace, 'Military Tribunals', *op. cit., supra* n. 60. Moreover, the Supreme Court was unnecessarily hasty in its *Quirin* decision, giving judgment only one hour after oral arguments had closed

[72] American Civil Liberties Union (ACLU), *Memorandum on Military Tribunals*, under III.

[73] Cf. T. Judah, 'The Star of The Hague', in: *The New York Review of Books*, April 25, 2002.

[74] Robertson, *Crimes against Humanity, op. cit., supra* n. 16, 509; One might also reconsider Hannah Arendt's thesis on the banality of evil, in: H. Arendt, *Eichmann in Jerusalem, op. cit., supra* n. 20.

[75] Neier, 'The Military Tribunals on Trial', *op. cit., supra* n. 60.

[76] 'Fact Sheet: Past US Criticism of Military Tribunals', see: http://www.hrw.org/press/2001/11/tribunals1128.htm; American Civil Liberties Union (ACLU), *Memorandum on Military Tribunals*, under V; Neier, 'The Military Tribunals on Trial', *ibid.*

[77] Neier, 'The Military Tribunals on Trial', *ibid.*

[78] 'As low as possible', since a criminal trial exemplifies only imperfect procedural justice: it seems impossible to design the legal rules in such a way that they always lead to the correct result, namely that a defendant is declared guilty if, and only if, he is guilty, in line with: J. Rawls, *A Theory of Justice*, Oxford 1971, 85.

[79] In the past, however, many death row cases testified to the opposite.

[80] L. H. Tribe, 'Trial by Fury', in: *The New Republic*, December 10, 2001, quoted in: Dworkin, 'The Threat to Patriotism', *op. cit., supra* n.31.

[81] J. Wallison, 'In favor of military tribunals', see: http://www.csmonitor.com.

[82] R. Dworkin, 'The Threat to Patriotism', *ibid*; C. L. Eisgruber and L. G. Sager, 'Military Courts and Constitutional Justice', *op. cit., supra* n. 59.

[83] The detention of British citizens in Guantanamo Bay placed real pressure on the so-called 'special relationship', although much of it behind closed doors. See: http://observer.guardian.co.uk/international/story/0,6903,1096508,00.html.

[84] Among others: S. Hoffmann, 'On the War', in: *The New York Review of Books*, November 1, 2001; T. Judt, 'America and the War', in: *The New York Review of Books*, November 15, 2001.

[85] Cf. the American attitude towards the Kyoto protocols and the Johannesburg summit. The US has not ratified many widely supported conventions, such as the conventions regarding land mines, prohibiting discrimination against women, protecting the rights of the child and the Additional Protocols to the Geneva Conventions. Robertson, *Crimes against Humanity, op. cit., supra* n. 16, 87; J.E. Alvarez, 'Do Liberal States Behave Better? – A Critique of Slaughter's Liberal Theory', in: *European Journal of International Law* 2002 (12), 183-246.

[86] J. Habermas, 'Bestiality and Humanity', in: *Constellations* 1999 (6), 269.

[87] J. Habermas & J. Derrida, 'Unsere Erneuerung. Nach dem Krieg: Die Wiedergeburt Europas', in: *Frankfurter Allgemeine Zeitung*, May 31th 2003.

[88] F. Fitzgerald, 'George Bush & the World', in: *The New York Review of Books*, September 26, 2002.

[89] See also: T. Judt, 'Its Own Worst Enemy', in: *The New York Review of Books*, August 15, 2002. See also the GLJ Kagan symposium, September 2003, http://www.germanlawjournal.com/past_issues_archive.php?show=9&volume=4.

[90] R. Kagan, 'Power and Weakness', in: *Policy Review* 2002 (113), 1; fortunately for the Europeans, Kagan adds that 'the US is a Behemoth with a conscience, a liberal, progressive society through and through'. The article was followed by a book *Of Pradise and Power* (New York, 2003), which added little to the main thrust of the argument. For an interesting comment on Kagan: D. Runciman, 'A Bear Armed with a Gun', in: *London Review of Books*, April 3, 2003.

[91] In his recent 'America's Crisis of Legitimacy' (*Foreign Affairs* 2004 (83), 87), Kagan mildly modified his position, arguing that '... Americans will need the legitimacy that Europe can provide ...'.

[92] See: e.g. L. Strauss, *Natural Right and History*, Chicago 1950, 181.

[93] Th. Hobbes, *Leviathan*, Ch XVII: 'The great LEVIATHAN, or rather, to speak more reverently, (...) that mortal god to which we owe, under the immortal god, our peace and defence.'

[94] I. Kant, *Reflexionen zur Rechtsphilosophie*, Akademie Ausgabe, Vol. XIX, 504 (No. 7740, see also: 7737).

[95] I. Kant, *Perpetual Peace – A Philosophical Sketch*, 98-99.

[96] For a similar line of thinking, see: R. Rorty, Post-Democracy, in: *London Review of Books*, April 1, 2004.

RALF GROETKER

LOOKING FOR MOHAMMED: DATA SCREENING IN SEARCH OF TERRORISTS

It's a well-known story. An ethnographer is visiting natives in the jungle and wants to take pictures of them. But they refuse, believing that the camera will take away something – something immaterial, but nevertheless important. Isn't it the same with informational privacy? Someone takes our name – a combination of letters – or our address, and puts it into a box, which happens to be a computer. What must happen, in order that putting someone's name or addresses into a box becomes a problem? – I will address this question by concentrating on the case of "data screening" or "Rasterfahndung" – which is a computerized search for wanted persons by means of descriptive profiles.

I. WHAT IS "DATA SCREENING IN SEARCH OF TERRORISTS"?

a. Metaphors of Screening

Two things come to mind when one thinks of "Rasterfahndung" – of raster scan, of data screening in search of criminals. The first thing is a scanning device – like a virus scanner, a sieve, filter or a net. Or, better, a crawler, crawling through a vast sea of data. Originally, a "raster" has been a system a parallel lines, etched onto a plate of glass for the purpose of printing. A "rastral" was a device for the making of lines on a sheet of music-paper. On a Dutch picture of such a rastral, dating from 1614 (which shows up if one is looking for "rastral" in "google"-for-pictures), the device is surrounded by an inscription. It says: "Aequabilitate" – constantly, with uniformity. Data-screening works in the same manner. The search goes on constantly, with uniformity. And often secretly.

The other thing often associated with "screening" is a medical image: The procedure of a quasi-bodily intervention or operation, a surgery, an *informational interference, an interference on personal rights*. Wolf-Dieter Narr, Professor for Political Sciences at the Free University Berlin, puts it this way:

> "In the information society, there can be mastery, without that bodies
> are being touched. That this calls for a new form of right and of
> protection, was the great insight of the judges who declared the
> "Volkszählungsurteil", the census-jurisdiction, in 1983."[1]

This idea of a quasi-physical interference has a great appeal. It goes back to Samuel D. Warren's und Louis D. Brandeis' essay "The Right to Privacy" from 1890. They write:

G. Meggle (ed.), Ethics of Terrorism & Counter-Terrorism, 301-318.
© 2005 Ontos, Heusenstamm.

"[M]an, under the refining influence of culture, has become more sensitive to publicity, so that solitude and privacy have become more essential to the individual; but modern enterprise and invention have, through invasions upon his privacy, subjected him to mental pain and distress, far greater than could be inflicted by mere bodily injury."

Thus, from the very beginning, the debate on privacy referred to a bodily injury as a model for the kind of harm caused through the intrusion into the personal sphere.

To sum up these two relatively vague ideas: Data screening is something like a quasi-corporeal injury, an injury of a rather ethereal or mental sort. And it is something going on automatically – like a virus-scan on the computer. It works in the background – but with so much conformity and regularity that no set of data will be left out. No-one will not be concerned.

b. Definition and examples

The method of profile searches has been developed in the early 1970ies in West Germany. It was – and still is – called "Rasterfahndung". The "Rasterfahndung" as a legal and social construct exists only in Germany. There is, for sure, no direct English or French translation for the word "Rasterfahndung", even though some of countries might engage in practices that are quite similar to a "Rasterfahndung".

One of the key aspects of the "Rasterfahndung" is that it involves data-flows from the private sector to the government. One of the most often cited examples of a "Rasterfahndung" in Germany is in fact *not* a "Rasterfahndung". When Hans-Martin Schleyer was held hostage by members of the Red Army Fraction (RAF) in 1977, the police headquarters initiated a kind of "pattern search" to find the kidnappers. Horst Herold, the chief of the Federal Criminal Agency, the Bundeskriminalamt (BKA), reasoned that the kidnappers would use an apartment in a modern, rather anonymous building, close to the highway. Herold thought that the apartment should be located in a distance not more than twenty kilometres from where the kidnapping took place, on the left side of the Rhine – because he didn't expect the kidnappers to take the risk of being caught in a control while crossing one of the very few bridges. The method worked out. The police found the place where Schleyer was kept. But the message was lost in the huge mass of calls and telegraphs in those days.

In fact, the search for Hans-Martin Schleyer meets only two of the three characteristics of the "Rasterfahndung". It involved the use of the computer – a machine much feared back in the seventies –; and it was a search not for a concrete person, but for a "pattern". The target was "a modern apartment building, close to the highway". But still, it was a search in the real world – not in a data-base. Therefore it was not a "Rasterfahndung".

"Rasterfahndung" is defined by the following three characteristics:

1. It is a search for non-determined persons, rather than for a particular individual that is known by name.
2. It is based on the computer.
3. It relies on data-bases that are not already in the possession of the police.

A few examples. In 1979 the German police used the "Rasterfahndung" to spot RAF-terrorists. They searched the data from electricity-clients in Frankfurt. The assumption was: Terrorists must be people who, when renting an apartment for the purpose of a conspiracy, whish to stay anonymous. Therefore they will pay in cash. They will also not be registered as the owner of an automobile or a driver's licence. They will not receive social funds for families. After sorting out the data, there where only two persons left on the list. One was a drug-dealer, the other one a RAF-Terrorist, Rudolf Heißler.

The "Rasterfahndung" also was applied in the war against drug-traffic. The police controlled flight passengers from Asia, who stayed in Europe just for a few days und who where travelling alone. With this method, about 350 drug-couriers were arrested; drug-traffic between the BRD and China and Malaysia almost stopped for a while.

After September 11, Germany initiated a "Rasterfahndung" to find potential terrorists. Related techniques were used in the USA – for instance the screening of flight passengers. That search relied and still relies on two different strategies:

a. The data is searched for interesting *relational* features: Are there passengers who paid with the same credit card, but booked different seats?

b. The search also relies on *indexical* features – it points out individuals whose data is in the "neighbourhood" of bad guys who are known by name.

Special software has been developed for this kind of searching, for instance by the American company "Systems Research & Development" (SRD). SRD developed a software called "NORA". NORA is a tool for "Non-Obvious-Relationship-Awareness". Normally data-mining tools like NORA are applied to detect gambling fraud, unusual patterns in credit-card usage, or to test the expected financial credibility of a client. But as pointed out, not only patterns are deteted. NORA has access to files from the FBI and from the Office of Foreign Asset Control (OFAC) of the U.S. Department of the Treasury, which is responsible for the ordering and the control of sanctions against rogue states. More than 4.000 data-sources flow into NORA; data from more than one million people, according to SRD-CEO Jeff Jones, are stored. NORA checks, if a given person is somehow related to a person on the bad guy list, if he has lived close to his home, has a similar phone number, ID-Number – or name.

One further point: Systems like NORA can be installed in the US, because there are not too many restrictions on the flow of information from private companies to the government and vice versa. Just read what Choice Point, one of the leading companies in that industry, says about itself on its website www.choicepoint.net:

"ChoicePoint Public Records Group provides access to billions of public records. [...] Through instant online screening services, comprehensive background checks and drug testing, ChoicePoint is well positioned to meet the varying employment needs of its corporate customers. It compiles a comprehensive report on an individual including current and previous addresses, relatives, assets, corporate involvement ..." (cf. EPIC (2002)).

Looking at these examples, a general question emerges. How *should* data flows, especially flows from the private sector to the government, be regulated? – There are several arguments that have to be considered.

II. WHAT'S WRONG WITH DATA SCREENING?

One initial assumption is that data-screening poses problems, because it involves the computer. Horst Herold, the former chief of the Bundeskriminalamt (BKA), says:

> *"The murderer as a height about 1,80 m, he has black hairs and works as a baker. He lives in a small town in southern Germany.* As these features do apply to a lot of persons, out of which the real suspected one must be filtered out, the search is difficult for the police. If one describes the sum of the features as as "Raster" (pattern), then the "Rasterfahndung" is probably as old as the fight against crime."

Herold also says: "Modern technology has no other impact as that the search in non-governmental data-bases can be done faster." We should wonder if that is true: If the only difference between a computer-aided search and a conventional search is the speed by which the search is conducted.

In skipping through the arguments pro and contra data screening, I will start with one major distinction, which refers to the two set of metaphors mentioned in the beginning. I propose to distinguish arguments that deal with costs that arise for particular persons on the one hand, and arguments that deal with the burden to society as a whole on the other. To put it roughly: The factor 'costs for particular persons' is expressed by the image of a clinic surgery, while harm to society as a whole is rather symbolized by the figure of the crawler. Considering the possibility of harm to the individual, I will again distinguish between two groups of arguments: arguments dealing immediately with informational privacy and arguments that point to other effects of data screening.

Dangers of screening

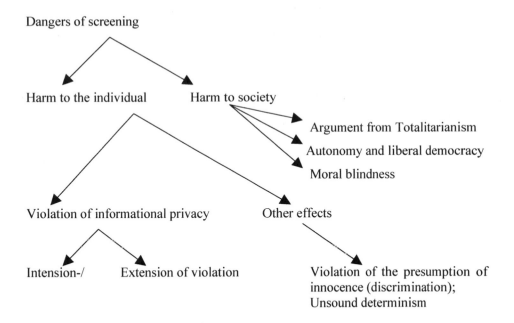

Harm to the individual

Harm to society

Argument from Totalitarianism

Autonomy and liberal democracy

Moral blindness

Violation of informational privacy

Other effects

Intension-/   Extension of violation

Violation of the presumption of innocence (discrimination); Unsound determinism

First, the arguments dealing with harm to the individual, but not with informational privacy.

Argument from the persecution of the innocent. Critics often say that computer-aided preventive search is problematic because it violates the presumption of innocence. Of course, this applies also to Horst Herold's baker. If the police searches all bakers in south Germany, with black hair and a height of about 1.80 meter sure there will be lots of innocent people bothered by the police. Among the group of people who are in possession of all the relevant properties, there will be some innocently suspected. From this, one can conclude both: that even a conventional search is an unreasonable intrusion into personal affairs – or that data screening is not any more harmful than conventional searches are.

But there is still one further difference between data screening and a conventional search that has to be considered. A screening or a "Rasterfahndung" is often not initiated, because a concrete criminal is suspected to be among a certain group of people, but because a certain group of people bears features that make them susceptible of being criminals – as was the case in the search-campaign after 9/11. Of course, in principle this strategy could also be pursued relying on purely conventional methods.

The difference between a conventional search and a search based on data screening is not a difference in principle, but in degree.

But still, the evaluation of the dangers of computerized profile searches has to be considered in relation to those of conventional searches. Data screening is regarded as being a softer intrusion into the personal sphere than a conventional search: No policeman is ringing at your door. And being a member of the raster-group doesn't necessarily imply that one is suspected of being guilty. Without the "Rasterfahndung", the proponent of the method says, much more people would have to endure searching. On the other hand: The search for profiles or patterns would hardly be affordable without the methods of modern, computer-aided data processing. In the end, data screening doesn't cause a reduction, but a proliferation of searches.

Besides the discussion about respective merits of conventional and computer-aided search methods regarding the presumption of innocence, there are other aspects to be considered.

A minor one is the *Argument from unsound determinism*. In some cases, profiles or patterns rely on a too deterministic conception of human nature. Well-known and crude examples for this from the history of criminology are for instance the works by Cesare Lombroso (*The Criminal Man,* 1876; *Crime: Its Causes and Remedies*, 1899) or later, by the German neurologist Johannes Lang (*Verbrechen als Schicksal: Studien an kriminellen Zwillingen*, 1929; cf. Nass (1981)). Both constitute attempts to trace the roots of crime back to biology. Today we face other questions: Is someone, who, after 9/11, wishes to baptise his child "Osama" (as it happened in Cologne), susceptible of committing a terrorist crime? The general outline of the question is clear. If a pattern is grounded on unsound scientific evidence, then a search that relies on that pattern is simply unlikely to have success. Those searches should not be conducted, be it for moral or for economic reasons.

A much broader scope of considerations is tangled by the *Arguments from autonomy, freedom and informational privacy*, which relate to the judicial issues of personal rights and personal freedom. This complex is what the metaphors of a quasi-bodily interference or operation mentioned above hint at. "Freedom" is a point that needs to be more closely considered. I propose to distinguish between the *extension* and the *intension* of "freedom". By "extension" I mean the group of people, whose freedom is concerned. Referring to the searches after 9/11, there are several candidates. We can distinguish between the freedom of individuals

— who are suspected of being a "sleeper" (that is, individuals who are regarded as potentially being a potential criminal: This is what "being potentially a sleeper" sums up to);

— who are suspected of being an ordinary, actual criminal (that is, individuals, who are regarded as potentially being a real criminal);

— whose data are being used in course of a search.

— The whole population, on which a search is conducted.

On the other hand, there are different "intensions" or different degrees of freedom:

Freedom of action. "Freedom" means, in its most obvious sense, freedom to act. Data screening, it is argued, is diminishing this freedom. How can that happen? The issue here is discrimination. If there is discrimination, then people will probably behave in a certain way to avoid being discriminated against. They will adapt. Those who are discriminated against, on the other hand, are violated in their freedom: they are not free anymore to behave as they want to, without feeling commented on, without having to fear oppressions. This might have severe effects on the system of democracy. Jutta Limbach, former President of the German Verfassungsgericht, puts it this way:

> "A democratic cultures is sustained by its citizens' willingness to engage and to express their opinions. This presumes fearlessness. Fearlessness might get lost, if the government starts to biometrically measure its citizens, to data-raster them and to electronically persecute their movements. [...] A "Rasterfahndung", which is applied without concrete suspicion and which follows a general search-pattern, probably has rather stigmatising and humiliating effects. Such a measure is more apt to create enemies than to detect sleepers." (Limbach 2002)

Freedom as autonomy. But "freedom" can mean more than freedom of action. Freedom can also mean self-determination or autonomy. Self-determination can be diminished even when freedom of action still is intact. The text of the German 1983-legislation concerning the "Volkszählung" refers to both aspects, conventional freedom and autonomy, in two passages, one following closely upon the other. The first passage resembles the words of Jutta Limbach: "Who cannot be sure that his participation on an assembly or a citizens-initiative is registered by the state (...) will maybe not participate." (Bundesverfassungsgericht 1983) Close by, one finds the other passage concerning *autonomy*, with the famous phrase in it that citizens "have a right to be informed about who knows what about them on which occasion" – "wer was wann und bei welcher Gelegenheit über sie weiß".

Why does it violate my privacy, why does it violate my informational privacy, when someone collects, stores, compiles or distributes "my" data? The answer, which the autonomy-theoretician holds for that question, is: Because it diminishes my capability to be the author of my own life – to control my 'picture', my image in the public. If someone takes my name and puts that name in a box, a box perhaps designated with a certain label, then this is something that I feel rightly concerned about. What is happening there is something happening to me.

To put it more general: Autonomy is the telos of freedom, the implicit idea of freedom. (I take this idea from Rössler (2001)). In order to live an autonomous life, we necessarily need to control who has access to our person. Control of access: this is what privacy is about. Informational privacy is just one dimension of privacy. But if we want to live autonomously, we cannot do without informational privacy. This is, briefly, the argument. Its relevance to the question of data screening is clear: Everything that data screening, or at least everything that the "Rasterfahndung" does, is a violation of the above stated principle concerning people's "right to be informed about who knows what about them on which occasion". This principle is violated if data collected for special purposes is being given to a third party – to the government, or to the police – without that the 'owner' of the data is informed and without that he has a chance to consent or to withdraw. It is against the principle, if a search pattern is kept secret, so that no member of a given population can know, whether or not he or she is concerned. The same holds true, if the search itself is kept secret. As a consequence, the individual cannot control the self-image that the raster creates. The weight of the damage depends on the kind of "image" that a data-cluster establishes. It is more troubling to find oneself in one cluster together with probable criminals than in a cluster made up of male students born in 1985, studying physics or chemistry.

From all this follows just, that informational privacy has a certain value. It is still an open question what importance we attach to that prima facie value in a situation where we have to balance the burden and the benefits of intrusive search methods, all things considered.

Even though informational privacy and other dimensions of costs arising for individual persons are important issues, we should not overlook the other factors. This happens easily, because one principle, which lurks behind the metaphor of the "Rasterfahndung" as a medical surgery, is that only *individuals* might possibly suffer harm from such kind of intrusive searching. Or even stronger: 'Only those individuals, whose data has actually been used for a search, can possibly be harmed.' But this principle is clearly wrong. If search profiles are not communicated to the public, if the conduction of a search itself is kept secret – then *nobody* can know whether or not his data are involved. And this is a violation of the principle of informational privacy, which is also expressed by the phrasing that "[a] form of society, where citizens cannot know, what someone knows about them on a certain occasion and who that someone is, would not be compatible with the right of informational self-determination" (Bundesverfassungsgericht 1983). What therefore has to bother us, is not only actual harm, but possible evil. In other words: Harm is not only caused by a concrete, actual search-operation. It's the whole 'architecture', which structures the flows of data from the private sector to the government, that should bother us, rather than the ad hoc initiation, the actual usage of the possibilities that such an architecture offers. It is because this architecture exists, that we cannot know, who knows what about us on what occasion – because we simply may not know that searches are going on. And that means: Even if there is no actual search happening, we cannot be sure, what someone could know about us on what occasion. And this mere *possibility* has a real impact on how we conceive of our autonomy. The *possibility* of a search poses an *actual* threat to our self-determination.

One metaphor, that spells out those virtual dangers of data-collection and surveillance is the panopticon. Originally, the "panopticon" is an architectural design for prisons – proposed by Jeremy Bentham. Michel Foucault has taken this design as a metaphor for social structures, the ambivalent character of which he describes in *Discipline and punishment* (1977/75). The key feature of the panopticon is the tower. All prisoners can be seen from the tower, but the prisoner itself cannot see whether or not there is someone watching in this tower.

In the modern world of "dataveillance" (a term coined by Roger Clarke (1988)), the situation as a whole is somewhat different: Even less than Bentham's prisoner, do we know *who* is looking, and *what* he is looking for. We simply don't know what happens to our data, when we cannot control how these data are communicated from the private sector to the government. And what we have to worry about is not, whether or not there is a watchman in that tower, but whether or not the there is some human consciousness "online". Everything is less concrete than in the original panopticon. Intimidation, therefore, is much less probable – because intimidation presupposes knowledge about the supposed observer. The scope of surveillance, on the other hand, is a great deal broader than in the original setting.

This whole setting poses a threat not only to the individual's informational privacy, but to society as a whole. Considerations that hint at the dangers of badly controlled data-flows from the private sector to the government usually take the form of a slippery-slope argument. There are several of those arguments to be made:

Argument from Totalitarianism. A very common and often cited argument refers to George Orwell's "1984". If, by any chance, our government should take on features of a totalitarian state, than this tendency would be significantly increased by the extend to which the government can exercise social control. Evidence for this is given for instance by Götz Aly and Karl Heinz Roth in their study about the bureaucratic background of the Nazi-regime (1984). Aly and Roth describe to what extent the German Nazi-Regime relied on bureaucratic techniques and social statistics (the ancient version of data mining) for circling out and deporting the Jewish population. Other, well-known examples for intrusive investigations in the past are related to US-McCarthyism and the maltreatment of Japanese-Americans during World War II (cf. Solove 2002).

Argument from moral blindness: Along with bureaucratic regimes goes another danger, which is associated with the name of Hannah Arendt and her thesis of the "banality of evil" in her study "Eichmann in Jerusalem". The objection differs from the argument of totalitarianism, because rather than pointing to the possibilities that a malevolent person or a mislead government would have with the help of data screening, it states that certain bureaucratic structures could have an impact on the way people form their intentions. According to Arendt, the greatest danger we face is not that man might unbind himself from the restraints of society. It is rather the surrender of independent and critical judgment by people who work in large organizations. Evil, says Arendt, is far more the product of people working in complex institutions, acting without personal reflection than it is something inherent in individual man. Bureaucratic data-regimes might represent this kind of complex institution. If this holds true, the danger of totalitarianism appears to be even more pressing, because the argument from totalitarianism and the argument from moral blindness can be combined.

Argument from the value of autonomy for a liberal democracy: This argument has already been mentioned under the aspect of "freedom of action". It also can be read the following way: Surveillance in general and computerized profile searches or "Rasterfahndung" in particular pose a threat to democracy, because there is a risk of an inhibition of those autonomous acts that are related to the *political identity* of a person. Acts concerned are, e.g., related to freedom of assembly; right of anonymous communication, anonymous reading.[2]

III. PUTTING THE PUZZLE TOGETHER

One thing is troubling about the two groups of arguments. The concept of "informational pricacy" and the reference to individual harm on the one hand and the group of "social harms" don't easily sum up to form a coherent whole. Rather, they seem to work against each other. When we justify "privacy" with respect to autonomy, then violations of privacy can only be objected to by the person who is concerned. If surveillance – or anything that comes close to this – happens with the knowledge and the consent of the person who is concerned, than privacy is not violated. This leaves some cases of intrusion uncovered.

What happens if there is, from the point of view of the individual, no strong incentive to protest against data screening? Often there is no such incentive, because the actual case of data-collection does not seem to be harmful. But from this doesn't follow that the aggregate of data-collections which aren't harmful by themselves will also be harmless in sum. If we rely to strongly on the idea that data protection is a personal business of those people who are directly concerned, then there will be no one who has a mandate to watch out for the dangers of aggregate data-collection. Better than complaining about the many people who are *not* concerned about their privacy, one should rather accept the fact that data protection is, to a great deal, a matter for experts.

Let's consider more carefully, how the different arguments can be but together. Before starting to balance pro and contra, good and evil, we should ask, whether or not there are reasons to oppose data screening, no matter what the hoped-for benefits.

First of all: the rights of informational privacy and likewise liberty-rights do not have the status of unconditional or absolute rights. They don't have this status in our constitutions, and they don't have this status in our moral thinking. Those rights can be waived – if there are important reasons for it. Maybe we would even accept to make privacy rights part of a consequentialist calculus: Maybe we would agree that a violation of privacy rights takes place in order to prevent an even greater amount of such violations in the future.

If we agree that intrusive data screening might be justified in at least some cases, we arrive at two groups of further questions: What should count as a legitimate reason for such as search? And what rules should be obeyed within such as search? Reasons of the first group can, to form an analogy to the terminology of the just-war-theorie, be subsumed under the heading of the *ius ad vigilationem*. Reasons of the second kind then refer to the *ius in vigilatione*. Of course, this comparison doesn't really fully work out, because there is not "state of search" with special rules, comparable to the "state of war". Also, the *ius ad vigilationem* relates to the *ius in vigilatione*, because the legitimacy of searches depends on what can reasonably be expected to happen within a search.

a. Ius ad vigilationem

It is useful to apply also the further framework of the just-war-theory to the discussion on the ethics of data screening. Following this analogy, we can spell out the different principles to be obeyed concerning the ius ad vigilationem.

The *causa justa*, the just cause for data screening is made explicit in at least some jurisdiction on the subject. The legal framework for the German "Rasterfahndung", for instance, demands that the police is entitled to engage in such a search only if there is a present danger for the existence or the security of the BRD, of a county, or for the life or the freedom of a person.[3]

Auctoritas principis: Acts of data screening in search of terrorists or criminals have to be allowed for and conducted by the proper authority. Basically, this principle calls for obedience to the law. (In just war theory, this principle attaches to the question what may count as a proper authority in international affairs. Regarding national security, the principle of authority rather seems to be a trivial point.)

Intentio recta: A search has to be conducted with the right intention – this, too, is a point of minor theoretical interest. But practically, questions of intention were widely discussed in the wake of the post 9/11-searches and legislative changes. A commonly expressed concern was that "was passed in the wake of 9/11 were things that had little to do with catching terrorists but a lot to do with increasing the strength of government to infiltrate and spy on conservative organizations".[4]

Proportionality: Given that data screening in search of terrorists is an intrusive search method, proportionality or adequacy is demanded by general privacy-protection guidelines. The German jurisdiction concerning the Volkszählung in 1983, for example, explicitly grants the "right for informational privacy". Constraints of that right, it says, "are allowed only in the interest of the common good. [...] Jurisdiction has to obey the principle of adequacy" (Bundesverfassungsgericht 1983). If the same ends can be reached by other methods, which impose lesser right-violations, than intrusive data screening sure is inadequate. Adequacy demands that success is possible and likely. All things considered, ends must be able to justify means.

All those questions were vigorously debated in regard to the search campaigns after 9/11. Appealing to the principle of adequacy, many critics simply argued, that the "Rasterfahndung" was not legitimate, because it was not likely to succeed. But there *were*, as mentioned, cases in the past, were the "Rasterfahndung" led to success. Still, opinions differ, regarding the success of the post 9/11 searching-campaign. Even if one stays with the fact that no terrorists have been arrested as a result of the current search, the outcome can be interpreted in quite different ways. Take, for instance, Jörg Schönbohm's interpretation, Innenminister for the State of Brandenburg:

> "If we have a "Rasterfahndung" with a negative outcome, then this also is an important result. [...] That's falsification. Falsification works in science. And this is not only science: this is real life. I personally feel much more secure, if I know, that there is no concrete danger and no suspected collaboration with terrorist organisations in those areas where we have Islamic communities in Brandenburg. We have, for instance, an institute for Aeronautic at the TU Cottbus. If there would be someone like Mr. Atta – someone like him we would catch now."[5]

So much for Schönbohm.

Still, the principle of adequacy is the general framework for a discussion on whether or not a search relying on data screening should be conducted. All the mentioned dangers, risks and side-effects have to be weighed against the expected benefits of such a measure. But even if agreement on all the principle could established, there still would be plenty of room for debate in every actual case. This is for several reasons. The first one concerns the facts: Our decision is a decision under uncertainty. We don't know, and we cannot know, what we really can gain by data screening, and we don't know what effects such a measure will have in the long run. Second: What we will opt for depends also on a series of value-judgements, on which we have anything far from a social consensus. It's a question of our normative self-conception – a question rather of the form "what do we *want*" than "what *may* we do". We swift from the objectivity-orientated realm of moral decision-making to the field of lifestyle and personal ethics.

Further more, decisions about the legitimacy of data screening are shaped by still another factor: the expectation of what will happen in the context of a search. These expectations are based on the rules that govern the conduct of searches – the ius in vigilatione.

b. Ius in vigilatione

Considering the legitimacy of different modes of search-conduct, again the question of *proportionality* comes up. Adequacy or proportionality within searches differs slightly from the adequacy of a search, all things considered. Within a search, it is interesting to see that the principle of adequacy may come in conflict with other rules, especially those governing the *protection of the innocent*, which is one form of avoidance of unjust discrimination. The police of the German county of Nordrhein-Westfalen was criticized for collecting not only the data of Arab students, but of all male citizens from 18 to 45 years of age. This was seen as a violation of the principle of adequacy, because more data than necessary (and more than in the other counties, which concentrated on the "Islamic" students) were collected. From this one should not conclude that it is necessarily better to concentrate on a smaller group of individuals: Those counties that took only the data of Islamic student, were criticized for laying grounds for unfair racial discrimination. Thus, the principle of non-discrimination and the privacy-protection from the principle of adequacy apply at different ends of the spectrum. If the focus group of the profiling is well-defined, rather small and publicly known, then discrimination is likely to happen. If the group is large and not strictly defined, it will be rather hard to make a convincing point concerning discrimination. Even though privacy and non-discrimination are often seen as interrelated topics, the two might diverge.[6]

Concerning non-discrimination and protection of the innocent, still further issues have to be addressed. One of the ways individuals can be harmed by data searches on other ground than privacy, is profiling caused by unlimited bureaucratic discretion. The police or other search agents might use their licence to skip through vast amounts of data in order to convict *minor criminals* (who are "innocent" regarding terrorist activity). This often goes along with certain forms of discrimination, as it is the case with the practice of racial profiling on US-highways: Officers can legally select a few speed-limit violators out of the large universe of such violators (e.g., coloured people) and stop them in order to search for drugs. One might find a parallel in the events following 9/11. Of the 130 Pakistan seized after 9/11, reports Jeffrey Rosen (2003), 110 were convicted of immigration violations, and 22 were convicted of robbery, credit card fraud, or drug possession. None was linked to the 9/11 attacks.[7]

Another issue is the risk of *mistaken identity*. The most troubling cases in America after 9/11, writes Rosen,

> "involved immigrants who were arrested and detained for months based on snippets of circumstantial evidence that they fit a terrorist profile and then turned out not to be terrorists. For example, a man named Hady Hassan Omar, was arrested on Sept. 12 and detained for seventy-three

days after he bought a one-way airline ticket on the same Kinko's computer used by one of the 9/11 hijackers. An Egyptian named Osama Elfar was locked up for more than two months because he had attended a Florida flight school and worked as a mechanic for an airline in Saint Louis."

Finally, relatively innocent people (non-terrorists) might face the burden of suffering inadequate punishment for *past actions*, which can be brought to general knowledge through data-screening. Rosen cites the case of a policy adopted after the murder of a child named Megan Kanka in 1994:

> "The laws, ostensibly designed to protect public safety, typically require all sex offenders, both violent and non-violent, to enrol in a public registry that is on the Internet."

A similar stigmatisation could occur regarding any kind of minor crime, such as shoplifting.

c. In vigilatione: Search engines

Some forms of data screening and data aggregation might seem apt to avoid these kinds of side-effects. Let's go back to the metaphors of "screening" once again. ""Rasterfahndung" is a search that goes on in the background. Constantly, with uniformity. No set of data will be left out. No one will not be concerned." All this can be regarded as a threat of intelligence-like machine power. But it may as well count as a means to avoid the many dangers caused by human failure, threatening personal privacy as well as the existence of the liberal state. Only humans can deliberately use data for other purposes as intended or apply search machineries to illegitimately spy on a certain individual. Only humans are victims of moral blindness.

The question is, how to limit the power of humans dealing with great amounts of personal data. Self-obligation won't do. What is needed is some sharing of control or power, a system of checks and balances, wherever a collection of data reaches a critical dimension. This job can be done by people sitting in a committee for the control of the secret service. But it can also be done by a machine. Suppose we could install a closed circuit of surveillance, with no human operator involved ...

The crucial point is the connection between the machine and a human being. We wouldn't bother, if a robot would care for the selection of data. We think, that encryption protects our privacy – because we are not afraid, the "the machine" will read our data. We don't feel bothered, if we know for sure, that there is neither a tape in the video camera, nor a human eye looking through the lens.

Data screening bears some aspects of such a automatic search engine. Take, for instance, the debate on the "negative Rasterfahndung", negative profiling, in Germany in the late 1970s. The BKA-chief Horst Herold proposed it as an "ethical clean" method. Whereas a positive search is a search for positive features, a "negative" search is looking for non-features. An example: We know that the murderer is *not* someone who has already retired. So the police hands its list of suspected individuals over to the governmental agency, which keeps the lists of those individuals who receive grants for the retired. The police ask them to delete all names of retired persons from their list. In the end, the police has cleaned its list – without that any police officer has seen the data of retired persons, without that the governmental agency had to loose control over its data.

Horst Herold assumed that this method was inoffensive from the point of view of data protection – because it served to discharge the people whose data were being involved and because the data weren't actually inspected by the police. Today, the distinction between "positive" and "negative" search is not longer discussed – maybe, because "positive" and "negative" is always a matter of definition (a "positive" search can easily be framed as a "negative" one), and surely because almost any real search is a combination of the two methods. But the argument still seem persuading. If nobody actually sees (or reads) the data, if the data doesn't actually flow from the private company to the government – then, certain problems won't arise from the beginning.

Similar considerations underlie the use of techniques of encryption today. Some CCTV-systems run by German police-stations, for instance, have a software installed, which automatically blackens that area of the screen, where a portion of the window of a private apartment appears, so that the police officer cannot see what is happening behind that windows without at least making the (criminal) effort of removing the device.

Data screening in general is a technique that has a certain "impartial" appeal – just because it works automatically. The technique itself makes it impossible for the police to go on "fishing expedition". The search-algorithm is absolutely objective. If you are not in the target group of the raster, than the machine keeps everything that it knows about you for itself. The only problem is: who is in control of the search-pattern? Who will ensure, that the pattern is not relying on ethical discrimination, or other forms of discrimination, in an unjustifiable way? The fact that a pattern is secret may also pose the threat of misguided use. All this could be avoided my making public the search pattern.

But if a search pattern becomes known publicly, then it will probably become ineffective. And if the search is likely to be ineffective, constitutional law will rule it out. There is some evidence, for instance, that the system used for the screening of flight-passengers used in the USA suffers from such a defect: As terrorists can find out about the pattern, they can easily get away uncaught (Chakrabarti/Strauss 2002).

Another argument against the publication of profiles is the threat of discrimination. If a profile is known, then people will try to behave in a way not to arise suspicion. People who bear all the relevant features will likely to be regarded as suspect persons.

Both objections arise only if the search pattern is made up of features which are just accidental to the criminal activity in question. Suppose a case were a subject cannot get rid of the features without loosing the ability to behave in a criminal way. Lawrence Lessig has once made up such a case:

> "Imagine a worm – a bit of computer code that crosses network wires and places itself on your computer – that snooped your hard disk looking for illegal copies of software. The FBI, for example, might spit this critter onto the Net, and let it work its way onto disks across the country. When the worm found an illegal copy of software, it would

send a message to that effect back to the FBI; if it found no such illegality, it would self-destruct. No difference in the operations of the computer would be noticed; the worm would snoop, as it were, deep underground." (Lessig 1996; vgl. 1999, 17 ff.)

Lessig thinks that the activity of such a worm wouldn't violate the privacy-protection rules granted by the American Constitution. But that's maybe not because Lessig is a proponent of worm-like search machineries, but because he is rather pessimistic concerning the workability of the American Constitution facing the features of the cyberspace world. In the framework of the Constitution, privacy is addressed by the Fourth Amendment. "The right of the people to be secure ... against unreasonable searches", it says there, "shall not be violated". Everything thus comes to down the question, what exactly has to count as an "unreasonable search". The common interpretation of the phrase regards "reasonable" in terms of reasonable expectance. Given the cyberspace world as it actually is, nobody can reasonable expected that no worm is snooping on his harddisk. Therefore, the Fourth Amendment offers no protection against this kind of device.[8]

Jeffrey Rosen (2004) describes a similar – but real – scenario. Referring to "Carnivore", he says: "The computer search ensures that no human being views the innocent e-mail; by focusing on the suspicious e-mails with laser-like precision, it avoids the dangers of executive discretion and unregulated snooping [...]." Provided that Congress has jurisdiction to review whether Carnivore is being used as the government promises, Rosen concludes, that "Carnivore now functions as a reasonable search tool which might be viewed as a model for other architectures of identification".

"Carnivore" is a tool employed by the FBI to screen email-traffic. Is serves to filter out mails related to persons, which are already suspected to be criminals or terrorists. "Carnivore" is not a "Rasterfahndung", because it is not a search for undetermined person. Neither constitutes Lessigs "worm" a "Rasterfahndung" – because the worm isn't screening databases, but real-world hard-drives. People who don't use email and who don't connect their computer to the internet, won't be bothered by Carnivore or the FBI-worm. But all three search methods are relying on the computer. They are automatically singling out facts about certain individuals.

The more likely an individual which is part of the target-group of the search algorithm belongs to the category "guilty", the lesser is the burden imposed on the innocent. In the worm-scenario, this burden is, as Lessig admits, "quite slight", even though "[o]ne might think that there is an insecurity for people who generally know that they might be watched; that this worm might be crossing their disk; that they are constantly open to surveillance by the government". But to those who are obeying the rules, the worm won't do any harm. Putting the issue of the constitutional legitimacy of such a worm aside: What ethical reasons are there to oppose the employment of likewise search-engines?

For the sake of the argument, let's take for granted that the search engine produces no false-positives. Suppose that the rules, the obedience to which the worm serves to confirm, are established by a democratic procedure and in accordance with constitutional norms. Suppose further, that misuse is excluded. What reason would there be to oppose the worm?

315

There would be, as mentioned, certain costs for the innocent. They would have to live with the knowledge that every violation of the rule will be detected (and possibly fined). Even those individuals, who intend to live in accordance with the rules, might prefer for themselves to have at least the possibility to violate rules without instant detection (taking or not taking into account the costs resulting from other people's real rule-violations). A similar consideration holds plausible for those, who do not intend to live in accordance with the rules. They should have, one could say, (and they surely will prefer to have) the possibility to violate rules without instant detection. The reason for this is, that it is just not likely to be effective to switch from a social system which builds upon the internalisation and general acknowledgment of rules to a system which is solely based on the threat of sanctions. Besides efficiency, this is also a question of moral self-esteem. Even minor criminals we do not want to treat as persons who are unable to acknowledge the validity of any agreed-upon rules. Therefore, a certain amount of rule-violation and minor criminal activity is something which we cannot reasonably wish to get rid of – even if we had the means to do this. A "worm" used by the FBI to detect illegal software-downloads would therefore be an device most of us would reject – and rightfully so. Thus, even though we could minimalize side effects and collateral costs of data screening, there are also objections regarding the *main* effects. It seems reasonable to limit the employment of data screening to the hard cases of rule-violation: to terrorism and major criminal activity – which is a point belonging to the topic of the *causa iusta* for a *vigilatio*.

But given that a terrorist act is likely to happen, that national security is threatened or that a major criminal activity has to be stopped, neither the appeal to privacy nor to privacy-related costs imposed on society as well as on individuals will, all things considered, presumably count as a reason against data-screening. The loss of control over the own self-image and authorship of one's life, the danger of totalitarianism or of moral blindness and likewise considerations are just too vague and too soft arguments to make up with the all too real possibility of physical harm, caused by criminal or terrorist action. "Slippery slope" always looses in cases of emergency. But it may well be that this is rather a result of preferences in argumentative style than a victory of rationality.

NOTES

[1] Interview with the author, December 2001.
[2] I am indebted do Daniel Solove (2002) for making these issues clear to me.
[3] This is the line pursued by the Landespolizeigesetz. The phrasing differs among the different german counties. Refering to these laws, judges in some counties decided that the searches conducted after 9/11 were illegal and had to be stopped. – Apart from searches by the police, a "Rasterfahndung" may also be conducted by the german secret services.
[4] Paul Weyrich, the president of the Free Congress Foundation, which had been a leading supporter of Ashcroft's nomination as attorney general, in conversation with The New York Times: Neil A. Lewis, "Ashcroft's Terrorism Policies Dismay Some Conservatives", *The New York Times*, July 24, 2002, p. A1.
[5] Interview with the author. August, 2002.
[6] Another instance where that might happen is in the area of genetic privacy (or health privacy) and insurances. Economists such as Achim Wambach (2000) argue that in these cases, the pareto-optimum can

be established in a regulatory regime which avoids the effects of information-asymetrie anti-selection and gives insurers rather unconstrained access to their clients health data.
[7] I take this from Jeffrey Rosen (2003) chap. 2.
[8] For the details on why the Fourth Amendment fails to deliver adequate privacy-protection, cf. Solove (2002).

REFERENCES

Aly, Götz and Karl Heinz Roth: *Die restlose Erfassung. Volkszählen, Identifizieren, Aussondern im Nationalsozialismus*, Frankfurt/Main, 1984 and 2000.
Brandeis, Louis D. and Samuel D. Warren: "The Right to Privacy", in: *Harvard Law Review*, 4/1 (1890), 193-220; http://www.lawrence.edu/fac/boardmaw/Privacy_brand_warr2.html.
Bittner, Jochen: "Löcher im Datennetz. In den Ländern kippt die "Rasterfahndung" – das BKA sammelt weiter", in: *Die Zeit* 12/2002.
Bundesverfassungsgericht: *Volkszählung. Urteil des Ersten Senats vom 15. Dezember 1983 auf die mündliche Verhandlung vom 18. und 19. Oktober 1983*, 1 BvR 209, 269, 362, 420, 440, 484/83 in den Verfahren über die Verfassungsbeschwerden; http://www.datenschutz-berlin.de/gesetze/sonstige/volksz.htm.
EPIC: "Paying for Big Brother: A Review of the proposed FY2003 Budget for the Department of Justice, February 2002"; http://www.epic.org/reports/paying_for_bb.pdf.
Chakrabarti, Samidh, and Aaron Strauss: "Carnival Booth: An Algorithm for Defeating the Computer-Assisted Passenger Screening System", in: *Firstmonday* 7 (2002); http://www.firstmonday.org/issues/issue7_10/chakrabarti/.
Clarke, Roger: "Information Technology and Dataveillance", in: *Commun. ACM* 31,5 (May 1988) 498-512; http://www.anu.edu.au/people/Roger.Clarke/DV/CACM88.html.
Foucault, Michel: *Discipline and punishment*. London: Allen Lane, 1977 (*Surveiller et punir. La naissance de la prison*. Paris: Editions Gallimard, 1975).
Grabenströer, Michael and Reinhard Voss: "Fahnder tappen noch im Dunkeln", in: *Frankfurter Rundschau*, 07.11.2002.
Herold, Horst: "'Die Position der RAF hat sich verbessert'. Der ehemalige BKA-Chef Horst Herold über Terroristen und Computer-Fahndung", Interview, in: *Der Spiegel* 37 (1966), 38-61.
Herold, Horst: "'Rasterfahndung' – unverzichtbares Mittel für die Polizei", in: *Die Welt*, 10.02.1986.
Krempl, Stefan: "'Rasterfahndung' in Berlin für unzulässig erklärt", in: *Telepolis*, 22.01.2002.
K. J.: "'Rasterfahndung' an Hochschulen im Visier der Datenschützer", in: *Heise Newsticker*, 03.04.02.
Lessig, Lawrence: "Reading the Constitution in Cyberspace", in: *Emory Law Journal*, Summer, 1996
—: *Code and other laws of cyberspace*. New York, NY: Basic Books, 1999.
Limbach, Jutta: Rede auf dem Deutschen Anwaltstag. München: 10. Mai 2002.
Nass, Gustav (eds.): *Biologische Ursachen abnormen Verhaltens. Beiträge der Grundlagenforschung zu aktuellen Kriminalitätsproblemen*. Akad. Verlagsanstalt, Wiesbaden, 1981.
Neuber, Harald: "Durchs Raster gefallen. Die neu etablierte "Rasterfahndung" stellt auch an Universitäten Unschuldige unter Generalverdacht", in: *Telepolis*, 26.09.2001.
Neuber, Harald: "Politischer Sprengstoff. Die Kriterien der "Rasterfahndung" werden in Berlin immer mehr ausgeweitet ...", in: *Telepolis*, 14.11.2002.
Not signed: "Viel Lärm um die Computerfahndung", in: *Quick*, 7.2.1980.
Not signed: "'Rasterfahndung': Eine neue polizeiliche Fahndungsmethode", in: *Cilip* [Bürgerrechte & Polizei] 6 (1980), 15-20.
Palm, Godehart: "Verbraucherdaten sollen sich zum Profil von Terroristen veredeln", in: *Telepolis*, 09.04.2002.
Plog, Karsten: "Fahnder visieren Studenten an. Hamburgs Polizei lädt 140 meist ausländische Jugendliche vor", in: *Frankfurter Rundschau*, 22.01.2002.
Prantl, Heribert: "Die Rasterfahndung ist nicht gestorben. Der ehemalige BKA-Präsident Horst Herold über Erfolgsaussichten verschiedener Ermittlungsmethoden", in: *Süddeutsche Zeitung*, 24.10.2001.
Reifenrath, Roderich: "'Für "Rasterfahndung" fehlen ausreichende Rechtsgrundlagen". Von Börner bestelltes Gutachten vorgelegt/Prof. Denninger: Aufgaben von Polizei und Verfassungsschutz trennen", in: *Frankfurter Rundschau*, 14.07.1984.

Rosen, Jeffrey: *The naked crowed. Reclaiming Security and Freedom in an Anxious Age.* New York: Random House, 2004.

Rössler, Beate: *Der Wert des Privaten.* Frankfurt am Main: Suhrkamp, 2001.

Schenk, Dieter: *Horst Herold und das BKA.* Hamburg: Hoffman und Campe, 1998, 397-402.

Schulzki-Haddouti, Christiane: "Rasterfahndung in Deutschland. Welches Datenprofil haben ,Schläfer'?", in: *Telepolis,* 03.10.2001.

–: "Nach Berlin kippt nun Wiesbaden die "Rasterfahndung"", in: *Telepolis,* 07.02.2002.

Seeber, Lothar: ""Rasterfahndung" und Datenschutz", in: *Kriminalistik* 5 (1981), 203-207.

Siebrecht, Michael: *Rasterfahndung. Eine EDV-gestützte Massenfahndungsmethode im Spannungsfeld zwischen einer effektiven Strafverfolgung und dem Recht auf informationelle Selbstbestimmung.* Berlin: Duncker & Humblot, 1997.

Simon, Jürgen/Simon-Ern, Gundel/Taeger, Jürgen: "Wer sich umdreht oder lacht ... "Rasterfahndung": Ein Beitrag zur Gewährleistung der Inneren Sicherheit", in: *Kursbuch* 66 (1981), 20-36.

Simon, Jürgen: "Die fragwürdige Sammelie. Datenschutz und "Rasterfahndung"", in: *Die Zeit,* 49 (1982).

Simon, Jürgen/Taeger, Jürgen: *"Rasterfahndung" – Entwicklung, Inhalt und Grenzen einer kriminalpolizeilichen Fahndungsmethode.* Baden-Baden: Nomos, 1981.

Sokol, Bettina: "Rasterfahndung" vor 20 Jahren und heute", in: Bäumler, Helmut (ed.): *Polizei und Datenschutz. Neupositionierung im Zeichen der Informationsgesellschaft.* Neuwied: Luchterhand, 1999, 188-198.

Solove, Daniel: "Digital Dossiers and the Dissipation of Fourth Amendment Privacy", *S. Cal. L. Rev.* 1083, 1098 (2002).

Wambach, Achim. "Die ökonomischen Auswirkungen von Gentests auf Versicherungsmärkte", in: Felix Thiele (ed.), *Genetische Diagnostik und Versicherungsschutz. Die Situation in Deutschland.* Graue Reihe, Bd. 20, Europäische Akademie: Bad Neuenahr, 2000.

Wanner, Stephan: *Die negative Rasterfahndung. Eine moderne und umstrittene Methode der repressiven Verbrechensbekämpfung.* München: Florentz, 1989.

FILIMON PEONIDIS

DOES THE SUPPRESSION OF PRO-TERRORIST SPEECH ENHANCE COLLECTIVE SECURITY?

> And while the sources of social oppression are indeed numerous, none has the deadly effect of those who, as the agents of the modern state, have unique resources of physical might and persuasion at their disposal.
>
> Judith N. Shklar, *The Liberalism of Fear*

Western democratic societies appear quite hesitant to extend the highly venerable freedom of speech to the public expression and broadcasting of pro-terrorist speech. In 1988 the British government ordered the BBC and the IBA to refrain from broadcasting anything coming from a person who was a member of a terrorist organization.[1] A few years later, the Greek government banned the publication of terrorist statements in the media, in an effort to minimize the influence the seemingly invincible organization *November 17* had on the Greek public.[2] The British government in 2000 decided to penalize the simple possession of written material praising terrorism.[3] In the United States, the legislative acts that followed the events of 9/11, as far as I can tell, do not seem to be directly concerned with the simple endorsement or publication of the claims of terrorist organizations, with one exception.[4] However, this does not imply that the traditional spirit of free speech has always made its presence felt: academics expressing unpopular views were asked to leave campus for their own safety;[5] journalists maintained that they were fired for their anti-Bush editorials;[6] cartoonists came under pressure not to be critical of the government;[7] and the State Department tried (unsuccessfully) to quash a Voice of America broadcast of an interview with Mullah Omar.[8] All these incidents raise significant issues. Are these reactions justified? Does pro-terrorist speech not belong to one of the broad categories of protected speech? Should we tolerate it even in times of emergency? Are there any distinctions within this type of speech that are significant from the perspective of freedom of speech?

I shall not approach these questions from the standpoint of a particular legal or constitutional order, although the thoughts expressed here have been influenced by legal developments in Western countries. In particular, I will be concerned with offering principled and plausible arguments against the view that the suppression of pro-terrorist speech enhances collective security. Echoing the spirit of Joel Feinberg's philosophy, the quest is not for legal measures "or useful policies but for valid

319

Meggle (ed.), Ethics of Terrorism & Counter-Terrorism, 319-328.

principles",[9] and the arguments are addressed to politicians, legislators and laymen alike. I will start by considering two essential conceptual clarifications.

CONCEPTUAL CLARIFICATIONS

Writing about terrorism demands that the author give his/her own understanding of this "essentially contested" and unfortunate term. Thus, for the purposes of this essay I mean by "terrorism" the politically–motivated, violent acts perpetrated consistently and systematically by small and organized domestic or foreign groups against selected targets (civilian or otherwise) in democratic regimes. For the most part these groups are aware that they cannot achieve their aims by overcoming their opponents in a full-scale confrontation. Thus, they try to make governments succumb to their demands by creating an unbearable climate of intimidation through the repeated use of force and the threat of further force. Many terrorist activities of this sort involve some kind of negotiation with the authorities. In other cases, however, they merely intend to deal a blow to their enemies without offering them any option of avoiding it. It is important to stress that the activities of these groups must be extremely violent. A political group that sporadically clashes with the police in demonstrations cannot be dubbed "terrorist". It has to be engaged in bombings, sabotage, assassinations, kidnappings, robberies and other acts of relative severity. I believe that the above description does not diverge significantly from the perception of terrorist activity prevailing in North America and in Europe – and in particular from the perception of those who have tried to censor pro-terrorist speech –, although it should be pointed out that it does not intend to exhaust the complex and multifaceted phenomenon of terrorism. It does not deal, for instance, with similar acts instigated by legitimate governments (state terrorism) or performed against authoritarian states.

The use of violence, instead of the usual means we possess to conduct democratic politics, creates a strong presumption against this type of terrorism. The blatant disrespect these people show for human life, which sometimes takes the form of an indiscriminate mass murder of innocent civilians, by far outweighs any sympathy we might feel for their cause. However, the above description leaves open the logical possibility – under specific conditions – of a more positive appreciation of terrorist activity. Suppose that democratic state A occupies state B by force. Consequently, a liberation movement which uses traditional political means to make A give B back its independence emerges in state B. Certain members of the liberation movement, weary of the inefficacy of peaceful tactics, start attacking selected government targets in state A. Perhaps, the route they have chosen to take might lead them nowhere, but is their decision unjustified? I think it is not, although this group falls within our description of terrorism.

Leaving aside questions of justification, which are peripheral to the main argument, I proceed now to a specification of "pro-terrorist speech". The category of expression in question can be divided into two subcategories of more limited scope. (a) Indirect pro-terrorist speech refers to expressive acts that originate from people who do not belong to terrorist groups or are associated with them and convey messages that are supportive of the latter's activities and beliefs. The statement "anyone who can blow up the Pentagon has my vote", reportedly made by a

University of New Mexico professor, is a clear example.[10] (b) Direct pro-terrorist speech refers basically to the statements that are issued by members or representatives of terrorist groups and constitute an essential part of their overall, operational plan. Through these means, terrorists try to achieve several objectives that are important to them: to assume responsibility for their actions, to express their demands, to make their views and policies known, to gain sympathy for their cause, to threaten and intimidate their enemies, to pay tribute to their own members, to open an informal dialogue with the authorities and so forth. Yet it is evident that these communications cannot reach a greater public, unless they are publicized by the written and electronic press. This is why the authorities impose restrictions on the press coverage of terrorist's speech.[11]

PRO–TERRORIST SPEECH IS POLITICAL SPEECH

Terrorism in the sense defined is a political phenomenon. "Unless", wrote Lorin E. Lomasky, "an individual or group represents itself as acting in the service of a political ideal or program, it will not be deemed terrorist".[12] Terrorists are distinguished from common criminals by the political inspiration of their activities. Whatever their ultimate motives – a determination to redress an injustice done to their people, a strong desire to bring about a classless communist society, their opposition to animal experimentation or the simple ambition to impose their will on a democratic public by force or threat of force – are, they all belong to the realm of the political. Even if these organizations argue on religious grounds, it is the political dimension of religion that guides their actions. This does not imply that there is always a discernible political goal served by terrorist action or that their leaders display even a rudimentary sense of instrumental rationality. Terrorism in many cases does not appear to be the "continuation of politics by other means" and it is not uncommon for the tactics of terrorists to contradict their strategies in a way that is most painful for them.

If terrorism is a political phenomenon, then pro-terrorist speech, in both senses of the term, is political speech. And in liberal democratic regimes there is a widespread consensus that political speech, whatever its source, should enjoy special protection.[13] This does not imply that this protection is absolute. Most people would agree that some reasonable restrictions concerning the time and place of political expression would be appropriate. However, when it comes to content regulation, it is important for any limitations imposed to be minimal and well defined. In addition, these restrictions should not reflect merely the government's dislike for the content of certain political utterances, but rather be guided by the absolute necessity to protect values and rights (including the very right to free speech) that are essential for the functioning of liberal democracy. Generally speaking, and certain mishaps notwithstanding, it is an achievement of our political culture that we do not prosecute anyone for the simple reason that the majority or the authorities believe that someone airs subversive, vituperative, mistaken and/or outrageous political views. When these views are publicly stated, as Justice Brandeis put it, "the remedy to be applied is more speech, not enforced silence".[14] All the above suffices, I believe, to establish a certain presumption against the suppression of pro-terrorist speech.

THE SECURITY ARGUMENT

At this point, a major objection is expected:

> We cannot envisage terrorists as a bunch of radicals or dissidents who
> protest against a democratic government and its policies. On 9/11 the
> United States was the victim of a brutal attack by a terrorist
> organization that would constitute a *casus belli* if it were carried out by
> a state and the same holds for all those countries that were targeted by
> al-Queda. No one in Western democratic societies can feel safe any
> more, until the war against terror is won. We have a case of supreme
> emergency and our first priority should be the security of our people.
> Thus, we have to curtail, as long as it is necessary, certain civil liberties
> and legal safeguards including the right to express pro-terrorists views.
> It is an unhappy situation but security has to trump liberty.

Here we can distinguish two different claims. (a) The general claim that in cases of emergency the state, and a liberal democratic polity in particular, must curtail civil liberties and suspend the rule of law to protect the safety of its citizens. (b) The specific claim that the suppression of pro-terrorist speech makes us safer from the evil of terrorism. I will start with the general assertion.

The state of supreme emergency, despite Carl Schmitt's early warning that here the exception is more interesting than a rule that proves nothing, has not received the attention it deserves in contemporary political philosophy.[15] One is entitled to pose afresh questions about the conditions under which a state of supreme emergency should be proclaimed and about who is entitled to make the necessary decisions. These considerations are beyond the scope of this essay and presumably beyond my competence.[16] Instead, I will grant that we are in a state of supreme emergency in a loose and non-technical sense and I will focus on the core of the general claim to examine its plausibility, on the assumption that under the current circumstances security is the supreme prudential value for most citizens.[17]

The supporters of the general claim speak as if we are facing an inevitable choice between two completely heterogeneous and unrelated things: civil liberties and security. However, what is forgotten here is that civil liberties have been campaigned for and constitutionally established to make the lives of ordinary citizens (and non-citizens who are subject to the state's jurisdiction) safer from a "clear and (always) present" danger: the abuse of public authority. No matter what other justifications can be summoned up on their behalf, it cannot be denied that we feel secure because we know, for instance, that we will not be sent into exile when our political opponents assume power or that we will not stay for long in prison without being indicted for a clearly defined crime. The enforcement of civil liberties and the rule of law do not, as a matter of fact, assuage our fear of decease, poverty and old age, but makes us not worry about an equally significant threat to our well being.

If this is the case, then the supporters of the general claim suggest that in an emergency the state should lower or suspend the protection we enjoy from its powers to protect us from another agent (a foreign state, a faction or a terrorist group) that is about to harm us. Is this a fair compromise? Is it something we are willing to accept, even if personal safety is our only concern? The reasonable answer is to demand to be protected from our terrorist enemies as effectively as we are protected from the abuse of state power. Thus the real trade-off should not be between civil liberties and our security but between the resources democratic governments devote to the protection of the life and property of the people and the resources channelled into other purposes such as education or public works. Since we know well that we can suffer significant harm at the hands of state authorities, it is prudent not to want to disavow our civil liberties and rights but to be ready to make other sacrifices to contribute to the government's effort to combat effectively the collective threat that has suddenly arisen. Yet, the fact that the loss of liberties and rights will be now legitimate, even for a limited period of time, whereas the actions of the hostile agent will never be, adds to our reluctance to accept the proposal put forward by the adherents of the general claim. Moreover, the situation is exacerbated by our reasonable fears that, once a decision of this kind is institutionalised, it acquires its own momentum and this makes repeal difficult, and that the suspension of one civil liberty may pave the way for harsher measures by eroding the moral commitments of those in power. As to the possible claim that terrorist organizations are deadlier than governments, one can compare the number of civilians that died in the 20th century because of the (justifiable or unjustifiable) decisions of democratic governments with the number of civilians killed by terrorists.

Here the following objection can be raised:

> You assume that in a supreme emergency the state will turn against innocent people or its political opponents,[18] whence, in fact, all these measures seek to apprehend and punish a handful of guilty terrorists. Anyone not associated with these individuals has nothing to fear.

However, this is easier said than done. The very fact that a liberal, democratic state resorts to these measures betrays its difficulty in identifying and apprehending the guilty few. But by suspending certain basic provisions of the rule of law, say by allowing the conviction of defendants even if they are not found guilty beyond a reasonable doubt, the chances of punishing the innocent increase significantly.

Let us grant, however, that no mistakes will be made, that the government will not use its newly acquired powers to gain unfair political advantage and that only "the real enemies of the people" will be affected by the suspension of civil liberties and the corresponding legislative constraints. Even then, we believe that the state has acquired an unfair advantage over us. Consider, for instance, the bulk of personal information the authorities might gather if all restrictions concerning respect for individual privacy were lifted. We do not want the state to know so much about us, even if we know that it does not intend to use all this personal information improperly. We remain vulnerable and rely solely on the authorities' good intentions, since we have now been deprived of any significant means of self-protection.[19] This brings us closer to a benevolent Hobbesian state, but it is small wonder that we cannot feel safer there, having experienced the liberties and safeguards of the modern liberal democratic state.

Leaving now the general claim, which no longer looks as powerful or persuasive as it used to, I turn to the specific claim that we must ban pro-terrorist speech as a means of protecting us from the evil of terrorism. Is there some truth in this contention? Is there some value in it, even if we discount any potential dangers to our security stemming from giving government the liberty to censor political speech? Let us start with indirect pro-terrorist speech. Do we feel more secure from terrorism now that we know that our fellow citizens will be penalised if they publicly express their sympathy for it? By definition these people are not associated in any way with terrorist groups. They are just spectators and commentators of the political developments and pose no threat to national security, unless we make the implausible assumption that anyone who does not explicitly condemn terrorism is a potential terrorist. But even if this were true, it would be in our best interests to let people make their views public. In a society where freedom of speech is guaranteed, citizens will tend to reveal their real beliefs and this will help us determine our attitude towards these individuals. On the contrary, if free speech is stifled, people will be unwilling to openly support proscribed views and this makes it easier for us to be deceived about whom we have to deal with.

With regard to direct pro-terrorist speech, I claim that the first-hand knowledge of it confers citizens certain advantages. It gives us the opportunity to learn something about the reasons behind these violent acts and this is preferable to remaining in a state of complete ignorance.[20] The knowledge of these reasons makes us participants in a substantive public dialogue about our collective reaction to this phenomenon, since we now share crucial information with the authorities. Our confrontation with terrorism has many dimensions. Some of them are necessarily cloaked in secrecy. Others, however, should be public. A state might have to change its foreign or domestic policy dramatically to combat the terrorist threat more effectively. These are important decisions that should be backed by a wide and genuine consensus that cannot be achieved without open, public deliberation. In this dialogue, information about the causes of terrorism and the terrorists' perspective is important. It is not my wish to assert that this information is significant because it will make the citizenry sympathetic to the terrorists' cause. It is equally significant when it leads citizens to the conclusion that this cause is incomprehensible or unfounded. It seems that by proscribing direct, pro-terrorist speech, we do not become safer and we are deprived of certain assets we need in our dealings with terrorism.

The retort may be that terrorist communications do not include only explanations and political analyses but they address serious threats to specific persons, groups or peoples. This makes the recipients feel unsafe and, thus, it constitutes a reason for the suppression of the above communications.

The decision to include threats in the category of proscribed or protected speech is not an easy one. A good starting point would be a brief analysis of the concept of threat. Following Kent Greenawalt,[21] we can distinguish between unconditional and conditional threats. In the first case, A informs B that he will harm her, although he is not morally or legally justified to do so, without giving the threatened party the option to avoid the impending harm. In the second case, A informs B that he will unjustifiably harm her, unless she complies with his demands. Conditional threats are of the form "I will do you x, unless you do y". Both types of threats are found in terrorist discourse. A terrorist group may threaten to punish its enemies *tout court* or to harm certain people in case its demands are not satisfied.

It is often argued that many threats made in the political sphere, albeit they might betray moral depravity or lack of moderation, should not worry us too much. According to one author "threats or implied threats of force or other sanctions affecting the well-being of the disputants, are always a part of the currency of the political debate".[22] Along these lines, the U.S. Supreme Court in *Watts v. United States*, 394 U.S. 705 (1969) reversed the conviction of an 18-year-old youth who said in a group of protestors "if they [i.e. the government] ever make me carry a rifle, the first man I want to get in my sights is L[yndon] B. J[ohnson]". The Court ruled that this assertion could not be interpreted as a "knowing and wilful threat against the President", but as "political hyperbole", that is a form of speech falling under the First Amendment. However, as it is attested by various legal systems and codes, not all threats fall into this category. From the moral, pre-legal point of view we adopt here, it seems that there is something seriously wrong with a certain type of political threat. In particular when

(i)   A threatens openly (conditionally or unconditionally) to inflict serious harm upon B and

(ii)   from the overall context it is inferred that A is determined and capable[23] of inflicting the harm upon B,

then we have a morally reprehensible act, even if A does not fulfil his threat. One reason is that it invades B's autonomy by making her do things she would not do in the normal course of events.[24] Another is that it undermines her sense of security and strikes fear in her. Unfortunately all the threats issued by al-Qaeda and other similar organizations belong to this category.[25] In the most tragic manner their leaders have already proved that they mean what they say, that they are ruthless and indiscriminate and, alas, unexpectedly effective. Thus, there is no question that their threats undermine our sense of security. However, it is again not clear that the suppression of direct pro-terrorist speech will restore our collective sense of security. First of all, it is highly unlikely for a democratic state to acquire such a firm grip on all communications, the media and the Internet to prevent terrorist discourse from reaching a greater public. But even if this can be achieved, the crucial point is that the feelings of insecurity, anxiety and uncertainty most of us have experienced after 9/11 are due to what they have done to us and not on what they say in their communications. It is of no comfort to be protected from becoming the final target of terrorist threats but to know that all these groups are fully operational. We should not put the cart before the horse.

CONCLUSION

I have argued that there is a certain presumption against the suppression of pro-terrorist speech and that considerations of collective security are not in principle strong enough to outweigh this presumption. This does not imply that there are no imaginable cases whatsoever where pro-terrorist speech should become subject to legal control for public safety reasons. There might be,[26] but the specification of all exceptions will require a detailed and legalistic approach that is beyond the scope of this essay.

How, then, should we as democratic citizens[27] treat those expressing pro-terrorist views we find absolutely mistaken, callous and appalling? What should we do with those who rejoice in the events of 9/11, Bali, Istanbul and Madrid? If these people are not in any way involved in terrorist activities, we can follow Mill's advice and endeavour to show them that they are wrong or avoid them and "caution others against them". This treatment might have undesirable consequences for them but any harm they suffer is the "spontaneous consequences of their faults" or choices, as we would now preferably say, and they are not "purposefully inflicted for the sake of punishment".[28] However, we are not entitled to take other measures against them. If they are engaged in terrorist activities, then it is our duty (and of course that of the law enforcement authorities) these individuals to be brought to justice and have a fair trial; not for their beliefs but for the wrongful acts they have committed.

NOTES

[1] See Brett V. Kenney, "The British Media Ban: The Difference between Terrorist-Related Speech and Terrorist Acts", *Notre Dame Journal of Law, Ethics and Public Policy* 6 (1992): 245-81.

[2] I discuss this ban in "Freedom of Expression and Terrorism", *Journal of Liberal Arts* (Thessaloniki) 1(1994): 57-70.

[3] This is what I make of article 57 (1) of the Terrorism Act 2000, which states that "a person commits an offence if he *possesses* an article in circumstances which give rise to a reasonable suspicion that his possession is for a purpose connected with the commission, preparation or *instigation* of an act of terrorism" [italics mine]. And if press reports are accurate, Charalambos Dousemetzis, a Greek student in England, was arrested and charged under the above article of the Terrorism Act 2000 for having a pamphlet and two rubber stamps related to *November 17* in his house. See "Charges dropped against suspected terrorist", http://www.thisisthenortheast.co.uk/the_north_east/archive/2003/0408/terrorist.news.html.

[4] The PATRIOT Act of 2001 (section 411) amended the grounds of inadmissibility of aliens for security and related grounds specified in the Immigration and Nationality Act (8 U.S.C. 1182 (a) (3)). Now any alien who "has used the alien's prominent position within any country to endorse or espouse terrorist activity, or to persuade others to support terrorist activity or a terrorist organization, in a way that the Secretary of State has determined undermines United States efforts to reduce or eliminate terrorist activities" is excludable. This in fact means that it is possible for certain individuals to be denied entry to the United States merely because of their beliefs.
There is no doubt that the above category of persons will suffer a setback in their interests but they are hardly *punished* for their pro-terrorist attitudes. Generally, we do not regard the exclusion of individuals from certain institutions for ideological reasons as punishment for their credos, if these persons have no pre-established right to participate in them. Atheists do not qualify for priesthood; neither do pacifists for a career in the military. In these cases, however, we do not claim that all these are *wronged* because of their ideological preferences. Thus a state cannot in principle be blamed for refusing entry to those who, say, publicly declare that its people deserve to be wiped off the face of the earth. After all, there is no unqualified universal right to immigrate or to visit any place in the world. The most it can be said here is that all relevant cases should be examined as fair-mindedly as possible by taking into account the special reasons each alien has for entering the country. For a general criticism of the Act, including the above provision, see David Cole & James X. Dempsey *Terrorism and the Constitution: Sacrificing Civil Liberties in the Name of National Security* (New York: The New Press, 2002).

[5] "College Staff Find Chilling Free Speech Climate", http://www.blacknewsweekly.com/bin29.html.

[6] Ellen Cronin, "Editor of the Courier Newspaper Fired Suddenly", 14 February 2002, http://www. caledonianrecord.com/pages/local_news/story/faebd52bf.

[7] Andrew Buncombe, "US Cartoonists under Pressure to Follow the Patriotic Line", *The Independent* (London), 23 June 2002.

[8] "Falling under the Spell", *Index on Censorship*, http://www.indexonline.org/news/110901/20011010_unitedstates.shtml.

[9] Joel Feinberg, *Harm to Others: The Moral Limits of Criminal Law*, Volume One (Oxford: Oxford University Press, 1984), 4.

[10] "College Stuff", op. cit.

[11] It is very likely that the rapid expansion of the Internet will make these bans obsolete in the near future. This new cheap medium of communication allows all sorts of terrorists and extremists to bypass national laws, to retain their anonymity and to reach diverse audiences all over the world. For the legal issues concerning the policing of the Internet as well as the various difficulties surrounding it, see Kathy Crilley, "Information Warfare: New Battlefields. Terrorists, Propaganda and the Internet", *Aslib Proceedings* 53 (2001): 250-64.

[12] "The Political Significance of Terrorism", in *Violence, Terrorism, and Justice*, edited by R. G. Frey & Christopher W. Morris (Cambridge: Cambridge University Press, 1991), 88.

[13] I will not rehearse the various arguments undergirding this consensus. For a recent general account see Cass R. Sunstein, *Democracy and the Problem of Free Speech* (New York: Free Press, 1993). I have discussed one of these arguments at length in "Deliberative Democracy and Freedom of Expression (in Greek)", *Epistimi kai Koinonia* 1 (1998): 29-56. I would only like to point out that the most eloquent defenses of political speech are given in periods of crisis. Meikljohn's masterpiece *Political Freedom* came out as a reaction to the communist witch-hunts that took place in the forties and the fifties in the United States.

[14] *Whitney v. California* 274 U.S. 357 (1927).

[15] Carl Schmitt, *Political Theology: Four Chapters on the Concept of Sovereignty*, translated by George Schwab (Cambridge, Mass.: The MIT Press, 1994), Introduction.

[16] Cf. the remarks of Andrew Arato in his "*Minima Politica* after September 11", *Constellations* 9 (2002): 46-52.

[17] Undoubtedly, there are many ways to attack the security argument. Within a liberal philosophical context one can appeal to the lexical priority of civil liberties in a well-ordered society or to the anti-consequentialist consideration that we are not justified in bypassing the rights of a small minority to bring about a collectively beneficial outcome. See respectively Rawls's *Political Liberalism* (New York: Columbia University Press, 1993) and Dworkin's recent articles "The Threat to Patriotism", *The New York Review of Books*, 28 February 2002 and "Terror and the Attack on Civil Liberties", *The New York Review of Books*, 17 November 2003. However, this is not the line I take in this essay, although I am in full agreement with the rights approach. Instead I will attempt a more internal criticism of the security argument by taking for granted its basic underlying premise. It is my belief that under the current pressing circumstances it is more imperative to convince conservatives not to opt for an oppressive state rather than liberals, who oppose any curtailment of civil liberties more firmly than anyone else.

[18] Cf. Waldron's remark that "we have to worry that the very means given to the government to combat our enemies will be used by the government against *its* enemies – and although these two classes "enemies of the people" and "enemies of the state" overlap, they are not necessarily co-extensive". Jeremy Waldron, "Security and Liberty: The Image of Balance", *The Journal of Political Philosophy* 11 (2003): 206.

[19] If we substitute "liberty" for "personal safety", we have the 17th century "neo-roman" argument British political theorists put forward in favour of a free and representative civil association. See Quentin Skinner, *Liberty before Liberalism* (Cambridge: Cambridge University Press, 1998).

[20] In some cases terrorist communications take the form of detailed political commentaries similar to those published in radical journals and magazines. This is the case with *November 17* who would like to have its say in almost every aspect of Greek domestic and foreign policy. The "collected written works" of the organization, about nine hundred densely printed pages, constitute an important document for the study of the Greek political scene after the restoration of democracy in 1974. See *The Proclamations 1975-2002: All the Texts of the Organization* (in Greek) (Athens: Kaktos, 2002).

[21] *Speech, Crime, and the Uses of Language* (New York: Oxford University Press, 1989), 90-1.

[22] P. Gilbert, "The Oxygen of Publicity: Terrorism and Reporting Restrictions", in *Ethical Issues in Journalism and the Media*, edited by Andrew Belsey & Ruth Chadwick (London & New York: Routledge, 1992), 145.

[23] Cf. Onora O' Neill's remark that "[w]hat constitutes a threat depends on what powers a threatener has to harm particular victims – hence also on the reciprocal of power, i.e. on the vulnerability of those threatened". See her "Transnational Justice", in *Political Theory Today*, edited by David Held (Cambridge: Polity Press, 1991), 300.

[24] I elaborate this claim in "Freedom of Expression, Autonomy and Defamation", *Law and Philosophy* 17 (1998): 1-17.

[25] On the contrary this is not true with respect to any threats made by citizens who simply sympathise with terrorist groups. These can be better characterised as "political hyperbole".

[26] I am thinking of cases where terrorists attempt to publicize stolen secret documents that would jeopardise national security. Or cases where the broadcasting of a threat would create such panic that more lives would be saved if the authorities and the media kept the public in the dark.

[27] It was said earlier that the arguments adduced concern individual citizens, legislators and politicians. I shall not discuss the media coverage of terrorism, which deserves separate treatment. This is a very perplexing issue, given the special moral obligations of media to the public, the unavoidably commercial character of most of them and the tremendous influence they exercise in the formation of public opinion. For various aspects of it, see S. Kleidman & T. L. Beauchamp, *The Virtuous Journalist* (New York: Oxford University Press, 1987), David L. Paletz & Alex P. Schmid, eds., *Terrorism and the Media* (London: Sage, 1992), Santo Iyengar, *Is Anyone Responsible? How Television Frames Political Issues* (Chicago and London: Chicago University Press, 1994), and Virginia Held, "The Media and Political Violence", *The Journal of Ethics* 1 (1997): 187-202.

[28] *On Liberty,* edited with an Introduction by John Gray (Oxford: Oxford University Press, 1991), 86.

VÉRONIQUE ZANETTI

AFTER 9-11 – A PARADIGM CHANGE IN INTERNATIONAL LAW?[*]

The terrorist attacks of September 11, 2001 upon the World Trade Center in New York and the Pentagon in Washington have sent shock waves through international politics and law whose consequences some compare to those of the fall of the Berlin Wall.[1] Within a few hours the whole world had been swamped by the spectacular and shocking images of the Twin Towers – emblems of economic and political liberalism – collapsing into themselves like a house of cards. Within a few days the international community had demonstrated unprecedented unanimity in its response, which translated with equal alacrity into decisions. Before long juridical facts had been constituted which doubtless will make their mark on future international legislation. I would like to recall some of the key moments:

- On September 12 President Bush deems the attack a crime, only later to speak of a "war" against the civilised world – a formulation immediately adopted by politicians in other countries and by a broad faction of the international press.[2]

- That same day, in less than a half an hour, the Security Council unanimously passes a resolution (resolution 1368) characterising the attack as a "threat to international peace and security" and conferring upon the victim state the right to act in self-defence.

- Still September 12: For the first time in the history of NATO article 5 of the Washington Treaty is provisionally invoked (and on October 2 definitively), calling for the solidarity of the allied nations.[3]

- On September 28 the Security Council votes – again unanimously – in favour of Resolution 1373, which affirms the decision made directly after the attack and endorses a package of concrete measures for the struggle against terrorism.

- On October 7, the first bombs fall on Afghanistan; after several weeks of intensively negotiating for the support of Arab leaders, the United States makes concrete its intention to wage war on the Al Quaida terrorist organisation. But beyond this, by setting their sights also on the Taliban regime, the Americans signal a paradigm shift: what could not be called a war as long as it is directed at a private organisation takes on the classical form of armed conflict between states.

As we can see, then, and as the media has often emphasised, the events of September 11 and the subsequent weeks, by shuffling and consolidating international alliances, have altered the geopolitical face of the world in record time and led to dramatic changes in international law. The unanimous acceptance of the resolutions, on the one hand, introduced a convention whereby measures aimed to prevent and combat terrorism are immune to the incalculable hazards of ad hoc acceptance by individual

329

Meggle (ed.), Ethics of Terrorism & Counter-Terrorism, 329-340.
© 2005 Ontos, Heusenstamm.

states.[4] On the other hand, decisions had to be made under pressure of urgency and shock for which international law was unprepared. Existing concepts had to be specified or adjusted to fit new realities: does a terrorist attack of such magnitude constitute an armed attack? Is the victim state in sole possession of the right to self-defence against such aggression, or must a legitimate response be made collectively? Who are the aggressors? Does the pursuit of an international terrorist organisation justify suspending the prohibition of the use of force against a third state? Politics may already have answered in practise; but the questions remain open, and I shall investigate them in this paper.

I make no claim to originality – neither for my method nor for my answers. Indeed, the gravity of the events immediately triggered considerable debate among legal scholars.[5] But unfortunately this debate has remained the exclusive province of experts; despite the importance of the issues, it has not crossed the threshold to a broader public.

I would like to state clearly that I am not a legal scholar but a philosopher, and that I would like to address the matters at hand philosophically. I do not want to appraise the soundness of the decisions that were made, but to analyse the normative significance and political consequences of the specific conceptual formulation of the events. It is no mere rhetorical exercise to apply the term "war" to a conflict and thereby to locate it within the framework of self-defence or collective response to an affront against peace and security. This appellation has consequences of extreme import for an incalculable number of people. The question whether there has been a paradigm shift in international law implies the further question as to the consequences of such a paradigm shift and as to what principles are to guide international law and politics.

Before examining the legal categories that have been called into question since September 11 I would like to sketch some of the characteristics of international terrorism and show how it challenges the classical typology of organised violence. I realise that my discussion may be open to the charge of over-simplification: there is, in fact, no such thing as terrorism as such. Rather, there are diverse structures with diverse motives, strategies and goals. But the scheme I present should at least demonstrate how helpless international law is to respond to a phenomenon that does not respect the traditional division of the world into sovereign states: the privatisation of violence presents a serious challenge to an international law designed for conflicts delimited in space and time and involving state-actors.[6] It was this void of appropriate legal concepts which enabled the US to justify its primarily unilateral military response; for a state that has never concerned itself much anyway with international documents, legal ambiguity is a welcome invitation to exercise its power with glib legitimacy.

I. CLASSICAL WAR VERSUS INTERNATIONAL TERRORISM

The theory of just war is rooted in a classical scheme of warfare that does not accommodate the forms of domestic or international conflict typical of the post-war era.[7] In the following I shall sketch the main points of contrast between international terrorism and this classical scheme.

- The Actors: Whereas conventional wars manifest the power of a state or alliance of states, terrorist actions are the work of individuals organised by leaders of private groups.
- Organisation: When conflict arises, states officially call on armed forces, which are organised vertically and hierarchically. Terrorist organisations, in contrast, operate underground. Although they often have a central leadership, they consist of scattered units which, for the sake of efficacy and flexibility, require a certain degree of autonomy. In structures modelled according to the Waben Principle, for example, a suicide commando learns the identity of his immediate superior and the nature of his task only shortly before going into action.[8]
- Strategy: The application of violence differs between the two forms of conflict. In a classical war, states aim for superiority in numbers and military technology. Civilian casualty is not a goal, but constitutes regrettable "collateral damage". Terrorist attacks, on the other hand, aim for psychological effect and media sensation. They invert the principle of proportionality by seeking to wreak as much havoc as possible with limited means.
- Funding: Classical warfare is financed centrally; taxation pays for weapons and soldiers. International terrorist organisations, in contrast, are financed de-centrally; they are supported by private donations, organised crime, drug and weapons trafficking, even charities.[9]
- Space: Whereas the location of a conventional war is more or less unambiguous, terrorism depends upon the unpredictability of its targets.
- Time: Financial and human costs impose strict limits on the duration of classical warfare. If an offensive campaign does not lead to quick victory, then it must also compete with time. But since terrorist groups do not seek to conquer, they need not reckon with time in the same way. They have at their disposal extended or even unlimited periods of time. This temporal indeterminacy serves as an effective psychological weapon.

Let us return to the conceptual formulation of the events of September 11 and its legal and political consequences. What was it, that occurred on that day? A terrorist attack or a declaration of war? Was there and armed attack? A threat to international peace? Who were the aggressors?

II. WAS THERE A WAR?

In classical international law the terms "war" and "armed conflict" apply only to conflicts between states. A state is at war when it fights against another internationally recognised state or against a revolting party. War can also be waged against a population, even when this population possesses no officially recognised territory (against the Palestinians or the Kurds, for example). But there can be no war against Osama bin Laden or Al Quaida, since they represent neither a state nor a revolting party.[10] For many legal scholars "a murderous attack on the citizens of a country do not represent an act of war, but simply a crime, for which the criminals and their co-conspirators can be brought to court".[11]

Granted, the attacks of September 11 were no isolated incidents: in 1993 bin Laden and his associates were implicated in an earlier attack on the World Trade Center; in 1998 they were involved in attacks on the American embassies in Tanzania and Kenya. Insofar as the attacks were part of an ongoing campaign designed to create an atmosphere of constant threat, one may say that they resemble a declaration of war. Indeed, it is precisely this repetitiveness to which the US refers in asserting its right to self-defence. But the fact remains that President Bush's slogan "we are at war" is legally false. Moreover, it is dangerous in that it opens the door to a unilateral administration of justice.[12]

It was not the passion of the moment that led Bush to this particular formulation. Nor was he taken in by the rhetoric of holy war employed by his enemies. On the contrary, he chose his words carefully, with an eye to their psychological, strategic and legal consequences. A declaration of war, as we know, does not call for the same sort of response as a criminal act.

As for the psychological aspect, calling a terrorist act a declaration of war emphasises the extent as well as the international significance of the catastrophe, and draws attention to the stated intention of the attackers to engage in a long-term conflict. In reality, a random or isolated act of violence is not the same thing as a declaration of war. In an interview on September 13, 2001, Colin Powell summed up this psychological effect: "(We are) speaking about war as a way of focusing the energy of America and the energy of the international community."[13] If the events of September 11 are understood as a declaration of war, then it becomes self-evident that the US must exercise its right to self-defence and respond with violence.

Then there is the strategic aspect. As the allies must have realised – not to mention the aggressors and those offering them refuge – the talk of war was not merely metaphorical. It would not have been very credible for the US to respond as one looks for a needle in a haystack. But, as we saw earlier, international terrorism operates from secret bases that are geographically and structurally scattered. Such an enemy would not do; he had to be given a face.[14] By territorialising the conflict, the US compelled it to fit the mould of a classical armed conflict between states. The Bush administration knew that it could count on the concurrence of its shocked population and on the passivity of other nations. But it is important to understand that the territorialisation of the conflict leads to a twofold paradigm shift, with considerable consequences for international law.

The first blow to the reigning paradigm occurs on the level of principles, when responsibility for the actions is extended from the terrorists to the state harbouring them. This state is charged with violating international resolutions insofar as it tolerates terrorists within its borders and refuses to take the appropriate measures against them. I shall return to this point when I deal with the question of the right to self-defence.

The second blow to the paradigm is political in nature. It has to do with a change of goals: the campaign to root out terrorism and the armed bases which support it metamorphoses into a war against the reigning Taliban regime. With this operation the US authorities manage to kill three birds with one stone: playing the card of the military superpower, they demonstrates resoluteness; they remove a long-unfriendly regime (which they earlier supported for quite some time); and in the event of victory, they can station troops in an a region whose proximity to the rich oil reserves lends it great strategic importance.

Finally, there is the legal aspect. According to the official reaction, the war began on September 11, not October 7, when the first bombs fell on Afghanistan.[15] We are referred, therefore, to the terms of the Geneva Convention of 1949 and its subsequent regulations, which prescribe that a military counter-attack must respect the principle of proportionality of employed means and the principle of distinction between military and civilian targets.

In the case at hand it is questionable whether either of these principles was respected. As for the principle of distinction, the US forces used not only cluster bombs – thousands of which lie unexploded on the ground, presenting a long-term threat to the Afghani people – but also degraded uranium bombs to destroy the bunkers where Al Quaida members were hiding. Nor did they respect accepted principles regarding the treatment of captured soldiers. Before an audience of representatives in Strasbourg on July 12, Irish journalist Jamie Doran presented film of what he asserted were mass graves in Afghanistan. Witnesses report that approximately 3000 Taliban fighters were forced after capitulating into a container where as many as half of them suffocated to death. A US soldier claims that surviving prisoners were tortured, killed and transported to mass graves.[16] And the principle of proportionality of employed means? Only terrorist bases or military installations that support them could come into consideration as appropriate military targets.[17] In this case, however, the American attack targeted not only terrorist bases but also the reigning government of Afghanistan. This, as I have asserted, represents a significant paradigm shift.

III. THE RIGHT TO SELF-DEFENCE

Countless legal scholars have emphasised the ambiguity, indeed contradiction, of the two resolutions – 1368 and 1373 – passed immediately following September 11.[18] The Security Council qualified the attacks, "like any act of international terrorism, as a threat to international peace and security". These words clearly suggest a course of action in accordance with chapter VII of the Charter, namely a collective response of military or non-military nature under UN leadership. But the Security Council went on to acknowledge "the inherent right of individual or collective self-defence in accordance with the Charter", thereby leaving the initial reaction to the discretion of the victim state. The wavering of the Security Council is a good indication of the insufficiency of international law to handle a non-state foe whose destructive capabilities are recognised by all.

But this contradiction is not the only sign that the international community was at a complete loss to deal with the violence of the attacks and the obvious threat posed by a group so well-organised and so unscrupulous. This helplessness is also betrayed by the unfortunate wording of the resolution: can one really make the claim that *any act of international terrorism* is a threat to international peace and security? There is good reason to doubt the soundness of such a claim, which neglects to differentiate degrees of catastrophe and, on top of it all, does not bother with a definition of "international terrorism".

Under article 51 of the UN Charter, a state has the right to defend itself when it is the victim of an "armed attack". But this right to self-defence is explicitly provisional, valid "until the Security Council has taken measures requisite to the preservation of international peace and security". Its role is, according to expert opinion,[19] subsidiary to the collective system of peace-keeping.

Since article 51 can be invoked only after an "armed attack", it is clear that everything depends upon the precise conceptual formulation of what happened on September 11. We may concede that the term "armed attack" is not limited to invasion by a regular army, but also includes "the dispatch by a state of armed bands or groups, irregular or mercenary soldiers to carry out acts of armed aggression against another state".[20] Not just any criminal act, however, is an occasion to exercise the right to self-defence.

In the present case there could be no doubt from the moment the attacks were qualified as a declaration of war that they would fall under the category of an "armed attack". This interpretation was confirmed when NATO invoked article 5, which asserts the right to collective self-defence in the event that one of the nineteen member states falls victim to an armed attack. With this, along with the Security Council resolutions, a new precedent has been created in the interpretation of international law.[21] It was nothing new for the Security Council to adopt a resolution characterising terrorism as a threat to peace and security, but invoking the right to self-defence was indeed an innovation, and many legal scholars fear its potentially subversive consequences.[22]

Such a reaction goes to show, once again, how much the traditional categories of international law were overwhelmed by the unprecedented magnitude of this misdeed committed by such a well-organised group. For the right to self-defence had previously been contingent upon a clearly defined set of conditions,[23] closely tied to the criteria for state exercise of force I discussed in part one.

1. The reaction of the victim state must be immediate.

2. The state against which force is applied must have been responsible for the initial aggression. The goal is to respond to an armed attack with a military counter-attack.

3. The application of force must cease when the initial attack has ended or when the Security Council has taken requisite measures.

4. The nature of the operation must be appropriate to the pursued aim, namely to put an end to the initial attack.

5. The state defending itself must respect the internationally recognised principles of conduct in war.

As we can see, the concept of a right to self-defence fits perfectly into the classical, state-oriented mould of international law: the aggressor, the aim and (at least in theory) the duration, are clearly given. But in this case the aggressor, the attack and the appropriate reaction are all matters of interpretation, indeed controversies. I shall examine each in turn:

The Aggressors: As for the direct aggressors, they were destroyed along with their weapons the instant they attacked. If this constitutes an "armed attack", it ends as soon as it has begun. The right to self-defence, then, does not come into the picture at all. Of course the indirect aggressors remain, who served as middle-men or provided resources for the attack. But it takes time to identify who they are, so a response to them could not fulfil the condition of immediacy.

Then there is of course the extremely difficult question whether a regime knowingly harbouring terrorists and refusing to comply with UN resolutions concerning the struggle against terrorism can be held responsible for such an act of aggression and treated as an aggressor.[24]

No one denies that the Taliban government – or de facto government – harboured terrorists and allowed them to use Afghani territory for military training. And no one denies that it provided them with material for organising and executing their plans. So there is no question that it shared responsibility for the attacks. This conclusion is confirmed by several earlier resolutions of the Security Council condemning the Taliban for refusing to co-operate. Resolution 1267 (1999) even refers in this context to a threat to international peace and security and draws a parallel between refusing to take measures against terrorism and encouraging terrorists to commit acts of violence.[25] In fact, the resolution goes so far as to charge the Taliban regime with creating an internationally insecure situation in which chapter VII of the Charter could justifiably be invoked.

But it is important to make a distinction between two questions. First: If a state refuses to co-operate against terrorism and, indeed, supports terrorism: does this suffice to suspend article 2/4, which prohibits the use of force against a state? Second: Can a state that harbours terrorists be equated with an aggressor and become the target of unilateral or collective exercise of the right to self-defence?

The distinction is important because of the different types of response to which it leads. In the first case the refusal to co-operate justifies the UN to take collective action to compel the fractious state to abide by its terms. The coercive measures, however, need not be of military nature. Resolutions 1368 and 1373 express on the one hand determination to take "all necessary steps in order to ensure the full implementation of this resolution". But, on the other hand, they make no mention of military action and limit themselves to a catalogue of legal and financial sanctions. In other words: as soon as one abandons the classical model of conflict, where the instances of power represent states, the ascription of responsibility becomes an extremely tricky affair with which no international document can help. As for the requirements imposed by the anti-terrorist resolutions of the Security Council, we can distinguish at least three levels:

a) Implication by omission: a state can be held accountable for failing to meet the requirements imposed by the Security Council. This may occur when a state neglects to take the requisite steps to control or cut off the financial resources on which terrorism subsists: when the state, for example, does not freeze the savings and capital of individuals accused of having connections with terrorism.

b) Implication by noncooperation: a state can be held accountable for refusing to fulfil obligations. It refuses, for example, to extradite terrorists or to share information that would help to identify leaders of international networks.

c) Implication by contribution: a state can be held accountable for assisting in planning or funding terrorist attacks.

The aforementioned plenary assembly declared that only this third set of conditions is sufficient to make a state guilty of an armed attack. In other words: it is not enough that a state has neglected to fulfil internationally agreed upon obligations, nor even that a state has violated essential regulations of an agreement. There must be evidence of a direct responsibility for the existence of a terrorist organisation or for the preparation of an attack. These three degrees of implication imply varying degrees of pressure that can legitimately be applied.

The Attack: it must be emphasised that the Security Council carefully avoided talk of an "armed attack" in both of its resolutions of September 11 and 28, preferring to speak of a "terrorist attack". Of course one could say that the magnitude as well as the instruments (passenger jets were indeed employed as veritable bombs) qualify this terrorist attack as an armed attack, even if the expression has traditionally been reserved for acts of aggression performed by states against the sovereignty and territorial integrity of other states. But even if one takes this step, it does not follow that one can extend the term "armed attack" to include the role played by the government harbouring the terrorists. "This raises first of all the question whether it is admissible to equate planning and assistance with criminal action."[26] And so we meet up again with the difficulty of identifying the aggressor.

The Reaction: by now it should be abundantly clear what position I take. Since I do not think that harbouring terrorist organisations can be equated with committing a criminal act, I do not consider the American military action against Afghanistan an appropriate response to the events of September 11. Having said this, it is important to recognise that there is another perspective from which to scrutinise my answer. The point of the proviso that a state exercising the right to self-defence must react immediately is to limit this reaction to the time required for the UN to prepare a collective response and take over the defence.[27] But the American reaction in this case has the peculiar characteristic of having begun almost a month after the initial attack. Furthermore, it is not limited to any particular time frame, nor to the purpose of stopping the initial attack. Its purpose, rather, is to prevent further attacks. Clearly, this represents a paradigm shift. The primary concern is no longer the terrorist attacks of September 11, but the threat presented to international peace and security by internationally organised terrorism.

The task of appraising and meeting this danger should fall to the UN Security Council. There is every reason for concern when the extent of repressive and preventative measures is left to the discretion of a particular state – all the more so, when, to quote George Bush, "this group and its leader [...] are linked to many other organizations in different countries, including the Egyptian Islamic Jihad and the Islamic Movement of Uzbekistan. There are thousands of terrorists in more than 60 countries."[28] Moreover, Bush declared at the beginning of the bombing campaign that all governments tolerating or supporting terrorism would be regarded as "rogue states". What the president forgot to mention on this occasion is that the US officially finances terrorist training camps and a school by the name of "Western Hemisphere Institute for Security Cooperation" where more than 60.000 Latin-American soldiers and police officers have been trained since 1946, many of whom have organised terrorist actions against prominent political figures and against the populations of Guatemala, El Salvador, Chile, Argentina and Columbia.[29] In 1996 the US government had to remove books from the curriculum which provided tips for terrorists, including recommendations for "blackmail, torture, execution and the arrest of witnesses' relatives" (ibid.).

I want to express the difficulty of determining the aggressors, the nature of the aggression and the appropriate response with a quote from de Cassese:

> "[...] We are confronted here with attacks emanating from non-state organizations, which may be hosted in various countries possibly not easy to identify and, what is more important, whose degree of 'complicity' may vary. It would be legally unwarranted to grant the state victim of terrorist attacks very sweeping discretionary powers that would include the power to decide what states are behind the terrorist organizations and to what degree they have tolerated, or approved or instigated and promoted terrorism. A sober consideration of the general legal principles governing the international community should lead us to a clear conclusion: it would only be for the Security Council to decide whether, and on what conditions, to authorize the use of force against specific states, on the basis of compelling evidence showing that those states, instead of stopping the action of terrorist organizations and detaining its members, harbour, protect, tolerate or promote such organizations, in breach of the general legal duty referred to above." (Cassese, op. cit.).

IV. CONCLUSION

Have the attacks of September 11 provided the occasion for a paradigm shift in international law? I hope it has become clear that I think the level of facts has to be kept distinct from the normative level. Looking at the facts – created by the resolutions of the Security Council and NATO, as well as by the military actions of the United States and its allies – the answer has to be "yes". This paradigm shift has four aspects, which I summarise as follows:

1) The terrorist attacks were equated with a declaration of war and conceptualised as an armed attack. This extends article 51 of the UN Charter – designed for attacks issuing from states – to criminal acts perpetrated by private individuals.

2) The terrorist attacks spurred the invocation of the right to individual or collective self-defence by the victim state.

3) Not only the direct aggressors were held accountable for the attacks, but an entire state, which violated multiple international agreements by harbouring Al Quaida and refusing to extradite its leader.

4) The delayed start and unlimited duration of the reaction of the victim state created a new precedent, whereby the right to self-defence can be exercised preventatively.

In view of the tragedy of the events and the proportions assumed by organised international crime, it is undeniable that we are experiencing de facto a shift in the application of international law. For this very reason it is important to consider the question whether such a factual rearrangement should be equated with a change in our normative consciousness. In other words, we need to think about whether the newly manifested brutality of international terrorism call for an alteration of the fundamental principles of international law.

I am not in a position to offer an answer to this difficult question. But I would like to mention a few points that seem to me important in connection with the aspects I have emphasised:

- Official reactions to the events of September 11 have stressed the international dimension of the catastrophe (expressed by the diversity of the victims' nationalities). Although the United States was clearly the main target on this occasion, the whole world has been alerted to the vulnerability of its cities, its infrastructure and its population to such unscrupulous and well-orchestrated attacks. The alacrity and unanimity of international response reflect solidarity: it is paramount that this solidarity be expressed in collective action. Any unilateral initiative may threaten the precarious balance.

- In view of the perfection of the technical means and the extent of the destruction, it is surely unavoidable to broaden the concept of armed attack to terrorist attacks of a certain magnitude. It is probably also necessary to expand the accountability of a state that harbours terrorists and allows them to use its territory for training and weapons-storage. Finally, the magnitude of the catastrophe forces us to accept that the right to self-defence will have to include a preventative element in cases where there is clear danger of further attacks by the same organisation. Considering the unscrupulousness of groups that would not hesitate to use nuclear or biological weapons, it would be somewhat absurd to expect that a state refrain from acting to prevent an attack that were sure to come. Having said this, I do not believe that a broader concept of "armed attack", nor an expanded accountability of a state for acts of aggression, nor even the necessity of prevention can serve as justification for a state to act unilaterally. It is the task of the Security Council to decide what measures are necessary and to identify guilty parties on the basis of incontestable evidence.

- The expansion of the right to intervene – corresponding to the expansion of the aforementioned concepts – is no *carte blanche* for the use of force. Measures taken against states or private criminals must be contained within appropriate bounds.

- Terrorist acts of a certain magnitude should be condemned as crimes against humanity. This implies the creation of an international criminal court, to which the US is currently in opposition. An international court would have the advantage of being able to speak on behalf of the entire international community. It would be protected from the charge of partiality.

- The expansion of the concept of accountability would entail that not only direct aggressors could be charged in an international criminal court, but also official members of a government guilty of assisting terrorists. But this would only be credible if all those responsible for state actions aimed to destabilise democratically elected governments or to spread terror in other countries, were tried and held accountable.

AFTER 9-11 – A PARADIGM CHANGE IN INTERNATIONAL LAW?

In summary, the tragic events of September 11 have undeniably brought about significant changes in international law. Nevertheless, it would be false to abandon the fundamental principles governing the international community, represented by the UN. On the contrary, the attacks have alerted us to the need to expand and improve our collective resources. They have reminded us how important an impartial justice system is. For as long as international law allows a few states to get away with (directly or indirectly) manipulating the interior affairs and the futures of other states, it will be opening the door to anarchy – to the greater benefit of terrorists.

NOTES

* This text was written immediately after the terrorist attacks of September 11, 2001. Even if many of the issues treated here are closely tied to the historical events, the normative questions they address remain entirely pertinent today.

[1] See for example Daniele Archibugi, "Terrorism and Cosmopolitanism", http://www.ssrc.org/sept11/essays/archibugi.htm.

[2] "The deliberate and deadly attacks which were carried out yesterday against our country were more than acts or terror. They were acts of war." See also Bush's speech: http://www.whitehouse.gov/news/releases/2001/09/20010911-16.html (or: http://www.whitehouse.gov/response/faq-what.html).

[3] "We know that the individuals who carried out these attacks were part of the worldwide terrorist network of Al-Quaida, headed by Osama bin Laden and his key lieutenants and protected by the Taliban. On the basis of this briefing, it has now been determined that the attack against the United States on 11 September was directed from abroad and shall therefore be regarded as an action covered by Article 5 of the Washington Treaty, which states that an armed attack on one or more of the Allies in Europe or North America shall be considered an attack against them all." Cf. http://www.nato.int/doc/speech/2001/s011002a.htm. See also Carsten Stahn, "Security Council Resolutions 1368 (2001) and 1373 (2001): What They Say and What They Do Not Say", *European Journal of International Law, Discussion Forum,* http://www.ejil.org/forum_WTC.

[4] Luigi Condorelli (2001): Les attentats du 11 septembre et leurs suites: où va le droit international ?", *Revue Générale de Droit International Public,* Paris, vol. 105/2001/4, 829-848.

[5] An important discussion took immediately place on the Web. See the excellent page of the European Journal of International Law: http://www.ejil.org/forum_WTC. For reactions from American legal scholars, see also ASIL (The American Society of International Law): http://www.asil.org/insights/insigh77.htm.

[6] Tomas Bruha; Matthias Bortfeld (2001): "Terrorismus und Selbstverteidigung. Voraussetzungen und Umfang erlaubter Selbstverteidigungsmaßnahmen nach den Anschlägen vom 11. September 2001", *Vereinte Nationen* 5, Oktober 2001, 161-167.

[7] See Mary Kaldors, "Reconceptualizing Organized Violence", In: Daniele Archibugi et al. (ed.) (1998), *Re-imagining Political Community,* Stanford.

[8] Cf. Peter Waldmann (1998): *Terrorismus. Provokation der Macht,* München. Footnote 5, p. 63.

[9] See Yael Shahar, "Tracing bin Laden's Money: easier said than done", http://www.ict.org.il/articles/articledet.cfm?articleid=387.

[10] Compare Jordan Paust (2001): "War and Responses to Terrorism", www.asil.orga/insights/insigh77.htm.

[11] Tomuschat, Christian (2001): "Der 11. September 2001 und seine rechtlichen Konsequenzen", EuCRZ 28, Heft 21-23, 535-545; here p. 536. See also Cassese, Antonio; Dupuy, Pierre-Marie, Pellet, Alain und Mégret, Frédéric, European Journal of International Law, Discussion Forum, op. cit.

[12] Compare with Alain Pellet (2001): "No, This is not War!", Discussion Forum, op. cit.

[13] http://usinfo.state.gov/topical/pol/terror/01091366.htm.

[14] Cf. Pierre-Marie Dupuy 2001: "The Law after the Destruction of the Towers", http://www.ejil.org/forum_WTC/ ny-dupuy.html.

[15] Cf. Luigi Condorelli (2001), op. cit.

[16] *Frankfurter Rundschau,* Juni 13, 2002, p. 1; *Le Monde,* June 14, 2002, p. 1.; See also Jamie Doran's article in *Le Monde Diplomatique* Nr. 582, September 2002, pp. 1, 16-17.

[17] As Cassese emphasizes: "[F]orce *may not* be used to wipe out the Afghan leadership or destroy Afghan military installations and other military objectives that have nothing to do with the terrorist organizations, unless the Afghan central authorities show by words or deeds that they approve and endorse the action of terrorist organizations." Op. cit.

[18] For example Cassese and Mégret, op. cit., as well as Carsten Stahn, "Security Coucil Resolutions 1368 (2001) and 1373 (2001): What They Say and What They Do Not Say", *European Journal of International Law, Discussion Forum*, op. cit.

[19] See for example Nico Krisch (2001): *Selbstverteidigung und kollektive Sicherheit,* Springer: Berlin, New York.

[20] Art. 3, paragraph g of the Resolution 3314 (XXIX) of the General Assembly, 14.12.1974. Cf. J. P. Cot and A. Pellet (1991): *La Charte des Nations Unies. Commentaire article par article.* Second expanded and revised edition, Paris.

[21] As Carsten Stahn emphasises (op. cit.), it is nothing new for the Security Council to deem terrorism a threat to international peace and security. In 1999, Resolution 1267 declared that the Taliban presented just such a threat by refusing to comply with Resolution 1214 (1998), which forbade all states to harbour terrorists within their borders. What is new about Resolutions 1368 and 1373 is that they acknowledge the right of the victim state to self-defence.

[22] In particular Cassese, op. cit.

[23] I shall assume here the criteria introduced by Cassese, op. cit. See also Tomuschat, op. cit.

[24] See for example Resolution Nr. 2625-XXV, (1970) as well as Resolutions Nr. 1189 (1998) and 1373 (2001) of the Security Council.

[25] This qualification occurs also in the Resolution 1333 (2000).

[26] Tomuschat, op. cit., p. 541.

[27] Compare Condorelli, op. cit., p. 838. For an detailed analyse of the right to self-defence, see Nico Krisch (2001), op. cit.

[28] Bush's speech before Congress, September 20, 2001, http://www.whitehouse.gov/response/faq-what.html.

[29] See George Monbiot, Guardian, 30 October 2001, http://www.zmag.org/zmag/articles/feb98herman.htm.

BIOGRAPHICAL NOTES

PER BAUHN

Per Bauhn is Professor of Practical Philosophy at Kalmar University College, Sweden. He has previously published *Ethical Aspects of Political Terrorism* (Lund, 1989) and *Nationalism and Morality* (Lund, 1995). Professor Bauhn lectured in Peace and Conflict Studies at Lund University between 1992 and 2004. His most recent book is *The Value of Courage* (Nordic Academic Press, 2003).

RÜDIGER BITTNER

Rüdiger Bittner is Professor of Philosophy at the University of Bielefeld. He is the author of *What reason demands* (Cambridge UP, 1989) and *Doing things for reasons* (Oxford UP, 2001). His fields are theory of action, moral philosophy and political philosophy.

C. A. J. (TONY) COADY

C. A. J. (Tony) Coady is Professorial Fellow in Applied Philosophy in the ARC Special Research Centre for Applied Philosophy and Public Ethics at the University of Melbourne. His books include *Testimony: A Philosophical Study* (Oxford, 1992).

He has published extensively on issues to do with war and political violence, and his book for Cambridge University Press on Morality and Political Violence is nearing completion.

MARCELO DASCAL

Marcelo Dascal is Professor of Philosophy and former Dean of Humanities at Tel Aviv University. His areas of research include the philosophy of language, history of modern philosophy, pragmatics, epistemology, political philosophy and, in the last decade, the investigation of the phenomenon of controversies. His most recent books are *Interpretation and Understanding* (Amsterdam, 2003) and *The Gust of the Wind: Humanities in a New-Old World* (Jerusalem, 2004; in Hebrew). Dascal has been active in the Israeli peace movements since 1969.

http://www.tau.ac.il/humanities/philos/dascal

CAROLIN EMCKE

Carolin Emcke is a political theorist and journalist. She has published on issues of cultural rights and recognition of collective identities. As a journalist she has covered human rights issues and regions of war all over the world, and the war against terror since 9/11 in New York, Pakistan, Afghanistan and Cashmir: *Von den Kriegen. Briefe an Freunde* (Frankfurt, 2004). Publications include: *Kollektive Identitäten – eine sozialphilosophische Grundlegung* (Frankfurt, 2000); "Between Choice and Coercion – Identitities, Injuries, and different forms of Recognition" (*Constellations*, Vol. 7, No. 4, December 2000).

RALF GROETKER

Ralf Groetker is a free lance Journalist, working for *Frankfurter Rundschau*, Deutschlandradio, www.telepolis.de and others. His recent work is centered around different topics related to privacy, ethical scepticism, and the history of perception.

TOMIS KAPITAN

Tomis Kapitan is currently Professor of Philosophy at Northern Illinois University. From 1981 to 1986 he taught philosophy and cultural studies at Birzeit University in the occupied West Bank. More recently, he has taught at the American University of Beirut and Bogazici University in Istanbul. His research is primarily focused on issues in metaphysics, philosophy of language, and international ethics.
   http://www.niu.edu/phil/~kapitan/index.shtml

HAIG KHATCHADOURIAN

Haig Khatchadourian is Emeritus Professor of Philosophy at The University of Wisconsin-Milwaukee. His publications include: *The Morality of Terrorism* (New York, 1998); *Community and Communitarianism* (New York, 1999); and *War, Terrorism, Genocide, And The Quest For Peace – Contemporary Problems In Political Ethics* (Lewiston, 2003). He is a foreign member of the Armenian Academy of Philosophy, a founding member of the International Academy of Philosophy, and a Fellow of the Royal Society for the encouragement of the Arts (FRSA) in England.

LAURENCE LUSTGARTEN

Laurence Lustgarten recently became a Commissioner of the Independent Police Complaints Commission, which oversees and investigates complaints against the police in England and Wales. The article was written when he was Professor of Law at the University of Southampton, where his research interests were broadly in public law and criminal justice; more particularly in policing and national security issues, comparativ constitutional structures and racial discrimination.
   Relevant publications: *In From the Cold: National Security and Parliamentary Democracy* (with I Leigh, Oxford: Univ. Press, 1994); "A Distorted Image of Ourselves: Nazism, 'Liberal' Societies, and the Qualities of Difference", in: *Darker legacies of law in Europe* (ed. N. Galeigh and C. Joerges, Oxford: Hart Publishing Co., 2003); *The Governance of Police* (London: Sweet & Maxwell, 1986).

GEORG MEGGLE

Georg Meggle is Professor of Philosophy at the University of Leipzig; initiator and first president of the Society of Anaytical Philosophy (GAP-Gesellschaft für Analytische Philosophie). Main topics of research: Action, Communication, Language (*Grundbegriffe der Kommunikation*, Berlin/New York: de Gruyter, [2]1997), Interpersonal Relations, Meaning of Life (*Sinn des Lebens*, München: dtv, [4]2002) and Ethics of War (*Terror & Der Krieg gegen ihn. Öffentliche Reflexionen*, ed., Paderborn: mentis, 2003). Papers relevant for the topic of this volume available also via: http://www.uni-leipzig.de/~philos/meggle.htm

THOMAS MERTENS

Thomas Mertens is Professor of Philosophy of Law, Faculty of Law at Nijmegen University, The Netherlands. He recently translated and published an annotated version of Kant's *Towards Perpetual Peace* in Dutch (Amsterdam: Boom, 2004). He has published on the ethics of war and peace from the perspective of authors such as Kant, Hegel, Arendt and Rawls. He is currently working on a monograph on law and morals during the Nazi era, with the provisional title: *From Weimar to Jerusalem*.

DANIEL MESSELKEN

Daniel Messelken has studied Political Science, Philosophy and French Studies at Leipzig University, Sciences-Po Paris, and Ecole Normale Supérieure Paris. He is currently working on his PhD thesis.
    http://messelken.de/

SEUMAS MILLER

Seumas Miller is Professor of Philosophy at Charles Sturt University and the Australian National University (joint position), and Director of the Centre for Applied Philosophy and Public Ethics (an Australian Research Council funded Special Research Centre).

OLAF L. MUELLER

Olaf Mueller is Professor of Philosophy at Humboldt-University, Berlin, Germany. He writes on topics in epistemology, metaphysics, ethics, and the philosophy of science. He published papers about pacifism (2004), analyticity (1998), and the refutation of skepticism (2001). His latest book concerns metaphysical implications of Putnam's proof against the brain-in-a-vat-hypothesis (*Hilary Putnam und der Abschied vom Skeptizismus*, Paderborn: mentis, 2003). Presently, he is preparing a monography about moral observation sentences.
    http://www.GehirnImTank.de

ALEKSANDAR PAVKOVIĆ

Aleksandar (Sasha) Pavković is Associate Professor of the Politics Department at Macquarie University, Sydney and an honorary senior Research Fellow at the Centre for Applied Philosophy and Public Ethics at the University of Melbourne. His publications include: *The Fragmentation of Yugoslavia: Nationalism and War in the Balkans* (London, ²2000). Apart from this, his main interest is in contemporary theories of secession: 'Secession as a defence of liberty: a liberal response to a nationalist demand' (*Canadian Journal of Political Science*, Vol. 37).

http://www.pol.mq.edu.au/about01.htm.

FILIMON PEONIDIS

Filimon Peonidis is an Assistant Professor of Moral and Political Philosophy at the Aristotle University of Thessaloniki. His primary academic interests are in moral philosophy with emphasis on Mill, Kant and applied ethics, and in political philosophy with emphasis on the history and theory of liberalism and the philosophical foundations of free expression. His work in Greek includes a book on the morality of lying, an edition of Constant's political writings and an annotated translation of Mill's Utilitarianism. His work in English includes *Autonomy and Sympathy: A post-Kantian moral Image* (forthcoming 2005).

http://users.auth.gr/peonidis

IGOR PRIMORATZ

Igor Primoratz is Professor of Philosophy at the Hebrew University, Jerusalem, and Principal Research Fellow at the Centre for Applied Philosophy and Public Ethics, University of Melbourne. He is the author of *Banquos Geist. Hegels Theorie der Strafe* (Bouvier Verlag, 1986), *Justifying Legal Punishment* (Humanities Press, 1989, 1997), *Ethics and Sex* (Routledge, 1999), and numerous papers in moral, political, and legal philosophy. Publications on terrorism and related subjects include "What Is Terrorism?" (*Journal of Applied Philosophy*, 1990), "The Morality of Terrorism" (*ibid.*, 1997), "Civilian Immunity in War" (*The Philosophical Forum*, 2005), and the edited anthology *Terrorism: The Philosophical Issues* (Palgrave MacMillan, 2004).

PETER SIMPSON

Peter Simpson is Professor of Philosophy and Classics at the City University of New York. He has published books and articles mainly in the area of moral and political philosophy and ancient philosophy. He was Visiting Fulbright Professor at Renmin University of China in Beijing in 2001-2002.

http://web.gc.cuny.edu/Philosophy/simpson.htm

UWE STEINHOFF

Uwe Steinhoff, Dr. phil., is Research Associate at the Oxford Leverhulme Programme on the Changing Character of War, University of Oxford. He worked on the younger Frankfurt School (*Kritik der kommunikativen Rationalität*, Marsberg, 2001) and has published articles on epistemology, postmodernism, political philosophy and ethics. He has recently finished a book on the ethics of war and terrorism and is currently working on war and non-state actors.

JANNA THOMPSON

Janna Thompson is an Associate Professor at La Trobe University in Melbourne, Australia and is Head of the Melbourne University Division of the Centre for Applied Philosophy and Public Ethics. She has written extensively on global justice, especially in reference to environmental problems, and she has recently written a book on reparation and historical injustice.

CHARLES P. WEBEL

Charles Webel is the Academic Director of the Center for Peace Studies and teaches at the University of Tromso, Norway, and at Walden University in the US. With David Barash, Charles Webel is the co-author of the highly acclaimed text *Peace and Conflict Studies* (Sage Publications, 2002), and he is the author of *Terror, Terrorism, and the Human Condition* (St. Martin's/Palgrave-MacMillan Press, 2005). He edits the scholarly book series *Twenty-First Century Perspectives on War, Peace, and Human Conflict* (St. Martin's/Palgrave Press).

VÉRONIQUE ZANETTI

Véronique Zanetti is Professor of Philosophy at the University of Bielefeld, Germany. Currently she is working on ethical aspects of international relations. She has written her habilitation on the ethics of humanitarian intervention and published several articles on the question in French, German and English. Other publications include: A monograph on Kant's concept of natural teleology (*La nature a-t-elle une fin?*, Bruxelles, 1994) and an important commentary on Kant's philosophy of nature and aesthetics (together with Manfred Frank: Bd. III von *Kants Gesammelten Schriften*, Bibliothek Deutscher Klassiker, Frankfurt/M., 1996, 1386 p., commentary p. 889-1355); with Steffen Wesche (ed.), *Dworkin: a Debate* (Bruxelles, 2000).

Philosophische Forschung
Philosophical Research

Edited by
Johannes Brandl • Andreas Kemmerling
Wolfgang Künne • Mark Textor

Georg Meggle (ed.)
Social Facts & Collective Intentionality

3-937202-08-0, Hardcover, 478 pp., EUR 138,00

Social Facts & Collective Intentionality: the combination of these two terms refers to a new field of basic research. Working mainly in the mood and by means of Analytical Philosophy, at the very heart of this new approach are conceptual explications of all the various versions of Social Facts & Collective Intentionality and the ramifications thereof. This approach tackles the topics of traditional social philosophy using new conceptual methods, including techniques of formal logics, computer simulations and artificial intelligence. Yet research on Social Facts & Collective Intentionality also includes ontological, epistemological, normative and - last but not least - methodological questions. This volume represents the state of the art in this new field.

Georg Meggle (Ed.)
Ethics of Terrorism & Counter Terrorism

3-937202-68-4, Hardcover, 410 pp., EUR 98,00

We are supposed to wage war against Terrorism – but exactly what we are fighting against in this war, there is nearly no consensus about. And, much worse, nearly nobody cares about this conceptual disaster – the main thing being, whether or not you are taking sides with the good guys.
This volume is an analytical attempt to end this disaster. What is Terrorism? Are terrorist acts to be defined exclusively on the basis of the characteristics of the respective actions? Or should we restrict such actions to acts performed by non-state organisations? And, most important, is terrorism already by its very nature to be morally condemned?

Mark Siebel • Mark Textor (Hrsg.)
Semantik und Ontologie
Beiträge zur philosophischen Forschung

ISBN 3-937202-43-9, Hardcover, 445 pp., EUR 93,00

Der zweite Band der Reihe Philosophische Forschung spannt zwei Kerngebiete der Analytischen Philosophie zusammen: die Semantik und die Ontologie. Was sind die Grundbausteine unserer Ontologie? Wie beziehen wir uns sprachlich bzw. geistig auf sie? Diese und weitere Fragen werden von international renommierten Philosophen aus historischer und systematischer Perspektive diskutiert.
Die Beiträge sind in Deutsch und English verfasst. Sie stammen von Christian Beyer, Johannes Brandl, Dagfinn Føllesdal, Dorothea Frede, Rolf George, Gerd Graßhoff, Peter Hacker, Andreas Kemmerling, Edgar Morscher, Kevin Mulligan, Rolf Puster, Richard Schantz, Benjamin Schnieder, Oliver Scholz, Severin Schröder, Peter Simons, Thomas Spitzley, Markus Stepanians, Ralf Stoecker und Daniel von Wachter.

René van Woudenberg, Sabine Roeser, Ron Rood (Eds.)
Basic Belief and Basic Knowledge
Papers in Epistemology
ISBN 3-937202-70-6, Hardcover, 293 pp., EUR 89,00

Over the last two decades foundationalism has been severely criticized. In response to this various alternatives to it have been advanced, notably coherentism. At the same time new versions of foundationalism were crafted, that were claimed to be immune to the earlier criticisms. This volume contains 12 papers in which various aspects of this dialectic are covered. A number of papers continue the trend to defend foundationalism, and foundationalism's commitment to basic beliefs and basic knowledge, against various attacks. Others aim to show that one important objection against coherentism, viz. that the notion of 'coherence' is too vague to be useful, can be countered.

ontos verlag

Frankfurt • Paris • Ebikon • Lancaster • New Brunswick

www.ontosverlag.com

Practical Philosophy

Edited by
Heinrich Ganthaler • Neil Roughley • Peter Schaber • Herlinde Pauer-Studer

ontos verlag
P.O. Box 15 41
63133 Heusenstamm nr. Frankfurt
www.ontosverlag.com

Frankfurt ▪ Lancaster